20/20

Twenty One-Act Plays from Twenty Years
of the Humana Festival

Smith and Kraus *Books For Actors*

THE MONOLOGUE SERIES
The Best Men's / Women's Stage Monologues of 1994
The Best Men's / Women's Stage Monologues of 1993
The Best Men's / Women's Stage Monologues of 1992
The Best Men's / Women's Stage Monologues of 1991
The Best Men's / Women's Stage Monologues of 1990
One Hundred Men's / Women's Stage Monologues from the 1980's
2 Minutes and Under: Original Character Monologues for Actors
Street Talk: Original Character Monologues for Actors
Uptown: Original Character Monologues for Actors
Ice Babies in Oz: Original Character Monologues for Actors
Monologues from Contemporary Literature: Volume I
Monologues from Classic Plays
100 Great Monologues from the Renaissance Theatre
100 Great Monologues from the Neo-Classical Theatre
100 Great Monologues from the 19th C. Romantic and Realistic Theatres

CONTEMPORARY PLAYWRIGHTS SERIES
Romulus Linney: 17 Short Plays
Eric Overmyer: Collected Plays
Lanford Wilson: 21 Short Plays
William Mastrosimone: Collected Plays
Horton Foote: 4 New Plays
Israel Horovitz Vol. I: 16 Short Plays
Terrence McNally: 15 Short Plays
Humana Festival '93: The Complete Plays
Humana Festival '94: The Complete Plays
Humana Festival '95: The Complete Plays
Women Playwrights: The Best Plays of 1992
Women Playwrights: The Best Plays of 1993
Women Playwrights: The Best Plays of 1994
EST Marathon '94: One-Act Plays
EST Marathon '95: One-Act Plays
Showtime's Act One Festival '95: One-Act Plays
By the Sea, By the Sea, By the Beautiful Sea: *McNally, Pintauro, Wilson*

GREAT TRANSLATION FOR ACTORS SERIES
Mercadet by Honoré de Balzac, tr. by Robert Cornthwaite
Zoyka's Apartment by Mikhail Bulgakov, tr. by N. Saunders & F. Dwyer
The Wood Demon by Anton Chekhov, tr. by N. Saunders & F. Dwyer
The Sea Gull by Anton Chekhov, tr. by N. Saunders & F. Dwyer
Three Sisters by Anton Chekhov, tr. by Lanford Wilson
The Coffee Shop by Carlo Goldoni, tr. by Robert Cornthwaite
Villeggiatura: The Trilogy by Carlo Goldoni, tr. by Robert Cornthwaite
Summer People by Maxim Gorky, tr. by N. Saunders & F. Dwyer
Ibsen: 4 Major Plays, tr. by Rick Davis & Brian Johnston
Spite for Spite by Agustín Moreto, tr. by Dakin Matthews
Cyrano de Bergerac by Edmond Rostand, tr. by Charles Marowitz
A Glass of Water by Eugène Scribe, tr. by Robert Cornthwaite

CAREER DEVELOPMENT SERIES
The Job Book: 100 Acting Jobs for Actors
The Smith and Kraus Monologue Index
What to Give Your Agent for Christmas and 100 Other Tips for the Working Actor
The Camera Smart Actor
The Sanford Meisner Approach
Anne Bogart: Viewpoints
The Actor's Chekhov
Kiss and Tell: Restoration Scenes, Monologues, & History
Cold Readings: Some Do's and Don'ts for Actors at Auditions

If you require pre-publication information about upcoming Smith and Kraus books, you may receive our semi-annual catalogue, free of charge, by sending your name and address to *Smith and Kraus Catalogue, P.O. Box 127, One Main Street, Lyme, NH 03768. Or call us at (800) 895-4331, fax (603) 795-4427.*

20/20
Twenty One-Act Plays from Twenty Years of the Humana Festival

Edited by Michele Volansky
and Michael Bigelow Dixon

Foreword by Jon Jory

Contemporary Playwrights Series

SK
A Smith and Kraus Book

A Smith and Kraus Book
Published by Smith and Kraus, Inc.
One Main Street, PO Box 127, Lyme, NH 03768

Manufactured in the United States of America
Cover and Text Design by Julia Hill

First Edition: December 1995
10 9 8 7 6 5 4 3

Library of Congress Cataloging-in-Publication Data

20/20 : twenty one-act plays from twenty years of the Humana Festival /
edited by Michele Volansky and Michael Bigelow Dixon; foreword by Jon Jory. -- 1st ed.
p. cm. -- (contemporary playwrights series)
ISBN 1-880399-98-9
1. One-act plays, American. 2. American drama--20th century.
I. Volansky, Michele. II. Dixon, Michael Bigelow. III. Humana Festival. IV. Series.
PS627.053A14   1995
812'.04108--dc20   95-45877
                                                   CIP

Acknowledgements

The editors wish to thank the following persons
for their assistance in compiling this anthology of one-act plays:

Jimmy Seacat
Alexander Speer
Wanda Snyder
Corby Tushla
Valerie Smith
Jeffrey Ullom
Linda Green
Suzan Mikiel
David Kuntz

Actors Theatre of Louisville

Actors Theatre of Louisville is the State Theatre of Kentucky. Founded in 1964 and guided by Producing Director Jon Jory since 1969, Actors Theatre has emerged as one of America's most consistently innovative professional theatre companies. For twenty years it has been a major force in revitalizing American playwriting with more than 200 ATL-premiered scripts in publication. The annual Humana Festival of New American Plays is recognized as the premiere event of its kind and draws producers, journalists, critics, playwrights, and theatre lovers from around the world for a marathon of new works. As the State Theatre of Kentucky, Actors Theatre performs annually to over 200,000 people and is the recipient of the most prestigious awards bestowed on a regional theatre: a special Tony Award for Distinguished Achievement, the James N. Vaughan Memorial Award for Exceptional Achievement and Contribution to the Development of Professional Theatre, and the Margo Jones Award for the Encouragement of New Plays.

Humana Festival of New American Plays

The Humana Foundation is the philanthropic arm of Humana Inc. Established in 1981, The Humana Foundation promotes worthwhile organizations that improve the health and welfare of communities throughout the United States. Humana Inc., one of the nation's largest publicly-traded managed care companies, offers a wide range of affordable health plans and services to employer groups and consumers.

Reflecting Humana's commitment to social responsibility and an improved quality of life, The Humana foundation supports nonprofit institutions in the areas of arts and culture, education, health and human services and community development.

Humana believes a higher quality of life can be achieved through the arts. As the sponsor of the Annual Humana Festival of New American Plays, The Humana Foundation is proud of its support of Actors Theatre of Louisville and a festival that brings the best and the brightest dramatic artists to American regional theatre.

Contents

Biographies

MICHELE VOLANSKY is the dramaturg/literary manager of Steppenwolf Theatre Company, where she serves as production dramaturg for the mainstage and studio theatres, as well as dramaturg for the playwrights in the New Plays Lab. She has worked with such playwrights as Kevin Kling, José Rivera, and Phyllis Nagy and with such directors as Anne Bogart, Tina Landau, and Lisa Peterson during her tenure as assistant literary manager at Actors Theatre of Louisville. She is the co-editor (with Michael Dixon) of *Kiss and Tell* and *A Brave and Violent Theatre*. She has guest dramaturged at the Atlantic Theatre Company, Philadelphia Theatre Company, Swarthmore College and Villanova University, where she received her M.A. in theatre/dramaturgy.

MICHAEL BIGELOW DIXON has served as literary manager at Actors Theatre of Louisville throughout the second decade of the Humana Festival of New American Plays. He's also held positions as literary manager at the Alley Theatre and literary associate at South Coast Repertory. He has been a Theatre Management Fellow at the National Endowment for the Arts, and has taught at North Carolina Central University, UC-Riverside, Rice University, and Action Theatre in Singapore. He has co-edited ten volumes of plays and criticism, and co-written more than twenty plays, fifteen of which are published.

Foreword

The one-act play is the perfect vehicle for personal obsession. You can get to the point, you can stay on the point, and you don't have to muddy the water with any of those tangential little subplots. It's equally true of character. The writers write about who they want to write about and when they are finished doing that, it's over. No butler, delivery persons or functionaries to slave over. "What characteristic can I give this damn uncle so that the audience will mistake him for a dimensional character?" Forget that.

It can also be written in a single gulp. A few long nights at the computer terminal and voilà! Because the writer is unlikely to regard the one-act as a career builder or a year of their life, they can bring spontaneity back to the work. "What are you writing, Mr. Chekhov?" "Oh nothing much, just an occasional piece, just passing the time."

These things might explain why so many important American writers work in this genre. Money wouldn't explain it, celebrity wouldn't explain it. The one-act is obviously a sliver they couldn't get out of their brains. One-acts, in a way, are literary acts of exorcism. In them (in my opinion) you find personal things about writers' lives, family, politics and fears much closer to the surface than in full-length work. If you want to know a writer better, go to their short plays, they didn't have their guard up when they wrote them.

This accounts for the sense of intimacy that one-act plays provoke. Audiences don't come loaded for bear expecting more than can be delivered. Actors don't feel they're climbing Mount Seagull or Mount Oedipus. Everybody brings to the event a relaxation of spirit that allows it into our head and heart.

This, in terms of atmosphere, is as close as theatre gets to "informal" with everybody looser, ready to talk and ready to act on impulse. For me, that means I remember them instead of confront them. It's very welcome. Think of them as palette cleansers if you will, but they have bite and tang and aftertaste.

Let them catch you by surprise. They're meant to.

Jon Jory
Producing Director
Actors Theatre of Louisville

Tough Choices for the New Century

A seminar for responsible living

by Jane Anderson

Ms. Anderson grew up in northern California. After two years in college, she dropped out to move to New York City to train as an actress. In 1975 she appeared in the New York premiere of David Mamet's *Sexual Perversity in Chicago.* She began writing in 1979 when she founded the New York Writers Bloc with playwrights Donald Margulies and Jeffery Sweet. She developed a series of characters and performed as a comedienne in New York clubs and cabarets. In 1982, her act was discovered by Billy Crystal, and she was brought to Los Angeles to be a regular on *The Billy Crystal Comedy Hour* which was taken off the air after three weeks. Ms. Anderson continued to perform in Los Angeles, receiving critical acclaim for her one-woman show, *How to Raise a Gifted Child.*

For several years she worked as a television writer, working on staff for several series, including *Wonder Years* and creating a short-lived show for Grant Tinker called *Raising Miranda.*

Her playwriting career began in 1986 with *Defying Gravity,* which premiered in L.A. and later received a W. Alton Jones Grant for a production at the Williamstown Theatre Festival. Her plays to follow were *Food & Shelter, The Baby Dance, The Pink Studio, Hotel Oubliette* (recipient of the Susan Smith Blackburn Prize) and several short plays, including *Lynette at 3 AM* and *The Last Time We Saw Her,* both winners of the Heideman Award. Her works are published and have been widely produced off-Broadway and in theatres around the country, including Long Wharf, The McCarter, Williamstown Theatre Festival, The Pasadena Playhouse, ACT, and Actors Theatre of Louisville.

In 1993, Ms. Anderson received an Emmy Award and Writer's Guild Award for her H.B.O. movie, *The Positively True Adventures of the Alleged Texas Cheerleader-Murdering Mom.*

Her film work includes: *Cop Gives Waitress $2 Million Tip,* renamed for release to *It Could Happen to You* (Tristar). Her film adaptation of *How To Make An American Quilt* is based on the novel by Whitney Otto.

Ms. Anderson is a member of the Dramatists Guild.

ORIGINAL PRODUCTION

Tough Choices for the New Century was first produced at Actors Theatre of Louisville as part of the Humana Festival of New American Plays in 1995. It was directed by Lisa Peterson with the following cast:

Bob Dooley . . . . Kenneth L. Marks
Helen Dooley, Arden Shingles . . . . Susan Knight

An earlier version of the play, Smart Choices for a New Century, *was originally produced by the McCarter Theatre.*

CHARACTERS

Our Seminar Speakers:

BOB AND HELEN DOOLEY: Bob has been giving his very popular preparedness seminars all around the country. Helen has recently joined the team and is an experienced volunteer for the Red Cross. They originally hail from Columbus, Ohio and currently reside in the Southern California area where Bob is a construction consultant.

ARDEN SHINGLES: Ms. Shingles is author of the bestseller, *Armed for Life.* She has been teaching seminars and workshops in self-defense for the past eleven years and was twice named Business Woman of the Year by the Austin Business Women's Association.

(Note: Arden and Helen may be played by the same actress.)

TIME: Present (whatever time curtain goes up)

PLACE : A Seminar Room

What people are saying after taking our seminars!

"I used to live my life in fear. Now I know that I have control over what happens to me."—*Grace Larkin, Michigan*

"I thought I was prepared before. Now I'm *really* prepared for whatever happens. And I feel great about it."—*Ron Held, Florida*

"I've turned my losses into gains. I learned a lot about positive thinking."—*Douglas Uley, Indiana*

TOUGH CHOICES
FOR THE NEW CENTURY
A Seminar for Responsible Living

As we enter the theater, we are given handouts [see Choices Itinerary *and* Questionnaire*] with a small stubby pencil and urged to fill them out while we wait for the seminar to begin. On the stage is a screen with slide thrown up:* Tough Choices for the New Century. *There's a chair and a table with a plastic pitcher of water and plastic cups for the speakers to use.*

Bob and Helen are already on stage setting up, going over notes, handing last-minute slides to someone on the Seminar Staff (can be played by the stage manager or one of the backstage persons). Bob and Helen are a nicely groomed, middle-class white couple. Bob's manner is energetic and folksy, a user-friendly kind of guy. Helen is maintaining a pleasant expression on her face but seems slightly cut off.

When the seminar begins, the lights in the audience should dim only slightly because we should feel that we're in lecture space rather than a theater.

BOB: *(To audience.)* Everybody here who's supposed to be here? Everybody in the right seminar? This is Tough Choices for the New Century. Now's your chance to escape! Terrific. My name is Bob Dooley and this is my wife Helen.

HELEN: Hello.

BOB: This is Helen's first time up here. I've been giving workshops for several years now and I've always bounced my ideas off Helen while we're sitting around the dinner table. And a few weeks ago, I finally said to her, "Honey, I think you'd have a heck of lot to share with people, why don't you come up and help me lead this seminar?" And it didn't take much convincing after that to get her to agree.

HELEN: I'm just here to keep an eye on him.

BOB: Well, I wish I were that handsome that you had to worry. Anyway, we're real lucky to have Helen with us and if you take a look at the schedule—everyone get one?, terrific—if you glance through your schedules you'll see that we have a really full weekend ahead of us. But you'll also have time to use the great facilities here. There's a beautiful pool, tennis courts, putting green, computer center, a Jacuzzi—Helen, I bet that's where you'll be headed for some quiet time.

HELEN: Oh, you bet, Honey.

BOB: Oh and Sunday afternoon, after the last talk, there will be a barbecue. So if you don't have to rush back home, we'd love you to stay and wind down with us, have some great food, chat about the weekend...Super. Let's get started. Helen?

(Helen changes the Slide. We see a map of America with large areas marked in red.)

HELEN: This is a government map showing every region that's been declared a national disaster zone in the past five years. Which means that by the year 2000, one out of every five Americans can expect to be directly impacted by a natural catastrophe.

BOB: Helen has family all over the United States and all of them have had their homes devastated in one form or another. Helen you want to tell us a little bit about that?

HELEN: Well, first my sister Renae and her husband lost their home in hurricane Andrew. Their roof was ripped off and everything inside their house was scattered and blown into the ocean—all their papers, family pictures, everything was gone. Then my brother and his family, they live in Iowa. When the floods came, they lost all their livestock—cows, chickens, pigs, they all drowned. Their house was under water for a month. Everything in the house—all their furniture, tax returns...family pictures, it all had to be thrown away. And then, oh gosh, my parents had just moved to Altadena, California, where they bought their retirement home. And they had just finished doing five months of work on the house—new carpeting, new wallpaper, new cabinets in the kitchen...

BOB: They found out that they had to put in new pipes...

HELEN: ...all new pipes, that's right—and finally when the last workman had left, and everything was new and clean and just the way they wanted it, my mother said to my father, "Now wasn't that all worth it?" and they went to bed that night, as my mother put it, with big smiles on their faces. But then around five in the morning, they were woken up by someone pounding on their door—

BOB: It was a fireman telling them that the hills were on fire.

HELEN: My parents were told that they had to evacuate. The fire was coming so fast, my mother didn't even have time to put in her teeth. She said that when they ran outside, they saw a giant wall of flames coming down from the hills—

BOB: She said it looked like a tidal wave from hell.

HELEN: I can tell it, Honey. *(To audience.)* —and in less than a minute the house caught fire like it was a cardboard box. They had to put my father in a wheelbarrow because he couldn't run from the fire fast enough.

BOB: *(To audience.)* Actually, what happened was— *(To Helen.)* ...sorry, Honey.

HELEN: Go ahead.

BOB: Helen's father wanted to stay and hose down their roof—

HELEN: Which was stupid.

BOB: —sure, that's not something we recommend in a situation like this, but Helen's dad is actually a pretty neat guy. Listen to this—after the fire, at age *seventy-six,* he took the insurance money they got for the house and bought a boat. He's already sailed to Hawaii twice. Now don't you wish we all had that kind of positive attitude on life? *(To Helen.)* Go ahead, Honey.

HELEN: Well, I was going to say that just the year before, my mother's sister who lives in Northern California had her house destroyed by the fire up there. And she had all the other family pictures…we had some pictures, but I couldn't find the album after the earthquake. So there are no more family pictures left.

BOB: OK, what is Helen saying here? If family pictures mean something to you, know where they are, keep them in a box that you can easily locate and slip into a backpack or the front seat of your car. What Helen is saying is, *be prepared.* Honey?

(Helen changes the slide to a photo of the famous casts of the victims of Pompeii.)

BOB: These are not statues. These are casts of actual people who were killed by the famous Volcano of Pompeii almost twenty centuries ago. As they ran back to their homes to collect their possessions, they were overwhelmed by sulfurous fumes and their bodies were covered by ash and lava, leaving this record of their struggle with death. Yes, this was tragic, yes this was awful, but the people of Pompeii *knew* they were living under an active volcano. They knew what was coming. Every morning when they woke up, they could look out their bedroom windows and see that mountain smoking. *What* was going through their heads? Were they just sitting there at their breakfast tables, saying "Well, Helena, looks like that volcano is going to give us another smoggy day," you know? I'm not putting them down, but the people of Pompeii just didn't want to bother themselves with preparedness. And that's why half the population ended up in a museum case.

(Helen changes the slide to another map of America, the regions marked in red, orange and yellow.)

BOB: Now some people have said to me, "Bob, my idea of preparedness is to not live in a place where I know disaster will hit." Good idea. But where? Take a look at this map. The red shows us where disasters are expected to occur at least once a year. The orange shows areas where disasters are expected every five years and the yellow shows where disasters are expected to occur every ten years. Let's take a look at where there aren't any colors—the Mojave Desert, gee, I'd sure like to move there, wouldn't you, Helen?

HELEN: Well, it would be restful.

BOB: But it wouldn't be home, would it? Would it, Helen.

HELEN: No, it wouldn't, Bob.

BOB: *(To audience.)* Everybody, if we look at this map you'll see that there's no point in running when there's nowhere to go. I don't want to see any of you pulling up stakes and moving to the so-called "safe zones." That's living your life out of fear. But I also don't want to see any of you living your life in denial. What's the middle ground here? How do we cope? Once again, it's that word again. I know you're going to get real sick of hearing me say it, but let's hear it, the P-word…

HELEN AND BOB: *(With audience.)* Preparedness.

BOB: One more time, louder, come on. *(With audience.) Preparedness.* Terrific. Helen?

(Helen changes the slide to: 1)Securing Your Castle 2) Securing the Family Jewels 3) Securing Your Identity 4) Securing the Right Perspective)

BOB: These are the four points of preparedness that we'll be covering this weekend. *(Using a pointer.) Securing Your Castle*—if you live in a fire area, replace your shake roof with tile, if you live in an earthquake zone, retrofit your foundation, if you live in flood country, add another story, live on the top floor. *(Pointing.) Securing the Family Jewels*—how do you protect your irreplaceables—birth certificates, tax returns, computer disks, pets.

HELEN: Family pictures.

BOB: Family pictures, one of Helen's favorite losses. We'll go over all of that later. Moving on, we have— *(Pointing.) Securing Your Identity*—this has to do with making sure that no matter where you are when a disaster hits, even if you're stepping out of the bathtub in your birthday suit, that you'll always have some form of identification on you. One of the biggest problems after any catastrophe is identifying the victims. If you're unable to communicate because of injury or death, you'll want relief workers to know who you are.

(Bob pulls his sock down. Helen looks away, clearly disturbed by this.)

BOB: I had my name and social security number tattooed on my ankle—any tattoo artist can do this for a reasonable fee, just make sure they're licensed and the needles are clean. Some people prefer to have the tattoo placed on a spot on their torso because sometimes limbs can get separated. But that's up to you. Helen can tell us another reason why IDs are so important. After the quake, Helen stood in line for eight hours to apply for emergency relief and when she finally got to the head of the line, they wouldn't give her an application because she didn't have any identification. Helen, what does FEMA stand for?

HELEN: Few Enlightened, Many Assholes.

BOB: *(Laughs.)* Excuse her French, but Helen had quite a time wrestling with the red tape. OK, let's look at number four: *(Pointing.) Securing the Right*

Perspective. I'd like to spend the rest of this time talking about this point. How do we keep our perspective on disaster? How do we not let a disaster depress us, or make us feel like a victim? Helen, what did your mother say after she lost her house in the fire?

HELEN: She said, "Well, I guess God didn't mean us to move to California."

BOB: *(To audience.)* All right, how many people here believe that God sends down disasters to punish us? Come on, let's have a show of hands. It's all right if you believe it, it's something we've all been taught—Helen change that slide for me please?

(Helen changes the Slide to a blow-up of a section of a contract with a particular sentence highlighted:)

BOB: Look at this, how many of you have ever signed a contract that had this clause in it? *(Reading the slide.)* "...the undersigned will not be held responsible in the event of war, civil disturbance, fire, earthquake, flood or any other *Act of God.* Act of God. Isn't that wild? Helen, what do you think about this?

HELEN: Well, I do believe there is a God.

BOB: But do you think he's out to punish us?

HELEN: No. *(Laughs.)* Well, I hope not.

BOB: *(To audience.)* Do you know what I think? I think that blaming God is just another excuse that people make for not preparing, "Well, if God's going to send an earthquake my way, I guess there's nothing I can do about it." Sorry, but I have to get tough here, that's just a bunch of you-know-what. I want all your minds to take a giant U-turn and start thinking in another direction—Honey?

(Helen changes the Slide that shows in large letters: A Catastrophe Is Nothing Personal.)

BOB: *A catastrophe is nothing personal.* I want this to become your mantra. I want you to print this on a T-shirt and wear it around for all your friends and neighbors to see. Come on, let's all say it together— *(With audience.)* *A catastrophe is nothing personal.* Helen?

HELEN: I never said it was, Bob.

BOB: But I think it helps us all to say it. You want to say it with us?

HELEN: All righty. *(Helen pours herself some water.)*

BOB: Come on, let's all say it again with Helen and me. One more time. *A catastrophe is nothing personal.*

(Helen deliberately drinks her water through this. Bob sees this.)

BOB: *(Flatly.)* Terrific. *(Bob goes over to the table, pours himself a cup of water so he can check on Helen. Quietly to Helen.)* How're you doing, Honey?

(Helen gives him a tight smile. A beat.)

BOB: *(Back to audience.)* Let's try something. *(Bob puts his cup of water down next to the pitcher.)* According to the laws of gravity, if I put this cup of water down on the table next to this pitcher...and I take a walk way over to here, I can be pretty sure that the pitcher and cup will stay where they are until I come back. The pitcher and cup are held there by gravity. Gravity is what keeps the world around us in place. Gravity is what gives humankind security. But what happens if I do this? *(Bob walks back to the table, puts his hands on the sides and jiggles it very slightly.)* This is what would happen during a three-point earthquake. Nothing much is going on, I notice some vibrations in the water but no big deal. All right, let's try a four-point earthquake.

(Bob jiggles the table even more. He glances at Helen who's watching him suspiciously.)

BOB: Well, that was kind of disturbing. I see that the pitcher has moved an inch or two and there's a little spillage. Oh well, but I guess I could still live with that. All right, here's a five-point earthquake. *(Bob jiggles the table until the pitcher just slides to the edge.)* Wow, close call. That will teach me never to leave something on the edge of the table. *(He slides the pitcher back to the middle of the table.)* How about a six-point earthquake?

(Bob rocks the table until the pitcher and cup fall off. Water spills all over the floor. Helen is splashed by the water, stands up. She's trying very hard not to react.)

BOB: And here's the seven-point. *(Bob picks up the table and throws it on the ground.)* And here's an eight point. *(Bob picks up the table and hits it over and over again on the floor until it breaks. Helen winces but doesn't move.)* Well, I guess it wouldn't have done me any good to duck and cover under that piece of furniture. *(To Helen.)* How are you doing?

HELEN: Just fine and dandy.

BOB: *(Calling backstage.)* Could we get some paper towels...? Thanks. *(To Helen.)* Honey, you did great. You really did.

(Someone on the Seminar Staff hands Helen a stack of brown paper towels. She starts mopping up the spilled water.)

BOB: *(Back to the audience.)* Let's talk a little about earthquakes. We'll be covering other disasters later. Honey, that's OK, they can do that.

HELEN: That's all right.

BOB: *(To audience.)* I like to start with earthquakes because they're the least predictable, the least controllable, and, seemingly, the most impossible to escape.

(Helen is obsessively drying a part of the floor with a paper towel making a Skishing noise.)

BOB: Thank you, Honey, that's terrific, thank you.

(Bob helps Helen gather up the paper towels. He hands them to a Seminar Staff person.)

BOB: Thank you. *(Back to audience.)* Helen and I have lived in the Southern California area for fifteen years and have been through several quakes. But in the last one, which was pretty wild, we had quite a lot of damage. *(To Helen.)* Honey, can we have those slides of the house?

(Helen forwards through a couple of disaster Slides and stops at a Slide of a kitchen destroyed by an earthquake.)

BOB: This is what happened to our kitchen. As you can see everything that was in the cupboards, on the walls, the counters, just flew out.

HELEN: *(Flatly.)* ...the blender, the coffee maker, the knives on the rack—

BOB: The knives on the rack, that's right—they ended up clear across the kitchen.

BOB: Thank God this happened at four in the morning. Can you imagine if Helen was standing there preparing a meal?

(Helen clicks to a Slide of kitchen knives stuck in the wall.)

BOB: We have a lot to be thankful for.

HELEN: Yes indeedy, we do. *(Helen snaps to the next slide—a dining room destroyed by the earthquake.)*

BOB: Here's our dining room. I don't know if you can tell in this picture, but we had a big china cabinet that fell down and all of Helen's knickknacks were broken to bits.

HELEN: My Hummels.

BOB: And of course you have to keep reminding yourself that these are only things.

HELEN: My mother gave me my Hummels. I'd been collecting them since I was a girl. There weren't even any pieces left that were big enough to glue.

BOB: But we're still in one piece, and that's what's important.

HELEN: The piano flipped over. On top of my Hummels.

BOB: The piano, that's right, and the dining room table, marble topped, you couldn't move it if you tried, but it flipped right over like it was made of balsa wood.

HELEN: The cat was hiding under the table. She thought it was safe. Our cat Muffin. She got her tail crushed.

BOB: —the table fell on her tail, that's right.

HELEN: She thought it was safe. That's where she went, under the table. We found her in the morning with her tail caught. The vet had to cut it off...

(Helen stops at a slide of Muffin with the stub of her tail bandaged.)

BOB: But here's something interesting—Honey, could you show us the next slide?

(Helen changes to a Slide of a water heater.)

BOB: The one thing that didn't move was the water heater. We had it strapped to the wall as a precaution. So preparedness really does pay off. We'll be talking later about wall-securing all your major appliances.

HELEN: If there are any walls left, you can't strap something to a wall that's going to come down.

BOB: No, you're absolutely right.

HELEN: My God, look what just happened in Japan.

BOB: OK, Helen.

HELEN: "Oh, the Japanese aren't scared of earthquakes. They've built everything to code."

BOB: OK. *(A beat. To audience.)* Fine, let's talk about Japan. *(To audience.)* First of all, Kobe was not a prepared city, all right? They don't have earthquakes in the western part of Japan. If this had happened in Tokyo, it would have been a completely different story.

HELEN: You don't know that.

BOB: Just wait a minute. *(To audience.)* I'm glad Helen has brought this up. This is a very important point. The other mistake that the Japanese have made, is that in their drive to become leaders in the world economy, they have given up the flexibility of the reed for the hardness of steel. You see, traditionally, houses in Japan were constructed of light materials—paper, wood, bamboo poles—and all activities—eating, sleeping, cooking—were done low to the ground. Pillows, instead of chairs, futons instead of beds, hibachis instead of stoves. The previous generations of Japanese were very smart. By tradition, they kept things very spare. They might have one small, pretty little vase with a single flower. If there was an earthquake, it might fall over but they could easily dodge it because they weren't running away from a hundred other things that were falling off the walls.

HELEN: No one lives like that, Bob.

BOB: That's right, and isn't that a shame. *(To audience.)* What I'm saying is, simple living is safe living. There was a couple in Northridge who were killed in the quake by their fifteen hundred-piece collection of depression-era ceramics. Now what's the point of that? Helen loved her Hummel figurines. But how often would she really look at them? Honey, how often would you say you actually looked at them, maybe once a year?

HELEN: It was more than that.

BOB: All right, once a month? The point being, after they were gone—well, this was months after, when we finally moved back into our house—I asked Helen one day, "Honey, do you miss your Hummels?" *(To Helen.)* And what did you say?

HELEN: I don't remember.

BOB: You said no. You said you didn't even remember what they looked like.

HELEN: I was still in shock.

BOB: But do you really need your Hummel figurines? Are they something you need every day to survive, like you would need a blanket or a jug for water or a bowl to eat your food in?

HELEN: We're not cave dwellers, Bob, there are certain things I like to have around.

BOB: So do I, but I'd feel pretty bad if you got clobbered on the head by one of my softball trophies. *(Laughs, to audience.)* All right, I think you all get my point. Let's move on. *(A beat.)* Let's take a look at the chair Helen is sitting on. Now according to the laws of gravity, a chair is a stable and safe place to rest. *(Bob grasps the back of Helen's chair.)* This is a three-point earthquake.

(Bob jiggles the chair slightly. Helen starts to look tense.)

BOB: Helen, did you feel much?

HELEN: Yes, I felt the chair shaking.

BOB: But you didn't feel like you were going to fall.

HELEN: No, Bob, I didn't.

BOB: All right, now let's try a four-point earthquake.

(Bob shakes the chair a little more. Helen tries not to react.)

BOB: How are you doing, Helen, you feel like you're falling off?

HELEN: *(Flatly.)* No, I don't.

BOB: OK, here comes a five-point earthquake.

(Bob shakes the chair harder. Helen grabs the sides.)

BOB: And here's a six-point earthquake.

(Bob violently rocks the chair back and forth while Helen grasps the sides.)

HELEN: Bob, please stop it.

BOB: All right, Helen wanted me to stop because she felt like she was about to topple over. That's because furniture of Western cultures has a high center of gravity. They aren't designed for earthquakes. Now let's look at the Japanese-style chair. *(Bob calls to someone on the seminar staff.)* Could I have one of our pillows?

(A staff member hands him an upholstered pillow.)

BOB: *(To audience.)* Later, we'll be showing you how to save your life in a hurricane with something as simple as a cushion from your couch. Anyway. How many of you have gone to one of those traditional Japanese restaurants that have a tatami room, you know, where you have to take your shoes off and sit on the floor on these funny little pillows, and your more adventurous friends are saying, "Come on, let's try it," and you're saying to yourself, "Geez, how am I gonna get through this meal without wrecking my back"? Well, I'm here to tell you that sitting Japanese-style is the best thing you can do for your posture, but more importantly it's the best thing you can do to save your life. *(Bob drops the pillow on the floor.)* Helen is going to try out this tatami pillow.

(Helen gives Bob a panicked look. Bob gently takes her arm, gets her to sit on the pillow. He kneels behind Helen, massages her shoulders.)

BOB: Boy, Helen is like a rock. That's from sitting in those Western chairs. *(Quietly to Helen.)* Honey, breathe, it's OK.

(Helen shuts her eyes.)

BOB: All right this is what would happen during a seven-point quake. *(Bob grasps the sides of the pillow, violently shakes it back and forth.)*

HELEN: *Bob stop! For God's sake, just stop!*

(Bob stops, puts his arms around Helen. She starts to sob.)

BOB: OK, that was scary for Helen, but there was no way that she was going to get hurt because she was so low to the floor. Helen, did you feel like you were going to fall over?

HELEN: *(Still sobbing.)* Don't do that to me again, I don't want you to do that again…

BOB: *(Hugging her.)* Shhh, it's OK.

HELEN: *(Over him.)* …this is not helping me, this is not what I need. It's not working, I don't like it, Bob…

BOB: *(Over her.)* Shhh, OK, OK, everything's OK, we're all OK… *(To audience.)* You see, for Helen, and many people, it's the fear of getting hurt that makes an earthquake so upsetting. But with the right preparation—and this is what I keep telling Helen…

(Helen throws Bob's arms off, gets up from the pillow and looks for her purse.)

BOB: Honey, you need my hankie?

(Helen shakes her head, finds a Kleenex in her purse.)

BOB: *(Back to audience.)* …what I've been trying to do for Helen is to help her separate her fear from the reality. Her fear is that there will be another earthquake and that she'll get hurt. The reality is, yes, there will be another earthquake, but no, she will not get hurt.

HELEN: You don't know that! How can you say you know that!?

BOB: Okay, Helen has brought up another good point. What Helen is saying is that there are no guarantees—Honey, is that what you're saying? —OK, but let's take a for-instance. There is no guarantee that anyone here won't be killed crossing the street. But your chances are better if you look both ways. And that's preparedness. You see what I'm saying? Honey?

HELEN: I get it, Bob, I understand. Thank you.

BOB: Great. Could you change the slide for me please? *(A beat.)* Please?

(Helen ignores him, wipes her nose with the tissue. Bob picks up the slide remote, changes the Slide to a textbook rendering of Indians around a tepee.)

BOB: Two-hundred years ago, our own Native Americans witnessed one of the biggest earthquakes ever to occur on this continent. But reports say that the Indian tribes did not experience any damage. That's because the Indians had a very simple lifestyle. Their tepees, which were made of hide and flexible poles, didn't collapse on their heads but gently swayed with the tremors. And, being nomadic, they didn't collect a lot of breakables. So instead of feeling terror when the ground started shaking, they felt wonder and awe and they all ran out and did a dance with Mother Earth.

HELEN: Well aren't they special and aren't I the poor sport.

BOB: That's not what I'm saying.

HELEN: Oh, I think it is.

BOB: No, listen to what I'm saying. What I'm saying is, that we should look at disasters as a learning opportunity. If you can let it change you in a positive rather than a negative way, then you're way ahead of the game. I

mean, look at your father learning to sail in his 70s. *(To the audience.)* —
he loses his home in a fire, now he's off following a dream.

HELEN: Oh please, my father is running away.

BOB: From what? He has nothing left.

HELEN: He has my mother, Bob.

BOB: Fine, but if she wants to shut herself up in a dark apartment, feeling sorry
for herself that's up to her.

HELEN: I don't want to have this discussion right now.

BOB: No, this is very useful. *(To audience.)* This is important. Excuse my
French, but Shit Happens. That's just a fact of life. So we might as well
face the music, practice our preparedness, and get on with our lives.

HELEN: He's a real trooper, my husband. *(To Bob.)* What did you say to me
during the quake?

BOB: I don't remember.

HELEN: *(To audience.)* This is at four in the morning and the bed is shaking
and I'm yelling at Bob to help me find my glasses. What did you say to
me, Bob?

BOB: OK, Honey.

HELEN: "Helen don't let me die, please make it stop, I don't want to die. Make
it stop. Oh Mommy make it stop."

BOB: I think to be fair, I was woken up from a dead sleep. Heck, we all got rattled, that's normal, but then you go on. You can't start sobbing every time
you think you feel an aftershock.

HELEN: If you'd let me sob, if you'd let me just Goddamn sob then maybe I'd
be all right.

BOB: Fine, but there comes a point when it turns into just plain whining and
self-indulgence.

HELEN: You're a horrible man. You're a fool. I hate you. Go to hell. *(Helen kicks
her chair over, walks off.)*

BOB: Helen? *(A beat.)* Honey? *(A beat. Bob sets the chair upright again.)*

BOB: Guess that was a seven-point-eight. OK. I'm going to bring out the next
speaker, but what I'd like you to do while we set up is for you to take a little mental tour of your house or apartment. In your mind's eye, look at all
the things you have on your shelves—picture frames, souvenirs from your
vacation, that set of commemorative dishes that you never eat on, trophies, the clay dog your child made in kindergarten, that glass jar filled
with pennies, that jumbo bottle of scotch your office chums gave you on
your birthday. Now imagine all these objects being hurled across the room
at your head at sixty miles per hour. Or imagine a wave of fire tearing
through your bedroom, spreading over your bed, the blankets, the bed-
spread, all those dopey little frou-frou pillows that you have to throw off
to get to the real pillows—imagine all of it starting to smoke in the terrible heat then *whoosh,* exploding into flames! And all those crappy plastic

knickknacks you keep throwing in the drawer of your bedside table—imagine it all melting into a bubbling, black ooze. And what about that guitar in the closet you never play, that walking stick someone brought you back from Scotland and *baskets,* how many of you keep collecting *baskets—Whoosh!* Or imagine being Noah sailing across the flood-swollen earth. Imagine the miles and miles of muddy, garbage-choked water, people's jetsam floating up, banging up against the side of the ark—*kachunk, kachunk, kachunk*—spooking all the animals inside, driving you nuts! Or imagine millions and millions of locusts swarming into your living room, devouring everything in their path, slipcovers, curtains, all those coffee table books you never read—*The Cat Lover's Handbook, (He makes eating sounds.) Hawaii from the Air, (More eating sounds.) The World of Hummel. (He makes extra vicious eating sounds.)* Imagine everything you own or love or *thought* you loved being destroyed in countless other ways. Imagine it all gone. Then ask yourself, "What would I miss?" *(A beat.)* What would I really miss? *(Bob takes his hankie out, wipes his mouth. Quietly.)* OK, terrific. *(Arden enters, a smartly-groomed woman, dressed in a short-skirted business suit and heels. She's carrying a metal briefcase. Bob perks up when she comes on, is clearly attracted to her.)*

BOB: Super. Everybody, say hello to Arden. *(With audience.)* Hello, Arden.

ARDEN: Hello, everybody. *(Arden looks around for the table, sees it smashed on the floor.)*

BOB: Oh, sorry. *(Looks backstage.)* Can we get another table out here, please? *(Someone on the Seminar Staff comes out with a new table, cleans up Bob's mess. Arden puts her case on the new table, opens it up, starts laying out a couple of handguns, a can of Mace, some other equipment.)*

BOB: *(Part of their routine.)* Arden, not to get personal, but you were married, once, weren't you?

ARDEN: That's right.

BOB: You and your husband ever have fights?

ARDEN: Like cats and dogs.

BOB: All part of a marriage, I guess.

ARDEN: Part of some, that's right.

BOB: Especially if there's been a lot of outside stress, wouldn't you say?

ARDEN: I'd say that.

BOB: But wouldn't you say that the stronger we become as individuals, the stronger the bonds become in marriage?

ARDEN: Strong minds make strong hearts, Yessir.

BOB: You bet. OK. *(To audience.)* I think the best introduction for Arden is to read this passage from her book: *(Reading.)* "There is no time when we're more vulnerable than during a disaster when resources are scarce and the police force is stretched to its limits. We must make sure that we aren't victims a second time around." Arden is one of the most knowledgeable people I know in the security business, and she's also a really, really super lady. I think you're going to get a lot out of her.

ARDEN: Thank you, Bob.

BOB: I'm going to stick around and give Arden a hand. Her partner, Rudy, had a little family emergency. His son, Brad— *(To Arden.)* Is Bradley all right?

ARDEN: They got his finger back on, yeah.

BOB: Thank God. Well, give him our best. Terrific.

ARDEN: Aren't we supposed to have water here?

BOB: Sorry.

(Bob runs backstage. Arden takes the slide remote, changes the Slide to Protecting Your Life.)

ARDEN: *(To audience.)* Hello everybody, I'm Arden Shingles and protecting your life is not just a privilege...it's your right. But it's more than just a right... *(She changes the slide: Your Responsibility.)* ...it's your responsibility. *(Bob comes back with another pitcher of water and cups, pours some water for Arden.)*

BOB: Sorry. Here you go.

(Arden takes the water, gives Bob the slide remote. She takes her time drinking the water, lets everyone wait. She hands the cup back to Bob, turns back to the audience.)

ARDEN: I'd like to tell you a story. There was a successful saleswoman who lived outside of Austin. She was headed for a sales meeting in Fort Worth. Instead of flying she decided to drive. She wanted to test out the brand new Lexus that her company had awarded her just that week. She had her fuzz buster on, the cruise control set at eighty, Garth on the tape deck...as she was driving, she started to notice that the air was gettin' kinda dusty. After about a mile she slowed down because she felt her car being rocked by a very strong wind. And there in the distance, heading in her direction, she saw a giant black funnel. It was a tornado. She stopped the car, knowing enough to open the windows a crack so they wouldn't explode. She then lay down on her front seat, shielding her face and praying to God that the twister would pass without doing her harm. Suddenly out of nowhere, a gigantic object falls out of the sky, lands on her car, shatters the windshield. The woman screams. Cut to, an hour later. The woman is now standing by the side of the road with an entire tree laying across the hood of her new car. She tries her car phone, it doesn't work. Great, so here she is, in the middle of nowhere, no phone, no help, it's starting to get dark, what is this woman going to do? She sees another car coming up the road. It pulls over, it's a Cadillac Seville. A nice-looking man gets out, early fifties, business suit, tie, gray at the temples—he reminds her of her boss. She glances through the window of his car, sees a briefcase on the front seat, a Business Week, a take-out coffee in the cup holder, the steam rising up over dash—the sight is so comforting, she almost cries. He asks if she needs help. She says, Yessir, yes, she certainly does. The man walks around to the back of his car and opens up his trunk. He pulls out a knife, holds it at her throat and tells her to get in. For two hours she's trapped in the trunk of his car while the man drives her around. She can hear him screaming obscenities at her from the front seat, telling her all the things he's going to do to her when they reach their destination—taking off her breasts with a hacksaw being the least of it, OK? Finally the car comes to a stop. The motor is turned off. She can hear him walking around to the back. She hears him putting his key in the lock of the trunk—"Are you ready to die like the bitch you are?" he says—and as he opens the trunk, she's ready with the .38 handgun she keeps in her purse. She shoots him twice through the chest and the man falls over dead. She climbs out of the trunk, her hands still shaking, and she uses the man's car phone to call the highway patrol—fully expecting that she might be put on trial for killing a seemingly innocent businessman. When the police arrive, they tell her that they had been trying to track down the suspect of a string of gruesome murders. They said that not only did she save herself, but she saved dozens of other women from a prolonged and horrible death. That woman is alive today because she was not afraid to take responsibility for her own protection. That woman is alive because she practiced aggressive, long-term thinking. That woman is alive. That woman is me. *(Arden goes over to a table and picks up a .38 revolver.)* During this talk, I'm going to give those of you who've never touched a gun before an opportunity to familiarize yourself with this piece of equipment. *(She snaps open the cylinder of the gun, holds it up and spins it to show that there are no bullets in the gun.)* This is a .38 double-action revolver, which is used and recommended by most police officers. I prefer a .38 to a .22 because it has guaranteed stopping power. Many women and also men are drawn to .22s for a first gun because they feel that a .22 might be easier to handle. Which is fine, but if you have an assailant who's on crack or any of your other substances, he might not even notice that he's been hit until he's back on the road, pondering what to do with your credit cards. But again, this is a personal choice.

(Arden hands the gun to Bob who takes it over to the audience to pass around. [Note: the gun should be real and not a prop gun. But for safety's sake, a part of it should be made inoperable.])

ARDEN: Pass it around, get to know it. This gun is not loaded, there are no bullets in the chamber. It doesn't have a mind, it doesn't have a will, it doesn't even have batteries. It is just a piece of metal, a collection of movable parts that do not move until you make them do so. Pull the trigger if you like. It will not hurt you. The devil is not hiding in the barrel. It is not "bad." Bad things are done by people, not by guns. Good people do not do bad things with guns. And conversely, good people do not turn bad if they have a gun, OK? By the year 2000, a firearm will be as common a piece of equipment as your car phone or pocket calculator. This should not scare you and this should not cause you despair. I'm a historian; I like to compare the Then with the Now; I like to let the past be my path to the future. Here's an example: when they first started putting electricity into homes, some people said, "Oh no we can't do that, it's too dangerous, someone's gonna kill themselves." They painted these scenarios of entire families laying dead on the floor, with their fingers in the sockets and their eyeballs fried. We can look back on that now and say, "Oh that was alarmist thinking." Hindsight is easy, I agree, but before we make an instant value judgment on something, it's good to first lay a grid on it. I'm an optimist-realist. What that means is that I look at what could potentially be bad and then figure out a way to make it good. Bob?

(Bob changes the Slide to a line graph chart on the projected crime rate up to the year 2000.)

ARDEN: Take a look at this chart. This is the reality, folks. I wish I could say that things in our country were getting better but sweet people, all you have to do is look at the numbers. And with all the riots, floods, fires, earthquakes, droughts—with all this happening, more and more people are saying, "Hey, the world's coming to an end, I don't give a blankety-blank about the law." You know? And the rest of us, the good people, the ones who, as Bob said, practice preparedness—we're going to have our little supply boxes with our batteries and canned goods, whatever, that we so carefully put together, and what's going to stop someone from walking up to us and saying, "Gimme"? And I hear, "Oh, I know it's really bad out there but there's nothin' I can do about it. Boo-hoo," you know? And I meet so many people, especially women who support this non-defense kind of attitude. They say, "Oh, I don't want to have a gun, my boyfriend says it's not feminine." Well what's feminine? *(Pause.)* You know? What's feminine—to look at me, I think you'd say that I was "feminine." Bob, would you say I was feminine?

BOB: I sure would.

ARDEN: There you go. But let's examine this for a minute. I know a lot of women who are ready to take responsibility for their own protection, but they say to me, "Arden, I just can't get behind using a gun." And that's a very natural reaction. As women, our traditional role has been to be life giver, not life taker. Yes, I agree with all of that. But as life giver, what am I going to do when there's been a hurricane, all lines of communication are down, my husband has gone off to find supplies, and a strange man has just kicked down my door?

(Arden picks up a ring of keys from the table, fits them between her fingers. Bob joins her for a demonstration.)

ARDEN: Here's a good one. How many of you have thought of this? "OK, I'm now going to defend myself with a bunch of keys sticking out of my knuckles."

BOB: "Watch out. I'm going to kill you, Lady."

(Bob does a simulated attack, disarms Arden then holds her in a grip.)

ARDEN: *(To audience.)* Now what? I am now free to be raped, disfigured and killed. *(Arden taps Bob to let him know to release her. Arden picks up a can of Mace.)*

ARDEN: OK, that didn't work, what if I keep a can of mace in my emergency supply box. Here goes.

BOB: "I'm going to kill you, Lady."

(Arden holds up the can of Mace, pretends to spray. Bob coughs twice then grabs Arden, holds her in the same grip.)

ARDEN: Oops, guess no one told me that most Mace sold on the market is so diluted that it's about as effective as a baby peeing on a rabid dog. Again, I am now free to be raped, disfigured and killed.

(Arden taps Bob. He releases his grip. Arden picks up a stun gun.)

ARDEN: OK, that was fun, now that all my broken ribs are healed and I've got most of my face back, I think I'll buy myself a stun gun. Now this is a great weapon. It won't penetrate a heavy coat or a leather jacket and in order for it to work at all you have to hold it against the struggling body of your two hundred-pound assailant for a full three seconds.

BOB: "Bitch! I'm going to kill you, Bitch."

(Arden looks a bit surprised by Bob's acting, then continues the demonstration, tries to zap Bob. Bob grabs her arms holds the gun away from his body then throws Arden in to a grip, holding the stun gun next to one of her nipples.)

ARDEN: Once again, it's open season on me. All right.

(Arden taps Bob. It takes him a little longer to release her this time. Bob starts to walk back to his chair. Bob suddenly rushes back at Arden. Arden grabs a gun from the table, and whips around taking a stance.)

ARDEN: "Stop right there! Advance any further and I'll shoot!"

(Bob immediately stops.)

ARDEN: "Slowly back away with your hands up. If you make any other movement I will kill you."

BOB: "Don't hurt me, Lady, please don't hurt me."

(Arden backs Bob up and makes him sit in the chair. She lowers the gun and walks back to the table, puts the gun back down.)

ARDEN: Which method of defense involved no physical contact between you and your assailant? Which method of defense protected your dignity as well as your life? And which method of defense involved the least amount of violence? It's like when we used to have nuclear weapons between us and the Russians, which I think was one of the biggest deterrents to war ever. In other words: the more *effective* your weapon is, the *less likely* you will have to use it. What we're talking about is deterrence, Folks. Not death, *deterrence.*

BOB: It's like preparedness.

ARDEN: That's right. See, I get crazy when people just make these blanket assumptions that all guns kill. That's like saying, oh, let's get rid of all cars because of all the highway deaths. Hey, fine with me—did you know that there are twenty times more fatalities caused by cars than by guns? And you don't see Car Control lobbies out there in Washington. You don't see anyone instituting a ten-day waiting period before you can purchase your new VW. What do you drive, Bob?

BOB: A Ford Bronco.

ARDEN: You like to buy American?

BOB: Wouldn't buy anything else.

ARDEN: Where are all our guns manufactured, Bob?

BOB: The good 'ol U.S. of A.

ARDEN: There you go. *(To audience.)* But it all comes down to this: deterrence equals power, power equals choice, choice equals life. Whoever has the gun, would you mind holding it up so Bob can collect it? By the way, the first thing Hitler did when he came into power? He took the guns away from the Jewish people. All things to think about.

(Bob hands Arden the .38.)

ARDEN: Isn't life funny? Lemme tell you one last story. I remember when I was a little girl, my family and I took a trip to the New York World's Fair. Anybody remember going to that? Anyway, there was this one exhibit called The City of Tomorrow. We stood in this long line that went into a room where you stood on a catwalk and looked down at a giant model of what a city would look like in fifty years. There were all these dome-shaped houses and weird-looking towers and monorails. And all the little people in the city looked kind of sealed in…and I don't know it all looked so strange to me that I got a sick feeling in my stomach. I started to cry and my mother asked me what the problem was. I told her my stomach hurt and she said that was because I'd been eating junk all day. And I said, no, my stomach hurt because the model of the city scared me, that I did-n't ever want to have to live like that. And my father looked down at me, and you know what he said? He said, "Don't worry, Girl, by the time the future gets here, you won't know the difference." *(Arden slowly starts loading bullets into the gun.)*

One last point. What happens if I put bullets in this gun and pass it back around? Maybe that gun would just continue to be passed from hand to hand. Or maybe it would stop with that one bad apple who's sitting among you. He or she would hold on to that loaded gun, cock the hammer and take advantage of us one by one. OK, but what if I gave every-one a loaded gun? You see how it all makes sense?

(Arden hands the loaded gun back to Bob. She exits.)

BOB: OK, folks. A lot to absorb. We're going to take a short break. Stretch your legs, there's water in the lobby. We'll see you back in fifteen.

(Bob puts the loaded gun in the case and snaps it shut. He picks it up and exits.)

END OF PLAY

WEEKEND ITINERARY

Friday, [appropriate date]

5:00-6:00 PM—Cocktail Hour and Mixer (Frontier Room, Main Lodge) *Please wear your name tags!*

6:30 PM—Dinner (Dining Room, Main Lodge)

8:00 PM—*Introduction to Getting Prepared* (Elk Seminar Room)

9:00 PM—Workshop (Elk Seminar Room)

Saturday, [appropriate date]

7:00-9:00 AM—Buffet Breakfast (Dining Room, Main Lodge)

10:00 AM—*Home Preparedness* (Elk Seminar Room)

11:00 AM—*Duck and Cover Workshop* (Elk Seminar Room)

12:30 PM—Lunch (Dining Room, Main Lodge)

2:00 PM—*Fire* (Elk Seminar Room) *optional

2:30 PM—*Floods and Mud slides* (Evergreen Seminar Room) *optional

3:00 PM—*Earthquakes* (Elk Seminar Room) *optional

3:30 PM—*Civil Disturbance* (Evergreen Seminar Room) *optional

4:00 PM—*Tornados and Hurricanes* (Santa Fe Seminar Room) *optional

4:30 PM—*Locusts* (Elk Seminar Room) *optional

5:00-6:00 PM—Cocktail Hour (Frontier Room, Main Lodge)

6:30 PM—Dinner (Dining Room, Main Lodge)

8:00 PM—Film-*Back Draft* (Evergreen Room) *optional

Sunday, [appropriate date]

7:00-9:00 AM—Buffet Breakfast (Dining Room, Main Lodge)

9:30-11:30 AM—*Defense Workshop* (Fitness Center) Please wear comfortable clothing.

12:30 PM—Lunch (Dining Room, Main Lodge)

2:00-3:00 PM—*FEMA and Insurance Workshop* (Santa Fe Seminar Room)

3:00-4:30 PM—*Building a New Life* (Elk Seminar Room)

5:00-7:00 PM—Barbecue and Cocktails (picnic area)

QUESTIONNAIRE

1) *Have you ever experienced one of the following* (please circle):

   a) Earthquake   b) Fire   c) Tornado   d)Hurricane   e) Flood   f) Landslide

   g) Riots   h) Locusts   i) Other_____

2) *If yes to #1, what kind of damage did you experience to your personal property?*

   a) none   b) slight   c) moderate   d) severe   e) total devastation

3) *Have you lost any family or loved ones to a natural or man-made cat-astrophe* (please do not include wars)?

   Please specify_____

4) *Have you recently moved because of a disaster? If yes, from where to where?*_____

5) *Which do you feel you would be most prepared to face?*

   a) Earthquake   b) Fire   c)Tornado   d) Hurricane   e) Flood   f) Landslide   g) Riots   h) Locusts

6) *Why are you taking this seminar?*

7) *What do you hope to get out of it?*

Out the Window
by Neal Bell

Mr. Bell's plays, including *Two Small Bodies, Raw Youth, Cold Sweat, Ready For The River, Out The Window, On The Bum* and adaptations of the novels *Therese Raquin* and *McTeague*, have appeared at such theatres as Playwrights Horizons, South Coast Repertory, the Mark Taper Forum, Actors Theatre of Louisville, La Jolla Playhouse and Berkeley Rep. The recipient of a 1992 Obie award for playwriting, Mr. Bell teaches at the 42nd Street Collective theatre-school in New York.

Out The Window is the co-winner of the Actors Theatre of Louisville 1990 Heideman Award and National Ten-Minute Play Contest.

ORIGINAL PRODUCTION

Out The Window was first produced by the Actors Theatre of Louisville in an Apprentice/Intern showcase on June 11, 1990. It was directed by Mark Hendren and had the following cast:

Jake	Josh Liveright
Andrea	Belinda Morgan

The play subsequently premiered professionally in the Humana Festival of New American Plays on April 6, 1991. It was directed by Bob Krakower and had the following cast:

Jake	Tom Stechschulte
Andy	Suzanna Hay

CHARACTERS

JAKE

ANDY

TIME: The time is the present.

SETTING: The action takes place in New York.

OUT THE WINDOW

A kitchen. Early morning light from the windows over the sink.
Up high, on top of the kitchen table, a wheelchair. In the wheelchair, Jake is
sprawled, completely out. He's wearing a wildly disheveled tux. In one dan-
gling hand he clutches an empty bottle. Jake is loudly sawing wood. The bottle
slips form his hand and hits the floor, with a crash that troubles Jake's sleep.

JAKE: *(Eyes closed.)* Who's there? *(He reacts to his shout.)* Oww! Jeez Louise, let me
try that again, little softer: Who's there? Andy? *(He feels the surrounding
air with his hands.)* Nothing. Me and my chair.
(Far off a cock crows.)
JAKE: Hit the snooze-alarm on that rooster, would you? I'm up. Well, almost
up. And I'd open my eyes, to greet the day and you, but I'm guessing that
light would not be what the doctor ordered, and speaking of tongue and
spirit depressors... One of my sweat-socks passed away in my mouth,
could you bring me a glass of water, see if I can just flush the sucker, yo,
Andrea, hey, little help...
(Again the offstage rooster crows. Jake winces.)
JAKE: And could somebody kindly get the hook for that bird?
(The rooster crows.)
JAKE: Do I live on a farm? Survey *says... (He buzzes "no.")* OK, did I go to a
party so trendy that animal acts were a part of the entertainment? Survey
says... I don't remember. Much about that party. At all. I recall a taxi-ride
through the Park. And then a mahogany elevator. And then a lot of
Republicans. People who *looked* like Republicans, anyway, bow-ties flap-
ping away...and then you wheeling me out of the madding crowd, and
into the dark and onto your bed, *somebody's* bed, whosever bed the party
was, and the rest is the kind of history you're condemned to
repeat...which I wouldn't mind, repeating, except next time, Andrea,
sweetie, baby, doll, I'd like to remember. The way you feel. The way you
taste. The way you move. For both of us. Remember all that, and not
black out and be shoveled back into my chair, like a sack of sheep-dip,
and shoved out into the hall or wherever I am, stark raving alone, if I *am*
alone, if I open my eyes...if I open my eyes and you've slunk
away–Andrea?... I'm going to feel, fair warning here, very crippled up
and very done in by Life, as I know it now, and extremely very sorry I
ever was born, it is going to get *that* ugly and whiny and borderline-truly-
obnoxious, I swear, so be it on your delectable head, if I open my eyes...
(He opens his eyes.) Andrea? *(He looks around.)* So you slopped me back in

my chair after all, and abandoned me halfway up the kitchen…wall…
(He looks down, suddenly realizing his chair is up in the air, on a table.)
…and screw a Mallard. I'm up on a table. *(Pause.)* Screw a green and yellow Mallard sideways. How'd I…like a giant entree, defrosting. How'd I
get up on a table?
*(Andy enters, her cocktail dress looking slept-in, toting an almost-empty bottle
of booze. She looks at Jake, in his chair on the table; then She squints at her bottle. Shrugging, she polishes off the booze and slumps in a kitchen chair.)*

JAKE: Hair of the dog that gummed your ankle?

ANDY: Arf.

JAKE: Little early for that.

ANDY: Go far away. *(Pause.)* I love you.

JAKE: I know.

ANDY: Despite your being high up on a table. By manner of means unknown.
(Pause.) And I'm marrying you.

JAKE: I appreciate the condescension.

ANDY: It isn't that. It's a lack of animal cunning–

JAKE: On whose part?

ANDY: Mine. My mother says I must subscribe to survival of the cutest.

JAKE: Your mother thinks I'm cute?

ANDY: I'm on the case. She's half-convinced. She worries about our children.

JAKE: You tell her that automobile collisions aren't passed along in the genes?

ANDY: The carelessness that gets you into them is.

JAKE: *She* says?…

ANDY: I wonder myself. Get down from there.

JAKE: *(Trying to find an excuse.)* In a minute. The air is clearer.

ANDY: Than what?
(Offstage, a mournful foghorn. Jake is surprised, and Andy is bothered.)

ANDY: And how, of course, would we *have* children?

JAKE: We do it.

ANDY: You never pop.

JAKE: Is that your mother's word? "Pop?"

ANDY: Get *down*.

JAKE: In what sense?
(The foghorn sounds again, louder.)

JAKE: I thought I heard a pop. Last night.

ANDY: Champagne. *Cheap* champagne. B-list people. Including us. That kind
of party.

JAKE: It was?
(She nods.)

JAKE: By the sea?

ANDY: No, not by the sea. And not on a farm. Though you babbled on about
both, before you went under. A farm with a yard running down to the

water. Some place in your head you read about. When you were a kid. Horsies neighing, and moo-cows moo-ing, and lobster lobbing, and foghorns moaning away…

JAKE: I thought I heard a rooster. A minute ago.

ANDY: Not this high up. On Central Park West. Unless—I suppose it's possible—animal sacrifice has trickled down to the horsey-set.

JAKE: —and foghorns.

ANDY: *No.*

JAKE: You heard them too.

ANDY: Get down from there *five minutes ago! (Pause.)*

JAKE: I don't know how I got up. *(Pause.)*

ANDY: You did it. Congratulations. I'm crying now.

JAKE: Why are you crying?

ANDY: Because you *did* pop. You sorry sodden son-of-a-bitch. You came inside me last night.

JAKE: I didn't.

ANDY: You did. We've been trying for how many months–fifteen? I'd fly, and you thought you never would. Ever again. But you did. Last night. You were finally up in the air *with* me. You went off like a Roman candle. And I was the sky you lit up. Way deep inside. But you don't remember.

JAKE: No, wait: maybe I do…

ANDY: You don't. So it never happened. *(Pause.)* It never happened at all. *Get off of this table! (Pause.)* How did you get on the table.

JAKE: An awesome wheelie? *(Pause.)*

ANDY: You drink too much.

JAKE: And if somebody lit your breath you could spot-weld. Give me a break. And where did *you* sleep last night.

ANDY: In a tub. But I know how I got in the tub. *(Pause.)* Why do you drink so much?

JAKE: I'm afraid.

ANDY: Of what? *(Pause; she suspects the answer.)* Of what?

JAKE: Of you. Of how you think you know me.

ANDY: Oh? Too bad. I *do* know you, pal.

JAKE: And what's the first thing that occurs to you–when you think about me? My sense of rhythm? My brain? My cock? My chair? *(Pause.)* My chair.

ANDY: What chair?

JAKE: Fuck *you.*

ANDY: No: fuck you *first.*

JAKE: Not *just* a man in a chair. You're smarter than that. But you start with that.

ANDY: I start with just a man–

JAKE: —about whom you know squat—

ANDY: —as do you of the *woman,* you pushy martyr—

JAKE: *A-ha!*

ANDY: I worship the ground you roll on, don't give me *"A-ha!"* Get off of that table you never should have got onto–

JAKE: Why not? I've seen *you* sit on tables before, all devil-may-care–

ANDY: –or I'm walking–

JAKE: Then *walk,* for the luvva Mike Wallace, you threaten to walk on me seventeen times a week, at least, and more in months with an "R," so stop sturming and dranging and *do* it! *Walk.*

ANDY: *You* walk!

JAKE: I can't!

ANDY: Then *roll.* *(Pause.)*

JAKE: Are you daring me to lay rubber? Step aside…
(Releasing the brakes on his chair, Jake starts to push forward. Andy stops the chair before it can topple over the edge.)

JAKE: Get out of my flight-path, lady.

ANDY: I doubt it severely, bud.

JAKE: You don't get it. Do you? How do you think I landed up here? I flew.

ANDY: I double-dee-doubt it.

JAKE: *(As the truth of it strikes him.)* I flew. Jeez Louise…

ANDY: Somebody put you up here. As a joke.

JAKE: Who? *(Pause.)* I'm not just a man in a chair.

ANDY: I know.

JAKE: You know that. But you don't know me.

ANDY: I know you didn't fly.

JAKE: Why not?

ANDY: If you could fly… *(Pause.)* I'm going to find a ladder.
(She starts to exit. He calls after her, stopping her.)

JAKE: "If I could fly…" *(He completes her unspoken thought.)* I could do any number of things. Walk, even.

ANDY: Stop.

JAKE: Start *hoping* again I could walk.

ANDY: *Stop.*

JAKE: Don't you think we should hope any more?

ANDY: I'd rather drink.

JAKE: I never thought I would come.

ANDY: You don't even know if you did.

JAKE: It's coming back. Look out the window.

ANDY: Don't change the subject–

JAKE: I'm not! Look out…
(Andy looks out the window and gasps.)

JAKE: We're in an apartment on Central Park West?

ANDY: We were…

JAKE: Can you see the Park?

ANDY: No.

JAKE: Lean out. Can you see the Gulf-and-Western Building? The Plaza? The street? The horse-and-buggies? Japanese tourists? Bicycle maniacs? Boomboxes? Road-apples? Anything? *(Pause.)*

ANDY: There's a farm. An old white clapboard farmhouse, up on a rise. And a lawn running down from the house to a rocky beach. The lawn is steep. It's all wildflowers...

JAKE: Fog?

ANDY: Yes. But the sun is burning through... What is it?

JAKE: It isn't a place I read about. It's a place I used to visit. When I was a kid. Great-Uncle-Somebody's farm. He died a long time ago, and I never went back... But I think I was happier there than I ever have been...

ANDY: How did we get...

JAKE: We flew. *(Pause.)*

ANDY: Fly off of the table, then. *(Pause.)* Fly yourself and your chair back down to the floor. Do it. Now. *(Pause.)*

JAKE: I think I've done enough for one day. I'm resting.

ANDY: I have to go. *(She starts to exit.)*

JAKE: I remember how we got here.

ANDY: How?

JAKE: You were sitting on me, you were bending over to brush my face with your hair, and I all of a sudden knew, if you moved again, I was going to shoot, for the very first time since I hurt myself, a lot of years in the desert and rain at last, and you started to move and I grabbed your ass, to hold the moment before I came, I could feel it all about to come down, this wind before a thunderstorm, you were licking my lips, I was holding you still, and holding you still, and just then...right then...we were standing beside each other, *standing* holding hands, in this milky light getting lighter, in Great Uncle Somebody's yard...Uncle *Norbert*...God, Uncle Norbert... and we started to run down the hill, that's what we'd do, back then, run down this hill to the water's edge...and the hill was so steep, you'd hit a place where you knew you couldn't stop anymore, if you tried you'd fall, so you'd just keep running, faster and faster, trying to move your legs as fast as the rest of your body was falling, you'd hear this roar in your ears, and the light on the water would blind your eyes, and all you'd want to do was run on forever. *(Pause.)*

ANDY: I had to hope you wouldn't die. And then I had to hope there was still a mind, in this body that hadn't died, and couldn't move. And then, when the mind came back, I had to hope it wasn't buried alive in a body that only lay there, month after month. And then when the body moved at all, the tip of one finger, a twitch, I had to hope it would move again. And that more would move. That your fingers could hold a pencil someday. That your sphincter muscles could hold your piss. That your penis could hold a boner. That you could hold me. So I could love your body! And come. Then I had to hope you could come too.

JAKE: I came.

ANDY: And now you want me to hope that you'll stand on a hill...

JAKE: I already have. I hope to again. Which I guess is by way of saying that hope is a complicated thing. You give me hope, and I don't know how. *(Pause.)* I also don't know how to get off of this table. *(Pause.)*

ANDY: I'll get a ladder... *(But she doesn't move.)*

JAKE: Do you understand what I'm saying? I can never run down that hill again. Except in you.

(Andy stares at Jake. Far off a rooster crows, and a foghorn sounds. The light in the room gets brighter.)

END OF PLAY

The Eye of the Beholder

by Kent Broadhurst

BIOGRAPHY

Kent Broadhurst has been active in theatre, film and television for many years. It was in 1980 while performing at Actors Theatre of Louisville that his work as a playwright emerged. His first play, the full-length comedy *They're Coming to Make it Brighter*, commissioned, produced and directed by Jon Jory, premiered on the mainstage in the Humana Festival of New American Plays and is now published by The Dramatic Publishing Co. Following this success, he was Playwright in Residence at ATL and wrote and also directed his second full-length comedy *Lemons* for the Humana Festival. Audiences voted it one of the five favorite plays of the entire first decade of Humana Festivals. The following fall, *Lemons* opened the season at The Group Theatre in Seattle. *Lemons* and *They're Coming to Make it Brighter* were both performed in Minneapolis at The Mixed Blood Theatre. His one-act play *The Eye of the Beholder* and it's companion piece *The Habitual Acceptance of The Near Enough* were premiered in separate ATL Humana Festivals and were chosen by ATL for the United States Information Agency sponsored Budapest, Australian, and Belgrade Tours during the mid-80's and have been published separately, along with *Lemons* by Dramatists Play Service. Both one-acts played The Kingshead Theatre in London, The Lunchbox Theatre in Calgary, Canada and subsequently have been successfully produced separately and together at numerous theatres and colleges across the country. Recently they were seen under the collective title, *Art Who?*, at the Ruth Bachofner Gallery in Los Angeles and the West Bank Cafe in New York City. Broadhurst was completed three new plays, the first entitled *Gala*, another entitled *Bound*, and most recently *Black Iris*, which he has also transposed into a screenplay.

ORIGINAL PRODUCTION

The Eye of the Beholder premiered in the 1982 Humana Festival of New American Plays. It was directed by Larry Deckel with the following cast:

James	Fred Sanders
Barney	Dierk Toporzysek
Leon	Bruce Kuhn

CHARACTERS

THE PAINTERS: They are equals but totally opposite in countenance and style. Both wear comfortable, timeless paint-stained clothes both to their own identity. They should seem to have been standing there painting side by side for centuries. Their working relationship is an equally ancient see-saw.

JAMES: over 30, fair, lean, chiseled intelligence, steady precision.

BARNEY: over 30, dark, husky, vigorously emotional, impulsive.

THE MODEL; LEON: over 30, well-muscled, powerful, but graceful. He wears a tan colored brief. He is standing on the model platform in a spotlight assuming a comfortable but eloquent classic pose.

Note: While originally written for three male actors, *The Eye of the Beholder* can be performed, with equal effectiveness, by a cast of three actresses, substituting the names Jane, Bella and Leona.

THE EYE
OF THE BEHOLDER

The setting is a painter's studio. There are two large and long-used, heavy wooden easels with a 28" x 60" stretched canvas (bigger if sight lines permit, but both are the same size) on each easel. The two paintings are in progress. The only other necessary furniture objects are a large table used by both artists to hold their palettes and supplies; a model's platform 18" high and 4' sq. and two wastebaskets. Their two palettes are side by side on the tabletop, rather like two backyards; a row of cans, jars, supplies, etc. separating the two. Both palettes (at least 2 ft. sq.) have many mounds and splotches of oil paints; the accumulation of many, many paintings worth. James's side of the table is a bit more organized and tidy than Barney's. Also on the table surrounding the palettes are each painter's tin cans holding brushes, bottles of painting medium and odds and ends. Each painter uses a roll of toilet paper to clean brushes between colors. The wastebaskets are nearly full of little wads of the paper swiped with different colors. Many are on the floor around the basket on Barney's side. All the objects and possibly the floor area around each easel (with the exception of the model platform) are stippled with myriad stray dots and splashes of paint; a random cross hatching from years of work being done in that precise area. (A dropcloth can be used under the entire acting area, Barney's side is a mess and James's fairly pristine.) The model's platform is gray, placed so as to complete a triangle with the two easels. The two paintings are of the same model done in James's and Barney's totally different individual style and expression. James's work is very precise and detailed, almost classical, tending to the Flemish-Dutch influence. Barney on the other hand, exudes a passionate impressionistic style; much thicker paint and vivid color. Both paintings should be as "good" as possible of the actor playing Leon; and done from the angle each painter has to the model. As the lights come up, the two painters are intently working from the model before them. They continue painting for a length of time; at moments absorbed in brushwork on the surface of the canvas, then studying the model, cleaning a brush, back to the palette for more pigment, etc. At some point Barney steps back to scrutinize his canvas with some distance. For a moment his eyes search the work, then shift over to the other painter's canvas. James remains focused on his own process, unaware of Barney's attention. Barney looks back to his own painting, then back to James's. He scans James's palette then his own, then back to James's painting, then back to his own, then to James's again.

BARNEY: …What is that, Cadmium Red Medium?…

JAMES: *(A beat.)* …Light.

BARNEY: …Medium Light?…

JAMES: …Just Light…Cadmium Red Light…

(Barney looks back and forth between the two canvases again.)

BARNEY: …Doesn't that make it too "pink"?…

JAMES: I cut it with Yellow Ochre.

BARNEY: I like that…mine looks muddy.

JAMES: That's because you're using Burnt Umber in there…it's bound to get muddy with Burnt Umber…

BARNEY: You use Burnt Umber.

JAMES: But I don't mix it *in*…I use it as a glaze over the top or for underpainting…I don't mix it *in*…

BARNEY: …Oh…

JAMES: …You're mixing it in, that's why it's muddy…

BARNEY: …Flesh tones are the hardest…to really make it look alive…there's no surface in the world like flesh…the way the light plays…Don't you feel that way?

JAMES: Of course I feel that way…that's why I like to paint from life…to have the actual living flesh in front of me.

BARNEY: *(After a beat.)* …Do you suppose I could have a squeeze of it?

JAMES: What.

BARNEY: Cadmium Red Light.

JAMES: That was the last of the tube…what's on the palette.

BARNEY: Oh…could I maybe borrow a small brush-full from that…

JAMES: …That's all I have.

BARNEY: Well, I know, but I'll pay you back soon as I buy some…I'd just like to try it on this one spot…just for the flush of the cheeks there…see what it looks like.

JAMES: …What if *I* run out…while I'm in the middle of using it?

BARNEY: Yeah, but I won't take that much…I just need a touch…for the cheeks…

JAMES: Take it.

BARNEY: *(As he takes some of the paint from James's palette.)* …I feel that you don't really want me to take it.

JAMES: TAKE IT.

BARNEY: You know how it is when you're inspired to do something… you have to act on the moment or you forget what it is you wanted to do.

JAMES: *You* do.

BARNEY: …That's what I said, you *do*.

JAMES: *You* do…*I* don't…I never forget what I intend to do. How can you forget?…You're looking at your painting and you see something it needs…it doesn't not need it the next time you're working on it.

BARNEY: Well, I do my best things impulsively...on the moment. I've found planning stifles my spontaneity...my style...

JAMES: I'd say lack of planning stifles your quality.

BARNEY: God, you have some nerve...you do...that's a purely subjective judgement. I find your pedantic regimentation rather...a...dry.

JAMES: Well, there's no accounting for taste...I suppose, if you consider proficiency in technical facility extraneous to the visitation of the muse, that's your prerogative...It would seem, however, that the skeleton holds up the flesh...the architecture has to be sound or no amount of surface dazzle is going to save it.

BARNEY: I'm not painting a building, for Chrissake...painting is an act of life...passion if you will.

JAMES: There's a chasm of difference between passion and slip-shod.

BARNEY: ...Slip-shod...*Slip*-shod...

JAMES: Well, you're never going to get the color you want, for instance, starting *out* with Cadmium Red Light and mixing white into it, of course it'll be too "pink"...it'll take tons of white to cut it...I knew you were going to do that when you took that much...you start with the white, and add a dash of Yellow Ochre, then just the smallest dot of Cadmium Red Light...Cadmium Red Light is a very strong color.

BARNEY: How can you be so Goddam sure I don't want it that pink...I might want it that pink.

JAMES: Well, you just asked me if Cadmium Red Light wouldn't make it *too* "pink"...I'm only going by what you said...if you want it "pink" pink, use Alizeron Crimson in it...*that*'ll make it pink.

BARNEY: I don't want it *blue* pink, for Chrissake...I know Alizeron Crimson...I know what Alizeron Crimson does...I use it all the time.

JAMES: I can see that...

BARNEY: ...What do you mean?

JAMES: Just that it's blatantly obvious that you're very *partial* to Alizeron Crimson...It's like a pubescent teen who's just discovering sex...you've got Alizeron Crimson everywhere...Alizeron Crimson is a chemically dominant pigment...you must use great discrimination when you use that overpowering a red or it just takes over anything you mix it with...That's why everybody you paint looks like an American Indian.

BARNEY: They do not.

JAMES: Of course they do...every figure you've done in the last two months looks like a slumbering Apache.

BARNEY: That's a *choice*.

JAMES: Then why did you complain that yours looks muddy.

BARNEY: It wasn't a complaint...it was a mere observation in the course of the work process...if you thought I was implying some sort of unhappiness...that's what *you're* reading into it.

JAMES: I was simply using *your* words.

BARNEY: ...I may have said "muddy," but it certainly wasn't a complaint.

JAMES: Well, "muddy" doesn't sound like someone who's delighted with the effect.

BARNEY: You really begrudge loaning me some Cadmium Red Light, don't you?

JAMES: I don't begrudge it at all...I wouldn't have given it to you if I begrudged it.

BARNEY: You're very hostile.

JAMES: Why would you say a thing like that?

BARNEY: You're certainly attacking me...I can hear it in your voice...I only asked in a spirit of camaraderie...I would have done the same for you, if I saw you were on a "roll"...

JAMES: A "roll" or a "rut" that may be true; but you're a very emotional person...you respond on an *emotional* level to everything...you would have given it to me or to a perfect stranger, because you want everyone to *like* you. While I, on the other hand, considered purely the demands of my own painting first and how much Cadmium Red Light I would be needing with respect to the area of the painting that I was working on at the time...The work comes first...If I had wanted to use a color I don't have...some of your Phthalocyanine Blue for instance...I would have made a mental note and proceeded to paint on some other area and the next time I got supplies, I would have bought my own Phthalocyanine Blue...Painting is fundamentally a solitary adventure, not a *team* effort...Thank God.

BARNEY: Then what do you need a model for?

JAMES: Because that's the subject, dammit.

BARNEY: But if you're so self-sufficient...such a fucking *purist*...then you should be able to do *without* a model...conceive it immaculately from some...invisible cosmic force field...

JAMES: Well, now you've drifted into hysterical babbling. I paint from a model because I find nothing inconsistent in the use of the subject before me for inspiration and factual source. It is my earnest endeavor to succeed in capturing the form I see before me on canvas and elevating it through my creative impression of it to the level of Art.

BARNEY: Well what the hell do you think I do?

JAMES: I think you take vandalous liberties and call it interpretation. I think you indulge in your emotional excesses and label it "style."

BARNEY: And it's that very, vigorous audacity and iconoclastic passion that makes *me* worthy of the title of Artist and you a plodding technician.

JAMES: How dare you!...After I have generously loaned you the last of my Cadmium Red Light for the execution, and I mean Execution, of your primitive daubing at the sacrifice of my own time and effort and expense.

BARNEY: THAT'S what it is...you're basically just cheap...you're afraid I won't pay you back for a lousy brush-full of Cadmium Red Light? Would you *like* some of my Phthalocyanine Blue? Because you're more than welcome to it...take a whole pile of it...take the tube...the thought of you standing there all this time coveting a dab of my Phthalocyanine Blue because you're too socially isolated to ask for some is appalling.

JAMES: I don't want your Phthalocyanine Blue!...I don't *need* your Phthalocyanine Blue...if on the spur of the moment I should happen to want to use blue, I can use Cerulean Blue...or Ultramarine Blue Deep with a little Viridian Green in it...I most certainly wouldn't resort to "coveting," as you put it, your damn tube of Phthalo Blue. The thing that is frustrating, however, is to give you the last of the goddam Cadmium Red Light and see it so crudely squandered and misused.

BARNEY: O.K., magic fingers, how would *you* use it. *(He refers to his painting.)*

LEON: Can I rest?

BARNEY: How can we work if you keep moving?

LEON: I just thought—

JAMES: A.a.agh...now you've moved your arm, it was higher...no, more to the left...no, the left...there... *(Back to Barney.)* I wouldn't presume to instruct you as to how you should use Cadmium Red Light...then it would be stamped with my indelible conceptual personality...it wouldn't be *your* painting anymore...you obviously have a totally differing concept of how the human body should be painted.

BARNEY: I have no "shoulds" in my paintings...I have no "shoulds" in my *life*...I paint on instinct!

JAMES: You urinate on instinct, that doesn't make it a work of Art.

BARNEY: All right, intuition.

JAMES: A better word, but intuition alone doesn't make Art. Everybody has intuition...you can't simply assault a canvas with intuition and expect to achieve a great work of Art.

BARNEY: I *expect* nothing...how can you *expect* some predetermined result from a painting yet to be done...a vision without form...Granted, everybody has intuition; but how many listen to it or would even recognize it if it threw up on them.

JAMES: How vivid.

BARNEY: Don't look down your academic nose at me. You can stand behind that sterile wasteland you believe to be a painting and pontificate on some obsolete traditional dogma all you want but it is by historical fact, the most stifling, stultifying, eclectic atmosphere possible to great Art!...Art must overwhelm!...Art must win territory from the unknown!...

JAMES: ... "win territory from the unknown"?...

BARNEY: Yes!

JAMES: Where did you hear that?…That's not yours…You heard that some-place…talk about eclectic.

BARNEY: I made that up just now.

JAMES: You did not…I can tell when you've heard some catchy phrase that's grabbed your emotional fancy and you can't wait to use it in a conversation somewhere…and that's the way you paint…You get swept away with someone else's ideas to the point where you think they're yours…Your vigorous defense of extempore is really someone else's ideas enthusiastically rearranged…You're simply not an original!

(Barney scoops up a spatula full of the Cadmium Red Light and thwacks it at James, hitting him squarely in the chest.)

BARNEY: That was entirely my own idea.

(James scoops up some Green and thwacks Barney in retaliation.)

LEON: Can I rest now, my foot's gone to sl—

JAMES AND BARNEY: NO!

JAMES: Do you feel better?

BARNEY: Yes!

JAMES: So do I!

(The two painters both scrape clean. James, with the Red from his chest on his spatula.)

JAMES: …Do you want this?

BARNEY: Yes, thanks.

(James puts the Red on Barney's palette. Barney returns the Green to James's. They resume painting. A silence.)

BARNEY: …What's the matter with me…I don't know what got into me…What a stupid…infantile gesture. It just proves conclusively everything you said about me. It's true…It's true…I'm an emotional mess…I actually threw paint at you because you're right.

JAMES: No…No, I threw paint back…You mustn't blame yourself, I provoked it…I was insulting and unfeeling and unjust…You're a *wonderful* artist!…You bring a vibrancy and sincerity to the work that I'm totally incapable of…I took advantage of your vulnerability and caring and pushed you into a corner…I admire your profound capacity for emotion…your willingness to hurl yourself…to rush toward your vision…and I think…deep down…I'm jealous of that…I'm cold…I am…I'm a *cold* man…unloving and dry just like you said…

BARNEY: NO…That's not so…That's an absolute untruth…Your sense of discipline has *always*—

JAMES: I'm like a dead man…a corpse…standing before the canvas trying to create life…vainly attempting to compensate for a barren and desolate soul…

BARNEY: I won't listen to you beating yourself like this…You have a dazzling, innate talent for structure and…and composition…I can only press my stupid nose to the glass in awe of such flawless precision...I watch you work sometimes and I could weep at the way your craft flows so effortlessly from your hand like a current...

JAMES: But why don't my paintings overwhelm??...I want to *stun* people...I want to jar some sacred crust loose...send a charge of *enlightenment* into the viewer.

BARNEY: YOU DO!

JAMES: I DON'T!...My work doesn't *thrill*...startle...My paintings only inspire indifference...and that's because they're vapid, thin...sterile...They have none of the bravado and ferocity you bring to the work...The sheer *danger!*...I think if I could do one painting...just once that was dangerous...I'd feel fulfilled...

BARNEY: You *will*...It's in you...like a vein of ore just waiting to be exposed...You merely need the right inspiration...something to crack the cosmic egg...a subject worthy of your technique.

JAMES: But you paint the same thing I paint and *you* have it...Your work sings with an unadorned brilliance of the primitive.

BARNEY: I'm a gorilla!...A big, clumsy bear with paint on my paws next to you,—Look! Look at what you've done there...the flesh...the movement, the spirit...you've taken this very...average-looking subject and made it noble...even epic...you've elevated the mundane...to Art.

JAMES: ART!...I don't even know what "Art" is anymore...

BARNEY: That's because it's indescribable...it can only be witnessed,—of course you don't know what Art is...no one knows What...Art...IS...That's why critics are pointless ultimately...

LEON: Art is the ever renewed, concentric approach and breaking through of selfhood towards infinity. The complete extinction of limitation...and the condensation of the universe to a microscopic focus and ever again...the establishment of a magic balance between soul and cosmos...The self dissolved and transformed into the whole.

BARNEY: Nobody asked you, Leon...

LEON: Well, I was just trying to help...I thought maybe if I gave you the answer...that I could rest.

BARNEY: But you're the model...

LEON: What difference does that make?...I thought you wanted to know what Art is...

BARNEY: But I want to know from somebody I know knows...How do I know *you* know...You're just the model...besides I said no one knows, what Art is.

LEON: I just *told* you what it is...Did it sound right or not?

BARNEY: What did you say?

LEON: I don't remember...

BARNEY: Well, there you are!

LEON: ...I remember the *thought*, I don't know if I remember the exact *words*...

JAMES: I remember exactly what you said...You said something about,—Art is the ever concentric breakthrough of selfhood from infinity...The complete extinction of the universe to a microscope, focused on the established magic and balance of the soul and the cosmos...The self dissolving the whole.

LEON: ...I didn't say that...Is that what you got?...That's not what I said...I can't believe I'm hearing you say that's what you thought I said...

BARNEY: You obviously didn't express yourself very clearly or we'd have understood what you said...which is why you're on that side of the easel...

LEON: I'm on this side of the easel because you're paying me to stand here...I didn't just happen along...There's plenty of stuff I could be doing.

JAMES: Meanwhile, you're not doing what we're paying you to do very well...I can't paint you if you're jumping all over the place.

BARNEY: However, sometimes when he moves like that...the brush moves with more...dash...like painting a blur in space...the strokes come out more vital as opposed to static...

JAMES: I won't dispute that...but if I'm trying to concentrate on the perfect rendering of a *form* in space that I've chosen to paint because its composition...its perspective or whatever is challenging and beautiful to my eye...then I damn well want it to stay that way till I can get it down on canvas...Particularly when I'm paying for it to do so.

BARNEY: God, you're practical...

JAMES: Just seems to me good sense.

LEON: Just because you're paying me...that doesn't shut down my mind...you asked a question and I gave you a perfect answer...and you didn't even hear it...and it seems to me your *eyes* aren't any better at picking up what's in front of you...I don't look like either of those paintings...That's not me...

JAMES: It's not supposed to be *you*...it's supposed to be "man"...if it were *you*...you'd be paying US...and it would be a portrait...You *represent* "man"...

LEON: But I *am* one.

JAMES: But your *a* man...not "Man"...the term "Man" implies a symbol...a synthesis of an enormous amount of information distilled into one...tangible... "glyph"...

LEON: One *what?*...

BARNEY: Don't ask him...

JAMES: ...a "glyph"...is a symbol...hieroglyphics were...*are* a set of symbols meant to convey certain highly evolved, esoteric and ancient information to only those who were capable of—

BARNEY: —Are you going to start on Ancient Egypt?...'cause I'm leaving ...you insist on bringing that up any chance you get and I will not put up with another 30 minute monologue on Ancient Egypt...I know *nothing* about it, so I can't dispute you on *anything*...and you take advantage of everyone's ignorance of the subject to lecture... and I told you that the next time you snuck it in, I would leave... *(He starts to put brushes into turpentine.)*

JAMES: O just relax!...I'm only using hieroglyphics as an example of a symbol...I'm not going to expound on Ancient Egypt...Although it's a fascinating topic and one that we could all benefit enormously from learning about if some of us would just—

BARNEY: —You think I'm fooling with you, don't you?...I *mean* it...ONE MORE WORD...

JAMES: All right, all right!...I just hate to see you so desperately protecting a pocket of ignorance that might be the very launch to a whole new consciousness for you, but I'm certainly not going to *thrash* awareness into you...

(Barney threatens again. James withdraws. They both resume painting without looking at Leon, who is no longer holding the pose. A silence.)

LEON: ...If I'm *a* man...then the painting is "Man"...is that what you're saying?...

JAMES: Right.

LEON: But the painting isn't "life"...it's just canvas and wood and paint and turpentine...I'M "life"...as the model, I'M "life"...the canvas isn't "life"...I'm *"Life"*...

BARNEY: Well, there's "life" and then there's *"Life"*...I can see life in the streets too; but, it isn't necessarily worth painting.

JAMES: That's a very good point...There's life that's merely going on... and then there's "Life" that sublimely reveals the best of what men can be.

BARNEY: ...One's boring, the other is inspiring...

JAMES: ...Exactly.

(They resume painting again. A pause.)

LEON: ...Are you saying I'm boring?

JAMES: You're not particularly *inspiring*...You have a good body but that's not the sum total of inspiration.

BARNEY: ...And I find that a good deal of the time, I *am* bored...that doesn't necessarily imply that *Leon* inspires boredom however.

JAMES: Now we're getting down to it...the ultimate and essentially primal question, then, is where does the inspiration come from *before* it does or doesn't take possession of the model in order that the painter is or is not inspired by what he sees...

BARNEY: That wasn't even coherent...You get lost in these obscure labyrinths of metaphysical speculation and absolutely deny entrance to any inspiration that might be ready to burst through...*wherever* it comes from...Who *cares* where it comes from?...

LEON: ...I don't think we're still on the point.

JAMES: You have to keep up, Leon...We can't keep going back for you.

BARNEY: What's the damn point?

LEON: You made a very disparaging slur regarding my ability and commitment...as an Artist's Model...professionally...and if you think you can do better then *you* get up here...I care just as much about *my* work as you do yours.

JAMES: *(To Leon.)* First of all, it would be *more* impossible for *him* to stand still than *you.*

BARNEY: There he goes with the "standing still" thing again...You still don't know when you've made your point, do you?...

JAMES: Well, that's fifty percent of the job!

BARNEY: —So is knowing when you've made your point!

LEON: The POINT IS—As the model, I'M "Life"...Right?...the canvas isn't "life"...I'M "Life"...*my existence* doesn't depend on being perceived.

JAMES AND BARNEY: Right.

LEON: ...The Life for the Art...or the Art for the "Life"...I can't "do" "Life"...I have to just "be"...and the closer I get to that...the more the inspiration that makes you want to paint me...so a polarity comes into being that results in Art...Both sides in the pursuit of Truth...or Beauty...or Art...or whatever...Right?

(Simultaneously:)

BARNEY: Right!

JAMES: Wrong!

JAMES: How can you assume that both sides have the same vision of it?...The only way you can be *some* what sure...is to exchange places...but I mean totally...and experience exactly what the other is experiencing...but that's impossible...because Leon can't paint... but you *can be painted!*...So...the only recourse is for you to simply *join* Leon...rather than replace him...Which might prove to be an inspiration...the next level up from "life" is relationship... which undoubtedly makes for a more complex and challenging subject to paint...compositionally... "Man" alone...that's one thing...but two Men, that's another thing...the potential for communication...Communication!...—That's what my work lacks. That may be the means to achieve a new level...instead of representing "Man" as solitary...paint him as "many"...but still "Man"...This may be the direction... *(A beat.)*

BARNEY: ...I think that's brilliant...it's a little hard to follow, but brilliant. The reason that *I* can't find the key to *my* painting is because I've never experienced *being* painted...What a breakthrough...

LEON: ...The main thing, is to find the rhythm of the stillness...and then relax...

BARNEY: "Rhythm of the stillness"...I like that.

LEON: Alignment...It's going to be a lot different now with two...The counterpoints of support and balance will be a lot different...but that's all right...Now look, whatever composition we eventually hit, that *is* the "One,"—we have to find who's the center of gravity in order to be able to maintain it...You have to lift against it *properly* and then relax within it until you cancel out effort...

(Barney strips down to his shorts.)

JAMES: This is very exciting now...I think we're right at the pulse of something...You can tell when you're on to something...YOU get enthused...I'm getting enthused...a whole new attack...and a certain "effortlessness"...

BARNEY: I know exactly what you mean...exactly...something right about it...As a painter myself, I can infuse Leon with what a painter *needs* by being in direct contact instead of an observer. *(He joins Leon on the platform.)*

JAMES: ...Are a.a...are you going to leave your hat on?

BARNEY: *No*...I'm not going to leave my hat on...I forgot it. *(He tosses his hat on his pile of clothing.)*

JAMES: I wasn't telling you to take it off...I mean it's a possible choice... It makes you more of a separate man from Leon...It makes you more of a *specific* man...as opposed to classic...It identifies you...whereas Leon has no definite identity...

BARNEY: Are you going to start directing?

JAMES: I'm merely giving you the benefit of my outside eye, so to speak...my impressions.

BARNEY: Well, how do you expect me to find the experience for myself if you tell me what do?...I thought this was what *I* needed to experience. I thought this was *my* experience.

JAMES: Of course it's your experience...but how can *you* tell what's harmonious to the viewer's eye...You've never done this before... You're a novice at this.

BARNEY: Typical of you to preclude the possibility of divine revelation...I might step into the light and get a direct message as to the perfect equation of harmony.

JAMES: Are you going to count on that?

BARNEY: NO, I'm not *counting* on it, but it's a *possibility*...Could you *give* me a minute, for Chrissake!

JAMES: Most definitely...I didn't mean to interfere with your experience.

BARNEY: *(To Leon.)*...Leon. *(They shake hands.)* It's good to be here.

LEON: My pleasure.

BARNEY: Now, let's see…the way I see it…we can either be in an antagonistic situation or a compatible one…God, I can already feel a new sensation.

LEON: That's the draft. You're unfamiliar with standing in the light without your clothes on…It takes a minute to get used to it, but I know what you mean…I feel it too, because I'm so used to being up here alone.

BARNEY: This is incredible…my mind is going nine million miles an hour…all sorts of combinations are available to us…it's hard to know which one will be the most successful.

LEON: I find you know it when you hit it.

BARNEY: Let's see…a.a.a. do you want to do something from Mythology or a.a.…contemporary?

LEON: This is your ball game…Whatever you want…

BARNEY: Well, let's see…a.a.a.…how about something like this? *(He throws a standard, standing wrestling hold on Leon.)*

JAMES: Are you going to wrestle???…Are you going to do "two wrestlers"?

BARNEY: You don't like this.

JAMES: Gee, I don't know…I was hoping for something a little more "epic".

BARNEY: Isn't this "epic"?

JAMES: Not really…It looks a little clumsy…I'm not judging, mind you…I just didn't think that's what we were going for.

LEON: It's not as easy as it looks, is it?

JAMES: Don't be smug, Leon.

BARNEY: Two wrestlers could symbolize the eternal polarity… Duality…Two forces pitted against each other in eternal but equal resistance.

JAMES: But that's not what you were *doing*…I mean if that's what you *want* to do, I suppose that's fine…but that's not what I got.

BARNEY: What if…Leon, you put your right hand on my left shoulder *(He does.)*…no, wait…your right hand on my *right* shoulder and… now step back a step…and I'll put my right hand on your right shoulder…

LEON: What'll I do with my left hand?

BARNEY: Just a.a.…just get rid of it…put it behind your back…now we'll lean in and support each other from falling with each of our right arms braced against each other's shoulder. *(They do this and freeze.)* Put your left knee forward a step…That's right…Good… Better huh?

JAMES: …You look like you're dancing.

BARNEY: Oh, Jesus Christ!…Well, look at it from another angle.

JAMES: *(He changes his angle to them a couple of times.)* …Well…it's a little better…but you still look like you're dancing.
(They break the pose.)

LEON: How about if…we don't necessarily relate to each other?…on a physical level…

BARNEY: Then what the hell's the point of me being here?

LEON: It was just a thought…

JAMES: It seems to me if you both had some common, essential "goal," that brought you into unified and yet diverse movement...something more—

BARNEY: I can't do this and concentrate, if you're going to just stand on the outside and pick at everything.

JAMES: Well, it doesn't appear that you have an innate gift for this...I was just trying to further the process along a little. *(Having great difficulty staying out of it.)*

BARNEY: I can sense you judging everything I do...Nothing is going to be right from your point of view because you're standing there thinking you could do this better.

JAMES: I wasn't thinking anything of the sort.

BARNEY: Impatience!...We're not all as driven for immediate results as you are...

LEON: How about "acrobats"?...We could do "acrobats"...

BARNEY: *I* don't know anything about "acrobats", dammit.

LEON: It's really very simple, it's all got to do with balance and thrust... a matter of weight and counterweight...You don't have to know anything about it, I do.

BARNEY: I don't want to do "acrobats"!

(James has begun stripping down to his shorts.)

BARNEY: What are you doing?

JAMES: You obviously need something to break the stalemate. The two of you are going around in circles, for God's sake. This could go on ad infinitum. You're clearly not getting anywhere by yourselves.

LEON: Actually, you know...He's right. Besides, there's no reason why he shouldn't have the experience with us...If he's included, he's no longer in a position to judge...*either* of us...and I've put up with it from up here longer than you have...

JAMES: Aside from that, since you've locked yourselves into indecision, the effect is simply confusion which is more irritating than when Leon was up there by himself.

BARNEY: All right...all right, I can accept that...I don't have to be alone to have my own personal experience up here...It's a platform originally designed for one, but come on...come on.

JAMES: *(Joining them on the platform.)*...Leon... *(They shake hands.)* Good to be here.

LEON: My pleasure.

(James and Barney also shake hands.)

LEON: I think maybe if we all just reach for the light.

JAMES: Good idea.

BARNEY: Fine by me.

(They all three instinctively and fluidly compose a complex interdependent composition with mutual support and counterbalance of weight; structurally

sound, yet capturing a feeling of motion. Leon is in the center, Barney to his left, James to his right. Leon should be the pivotal support; James and Barney extending out and away from him. As they do this, all the lights but the beam from overhead, lighting the model's platform, unobtrusively disappear but for a slight blue-grey tint. They should become a living sculpture frozen in space, harmonious from all angles.)

BARNEY: *(After a pause.)* ...James...are you there?

JAMES: Yeah...I can't see you...You're there...right?...Barney?

BARNEY: Right.

LEON: *(A beat.)* ...O.K. steady...now...LIFT.

(They remain motionless as the light slowly fades to black.)

END OF PLAY

How Gertrude Stormed the Philosophers' Club

by Martin Epstein

For Ellen

How Gertrude Stormed the Philosophers' Club was one of the hits in the annual SHORTS Festival produced by the Actors Theatre of Louisville (A.T.L.) in 1985. With a novel twist on the theme of women's liberation, the playwright offers his view of what happens when a sanctuary for philosophic males is invaded by a progressive female. Reviewing the play for the Louisville *Courier-Journal,* William Mootz writes: "Epstein's comedy is anything but conventional, and the destiny of Edgar and Edward is anything but predictable. By play's end, Epstein has taken them on a bizarre and surreal journey toward self-enlightenment…[The play's] dramatic progress is accompanied by a series of time bombs, whose explosions focus our attention and warn us to tread warily through Epstein's labyrinthian deceits and complications." The reception of the play prompted A.T.L.'s artistic director Jon Jory to revive the play for the 1986 Humana Festival of New American Plays. An earlier play, *Autobiography Of A Pearl Diver,* was presented in A.T.L.'s 1981 Humana Festival.

Mr. Epstein has also worked closely with The Magic Theatre of San Francisco, which has produced a number of his plays, including *Autobiography of a Pearl Diver, Charles the Irrelevant, The Man Who Killed the Buddha, Off Center* and *Possum Song*–the last three directed by the author. In its San Francisco production, *The Man Who Killed the Buddha* received the Dramalogue Award for the best play of the 1981 season.

Other groups which have produced Mr. Epstein's works include the Odyssey Theatre in Los Angeles, the Round House in Silver Spring, Maryland, the Detroit Repertory Theatre, the New Theatre of Brooklyn, and the Bay Area Playwrights Festival in Mill Valley, California.

From 1980 through the present, Mr. Epstein has been a playwright-in-residence at the Padua Hills Playwrights' Festival, where he directed the premiers of a number of his plays.

Mr. Epstein's plays have been published in *West Coast Plays, Plays from Padua Hills,* and in the *Plays in Process* series from the Theatre Communications Group. His playwriting efforts also have been rewarded with a Rockefeller Fellowship.

Currently, Mr. Epstein lives in New York, where he is on the Dramatic Writing Faculty at The Tisch School of the Arts (NYU).

ORIGINAL PRODUCTION

How Gertrude Stormed the Philosophers' Club premiered in the 1985 Shorts Festival at Actors Theatre of Louisville and was presented in the 1986 Humana Festival of New American Plays. The original production was directed by Frazier Marsh with the following cast:

Edgar ....Dana Mills
Edward ....Frederic Major
Jason ....Christian Kauffmann
Gertrude..Peggity Price

CHARACTERS

    EDGAR: a philosopher, fortyish, corduroy jacket, pipe
    EDWARD: a philosopher, fortyish, tweed jacket, pipe
    JASON: a waiter, fortyish
    GERTRUDE: the right fielder for the Queen Kongs, thirties
SETTING: The Philosophers' Club.
TIME: Now.

HOW GERTRUDE STORMED THE PHILOSOPHERS' CLUB

S<small>CENE</small> O<small>NE</small>

The Philosophers' Club: a comfortable reading room. Two large dark leather armchairs. A small table near each. Rear wall: floor to ceiling bookshelves with fine old hardback editions. Upstage left, a bust of Socrates on a pedestal. Upstage right: a waiter in a cutaway white tux. Edward in armchair, down right (the Nietzsche chair). Edgar, up left in the Wittgenstein Chair. The names, Nietzsche, Wittgenstein are present on small tags on the chairs to identify them. Lights up. The men smoke their pipes.

EDWARD: You know, I'm glad there are places in the world like The Philosophers' Club, where a man can go solely to think.

EDGAR: There we agree.

EDWARD: What a privilege to be able to come here and check one's body at the door, so to speak.

EDGAR: You make it sound a lot simpler than it is.

EDWARD: You find it difficult to check your body at the door?

EDGAR: Sometimes.

EDWARD: Hm.

(Edward signals the waiter for another round of drinks. Waiter exits. Edward and Edgar smoke.)

EDWARD: There's one other thing, you know, I love about this club.

EDGAR: What's that?

EDWARD: Read my mind.

EDGAR: *(Smiles.)* Yes, I agree with you there, too. If they want to have a Philosophers' Club of their own, they have every right, of course, to get together and start one.

EDWARD: Yes. But can you imagine one of *them* even conceiving such an idea? *(They smoke.)*

EDGAR: Well, you know, they *are* making progress.

EDWARD: Oh yes! On my way over here, I passed through the park. There was a softball game going on, and though I've never been all that interested in the sport, I found myself strangely *compelled* by some irregularity I couldn't quite put my finger on. It took me almost a full inning before I realized there wasn't a single man on either team.

EDGAR: They played that well, did they?

EDWARD: They looked damn attractive in their uniforms, too. Cleats and everything.

EDGAR: Cleats.

(They smoke.)

EDWARD: They're also learning how to fix cars.

EDGAR: Um.

EDWARD: It's a veritable revolution, I think…

EDGAR: Therefore, I am.

BOTH: *(Smiling.)* Um.

(Jason, the waiter, enters, carrying a tray loaded with drinks.)

JASON: Gentlemen, your drinks.

BOTH: Ah!

JASON: *(Placing a drink on Edward's table.)* One cognac, up.

EDWARD: *Merci.*

JASON: *Pas de quoi, Monsieur. (Placing drink on Edgar's table.)* And one gin and tonic with a twist of lime.

EDGAR: Thank you, Jason.

JASON: You're very welcome, Sir. *(He sets the tray on the serving stand.)* And for myself, seven double martinis. I hope you don't mind if I join you in a little toast. *(He takes a martini.)*

EDWARD: I think I do mind, Jason.

JASON: Oh?

EDWARD: You're an employee here, are you not?

JASON: Yes, sir.

EDWARD: Well, why don't we just keep it that way. Go drink in the kitchen if drink you must. *(He sips his cognac.)*

EDGAR: I'll be glad to join you in a toast, Jason.

JASON: Thank you, sir.

EDGAR: Why don't you propose it.

JASON: *(Lifting glass.)* To my last day of bogus freedom on this soon to be extinguished planet.

EDGAR: I'll drink to that.

(They both drink.)

EDWARD: I'm afraid that little toast may cost you your job, Jason.

EDGAR: Oh come off it, Edward.

EDWARD: Edgar, I don't like disturbing the natural order of things. The man is a servant!

(Jason lifts a toothpick and olive to his mouth.)

EDWARD: Jason, if you so much as nip a corner of that olive in my presence, your waiting days at The Philosophers' Club are over.

(Jason nips the olive. Edward rises. Jason pulls a Saturday Night Special from his cummerbund.)

JASON: Sit down, sir. Please.

(Edward sits.)

EDGAR: *(Laughs.)* Bravo, Jason!

JASON: *(Turning the gun on him.)* Hush!

EDGAR: *(Raising his hands slowly above his head.)* I have no money on me...

(Pause. Jason turns the gun back to Edward.)

JASON: These olives are a little off. *(He eats the rest of it.)* You know, many years ago I took an extension course in Philosophy. We read Plato's *Symposium.*

EDWARD: A splendid little book.

JASON: Yes? I remember there was a lot of talk about love. Queer love, as I recall. Fag love. But no where in the whole of that splendid little book, does old Socrates ever discuss what to do with a faggot downstairs neighbor who refuses to turn down his stereo in an apartment complex where the walls are already paper thin, and just the sound of him munching his morning Cornflakes is enough to drive me off my conk! *(He has polished a off second double, eats the olive.)* Notice how quietly *I* chew, gentlemen! *(He chews.)* That is because I am basically a conscientious person. I respect the privacy of others. *(He takes third double.)* But for the last seven years —and I am now going to drink one double martini for each of them—*(He drinks.)* For the last seven years, I have had to endure—Christ, these olives are positively rancid! *(He chews.)* Gentlemen, do you have any idea what it's like to have that disco beat in your head for six, eight, sometimes twelve hours at a stretch?

EDWARD: No.

EDGAR: Have you tried communicating with him?

JASON: Yes. I have. Tried. Communicating. *(He drinks a fourth double.)* I have also tried pounding on the floor with a broom handle, a steel claw hammer and a bowling ball. But all he does, gentlemen, is turn the volume up, *up, UP!* He slams his doors, talks for hours on the phone in a shrieking tone of voice, in which he is joined three to five nights a week by a whole chorus of his "friends" who sit around through the wee hours of the morning doing their Tallulah Bankhead imitations. *(He eats an olive, makes a face.)* Or if they happen to be in a more serious mood, he'll play his Great Moments in the Life of Hitler album, and let us not speak of how *that* scene usually ends. *(He takes a fifth drink.)* Gentlemen, I want to make one thing perfectly clear. I am not *(Exhaling hard.)* ho...mo...pho...bic! I'm not going to kill my downstairs neighbor because of his sexual politics, or his putrid taste in music. I'm going to kill him because I can no longer tolerate the *quality* of his life. *(He raises an olive in front of his face, looks at it.)*

EDGAR: Jason?

JASON: Hm? *(An olive into his mouth.)*

EDGAR: What is it, exactly, you'd like from us?

JASON: *(Picking up sixth drink.)* Confirmation.

EDGAR: Confirmation?

JASON: Gentlemen– *(He lays gun down on the arm of Edgar's chair, picks up seventh drink in his other hand, looks from one to the other.)*–I need to *know*, from a purely objective point of view–does a man not have an *obligation, regardless of the consequences,* to rid the earth of a life he *knows* is absolutely the shits? I shay he does, what do you shay?

(Edgar picks up the gun and fires point blank. Jason falls. Pause.)

EDWARD: Edgar?

EDGAR: Yes?

EDWARD: What have you done?

EDGAR: I answered his question.

EDWARD: You realize there'll be consequences?

EDGAR: No matter. I did what had to be done. *(He fires four more shots.)*

EDWARD: You're something of a perfectionist, aren't you?

EDGAR: Edward?

EDWARD: Yes?

EDGAR: I feel sick.

EDWARD: Mentally or physically?

EDGAR: *(Trying to think.)* Physically.

EDWARD: No one's ever thrown up in The Philosophers' Club. Not even on the steps. Is there anything I can do?

EDGAR: Help me think.

EDWARD: Therefore, we are?

EDGAR: Yes!

EDWARD: What would you like to think about?

EDGAR: My immediate paralysis.

EDWARD: What about it?

EDGAR: I'm not sure. But if a man shoots another man once, and then shoots him four more times, it seems to me he should know for sure that he's accomplished something.

EDWARD: Well, you did put him out of his misery.

EDGAR: It doesn't seem like enough.

EDWARD: Perhaps we should think about your options, then?

EDGAR: I can't seem to focus on any.

EDWARD: It seems to me there are basically two.

EDGAR: Yes?

EDWARD: A) You can turn yourself in. B) You could make a run for it.

EDGAR: Could you elaborate a bit?

EDWARD: A) Should you turn yourself in, you'll be processed in the usual manner and most likely you'll be found incompetent to stand trial.

EDGAR: *Incompetent?*

EDWARD: Assuming you play your cards right with the psychologists.

EDGAR: They'll turn me over to the psychologists?

EDWARD: Inevitably.

EDGAR: Let's move on to B.

EDWARD: B) If you make a run for it, you'll be a fugitive.

EDGAR: A fugitive?

EDWARD: Haven't you ever seen any movies about fugitives?

EDGAR: I can't remember any at the moment.

EDWARD: To begin with, you'll never be able to use your Visa or MasterCharge again. You won't be able to take books out of the public or university libraries. You'll have to give up the apartment you've been holding up in for the last sixteen years and "take it on the lam."

EDGAR: Take it on the lam?

EDWARD: It means running, hiding, slinking. It means everyone from your parents through your friends would be a potential enemy.

EDGAR: No more casual conversations with the checkout girls at Safeway...

EDWARD: An immediate lien on your grandmother's trust fund.

EDGAR: No more money from the National Endowment...

EDWARD: And you'd be hunted round-the-clock.

EDGAR: Hunted?

EDWARD: By a group of dedicated professionals with electronic equipment beyond your wildest imaginings. Not to mention what would happen to you in your dreams.

EDGAR: My dreams?

EDWARD: Where I assume you'll be pursued by "forces" far beyond anything the police or F.B.I. could possibly send after you. *(Pause.)*

EDGAR: Well, I refuse to have anything to do with the psychologists!

EDWARD: Then you *choose* to be a fugitive?

EDGAR: Yes! *(He tries to rise, falls back into chair.)*

EDWARD: Edgar?

EDGAR: What?

EDWARD: You haven't enough physical energy to be a fugitive.

EDGAR: Well, then, there's always a third option. *(He raises the gun to his temple.)*

EDWARD: Are you thinking of killing yourself?

EDGAR: There's one bullet left.

EDWARD: There's also a fourth option, you know.

EDGAR: A fourth option?

EDWARD: Suppose I were to take the blame.

EDGAR: You?

EDWARD: Um.

EDGAR: *(Lowering the gun.)* Would you really do that for me, Edward?

EDWARD: Don't be absurd.

EDGAR: *(Raising the gun.)* Oh.

EDWARD: I would, however, do it for myself.

EDGAR: *(Holding gun to his temple.)* Explicate.

EDWARD: Suppose an innocent man confesses to a crime he did not commit…

EDGAR: And confesses sincerely enough to be believed, go on!

EDWARD: The psychologists ask him questions. From his answers, they determine: A) that he is not only competent, but B) that the crime was also premeditated, and even C) that the killer is unremorseful as well as D) thoroughly pleased with himself! What do you think they'd do to such a man?

EDGAR: They'd sentence him to death, obviously!

EDWARD: And they'd be *so hopelessly wrong,* wouldn't they!

EDGAR: Would you really sacrifice you life just to make fools of the psychologists?

EDWARD: Yes! And while I'm at it, I'd also enjoy giving my wife and children a little something to broaden their outlook a bit.

EDGAR: Explicate.

EDWARD: My family takes an almost sadistic pleasure in constantly reminding me what a predictable guy I am. *(Pointing to Jason.)* And suddenly the method is at hand wherein I could turn their little bourgeois world upside-down! *(Reaches for gun.)* Edgar, I would definitely like to take the blame. Provided, of course, you agree.

EDGAR: *(Handing him gun.)* I agree.

EDWARD: Good. The crime is mine, then. *(He fires the last shot into Jason's body.)*

EDGAR: Christ!

EDWARD: What?

EDGAR: Do you realize the implications of what we're doing?

EDWARD: *(Shakes head.)* Nnnnn.

EDGAR: We're destroying the whole concept of the philosopher as a being who checks his body at the door.

EDWARD: *We?* Excuse me, but whose ass is actually on the line?

EDGAR: Literally, yours. Philosophically, mine.

EDWARD: *(Thrusting the gun into Edgar's stomach.) All you've ever done is play word games, you son-of-a-bitch!*

EDGAR: I beg your pardon?

EDWARD: Sorry. That was way out of line.

EDGAR: I'll just pretend I didn't hear it. *(Pause.)* So what happens now?

EDWARD: You return to your apartment a free man.

EDGAR: And you?

EDWARD: I take our former waiter and this weapon to the nearest police station.

EDGAR: You won't change your mind once you get there?

EDWARD: *(Hoisting Jason onto his back.)* Edgar, in the twenty-six years we've known each other, have you ever known me to change my mind?

EDGAR: Can I help you with him?

EDWARD: You can help by getting on your own way!

EDGAR: Shall I visit you in jail, then?

EDWARD: Edgar, I think–

EDGAR: Therefore–

EDWARD: It would be better if the two of us never saw each other again!

EDGAR: Yes, well, I'll follow the case in the papers.

EDWARD: I'm sure you will.

EDGAR: Good luck.

EDWARD: Good luck to you, too.

EDGAR: I go this way, I guess. *(He exits, left.)*

EDWARD: And I go this way. *(He exits right. Lights dim quickly to black.)*

SCENE TWO

Spot up. Enter Gertrude: She wears a softball uniform, the name of her team across the front: The Queen Kongs. She carries a baseball bat in one hand, the other is gloved. She addresses the audience.

GERTRUDE: Hi. I'm Gertrude, and I think it's time I put in an appearance, see-ing as how my name dominates the title of this play. I guess that last scene demonstrates once for all that whenever men gather together to think, inevitably they kill. *(Pause.)* If you're wondering what women do when they gather together to think, I can tell you that, too: I've just come from our team locker room. I play right field for the Queen Kongs, and we lost our season opener to the Green Barettas. Seventy-four to nothing. And though I didn't play any sloppier than the other girls, I made the mistake of trying to cheer my fellow Kongs up: "Hey, Kids, come on, it's only a game!" Well, believe me, if I hadn't grabbed my stuff and run, I'd have ended up as dead as that waiter. Only it wouldn't have been as cleanly done. *(She moves about, taking in her surroundings.)* Now the question still remains, what am I, Gertrude, doing in The Philosophers' Club? I sup-pose I can give you some possible answers: A) Maybe I'm fatally attracted to men with a certain quality of m-i-n-d. B) Perhaps I heard that the Philosophers' Club has a *men only* policy, and that kind of *thinking* gets me in my t-w-a-t. C) I might have been on my way back from the ball-game and I had to find a bathroom, quick. D) Maybe I don't know what I'm doing here. *(Sound of door slam.)* Anyway, I think I hear someone coming. I hope it's a philosopher so I can get to the bottom of this mys-tery. Shhh. I'll just plop myself down here in the Wittgenstein chair and pretend I'm asleep.

(She does this. Enter Edgar. He crosses to spot where Jason fell, gets down on his hands and knees, whispers Bang and falls. Edward enters, closing door. Edgar scrambles to his feet.)

BOTH MEN: It's you!

EDWARD: I thought we agreed never to see each other again!

EDGAR: We did agree!

GERTRUDE: *(Aside.)* I'm in luck. It's *two* philosophers!

EDWARD: So what are you doing here, then?

EDGAR: I don't feel right about what happened here a short while ago.

EDWARD: Refresh my memory, will you?

EDGAR: I *did* shoot that waiter, didn't I?

EDWARD: We both shot him.

EDGAR: But I shot him first. And I shot five times.

EDWARD: So?

EDGAR: So I've been thinking…

EDWARD: Therefore?

EDGAR: I'd like my crime back.

EDWARD: Why?

EDGAR: Because even though you took the blame, I still feel guilty, damnit! I *feel* like a fugitive!

EDWARD: Well, perhaps you'd best learn to live with it.

EDGAR: Why?

EDWARD: Stop and think a moment about something besides your own existential five-and-dime sized universe, and you might ask me how it is I happen to be standing here, rather than sitting in a jail cell surrounded by the psychologists!
(Gertrude snores lightly.)

EDGAR: Edward, I don't give a shit why you're standing here. I just want my crime back!

EDWARD: And suppose I told you there was no crime?

EDGAR: I fired five bullets into that waiter, Edward!

EDWARD: But suppose it wasn't any of those five bullets that killed him, Edgar!

EDGAR: What else could have possibly killed him, Edward?

EDWARD: Botulism!

EDGAR: Botulism?

EDWARD: The martini olives were contaminated.

EDGAR: The martini olives?
(Gertrude snores a bit louder.)

EDWARD: According to the computerized police autopsy report, our waiter died of botulism forty-three hundredths of a second before your first bullet hit him! *(Pause.)* We're both innocent!
(Gertrude snores louder.)

EDWARD: What is that horrible sound?

EDGAR: It's coming from the Wittgenstein chair.
(They both move toward it, discover the sleeper.)

EDWARD: Who is this?

EDGAR: Don't know. Never seen him before.

EDWARD: Well, whoever he is, he has obviously not checked his body at the door!

(Gertrude moans.)

EDWARD: And what's he doing in a baseball uniform?

EDGAR: He plays for a team called The Queen Kongs.

EDWARD: Shouldn't it be The King Kongs?

(Gertrude mumbles.)

EDGAR: Shhh. He seems to be dreaming.

GERTRUDE: Oh, Papa...

EDGAR: About his father.

GERTRUDE: *(Rising.)* I have to find it, Papa.

EDWARD: Edgar...

EDGAR: Shhh...

GERTRUDE: *(Moving.)* I found it once, I'll find it again.

EDGAR: He's sleepwalking.

(Gertrude turns toward the bookshelves. Her name is in large black letters across her back, together with the image of a Kong type gorilla face.)

EDWARD: His name is Gertrude.

EDGAR: Impossible. Gertrude is a woman's name.

GERTRUDE: Please help me find it, Papa.

EDWARD: Edgar...

(Gertrude takes a book from shelf, opens it, drops it.)

GERTRUDE: It's not here.

EDWARD: Edgar, there's a woman in The Philosophers' Club.

EDGAR: Impossible. We pay dues to keep them out.

(Gertrude flings a handful of books.)

GERTRUDE: Not here!

EDWARD: Use your eyes, for Chrissake! She's going after our books!

GERTRUDE: *(Flinging books from shelves.)* Not here! Not here! Not here!

EDWARD: Damnit, she'll destroy our entire library!

EDGAR: *(Holding him.)* Shhh. It might be even more dangerous to wake her!

(Gertrude tears into library, sending books out by the armful.)

EDWARD: What do you propose we do?

EDGAR: We should ease her into consciousness, obviously.

(Gertrude has begun to climb the bookcase.)

EDWARD: Ease one of them into consciousness? Oh go on, Edgar. You ease her into consciousness. I'll observe.

EDGAR: *(Moving closer.)* Gertrude?

GERTRUDE: *(Stops.)* Papa, is that you?

EDGAR: Yes, dear.

GERTRUDE: *(Climbs back down.)* Oh, Papa.

EDGAR: How are you, sweetheart?

GERTRUDE: I'm in so much trouble, Papa.

EDGAR: What's wrong, my darlin' girl?

GERTRUDE: I can't find it anywhere, Papa.

EDGAR: Find what, Gertrude?

GERTRUDE: It.

EDGAR: It?

GERTRUDE: Oh Papa, softball did not come easy to me.

EDGAR: Softball?

EDWARD: See if there's any link between softball and *it*.

EDGAR: Shhh…

GERTRUDE: I was always afraid the ball would disfigure my face.

EDGAR: One has to have courage, daughter.

EDWARD: It!

GERTRUDE: But everyone could smell my fear. They always chose me last. They put me in right field.

EDWARD: That's where they used to stick me, too. Ask her what *it* is?

GERTRUDE: But nothing ever happened in right field…

EDWARD: Thank God. It gave me lots of time to think!

GERTRUDE: Until that incredible afternoon when Coco Butterwrack connected!

BOTH: Coco Butterwrack?

GERTRUDE: She hit the ball almost as high as the sun. Oh, Papa, for a small eternity, it seemed to hang there. Then it began to fall…slowly…toward me…the right fielder. And I thought: Here it comes! Here comes doom! And there's no where to run! So I stuck out my glove and—*smack!* There it was, the ball…

EDGAR: It felt good, Gertrude?

GERTRUDE: Good doesn't begin to describe it, Papa. Later that day, I came home, you were sitting in the living room, smoking your pipe. You looked at me, and you knew something was *different*. And you said: "Hi, Gert, what you been up to?"

EDGAR: *(Soft.)* Hi, Gert, what you been up to?

GERTRUDE: And I said: "I've been playing softball, Papa." And you said: "Oh, yeah?"

EDGAR: Oh, yeah?

GERTRUDE: And I said: "Yeah. And I been playing hard!" And you said: "Oh, yeah?"

EDGAR: Oh, yeah?

GERTRUDE: And I said: "Yeah. And I got real dirty, Papa!" And you said: "Oh, yeah?"

EDGAR: Oh, yeah?

GERTRUDE: And I said: "Yeah!" And the two of us were beaming so hard we couldn't look at each other we were that embarrassed. And even poor Ma, who never wanted me to do anything more than spell properly and stay clean, Ma stood at her ironing board nodding and smiling even though she didn't know what the hell was going on!

(Gertrude, leaning back, lets her full weight rest against Edgar, who doesn't

quite know what to do with his hands, which have come up under her arms. Edward relights his pipe, watching.)

EDGAR: What was going on, Gertrude?

GERTRUDE: I was filling up with *it,* Papa!

EDGAR: It?

EDWARD: Will you establish the identity of *it,* for Chrissake!

EDGAR: What *it,* Gertrude?

GERTRUDE: I was filling up with The Secret Exaltation, Papa!

BOTH: The Secret Exaltation!?

GERTRUDE: *(Nodding.)* Yes, because I knew for a fact that if I could catch that ball, I could catch *anything! (She folds his hands gently in her own.)* Oh, Daddy.

EDWARD: Edgar, don't you think this little masquerade has gone far enough?

EDGAR: Shhhh.

(Edgar and Gertrude walk together in this position.)

EDWARD: *(Insistent whisper.)* Edgar, in the language of the psychologists, you may be exploiting this women's oedipal proclivities!

EDGAR: Edward, in the language of the psychologists, perhaps she's exploiting mine! *(They continue to walk this way. The scene should build with a real and dangerous heat.)*

EDWARD: May I remind you what happened the last time you put your mind at the mercy of your trigger-finger?

EDGAR: Nothing happened. We got off scott free!

EDWARD: You may not be as lucky this time.

EDGAR: I'll take my chances.

(They continue walking.)

EDGAR: Come, Gertrude.

GERTRUDE: Where are we going?

EDGAR: Someplace deep, someplace soft: the Nietzsche chair.

(He stops by the Nietzsche chair. They kiss.)

GERTRUDE: Wait.

EDGAR: What is it?

GERTRUDE: You're not really my father, are you?

EDGAR: *(Pause.)* No.

GERTRUDE: *(Turning back for another kiss.)* Well, okay, then.

(Edgar moves in for the kiss. Gertrude ducks under, comes downstage to audience, her hands making the time out sign. Edgar and Edward freeze.)

GERTRUDE: Time out! I'm afraid I'm having some difficulty with the scene that's coming up. The author would just love Gertrude and Edgar to tumble into the Nietzsche chair and go at it hot 'n heavy.

EDGAR: Yeah.

GERTRUDE: I personally don't get off on the idea of being fucked in my sleep. By *anyone! (She backs up.)* So we've decided on a little compromise.

(Whispers to Edgar, while pushing him onto the Nietzsche chair.)

GERTRUDE: Okay, play ball.

EDGAR: *(Falls into chair and begins making love to it.)* Oh, Gertrude! Darling Gertrude!

GERTRUDE: *(Standing to the side, she plays.)* Go on, do it to me, baby!

(Edward moves in, watching Edgar make love–tenderly–to the chair. He moves off, crosses toward the bust of Socrates, addressing it.)

EDWARD: I had an erotic experience once.

GERTRUDE: Ummm!

EDWARD: I was thirty-two at the time.

(Edgar and Gertrude sounding.)

EDWARD: Just completing my Ph.D. at UCLA.

(Sound.)

EDWARD: Newly married.

(Sound.)

EDWARD: Preparing for my orals.

(Edgar does a hand stand, his legs straight up in the air.)

EDWARD: I remember I was on line in the student cafeteria, standing next to a young lady in a paisley dress. Lying on the tray next to her turkey sandwich, Kant's *Critique!*

GERTRUDE: Oh you dirty dog!

EDWARD: On my tray, Hegel's *Phenomenology* and a bowl of watery borsht.

GERTRUDE: Oh you dirty filthy sweetheart dog!

EDWARD: Our eyes met!

GERTRUDE: *Ah!*

(Gertrude can participate with mimetic gestures.)

EDWARD: The recognition was immediate. "We must talk," I said. "Before or after we screw, you choose," she replied. "After," I said.

GERTRUDE: *Oh!*

EDWARD: We got to her apartment, we took off all our clothes, she handed me her hairbrush: "Brush," she said.

GERTRUDE: *Ou!*

EDWARD: "Go on, baby, brush!" And so I brushed. *(He combs her invisible hair, perhaps the busts head.)* And I brushed! And I brushed!

GERTRUDE: Oh baby!

EDWARD: *(Brushing.)* Her hair was thick and black and henna rinsed.

GERTRUDE: Oh honey!

EDWARD: And as I brushed I could feel the darkness sift from her body to my own…

GERTRUDE: Oh sugar!

EDWARD: And as I brushed something in me darker still began to throb and stretch: to show it's ivory teeth and claws.

GERTRUDE: It's happening…

EDWARD: And as I brushed, I wasn't Edward anymore, I was all fur and throbbing darkness staring at the back and shoulders and buttocks of a girl whose scent was urging me to spring!

GERTRUDE: It's happening!

(Edward purrs.)

GERTRUDE: It's happening!

EDWARD: And I knew if I let that beast break from the cage of my existence, it was good-bye my new wife, good-bye my Ph.D., good-bye my academic career, good-bye western civilization—*(With each of the above named, Gertrude lets out an equivalent sound.)*—And with the beast already en route through the air, I performed what I consider still to be the single most definitive act of my life: I grabbed my pants and ran! I grabbed my shoes and socks and ran! I grabbed my *Phenomenology of the Mind* and I ran! *(Gertrude orgasmic. Edward chokes the statue.)*

EDWARD: Fool! Idiot! Coward! Why! *(Slapping himself.)* Oh, hypocrite, why! Why! Why! Why! Why! Why! Why did you run away? Oh, why?

(More Gertrude.)

EDWARD: Because if I had stayed, I'd have devoured her, that's why! If I had stayed, I'd have eaten her alive!

(Edgar has descended, slowly, his legs folding down and the rest of his body crumpling up on the floor. Edward, too, on his hands and knees.)

EDGAR: Edward?

EDWARD: What?

EDGAR: Help me think.

EDWARD: What about?

EDGAR: Gertrude.

EDWARD: Gertrude?

EDGAR: Am I dreaming her, or is she really out there?

(Edward crawls across books and over to the Nietzsche chair. He observes.)

EDWARD: You're dreaming her.

EDGAR: Merciful God, please, let me go on dreaming.

(He collapses on his side, curls up. Edward, staring at the empty chair, purrs.)

EDGAR: What was that?

EDWARD: That was panther language.

(Gertrude sings a very haunting, wordless melody.)

EDGAR: Edward?

EDWARD: *(Staring at the chair.)* What?

EDGAR: My dream is singing.

(A light purr from Edward.)

EDGAR: I'm afraid to move, I'm afraid to breathe.

EDWARD: *(Rising on his knees, leaning over the chair.)* Well, I'm not afraid.

(He purrs loud. Gertrude stops singing, screams as though waking from a nightmare. Edward does a double-take; Edgar sits up, wide awake. Edward growls at Gertrude. She grabs baseball bat, makes as though to strike.)

EDWARD: No! Don't hit me! I didn't do anything! Hit him. He's the guilty one! He's the fugitive!

GERTRUDE: You, fugitive! What the hell is going on here?

EDGAR: Gertrude, I love you.

EDWARD: Gertrude, he had congress with you on the Nietzsche chair!

GERTRUDE: Congress?

EDGAR: Marry me, Gertrude.

GERTRUDE: I must still be dreaming.

EDWARD: Maybe we're all still dreaming. *(He turns his gaze back to the Nietzsche chair, and from this point on he will continue to look at it as though she were still lying there.)*

EDGAR: Oh Gertrude, I've listened to your theme.

GERTRUDE: My theme?

(Edgar sings a bit of Gertrude's theme.)

EDWARD: You sang it for us in your sleep.

GERTRUDE: I don't remember.

EDGAR: Oh Gertrude, before I heard your theme, I lived like a one man Diaspora.

GERTRUDE: A one man who?

EDWARD: He lived alone.

GERTRUDE: Oh yeah, alone.

EDGAR: I lived for no one but myself.

GERTRUDE: Sure. I know that scene.

EDWARD: We all know that scene.

EDGAR: No one knows that scene the way I know that scene!

EDWARD: He always has to be the king!

EDGAR: That's right!

EDWARD: Why?

EDGAR: Because I *am* the king, Goddamnit!

EDWARD: King of who, sir? King of what?

EDGAR: I am the Fugitive King of the Earth!

EDWARD: Oh really?

EDGAR: Oh Gertrude, before I heard your theme, I ruled over my whole imaginary universe like a crazed despot! Because I felt like a fugitive, I wanted everyone else to feel like a fugitive! Yes, I sat upon my mental throne, and I banished all the people! I banished the cities! I banished the nations! I sent the sun and the moon and the stars into perpetual exile!

EDWARD: His Fugitive Majesty is raving!

(This scene can turn operatic, with Gertrude catching Edgar's fever, so that she bursts into a refrain: "Come home, come home, come home, etc.")

EDGAR: *(Singing Gertrude's theme.)* But now that I've heard your theme, Oh, Gertrude, I want my kingdom to come home! *(Singing.)* Mother, Father, come home! Baby Sue! Brother Tom! Come home! Childhood playmates and friends of my youth, come home! Office workers, insurance salesmen, secretaries, real estate agents, come home! *(All this, of course, to the house.)* Plumbers, doctors, hat check girls, salad chefs, taxi drivers, home! Farmers, garbage men, physicists, movie stars, home! Thieves, pimps, prostitutes, congressmen, home! CIA agents, come home! Moscow! London! Peking! Dallas! Los Angeles, *please–(Or whatever city the play is being performed in)–Come home!*

(Gertrude continues to sing as he speaks.)

EDGAR: No one need ever pay another dollar to the psychologists! All your fugitive guilt is hereby forgiven! Edgar, King of the Fugitive Earth declares a universal amnesty! *(Spoken.)* Oh, Gertrude, rule with me! Say you'll be my queen!

EDWARD: *(Still focused on Nietzsche chair.)* Gertrude, the Fugitive Queen!

EDGAR: No, no! Be Gertrude, Queen of the Secret Exaltation!

GERTRUDE: Queen of the Secret Exaltation?

(He sings. She sings. They sing. She slides to her knees beside him.)

GERTRUDE: Oh, your Fugitive Majesty, that's a very hard offer to resist!

EDWARD: Resist it anyway!

GERTRUDE: Why?

EDWARD: Because as pretty as it sounds, it's basically a crock! *(He mimics Edgar's singing.)* That's the way all fugitives sound when they think they've fallen in love!

EDGAR: I think I'm in love, therefore, I *am* in love! Gertrude, I have a comfort-able income. We'll honeymoon in Mexico!

EDWARD: Don't say yes until you've heard my proposal!

BOTH: Your proposal?

EDGAR: You can't propose, Edward. You're a married man! The father of three. Old predictable, they call him!

EDWARD: *(Edward roars!)*

GERTRUDE: Why do you keep roaring that way?

EDGAR: He thinks he's a panther.

EDWARD: I think I'm a panther, therefore, I *am* a panther!

EDGAR: Marry me, Gertrude!

GERTRUDE: Shhhh.

EDWARD: Gertrude?

GERTRUDE: Yes?

EDWARD: How would you like to nourish the beast of your choice?

GERTRUDE: Nourish the beast...?

(Edward purrs.)

EDGAR: Gertrude, marry me.

GERTRUDE: Shhhh! Will you let him talk!

EDWARD: Yes, Edgar, let me talk. *(A light purr.)*

GERTRUDE: Just what do you mean "nourish the beast of my choice," Panther Man?

EDWARD: Listen, Gertrude: since the advent of our birth, the eye of the beast has been fixed on each single one of us. Fixed on the movement of arms and legs. Fixed on the turning of heads, the blinking of lids. Fixed on the wriggling of fingers and toes...

EDGAR: Gertrude, may I point out in passing that old Panther Man's gaze is presently fixed on nothing!

EDWARD: Panther Man's gaze is presently fixed on the real you, Gertrude! *(He purrs.)*

GERTRUDE: The real me?

EDWARD: Gertrude, you will never be more than you were when you lay sprawled across the Nietzsche chair, singing your theme.

GERTRUDE: What, exactly was I?

EDWARD: You were your essential self. *(He purrs.)*

GERTRUDE: But you say I was asleep, dreaming...

EDWARD: You were your essential self, Gertrude!

GERTRUDE: *(To Edgar.)* Is what he's saying true?

EDGAR: Gertrude, Edward's an *idealist:* he cannot deal with anything unless it's not really there!

(Edward roars, his gaze fixed on the Nietzsche chair.)

GERTRUDE: But he's looking at what he calls "the essential me" with such genuine sincerity.

EDGAR: What you call his "genuine sincerity" is a misnomer for his genuine psychosis. Gertrude, believe me, even if he wanted to, there is no way he *could* turn his gaze.

EDWARD: Oh yes I could.

EDGAR: Oh no you couldn't.

EDWARD: Oh yes I could!

EDGAR: Oh no you couldn't!

(Edward roars, begins to turn his gaze.)

GERTRUDE: Oh King Edgar, the Panther Man is turning his gaze!

EDGAR: Gertrude, say you'll marry me!

GERTRUDE: In another moment, he'll be looking right at me!

EDGAR: But he still won't be seeing *you*, Gertrude! He'll be seeing *her!*

GERTRUDE: Who?

EDGAR: The you you were! Gertrude!

(Edward, fixing his gaze on her, purrs.)

GERTRUDE: Too late! Oh, Mr. Panther-Man!

EDGAR: Damnit, woman, I'm the one who's had congress with you!

EDWARD: *But I'm the one who's going to eat her alive!*

GERTRUDE: Eat me alive?

EDWARD: Be eaten by me, Gertrude, or be eaten by *time!*

GERTRUDE: Be eaten by Time?

EDWARD: Tick tock, tick tock—*(Turning his gaze back to the Nietzsche chair)*—tick tock…

GERTRUDE: Oh God, *Time!*

EDGAR: *(Edgar can sing these lines, softly.)* Gertrude, we'll have a family! We'll make the future!

EDWARD: Tick tock, tick tock…

GERTRUDE: Oh God, don't stop looking at me! Panther Man!

EDWARD: Tick tock, tick tock, tick tock…

EDGAR: *(Singing these lines a bit louder.)* A house with a garden! A dog! A pussycat!

(Edward purrs.)

GERTRUDE: I'm sorry, your Majesty, but I feel driven to him.

EDGAR: Driven? Why driven?

GERTRUDE: I donno. Because he's my essential destiny, I guess.

EDGAR: Oh Gertrude…

GERTRUDE: It's all right. Ever since I was little, I've had a premonition this moment was on it's way. *(She lies down across the Nietzsche chair.)* All right, Mr. Panther Man, I'm ready. Devour me.

EDWARD: Sing your theme, Gertrude.

(Gertrude sings her theme. Edward lifts her arm, growls.)

GERTRUDE: Could I make one small request before you eat me, Panther Man?

EDWARD: Hurry.

GERTRUDE: If it's all right with you, I'd like to leave my uniform to my husband, Stuart.

(Edward tries to roar but gags.)

EDGAR: Your husband, Stuart, Gertrude?

GERTRUDE: We've been married seven years, and I'd like him to have a remembrance.

(Edward gags.)

EDGAR: Why didn't you tell us you were married, Gertrude?

GERTRUDE: The subject didn't come up till now.

EDGAR: But you allowed us both to assume you were *free.*

GERTRUDE: Yeah, well…

EDGAR: *(Imitates her.)* Yeah, well, my colleague and I don't particularly enjoy pissing into the wind, Gertrude! Why did you allow us to make such fools of ourselves?

GERTRUDE: Curiosity…

EDGAR: Curiosity?

GERTRUDE: I don't normally spend much time around guys who are so…verbal.

EDGAR: Stuart doesn't talk?

GERTRUDE: Stuart talks…only he doesn't really say too much.

EDGAR: What does he do for a living, your Stuart?

GERTRUDE: He's in construction.

(Edward gags.)

GERTRUDE: Hey, you guys, I wouldn't want you to get the idea I was a tease or anything.

(They look at her.)

GERTRUDE: I'd have left Stuart like that for either of you.

EDGAR: Does that mean we still have a chance?

GERTRUDE: Uh–no.

EDGAR: Why not?

GERTRUDE: I donno. Taken separately, either one of you is a terrific catch. But together, you kind of cancel each other out.

EDGAR: So we do.

GERTRUDE: And then there's my three kids.

EDGAR: You have children, Gertrude?

GERTRUDE: Sandy, Ducky and Orlando.

EDWARD: Six more and you could start your own softball team.

GERTRUDE: Do you still want to eat me, Panther Man?

(Edward, shaking his head "No," slips back into the other chair.)

GERTRUDE: Just as well, I guess. I'm expected home for dinner. I promised the kids my lasagna. I'd invite you guys, but the kids are absolute pigs at the table, and I'm afraid Stuart would find you both a little weird.

(Pause. Gertrude turns her head, sighs. She doesn't move.)

EDGAR: Gertrude?

GERTRUDE: Yes?

EDGAR: What seems to be the problem?

GERTRUDE: I donno. All of a sudden, I just don't feel like going home anymore.

EDGAR: Why not?

GERTRUDE: Because the whole scene is all so predictable.

(Signs of life in Edward, who turns his head in her direction.)

GERTRUDE: I can already see just how everything will happen. I'll open the door. Stuart and the kids will all be huddled in the living room round the TV set, watching the ball game. "Hey, Babe," he'll say, lifting the can of Schlitz in his hand. "How'd the Kongs do?" "We lost," I'll say. "What score, Mom?" "Seven to six, honey." "Oh, tough luck," they'll shout. "Well, commere anyway, an' we'll give you a great big loser's hug." And while they're all hugging me, I'll burst into tears. And they'll all think I'm crying because The Queen Kongs lost, but that's not what I'll be crying about. I'll be crying because there's no way in the world I can tell any of them what happened to me at The Philosophers' Club, and make them understand. *(She has risen, a bit weepy.)* I mean, "Hey, you guys, this afternoon I had congress with The Fugitive King of the Earth! And then, I was almost eaten alive by a Panther Man! And both of them proposed, and promised to fill me with The Secret Exaltation, but I chose *you* instead— *(Now she is caught up in her own discovery.)* —Instead of The Secret Exaltation, I chose to come home to *you! (She is talking to them via the house.)* Stuart…Sandy… Ducky…Orlando…I chose *Death* today for you… *What did you choose for me, you selfish, inconsiderate, filth-making bunch of predictable sons of bitches?* —And then, they'll all look at me like they've never seen me before. Yeah. And Stuart will drop his Schlitz and fall to his knees and cover his face with his hands and weep! Yeah! And Sandy will scramble for the Electro-lux and vacuum all the popcorn from the shag rug, *yeah!* And Ducky will collect all the empty soda bottles and throw them neatly into the trash, *yeah!* And Orlando will go to the fridge and fix me a gin and tonic strong enough to knock over an elephant, *yeah!* And then we'll all sit down *together* at the table, and like civilized ladies and gentlemen, we'll eat lasagna, and have some meaningful conversation, *yeah! (The bat is raised in one hand. Gertrude is almost transfixed.)* Hey, you guys?

EDGAR: Is she talking to us?

EDWARD: I hope not.

GERTRUDE: Now I know why I stormed The Philosophers' Club!

BOTH: Tell us, Gertrude.

GERTRUDE: So I could meet your two amazing minds and fill up with it!

BOTH: It?

(Gertrude sings her theme.)

BOTH: The Secret Exaltation!

GERTRUDE: Yeah! *(She turns; over to Edgar.)* Thank you for the congress, your Majesty. *(She gives him a sweet kiss.)*

EDGAR: Gertrude.

GERTRUDE: *(Over to Edward.)* And thank you for the beast. *(She gives him a sweet kiss.)*

EDWARD: *(Edward purrs, a bit despairingly.)*

GERTRUDE: *(To audience.)* And thank you for—I donno—just being there. *(She blows them a kiss.)* I'm going home to my family now! *(She turns, begins singing her theme, exits. Pause.)*

EDWARD: Edgar?

EDGAR: Hm?

EDWARD: I think…

EDGAR: Therefore…

EDWARD: I hate my life.

EDGAR: Yes, well, I hate mine even more.

EDWARD: Edgar?

EDGAR: Hm?

EDWARD: I don't suppose you'd consider…

EDGAR: A double suicide?

EDWARD: …Switching chairs.

EDGAR: Switching chairs?

EDWARD: It would be a great comfort to feel as though some kind of physical mobility were still possible.

EDGAR: Yes, one could almost imagine a whole new world if some kind of physical mobility were still possible.

EDWARD: Shall we give it the old college try?

EDGAR: I don't see that there's anything left to lose.

EDWARD: *(With great effort.)* I rise…

EDGAR: Therefore, I also rise…*(He does so.)*

EDWARD: I take a step! *(He takes a step.)*

EDGAR: Therefore, I take a step! *(He takes a step.)*

EDWARD: I take a second step!

EDGAR: Therefore, we walk!

EDWARD: We walk towards each other! *(They meet, take each other's hands.)*

EDGAR: Panther Man!

EDWARD: Fugitive King of the Earth!

(They sing Gertrude's theme. Continue to walk to their respective new chairs, turn, collapse. A great feeling of achievement as each fetches for his pipe and tobacco.)

EDWARD: Well, now, that's done, we'll have to speak to the Club Management about providing us with a new waiter.

EDGAR: Yes. A waiter who knows what it means to check his body at the door, hm?

(They look at each other.)

BOTH: There we agree!

(They light and smoke their pipes. Edgar hums Gertrude's theme as they puff, puff, puff. Lights dim.)

END OF PLAY

Chemical Reactions
by Andrew Foster

BIOGRAPHY

Andy Foster's other plays include *Reunion*, winner of the Villager's Off-Broadway Excellence in Writing Award in 1979; *Options*, which was produced in New York by New York StageWorks and in Los Angeles by Theatre 40; *American Abroad*, workshopped by Manhattan Theatre Club and *Talking Dirty*, seen at New York's West Bank Theatre Bar. *Chemical Reactions* has received more than 20 productions since its premiere and was published in Best Plays, 1989.

ORIGINAL PRODUCTION

Chemical Reactions premiered in the 1987 Humana Festival of New American Plays. It was directed by Ray Fry with the following cast:

Bern ....Peter Zapp

Ike ....Fred Sanders

CHARACTERS

BERN: Early twenties, sizable, not smart but not incurious about his surroundings. An unconsciously funny person with quite sensational timing.

IKE: Late twenties, harder and more complex–a short prison background, a lackey in the crime world, there only for the occasional and unthreatening easy buck. He still has a conscience simmering away. Lean and wiry.

LOM: Late thirties, he sounds like a large man. He is a laid-back and humorous man, but the kind that is very protective of family and friends. His humor in this case is born of desperation as he tries to shield himself from the situation.

SCENE NOTES: The characters can be New Yorkized or Chicagoized or St. Louisized in accent—there is no necessary location although the inspiration is in New Jersey's eastern marshland dumpsites and New York's much publicized Mafia pizza takeovers.

The 'special effects' of falling barrels can be handled just offstage by having Ike roll Lom away during his fight with Bern. That allows a couple of visible barrels to topple and flash powder and a fire extinguisher to handle the rest. The barrel should be thoroughly cleaned and have interior handles as well as padding for the occupant. The barrel should also have bullet holes and slashes to allow good air movement.

SETTING: The play takes place in a dumpsite just before dawn.

CHEMICAL REACTIONS

In the Blackout the sound of a truck engine revving, slowing and shut off. The ticking of the hot engine. One door opening and closing. Lights up on the truck, halfway through a sagging gate into a fenced off section of a dump. Its back is facing us. The bed is filled with industrial barrels. On one side of the dump there is a pyramid of weathered barrels similar to the ones in the truck. Pieces of old crumbled iron scatter the grounds. There are an array of warning signs on barrel and fence. The light is pre-dawn, cold and misty.

BERN: Sheez. This is a dump.

> *(Bern walks from the truck into the dump. He is about to put non-dairy creamer into his cup of coffee. His footsteps slop in the mud, a sucking kind of noise. A background static of someone looking for something and clattering things around in his efforts.)*

IKE: *(From the truck.)* Damn.

BERN: *(Leaning against a barrel, looking at the creamer label.)* Di-sodium gluta-mate. Polysorbate. Soybean protein. Soy extract. Two percent carbonate bisulfate. Emulsifiers, artificial flavorings and colorings…

> *(Another door slam and footsteps approaching.)*

IKE: We must of left the gloves at the warehouse. Careful you don't get no goop on your hands. Next time say something when I call, huh?

BERN: Cremona.

IKE: What?

BERN: Cremona. They don't give you milk no more, they give you cremona.

IKE: Cremola, Bern, it's cremola. Cremona sounds…filthy.

BERN: It's what my gal calls it. Cremona. She says I ought to sell the stuff, I drink so much.

IKE: It's 5:30 in the A.M. Would you cap your mouth?

BERN: Guess I'm just a morning person. *(He slurps his coffee.)*

IKE: You are a morning fruitcake is what you are!

> *(Bern gets excited by the sunrise, which is beginning to lighten and redden the dump.)*

BERN: Hey! Hey! Hey! Red sky in morning, sailors take warning. No fishin' today. We should a been out there last night…

IKE: Tonight's another day.

BERN: …pullin' in them blues, snappin' and twistin'. Oh yeah, better than this.

IKE: Easy money here, kid. Don't forget that. You do this one, you get time to spend it.

BERN: I don't want to sound ungrateful, Ike. Thanks for callin' me in.

IKE: Would I call anybody else? Huh?

BERN: Nah. Not since you go out with my sister.

IKE: Drink your coffee. There's work to do.

BERN: I don't care you're goin' out. Don't get me wrong, I ain't one of those jealous brother types, one of those guys can't imagine his sister havin' fun, goin' places, seein' people...

IKE: That's real of you, trustin' the two of us like that.

BERN: Just so you stay off her. *(Bern finds this very funny.)* Otherwise I have to box those big ears you got. Huh? Huh? *(Bern is up and dancing, right, left, right, shadow boxing. He exhales puffs as he punches and jabs.)* Whooo! Whuff! Hunh! *(Bern spills coffee from the cup he is still holding. A splash lands on Ike.)*

IKE: Hey! No, look at this stain!

BERN: It's not like it's Sunday dress man. It's not your disco drawers.

IKE: Aww, Bern! Damn it! You always have five cups of coffee and I get one all over me. Would you finish so we can get a move on?

BERN: All right, I'm sorry, I am sorry. I am your slave! *(Sound of the coffee cup as he crumples and drops it.)* Let's get to work!

(Pause. Ike is watching Bern, shaking his head.)

BERN: What're you looking at?

IKE: Anybody ever teach you to pick up after yourself?

BERN: Hey, all right, this is a dump already. You want maybe I should sweep up? Jesus, we have a truck loaded with these big cans of friggin' Comet cleanser or whatever, we bringin' it to some garbage place with, I mean, look at that thing of barrels...

IKE: What thing?

BERN: You know, it's what those Egyptians called it, pyramid! I mean all these barrels, all this old junk, and you're flappin' about some cup! Some rubber cup!

IKE: Foam.

BERN: Foam rubber.

IKE: It's Styrofoam. Foam rubber they use for other things, like those false titties. Does that cup feel like false titties?

BERN: *(Disdainful.)* I wouldn't know.

IKE: *(Cracking up.)* All right...Let's get a move. We got to be out of here before they open this dive.

BERN: You see me disagreein'? So what's the deal, we just gonna jam these cans up against them others? *(He whacks the side of a barrel. A dull full thunk.)*

IKE: Hey! We do not whack, we do not jam. These things is loaded with some kind of sludge, we jam them, they probably glom up in our faces.

BERN: They're not gonna glom, it's in a steel can.

IKE: We ease 'em on over, okay? We do not jam.

BERN: Okay.

IKE: You want to jam, let me get out of the way.

BERN: I'm just sayin' if we ease let's ease at high speed, cause this is a dump!

IKE: Come on, let's go.

BERN: Know what I mean, Jesus, it is ugly. Looks like crucifixion day, hey, you know that film? You know that story about John Wayne, the Duke? This guy told me. The Duke is playin' this dude who is casin' Christ on the Cross?

IKE: I don't know the story, let's get goin'.

BERN: He's sayin', "he must a been the Son a God." *(Bern does a good John Wayne imitation.)* Some clown comes up to the Duke, says, put a little respect, a little 'awe' into your line, champ. Duke nods and comes out with… "Awwwww, he must a been the Son a God."
(Ike is not impressed.)

IKE: Grab a hand.

BERN: All right, yeah, anyway, like I said, this is a dump.

IKE: Bern. Just take it easy, all right? You're not spendin' your vacation here. We get this done, d-o-n-e, then we go get paid, p-a-i-d. Leave with some bucks, have a good time.

BERN: All right, Ike, I am not remedial, okay? You sure they're gonna p-a-y?

IKE: Johnny Olander does not dog out on his debts, he's got an organization. Now give me a hand.

BERN: Look, I'm sorry to be a little, you know, a little, I don't know, like nervous. I was seein' this movie about stuff like this, you know, where these two chemicals meet up and start doin' a real number on each other.
(They start to pick up a barrel. Exhalations as they pick up the barrel. Bern talks with effort as they carry the barrel.) So in this movie, it's like a warehouse but it feels like this dump, big barrels, spooky lighting, and these two chemicals just snake out from these two cans, man they just flow on over to each other like with these fingers, Ike, and when they fix on each other you get this blob and it kind of pulses its way into a real ugly mess.

IKE: Got it? It kind of glommed up, huh? Let's go.

BERN: How do you mean?

IKE: Like I told you earlier, it glommed up, like in our faces, which is why we're easin' these barrels, not jammin', right?

BERN: I'm easin', I'm easin'.

IKE: Down right here. Careful.
(Grunts as the barrel is put down.)

BERN: I was just trying to tell you why I feel a little freaky.

IKE: Freaky?

BERN: That's what my mom says when she's a little off and that's exactly how I feel today.

IKE: You gonna feel freaky when we get paid? Cause if you feel freaky in front of Johnny Olander I don't want to be there, right? Let's go. Number two.

(More groans of effort as they lift a second barrel.)

BERN: I'm just tryin' to tell you this is a lousy place.

IKE: I know that for Christ's sake, it's a dump.

BERN: That's exactly my point.

IKE: You're actin' like it's some kind a mausoleum.

BERN: There is no such word.

IKE: You'd know, right? Watch your hand.

BERN: You're a real fool sometimes. There's nausea...

IKE: Will you watch your hand? There's goop...

BERN: And there's like, hell I don't know, auditorium, but there's no mausoleum.

IKE: ...it's suckin' out of that barrel, just like you...

BERN: And if there was, you'd still be a jerk to say it.

IKE: Crusty, real crusty goop, right on your old paw right about...now.

BERN: Hey! Hey! What is this crap?

IKE: Somethin' just dying to bust its way through your skin and join up with some good eatin'!

BERN: Ahhhh! Dammit! Ahhh! Help me, help my hand!

> *(Bern reacts in panic. The barrel drops, a solid thunk! The sound of the barrel dropping and Ike's protest as he pulls away just in time.)*

IKE: Bern! Don't drop no barrel on me, my finger was in there!

BERN: Damn! Look at this stuff. What is it? *(Bern tries to clean his hand off.)*

IKE: Wipe it with a rag. Phewww! What a lousy day.

> *(A strange sound.)*

LOM: Ohhhh. Ohhhh.

> *(Bern looks around wildly. Ike doesn't notice anything.)*

IKE: Quiet, Bern. Your hand's all right.

LOM: Ohhhh.

BERN: Can't you hear that? That's not me!

> *(There is a metallic thump. Ike is startled. Both start backing off and looking around.)*

BERN: It's some kind a blob, some kind a weird thing!

IKE: Would you shut up?

LOM: Ahhhh. Acchhhh.

> *(Another thump sends Ike tripping backward.)*

IKE: It's just some kind a noise, Bern, it's all right.

> *(The barrel begins rolling and creaking.)*

BERN: I never should a come to this dump.

> *(The noises are coming from inside and have that metallic echo. The noises move from awakening to surprise, to panic, to anger, as Lombardi comes to.)*

LOM: Ohhh. Rrrrrrr. Yaahhh.

BERN: Jesus, let me run! Let me run!

LOM: Yahhh! Yahhh!

> *(The barrel is rocking and creaking violently.)*

IKE: Let's get out of here! *(He starts for the truck.)* Bern! Come on!
(Bern is rooted to the spot.)

BERN: I can't move! I can't run! Jesus help me!
(The barrel stops rocking. From inside, the sound of tears. Ike and Bern are both silent and still.)

LOM: Damn. Damn. *(More crying.)*

BERN: What kind of blob is this?

LOM: *(Finally reacting to the voices.)* Hey. Hey! Hey! Hello?

IKE: There's some guy in that barrel.

LOM: Binxie! I'm over here, I'm okay. Gator!

BERN: Who's he talkin' to?

IKE: I don't know.

LOM: Binxie! Over here!
(Ike and Bern look around, still scared and unsure.)

LOM: Hello? Gator? Is anybody out there? Is anybody there?
(A long pause.)

BERN: *(A sigh of tension.)* Yeah.

LOM: Oh, people! Oh, yeah, people! I am so glad to hear people!

BERN: *(As if to an alien.)* What did you expect to hear?

LOM: Who are you guys? *(Pause, then with an edge of desperation.)* Hello? You still there?

BERN: Yeah.

LOM: Good. Who are you?

BERN: Bern.

IKE: Ike.

LOM: Hi. Hi. Hi. Bern and Ike. Can you let me out?

IKE: Who are you?

LOM: Lombardi. Would you let me out?

BERN: Lombardi who?

LOM: Just call me Lom, Ike, but get me out of here.

BERN: That was Bern speaking.

LOM: I don't care if you're Frank frigging Sinatra, let me out!

IKE: Take it easy.

LOM: Take it easy? Get me out! Get me out!
(The barrel starts rocking and creaking again. It begins rolling towards the large pile of old cans. Bern and Ike move to it and try to hold it steady.)

BERN: Mister! Calm down, come on, you're gonna knock this whole place to hell.

IKE: You want us to get you out? Calm down!
(Pause. The barrel stops. We can hear Lom breathing heavily. Bern and Ike take a closer look at the barrel. Ike whistles.)

IKE: You been welded.

LOM: What?

IKE: You been welded in. Good job. You're lucky there's holes in the barrel.

LOM: I feel lucky. I feel real lucky.

BERN: *(Fingering the seams.)* Wow. Looks like somethin' from auto shop.

IKE: So what are you doin' in there?

LOM: Where?

IKE: In the barrel.

LOM: What do you mean, what am I doin'? Let me out!

BERN: He's stuck in there, Ike!

IKE: No, I mean, is it some kind a prank or what?

BERN: That's a filthy joke to pull.

LOM: Hey! Binxie! Jumbo!

    (Pause as Ike and Bern again look around.)

IKE: Nobody here, man.

LOM: Nobody else?

BERN: Just us.

LOM: Great. The Ike and Bern show. Where the hell is here?

IKE: In a dump.

LOM: I am in a dump?

IKE: Yeah.

BERN: We was droppin' off these barrels of chemicals...

LOM: *(Desperate cry.)* Binxie! Shhhooo, no Binxie...oh God.

BERN: You want to listen?

LOM: Do I have a choice?

IKE: Hey, who is this Binxie?

LOM: My slice man.

BERN: *(Faintly alarmed.)* He carries a knife?

LOM: He sells slices, you know? Slices.

    (Bern and Ike look at each other. Both shake their heads silently.)

LOM: You seen him around?

BERN: Nobody's here. We're in a dump.

LOM: Yeah, well, I live in a dump, I work in a dump, it'd be a miracle if I wasn't in a dump right now. *(Lom finds this almost funny.)*

BERN: Sort of like what Bette Davis would have said.

LOM: You know her personal?

BERN: Yeah, I seen her movies. This is like a movie, you know? It's like a movie.

LOM: Got you, sport. Listen, you guys figuring how to crack this thing? I tell you, I don't feel so good.

BERN: I told you, it's like a movie, we'll get you out.

IKE: I don't know why you're in there, mister.

LOM: The point is I am.

IKE: It's a pretty heavy thing to do. I mean, somebody must be carrying the ax for you. Some kind of contract. Hey, how come you didn't say nothing all the way here?

LOM: All the way where?

IKE: In the truck when we was bringing you here.

LOM: You brought me here? You guys brought me here? Did you put me in here? Did you?

BERN: Hey, no, we thought you was chemicals.

LOM: Chemicals?

BERN: Yeah, you know, chemicals nobody wants.

LOM: Do I sound like chemicals?

BERN: Well, you got warnings like chemicals…

LOM: Do I sound like chemicals you have known?

BERN: No.

IKE: He thought you were a blob.

LOM: A what?

IKE: You know, like a blob.

LOM: Like a dead guy?

IKE: Like a live guy made out of chemicals.

LOM: I am a normal guy. I am not a blob, I'm just a normal guy.

IKE: Why didn't you say something?

LOM: Are you kidding? I was out!

IKE: Out drinkin'? Out takin' a walk?

LOM: Like knocked out. And I got stuff all over me, I don't know, I think it's blood, maybe it's sauce.

IKE: Sauce?

LOM: Tomato sauce, what's wrong with you?

BERN: *(Puzzled by this sauce thing.)* You feelin' all right?

LOM: Oh I can't complain. How about yourself?

BERN: Fine thank you.

IKE: That's good, Bern, that's really good. You want to maybe pass the guy in there a copy of your last physical, really make his day?
    (A banging on the barrel.)

LOM: You guys gettin' me out? I don't hear nothing happening!

IKE: *(Exasperated.)* Where did you come from?

LOM: You brought me here, you tell me!

BERN: *(Matter of fact.)* From Johnny Olander.

LOM: Johnny Olander?

IKE: Bern, you shut your mouth!

LOM: That jerkface? That asshole?

IKE: You know Johnny Olander.

LOM: That's my goddam partner.

BERN: He's your partner and he put you in the barrel? That is bad.

LOM: I didn't know he was my partner. He walks into my joint one day and he wants a slice, so Binxie cuts one up for him, slides it right over. This clown says "Glad we have you on board, kid, you got a nimble blade there." Ruffles his hair. 'Nimble blade,' little faggot gangster. Binxie looks all puzzled like a dog, which is how I felt. And I said "On board what?" He says "Lombardi! I'm your partner, you got a faulty connection or what?" Things went down the chute from there.

IKE: He was takin' over your joint, a pizza joint, huh?

LOM: Says I can stay but he gets half. Bull! I'm not takin' that!

IKE: So you end up in a barrel. *(Pause.)*

LOM: I thought he was jokin'. It's dark in here. There's these little slits in the barrel, little slices of light. Hey! Give me the whole pie!

BERN: *(Looks around.)* What pie?

LOM: Sun out?

BERN: It's real foggy. *(He shivers.)* It's like a movie.

IKE: We know.

LOM: This blob wants out!

BERN: Okay. *(Bern starts looking over the barrel.)* Don't move, I'm like looking for a weak spot.

IKE: Why didn't you let him have half your joint?

LOM: I'm not dancing to that tune.

IKE: He's getting the whole place now!

LOM: I'll put him in jail. Him and his insects. He says to me "you gonna wind up dead." Hey, I say what you gonna kill me for? My Neapolitan or my Sicilian? Please tell me, my customers argue this all day! *(Lom laughs.)*

IKE: You got bravado, man.

LOM: You know what he gives me for half? A bunch of chemicals! He says he got some supply house. I said I don't need chemicals. He gets this leer and says, "without chemicals life would be impossible." I say maybe life but not good pizza.

IKE: I bet you had him rollin' in the aisle.

LOM: Then Binxie pulls his roto-rooter on the guy.

BERN: His what? He's got a what?

LOM: What he calls his blade. God let me out. I can't joke on you boys, I want some air, I'm feelin' mushed. Air!

(Bern shrugs at Ike, no luck on welds.)

IKE: Olander didn't intend you to get out. I don't know what we can do.

LOM: Can you sit me up? I can't think lyin' down.

IKE: I really don't know what to do.

BERN: What do you mean? We get him out, guy's in a barrel, we let him out.

LOM: I give you free pizza.

BERN: You don't have to do that.

LOM: For the rest of your lives, no joke.

IKE: Great, we get pizza for two maybe three weeks.

BERN: Ike…

IKE: We let him out we won't be eating pizza, we'll be on the pizza. Olander…

BERN: We don't know what's goin' down, we just let some dude out of some barrel.

IKE: Don't talk to me Bern, this is serious.

LOM: I see what you mean. How about sittin' me up so I can think?

(Ike kicks the barrel viciously.)

IKE: Just knock it off, cut the cute jokes!

LOM: I'm tired of bein' on my back! Is that all right? I just feel like sittin' up. You don't want my pizza for life deal, that's your choice. I just feel like a change of scene, nothin' major, I want to sit Up!

BERN: Let's sit the man up!

IKE: This is not the time for one of your acts of generosity.

LOM: For God's sake, I'm goin' crazy lying down in this barrel!

(The barrel begins creaking and rolling.)

BERN: Calm down. Calm down. I'll get you out.

(The barrel slows.)

BERN: How long you been in there?

LOM: I don't know. Long enough, if you know what I mean. *(A sob.)*

BERN: Hey guy…

LOM: It's okay, it was worse at night. I woke up somewhere at night. I knew I died. I knew it. And, ohhh, I don't know, it was dying and finding there was nothing, you know? No silver, no light, no nobody at all, dark, nothing and you were, you know, gonna be awake for all of it! This is better than that. *(Pause.)*

IKE: All right, Lom. We'll set you up. Bern, grab hold.

(They lift the barrel and set it upright.)

LOM: *(Groans and then a sigh.)* Thanks. Thanks. Don't mean to be such a burden. Mom was right. She always said I spent too much time in the can.

(Ike looks at his hand. There is blood on it. He smells it.)

IKE: Not pizza sauce.

LOM: My old momma. Hey, is it still light out?

BERN: Yeah.

LOM: I thought so. How come? Is it daytime?

IKE: What do you think?

LOM: Might be lights or somethin'.

BERN: It's morning.

LOM: Nice day?

IKE: It's foggy. And it stinks in this dump.

LOM: Stinks in this dump too.

IKE: Shut up and let me think.

LOM: Guys, let me say something here. You want my half the pizza joint, I ain't against talkin', but let's make an agreement here pretty soon. Okay?

BERN: Half your joint?

LOM: Would you like that?

BERN: What joint is it?

LOM: The Vesuvious on Central.

BERN: You're kiddin'!

LOM: That's the place.

BERN: I had a slice there. Is that the place with that mural?

LOM: The dancing girls of Pompeii. Yeah.

BERN: That is a great mural.

LOM: You been there?

BERN: I been there, I wanted a copy of that mural. Guy told me there was just one in the whole world. That is amazin'.

LOM: What you look like?

BERN: Me?

IKE: He looks like a jerk. Bern. We got to take a walk and talk this out.

(There is severe coughing from inside the barrel. Ike and Bern stare at the ground. Bern leans down, touches and stands his finger, dappled with blood.)

LOM: *(Weakly.)* Guys?

(Bern and Ike are lost in thought.)

LOM: Hey! Guys? Guys! Anybody there? Oh God, oh Jesus, don't let them leave, don't go away! Please! Guys!

BERN: We're here.

IKE: We're here, Mr. Lombardi.

LOM: You want the whole joint. Is that it?

IKE: We didn't know you were in the barrel. We didn't know there was anything wrong at all.

LOM: Yeah, yeah I believe that.

IKE: We was hired to dump chemicals. You was just in one of the barrels.

LOM: I understand, I know.

IKE: Olander is a powerful man, our employer…I don't know what to…

LOM: We nail him.

IKE: I got a bit of a record, Mr. Lombardi, you know parole…

BERN: This is bullshit, I'm getting a crowbar.

IKE: Bern!

BERN: Cut it, Ike, I don't like it when you get all polite and weasely.

IKE: You be in trouble you get him out.

BERN: I can't worry about that.

IKE: You don't know how to worry, you don't know the word, you don't know think, worry, plan, you don't know jack!

BERN: *(Disagreeing.)* I know!

IKE: Yeah, you think you can walk into something like this and come out ahead? Isn't that your plan, to come out ahead? My man, you are not thinking straight. Arrow, remember? Arrow-straight! Nothing in your way but air. You do this, this is in your way. I double guarantee it.

BERN: What are you talkin'?

IKE: I am talking what you gonna do? You want to be a hero, you want to tell the police?

BERN: You're afraid of the cops, you little pisser!

IKE: You want to walk in with a gangland killing, no witnesses, just us? You want go against Olander?

LOM: Listen boys, I'm hearing you. I agree, see? Maybe I just go back, get Lucie and Binxie and disappear.

IKE: Disappear? Now that is rich. Guy's in a barrel he's worried about disappearin'.

BERN: I'm getting a crowbar.

IKE: Think it out!

BERN: I can't let this guy die, I ate his pizza.

IKE: You clown, you joker, he is dyin'! You saw the blood, you saw the bullet holes in the can! He is gonna pass on and leave us to sing the songs. You want to go against Olander for a dead man because of pizza?

BERN: Don't mess with my head!

IKE: You are an idiot! An idiot!

(Bern goes to the truck.)

LOM: Listen guys, tell me something, tell me you're letting me out.

IKE: There's only one guy here and I can't say that, Mr. Lombardi.

LOM: I'm in a barrel, you let me out! What kind of place are we talkin' about, leavin' me stuck in a barrel?

IKE: This place, man, a dump, so shut up!

LOM: You lyin' to me!

IKE: You are in a dump, clown! You hear somebody sayin' it's Times Square?

(Bern reenters with crowbar. He goes to the can and tries to jam the tip of the crowbar in the edge of the can.)

IKE: *(To Bern.)* Listen to me, I try to tell you things about the world, the real world.

LOM: Get me out!

BERN: I'm letting him out.

IKE: Look at you, you need a blow torch. You gonna hurt yourself, then I say I told you so.

BERN: I'm getting him out.

IKE: Bern, we have to split and split now. The dudes come and this place opens and we are stuck to the fucking wall!

BERN: Shut up!

(Bern is jamming at the can. Ike comes and tries to grab the crowbar. The bar hits the can with a clang!)

LOM: Ahhh!

BERN: No!

IKE: Damn it, get away from the can!

(The barrel rocks as Lom panics. Bern and Ike fall back against it and it rolls

against the pyramid of barrels. A massive creaking like a piece of crumbling glacial wall as the pile totters.)

IKE: Watch out!

(The pile gives way, burying Lom's barrel. A hissing of liquid and smoke. Bern and Ike, exhausted, hyperventilate, stare at the smoking wreckage. Pause.)

BERN: Lom? Mr. Lombardi? *(Pause.)* Lombardi? *(He bangs lightly on a barrel. A hiss of smoke. He coughs.)* Oh no. No. *(Pause.)*

IKE: I didn't knock those barrels over. I didn't mean it.

BERN: Lom! Hey, Lom!

IKE: I wanted him out as much as you did.

BERN: Lombardi!

IKE: I just needed to think it through.

BERN: Come on, he's in one of these.

(They roll away one barrel.)

IKE: Watch the goop.

(They both cough.)

BERN: Oh shit, oh man.

IKE: Bern. I'm sorry.

BERN: Lombardi! *(He reaches under another barrel. A hiss and flash of light and he yells in pain.)* Ahh! Oh damn! My hand!

IKE: Get it out! Get it away!

(Bern gets the hand free, holding it by the wrist.)

BERN: Oh God, oh God!

IKE: Give it to me, man, let me see it.

(More smoke as Ike grabs the hand and checks it out. A growing noise of chemical combinations. Bern is in pain. Torn between the pain and the search.)

IKE: Let me wrap it, here, hold still. *(He rips his shirt.)* Jesus, whole place is leakin'…

BERN: Ahh. Got to find him.

IKE: Damn barrels could blow…they could burn.

BERN: Don't scare me.

(Fear is exactly what Ike is looking for.)

IKE: Glom, that's what's happening. Probably already got him…

(He can feel Bern's sudden response.)

BERN: What are you sayin'?

IKE: Place is glommin' up. Look, Bern, over there, those chemicals, they're snaking man, they're snaking around like fingers.

BERN: You are cold, man, really cold.

IKE: They're doin' a dance, they're flaggin' a ride on over to each other, they're gonna glom!

BERN: They are?

IKE: They're gonna pulse into a real blob.

BERN: Like in the movie, in the warehouse…

IKE: It's almost too late, it may be too late…

BERN: We gotta get…we gotta…

IKE: It's gonna slide right out and suck us dry!

BERN: Go. We gotta go! *(Bern begins to cry.)*

IKE: Good, good buddy. Everything be all right, we do that, right now.
(He turns with Bern and comes face to face with the truck.)

IKE: Oh no.

BERN: What?

IKE: Ohhh. Oohhh man. We can't leave yet.

BERN: What do you mean we can't leave?

IKE: We have barrels to unload.

BERN: It's glommin' up. You said. You said we could leave, we gotta go!

IKE: We can't be tied to the barrels, we gotta get them off the truck.

BERN: You should a thought of that before you tried to make me pee my pants.
You're a mutt! A mutt! A sucker, an asshole, a fucking weenie! Why did
you get me into this?

IKE: Get you in…? Did I call you, as a favor, did I ask you, as a friend? You
have to say yes? Dint you want to come?

BERN: I'm not going to be seeing any more of you. I'm not.

IKE: Don't act like I set this up, I'm a sucker? Fine. I am, look at this! I am.
God, God I am! *(Ike is nearly collapsing.)* So fine, we do what you want to
do, you call the shot, you think I know what this is all about? Go on
Bern, you tell me, what do we do?

BERN: Me?

IKE: I don't know what to do, Bern, what do we do?

BERN: Oh. Ohhh. We…we… *(Pause. A discovery—Bern thinks something
through.)* We get the barrels off the truck.
*(Pause. Ike nods. They turn to the truck. Ike waits for Bern's orders. Bern
looks confused.)*

BERN: We ease it, okay? Ease it on over.

IKE: Sure, Bern.
(They pick up a barrel and start to heave it along.)

BARREL: Ohhhh. Ohhhh.
(It's the barrel they are carrying. They panic.)

IKE: Gahhh!

BERN: Ahh!
(They get off the truck and away from the barrel.)

IKE: No, not another, I don't believe it!
(Bern looks at his hand in horror.)

BERN: Oh God, ahhh…

IKE: What is it man, more goop, some chemical?

(He wordlessly wipes his hand across the T-shirt. A bright red slash of a stain. It's blood.)

BERN: *(Looking at the blood.)* Ohh God.

(Another noise, from the side. They look, backing towards each other.)

BARREL #2: Ohhh.

(Then another groan from one of the pyramids. They both look front, trying to place it.)

BARREL #3: Ohhhh.

IKE: The barrels are alive.

BERN: The whole place is alive.

IKE: Can't we even...leave?

(Pause.)

BERN: Ike, I know this place, like I recognize it, it's like I'm awake but not really, like you know, like I'm watchin' some kind of...

IKE: Movie...

BERN: Yeah. Like a movie, that I've never seen.

(More groans. Ike and Bern stare at each other as we Fade.)

END OF PLAY

What She Found There
by John Glore

John Glore's plays include *The Company of Heaven*, which was commissioned by South Coast Repertory and premiered by SCR in the fall of 1993; *Wing of a Thousand Tales* and *Folktales Too*, two plays for young audiences, commissioned and premiered by SCR and subsequently produced dozens of times across the country and in England; an adaptation of *The Stinky Cheeseman and Other Fairly Stupid Tales*, which had an extended sold-out run at SCR in June 1995; and numerous short plays, one of which, *What She Found There*, won the 1990 Heideman Award given by Actors Theatre of Louisville, which produced the play in its 1991 Humana Festival. *What She Found There* is included in an anthology published by Samuel French. *Wing of a Thousand Tales* and *Folktales Too* are both published and licensed by I.E. Clark, Inc.; *The Company of Heaven* is published by The Dramatists Play Service. Glore has been literary manager for South Coast Repertory in Costa Mesa, California since 1984, a position he took after serving for three years as literary manager for Arena Stage in Washington, D.C. He teaches playwriting in SCR's Conservatory program and has also taught playwriting for the extension division of the University of California, Irvine.

ORIGINAL PRODUCTION

What She Found There is the co-winner of the Actors Theatre of Louisville 1990 Heideman Award and National Ten-Minute Play Contest.

What She Found There premiered in the 1991 Humana Festival of New American Plays at Actors Theatre of Louisville. It was directed by Jon Jory and had the following cast:

Lou ....V Craig Heidenreich
Celia ....Jennifer Hubbard

CHARACTERS

LOU

CELIA

SETTING: The action takes place in a motel room.

TIME: The time is the present.

WHAT SHE FOUND THERE

A low-rent motel room. The floor is covered by downtrodden carpet squares in a checker-board pattern. A man's shirt has been draped over the mirror on the dresser. On the upstage wall above the bed hangs a painting depicting all the king's horses and all the king's men trying to put Humpty-Dumpty back together again.

As the lights come up, Celia, a young lady who looks and is dressed exactly like the famous Tenniel etchings of Lewis Carroll's Alice, is just pulling up her left stocking and straightening the horizontal stripes. She hums happily to herself. Lou, a nondescript, slightly ragged man in his twenties, is still in bed, apparently naked under the covers. He looks at Celia with a vaguely troubled expression. Note: In the tradition of other Alice plays, Celia is actually portrayed by a young adult.

LOU: *(Pause.)* This was *how* long ago?

CELIA: *(Faintly British.)* One hundred and twenty years.
(Pause.)

LOU: Now wait. Lem-me see if I got this straight. She climbed up on the fire-place thing—

CELIA: —the mantle—

LOU: —and she went *through* the mirror—

CELIA: *(Correcting him.)* —looking-glass—

LOU: —right through it without breaking the glass and ended up on the other side. And *you...* *(He makes a vague gesture with his arms.)*

CELIA: ...came out. I came *out*. I passed through *her*, to be precise, my head through her head, my breast through her breast, my hips through her hips, and my toes through her toes. Not at all an unpleasant sensation, after the initial shock—rather like being squeezed out of a tube of tooth cream.

LOU: And you've been wandering around in the real world ever since.

CELIA: No, I've been wandering around in *this* world ever since.

LOU: One hundred and twenty years.

CELIA: Yes. *(Pause.)*

LOU: How come you look so young?

CELIA: As long as I'm in your world I don't age. She doesn't either, for that matter, while she's in Looking-Glass World.

LOU: Jesus, you telling me I just made it with a hundred-thirty-year-old woman?

CELIA: If you'd care to look at it that way. Of course I have the body of a thirteen-year-old.

LOU: Tell me about it. *(Pause.)* You know, before—the way you talked and all, you seemed like—I thought you were older, *much* older. Than thirteen, I mean. I thought you were, like, young for your age.

CELIA: And so I am. *(She smiles. Pause.)* I so enjoyed playing with your puppy, Louis.

LOU: You what again?

CELIA: Your puppy. It's a naughty little thing, but then they all are. I'm sorry if I hurt its feelings when I giggled, but it has such a funny little pouty little mouth.

LOU: There you go with that "little" stuff again.

CELIA: My apologies. *(Beat.)* Of course *your* puppy doesn't talk. *(Beat.)*

LOU: No.

CELIA: Back in Looking-Glass World my uncle's puppy used to talk to me all the time, and it said the most impertinent things! Needless to say, he wasn't really my uncle.

LOU: Right.

CELIA: But *your* puppy doesn't make any noise at all.

LOU: Well—

CELIA: *(Gleefully.)* And now I shall recite a poem for you! *(Launching into it forthwith.)* In the garden, late at night—

LOU: —Whoa, whoa!—

CELIA: I found my way by candlelight
To a secret place which no one knows
Where the giggle sleeps and the yumyum glows.
Past the pussy-willows and—

LOU: Stop already!

CELIA: What is it?

LOU: You know on this side of the mirror we usually light up a cigarette or something.

CELIA: Beg pardon?

LOU: *After.* You know. We don't go in much for poems.

CELIA: I see. You don't wish to hear the rest, then?

LOU: Maybe later.

(Celia pouts, turning her back to him and making designs on the floor with the toe of her shoe.)

LOU: Look, it's nothing personal, it's just—I'm kinda discombobulated is all. I mean I've heard some weird stories before, but—

(She continues to pout, back turned.)

LOU: So. You do this kinda thing often?

CELIA: *(Still pouting.)* Not at all. I've never done it before.

LOU: Oh *Christ,* now you're telling me I just made it with a hundred-thirty-year-old virgin!

CELIA: *(Turning and giggling.)* Don't be silly! I've done *that*. I've just never done it in a bed.

LOU: Where'd—

CELIA: Oh, behind the Times Square Coca-Cola sign, in the control tower of John Wayne International Airport, in the batter's box at—

LOU: Okay, okay. *(Pause.)*

CELIA: *(Not able to resist adding.)* Twice at Disneyland. *(Singing.)* It's a small world after all.

LOU: How many guys would you say you've—

CELIA: Hundreds. And you, Louis, do you always use the bed?

LOU: *(Defensive.)* Yeah!—well—once on a fuzzy rug in the—

CELIA: *(Delighted.)* How peculiar you are, Louis!

(He has grabbed his undershorts and is putting them on under the covers.)

CELIA: Careful your little puppy doesn't bite you.

LOU: Right. Listen, I really enjoyed this and everything—

CELIA: Are you going to woo me now?

LOU: Woo you.

CELIA: It's customary. In Looking-Glass World, after the boy has his way with a girl he has never met before, he proceeds to woo her, beginning with passionate kisses and working his way gradually to exchange of pleasantries and courteous introductions. And then they part forever. The old ways are still the best, Louis, don't you agree?

LOU: Look, I was just—I don't know if I'm ready for, like you say, pleasantries and courteous whatevers.

CELIA: Everything in its time. *(She has wandered over to the window where she lifts a slat of the venetian blinds and peers out.)* I'm so glad you picked me up when you did. I was exhausted by the bewildering talk of that dirty woman with the shopping cart. She did seem quite certain, however, in her prognostications about the end of the world.

LOU: Crazy old bat.

CELIA: What is it that you're transporting in your lorry?

LOU: In my what?

CELIA: Your lorry, your "truck."

LOU: Oh. Hazardous waste. Hauling it to the dumpsite upstate.

CELIA: Hazardous waste. I once thought that referred to banana peels on sidewalks—tin cans with jagged lids, things of that sort. *(Still looking outside.)* Oh look! That boy is brandishing a windshield wiper and expostulating with great fervor to a fire hydrant. At last a breath of sanity in this senseless world!

LOU: *(Pulling on his trousers.)* Prob'ly on angel dust.

CELIA: Angel dust? Yes, we have that in Looking-Glass World, too. I once sprinkled some on a hitching post and it turned forthwith into a heliotrope.

LOU: Yeah, well, this ain't that kind of angel dust.

CELIA: *(Turning from the window.)* How this wiper-wielding warrior makes me long for my Looking-Glass home!

(She has become sad. He studies her for a moment.)

LOU: Why don't you go back?

CELIA: I can't, of course. I must wait for *her*, and she will never come back now. She knows full well that we both would crumble into dust as soon as we returned to our rightful sides of the looking-glass. So I must continue to live in this backward world and do my best to forget what I've left behind.

LOU: That why you covered up the mirror?

(She doesn't answer. Suddenly her mood changes again, but there's a willful edge to her cheer.)

CELIA: Shall we play a game of wormy-wiggle? What fun! *(She delivers the following in a manic burst while she turns chairs upside down, scatters towels and clothing over the floor, knocks over a lamp, etc. By the end of the speech, the room is a shambles.)* Now the rules are really very simple, Louis, so pay attention, the object of the game being to outfox one's opponent through a carefully developed subterfuge involving randomly chosen items from the environment arranged in such a way as to disguise the true nature of the player's emotional landscape, your objective on the other hand being to unearth the subterranean secret by means of intuition, canny examination of archaeological artifacts, and a series of yes or no questions, with a time limit to be agreed upon by both contestants prior to start of game, after which we change sides and the rules are completely disintegrated in favor of general anarchy and wild good fun. Ready? *(She takes in his expression of utter exasperation.)* Oh you've guessed the secret already, haven't you?! What's the point of playing when I'm not allowed to win. *(Pause.)*

LOU: I'd better hit the road.

(Gets up, looks for his t-shirt under the bed, finds it, puts it on. Celia looks around at the cluttered room.)

CELIA: Do you know what I like least about this place, Louis?

LOU: Hey look, it was convenient and cheap.

CELIA: *(Not hearing him.)* Entropy. The tendency of all things in your world to move away from order towards chaos. In my own world, it's the opposite. Dust floats up off one's furniture and through the air and gradually drifts together to be molded by the wind into great mountain ranges. Swarms of locusts descend upon a barren field and then lift away again, leaving waves of wheat behind them. Ancient monuments rise up out of ruins and, as time passes, become pristine and proud. A hole in the knee of a little girl's stocking grows smaller and smaller until it disappears altogether. And of course as the people of Looking-Glass World grow older, they *find* their innocence. What a muddle.

(She plops onto the edge of the bed. Her sadness has become deep and very old. Louis looks at her. He ambles over to the dresser. He removes his shirt, revealing the mirror. He looks at himself as he puts on the shirt and buttons it. He turns and looks around at the mess in the room. He tells the following as though it's an amusing anecdote; she begins to listen as though it's a fairy tale.)

LOU: One time, when I was a kid, it was just me and my dad and his dad living in a one-bedroom place, and Dad and Grampa always used to go out drinking. They were both drunks. Anyway, this one night I was home alone, I was about thirteen, fourteen, and I decided to drink a six-pack of beer. You know: "I'll show them." So I did, I drank all six cans. By about the fourth can I was feeling pretty crazy, and I started trashing the place, turned over all the furniture, spilled food, papered everything with TP—basically turned the place upside-down. After the fifth can I was crying 'cause...I guess I just felt really bad about messing things up. And after the sixth can I got sick. Barfed on the linoleum floor in the kitchen, went into the bedroom and passed out. Later on, I heard my dad and Grampa come in. They yelled at each other for awhile, then the door slammed and my dad's yelling disappeared down the street. The place got real quiet but then all of a sudden I heard this heavy thump. It scared me. I got out of bed and snuck back out into the living room but nobody was there. So I turned and looked in the kitchen and I saw my grampa. He had slipped on my puke, and he was just lying there on the floor, kinda bumbling around. He looked like one of those turtles on its back—trying to turn the world rightside up again. *(Laughs humorlessly.)* I just looked at him. He was really messed up, mumbling, groping—he coulda been hurt bad for all I knew. But I just looked at him. *I* was the *kid*... My grampa, he used to play the piano, you know, jazz, classical, when he was a young man. I guess he was really good, 'cause he was gonna maybe go on tour or something. But then he had to take a factory job during the Depression, to support Gramma and my dad. He lost parts of three fingers in the machines. Couldn't play anymore after that. So. That's my story. *(Pause.)*

CELIA: *(Still in story-land.)* Was your granddad a land turtle, a sea turtle or a mock turtle?

LOU: *(Smiling for the first time.)* Mock turtle, I guess.

CELIA: Yes, I thought so. *(Matter-of-fact.)* I'm sorry I never knew your granddad, but I do know that in Looking-Glass World he never stopped playing the piano.

LOU: *(Turning to look in the mirror.)* Yeah?...

CELIA: Furthermore, most of the really great Looking-Glass musicians have some turtle in them.

LOU: *(Sitting down next to her.)* You know, I don't think you're half as strange as you make out to be.

CELIA: Yes, well, after a hundred-twenty years, I suppose a certain degree of assimilation would be inevitable. *(Pause.)* Would you like to go again? We can do it in the bed, if you want.

LOU: I think maybe I'd rather hear your poem now.

CELIA: *(With a giggle.)* Why Louis, you impetuous mandrill! You must put me in the proper mood first!

LOU: Then tell me your name.

CELIA: *(Suddenly shy.)* I'm called Celia.

LOU: Celia. *(Pause.)* It is a great pleasure to make your acquaintance, Celia.

CELIA: *(She blushes.)* Thank you, Louis.

(They sit next to each other quietly, looking at their thoughts in the mirror. The lights fade to black.)

END OF PLAY

The American Century
by Murphy Guyer

Murphy Guyer, an actor and director as well as a writer, began his playwrighting career in 1980. His first play, *Eden Court*, was originally produced at the People's Light and Theatre Company in Malvern, Pennsylvania. In 1981 it was selected for that year's Humana Festival of New American Plays at the Actors Theatre of Louisville. It was subsequently produced at the Promenade Theatre in New York. His one-act play, *The American Century*, and a later full-length, *The Metaphor*, have also been presented at past Humana Festivals. *The American Century* has since been translated into German and Russian and has received productions in Berlin, Moscow and more recently at the 1994 Dublin Theatre Festival. His play *The Enchanted Maze*, originally staged at the Eugene O'Neill Playwright Conference in 1990, has also been translated into Russian and has been produced in Moscow, St. Petersburg, and Tbilisi. It received its American Premiere at the Cleveland Play House in January of 1996. His new play *Rendezvous With Reality* premiered at the Wilma Theatre in Philadelphia in 1995. Other plays include *The Interrogation, The Realists, The World Of Mirth, Coming Of Age In Samoa, Loyalties,* and *The True Satirist*. Murphy has received grants and fellowships from the National Endowment of the Arts, The Pennsylvania Alliance of Theatres, The New Jersey Council of the Arts, and the Steinbright Foundation.

ORIGINAL PRODUCTION

The American Century was originally produced by The People's Light and Theatre Company. At Actors Theatre of Louisville, it appeared in the 1985 Humana Festival of New American Plays. It was directed by Jon Jory with the following cast:

Woman	Debra Monk
Man	Christian Kauffmann
Stranger	Dana Mills

CHARACTERS

WOMAN

MAN

STRANGER

TIME: The play takes place in the Spring of 1945.

THE AMERICAN CENTURY

The time is Spring of 1945. The place, an American kitchen. It is spacious, sunny, and cheerful. The comforting hues of a Norman Rockwell illustration. Furnishings include an icebox, a bread box, a cathedral radio, and a round table with four chairs which should be centrally located. As the House Lights slowly fade, the final bars of Tommy Dorsey's "On The Sunny Side Of The Street" crossfade from the house speakers to the cathedral radio. The song ends, and in the darkness we hear the mild, resonant baritone voice of a forties disc jockey.

RADIO: "Leave your worries on the doorstep. Life's sweet. On the sunny side of the street"…That it is. Mister Tommy Dorsey and his orchestra. This hour of music dedicated to the boys on the boats. Yes girls, they're coming home. Soon they'll be walking down Main Street just as we remembered them. Let's sprinkle those memories with a little stardust, shall we? Artie Shaw.

(The Artie Shaw version of "Stardust" plays. Lights rise on a woman washing dishes at the sink, her back to the audience. Sunlight streams in through the window. She is a pretty woman in her mid-twenties. She works efficiently and thoroughly, but her mind is elsewhere. After a pause, a door closes offstage. The Woman calls out more from habit than interest.)

WOMAN: Mother?

(A Man appears in the doorway. He wears a full dress army uniform and a cap. He carries a duffel bag. He stands quietly and watches the woman from behind. Unaware of his presence and still preoccupied with her own thoughts, the Woman calls out again.)

WOMAN: Mother, what are you doing back so early?

(Suddenly the Woman freezes. Without turning she realizes who is behind her. The dish slides from her hand. She takes a moment to muster her courage and then turns. They stare at each other breathlessly. The Man slowly puts down his duffel bag and removes his cap.)

WOMAN: …Is it you? Is it really you?

MAN: It's really me.

(She runs to him and flings herself into his arms. Holding each other as if they'll never let go, the woman speaks in a passionate rush of emotional need.)

WOMAN: I knew it was you. I just knew it. I don't know how but I did. I was afraid to look. I was afraid that if I turned around you'd be gone. *(Pulling back to look into his eyes.)* But you're really here.

MAN: I'm really here.

WOMAN: *(Embracing him again.)* Oh God I've waited for this for so long. I kept telling myself that if I could just make it through one more day. But so many days. So many years. *(Pulling back once more.)* Oh Tom don't ever leave me again.

MAN: I won't.

WOMAN: Promise! Promise me you won't ever leave again!

MAN: I promise, I promise. Now come on, stop cryin. I'm back. And I'm here to stay.

WOMAN: I love you so much.

MAN: And I love you.

(They stare at each other longingly for a moment and are about to kiss when suddenly she pulls away frantic with fear.)

WOMAN: Oh God, are you all right?! You're not hurt are you?!

MAN: No, no, I'm fine.

WOMAN: Are you sure?! You weren't injured or wounded—

MAN: I'm fine, I'm fine. Everything's fine.

WOMAN: *(In an emotional panic.)* It's not fine! You had me worried half to death! Why didn't you write or call and let me know you were coming?!

MAN: I couldn't. I didn't have time. They shipped us out before I had a chance to—

WOMAN: Well it's not fair! Look at me! I'm a mess!

MAN: You're not a mess.

WOMAN: My hair is dirty, this old rag dress—

MAN: It doesn't matter.

WOMAN: How could you do this to me! It's not fair!

MAN: Margaret—

WOMAN: I had it all planned! I had new stockings and lipstick,—

MAN: Margaret it doesn't matter! I don't *care* about your stockings or your lipstick. I care about *you*. The way you are.

WOMAN: *(With girlish despair.)* I'm old.

MAN: No you're not.

WOMAN: When you left I was young and pretty and now I'm old and ugly.

MAN: You're even more beautiful than I remembered you.

WOMAN: You're just saying that.

MAN: And I'd love you even if you weren't.

WOMAN: *(Impulsively embracing him.)* Oh Tom I'm sorry. I'm acting like a spoiled schoolgirl.

MAN: I understand.

WOMAN: I guess I'm just so used to worrying.

MAN: Well you can stop now. It's over.

WOMAN: It is, isn't it. It's really over.

MAN: It's really over.

WOMAN: What was it like? Was it awful?

MAN: *(With a self-conscious shrug.)* ...Sometimes... *(Changing the subject.)* I don't know—I don't want to talk about it—it's over, it's not important anymore. What's important is us. I want to talk about us. Margaret, listen, sit down, I gotta tell ya somethin.

WOMAN: What is it? Did something happen?

MAN: Oh I'll say something happened.

WOMAN: What?

MAN: ...Ready?

WOMAN: What?! What?!

MAN: I got a job...Yeah, can you believe it?!

WOMAN: But, but when, how?

MAN: One of the guys from my squad is a vice president of a bank over in Fairview. He promised to have a job waitin for me when I hit stateside. A *good* one too. He said they were *lookin* for guys like me. He said that with a service record like mine the opportunities were unlimited.

WOMAN: Tom that's wonderful!

MAN: And that's not all. Wait till you hear this. He said he knew of a house for us. Yeah. About twenty miles from here. He said it's a bit run down right now but that with a little work it'd be just perfect. It's got a garden in the front. Two acres of land in the back. And three floors!

WOMAN: But how will we be able to afford it?

MAN: It's all taken care of. The government is giving out these special loans to GIs who wanna buy a home but don't have the down payment. My application's already in. Everything's set...And listen to this! *This* is the best part of all!...Every month I've been puttin aside a little bit of my pay. You know, so that'd we have somethin to get started with. Anyway it added up to over five hundred dollars.

WOMAN: Five hundred dollars!

MAN: And on the boat comin back I got in a poker game with a bunch of COs.

WOMAN: Oh Tom, you didn't *lose* it!

MAN: *Lose* it! I *doubled* it! I drew to an inside straight and I won! One thousand dollars!

WOMAN: A thousand?!

MAN: A thousand bucks! A thousand smackers! And it's all ours, free and clear! We're in clover Margaret. We're on our way. All those years of lookin for work that was never there? Of scrapin pennies to pay the bills? They're over. We're gonna have that big house. And that big car. Everything we always wanted.

WOMAN: Everything?

MAN: Enough to keep you in stockings and lipstick for the rest of your life.

WOMAN: I can hardly believe it.

MAN: Believe it Margaret. It's true.

WOMAN: Our very own house?

MAN: Just waitin for us to move in.

WOMAN: With three floors?

MAN: And six bedrooms.

WOMAN: Six!

MAN: That too many?

WOMAN: *(Blushing.)* …No.

MAN: We're gonna have that big family Margaret. We're gonna have kids playin and laughin in every corner of that house.

WOMAN: Oh Tom.

MAN: And we're gonna give those kids everything we never had. The best schools, the best doctors,—

WOMAN: And the first one will be a boy.

MAN: Yeah. And he'll be strong and healthy!

WOMAN: And smart and handsome!

MAN: A ballplayer. Another Duke Snyder!

WOMAN: Or a doctor! Like Albert Schweitzer.

MAN: Or a banker, like his old man.

WOMAN: And you can take him to watch the Dodgers play baseball.

MAN: I'll take him everywhere. Dodger games, fishing trips, the circus.

WOMAN: We can take the whole family on trips up to Mountain Lake.

MAN: Sure. We'll get our own little summer cottage.

WOMAN: What, you mean *buy* one?

MAN: Hey, I'm gonna be a banker. I'll just give myself a loan.

WOMAN: You're terrible!

(They laugh together.)

MAN: Margaret, from here on out it's gonna be nothin but the best. You know, when we were drivin through those small towns in France. God you shoulda seen it. The roads were jammed with people. Hangin from the street lamps. Leanin out the windows. And they were all cheerin and screamin and wavin American flags. And the women were holdin up their kids for us to kiss. And this one kid grabbed me and held me around the neck, and I looked into his eyes and…I don't know. I don't know how to explain it. I just felt that…that somehow it'd all been worth it. It's a new world Margaret. It's a whole new ball game. *That's* what I felt like when that kid hugged me. Like anything was possible. Like there wasn't anything we couldn't do, anything we couldn't have, once we put our minds to it. And it's all out there. Just waitin for us to grab it. A life more wonderful than we ever *dreamed* was possible…We made it Margaret. We're home.

(Tommy Dorsey's "Getting Sentimental Over You" comes on the radio. Hearing it, they both look at the radio. They look at each other and laugh. Man crosses to the radio and turns up the volume.)

MAN: May I have this dance?

(The woman rises from her chair. He approaches her awkwardly and, not

entirely sure of himself, he places his hand on her hip and begins to dance. After a few steps they look into each others' eyes and slowly come to a stop. They kiss. Tentative at first and then passionately. He pulls away, looks at her for a moment, and then sweeps her up into his arms. He carries her to the kitchen table and gently lays her down. Lying on top of her, he kisses her again. Suddenly the lights begin to flicker wildly and static crackles loudly from the radio. A few moments later we become aware of another presence in the room...A stranger...He is a slack-jawed, slovenly dressed man in his thirties. He wears an Hawaiian shirt over baggy army fatigue pants and sneakers. He carries a camera around his neck. He stares at the couple on the table in gaping astonishment.)

STRANGER: Oh my God.

(The man and woman leap from the table as the stranger struggles to remove the camera from its case.)

MAN: ...Who's he?

WOMAN: I don't know.

MAN: You don't *know?*

WOMAN: He does look familiar.

STRANGER: *(To the stubborn camera case.)* Come-annnnn.

MAN: *(Expecting the worst.)* All right Margaret, who is this guy?

WOMAN: I have no idea.

MAN: Well then how did he get *in* here.

WOMAN: I don't know, stop snapping at me.

MAN: *(Controlling his irritation.)* I'm not snapping at you, I just wanna know who he is.

WOMAN: Well I'm sure I haven't got the vaguest notion.

MAN: *(Turning off the radio.)* Hey you! What the hell you doin here?

WOMAN: Tom. Watch your language.

MAN: Well who is he?

STRANGER: *(Fearfully.)* Who? Me?

MAN: Yeah, you.

STRANGER: Uhh...nobody. I'm nobody. I'm not here. Look, just go on with what you were doing and—

MAN: Whatta ya mean you're not here. You're standing in my kitchen. Whatta ya think I'm blind?

WOMAN: Mother's kitchen.

MAN: What?

WOMAN: This is mother's kitchen.

STRANGER: Oh right! I thought it looked familiar!

WOMAN: Have you been here before?

STRANGER: I recognize the doilies. And the smell. It's that baking smell.

MAN: Who are you anyway?

STRANGER: Smells like cake or pie or somethin.

MAN: And how did you get in here?

STRANGER: *(Opening the bread box.)* Wow! Homemade bread!

MAN: What the hell is goin on here?!

WOMAN: Tom! Mind your tongue.

MAN: Margaret for godsake, a complete stranger is wandering around our house.

WOMAN: It's mother's house. And I'm sure there's a perfectly reasonable explanation.

STRANGER: Hey great radio.

MAN: Well I'd like to hear it.

STRANGER: Me too. How do you turn it on?

WOMAN: He's probably one of mother's salesman friends. They like to drop by for coffee and cake.

> *(Stranger turns on radio.)*

MAN: Hey you.

STRANGER: *(His ear to the radio speaker.)* Great.

MAN: We don't want any. Now turn that thing off and get the hell out.

WOMAN: Tom!

MAN: What?

WOMAN: What is wrong with you! What's happened to your manners?!

MAN: Manners!

WOMAN: Yes. Manners.

MAN: *(Thoroughly confused.)* Margaret I just got back from a World War.

WOMAN: That's no excuse to be rude. If you can't keep a civil tongue in your head then don't bother opening your mouth.

STRANGER: *(Peering into the back of the radio.)* God, look at the size of these tubes.

WOMAN: *(To Stranger.)* Excuse me.

STRANGER: They're enormous!

WOMAN: Excuse me.

STRANGER: *(To Woman.)* Hey do you guys get Jack Benny on this thing?

WOMAN: On Sunday, yes. Why? Do you like Jack Benny?

STRANGER: Oh yeah, he's my favorite.

WOMAN: Really? Mine too.

STRANGER: Yeah, he's great, isn't he?

WOMAN: I listen to him every week.

STRANGER: "This is a stick up. Your money or your life."

> *(Woman plays along and takes the pause.)*

STRANGER: "Well?"

WOMAN: "I'm thinking, I'm thinking."

> *(They laugh uproariously together.)*

MAN: *(Dryly.)* Margaret.

WOMAN: Hm? Oh. Yes. Look, uh, Mister…?

STRANGER: Call me Tom.

WOMAN: Really? My husband's name is Tom. His name is Tom too Tom. Isn't that funny?

(Man stares.)

WOMAN: Yes, well, tell me Tom, just what is it that you sell?

STRANGER: Sell?

WOMAN: Aren't you a salesman?

STRANGER: No. I mean I work in a second-hand bookstore on occasion. You know, between semesters. But that's not why I'm here.

WOMAN: Then why exactly *are* you here?

STRANGER: *(With growing anxiety.)* Well...I'm really not. I mean not *really.*

WOMAN: You're really not what?

STRANGER: Well I *am.* I mean obviously I *am.* Kind of.

WOMAN: You are what?

STRANGER: Alright look, first of all, this is not how it was supposed to be, alright? I mean nobody said anything about it being inter*act*ive. And you're not at all the way I expected you to be. Not that I expected that what*ever* you were would make me feel any better. I *never* expect anything that'll make me feel better. And even when I expect something that'll make me feel bad it always ends up making me feel a lot worse than I expected. I mean no matter how much time I spend trying to imagine the absolute worst that could possibly happen, no matter how many depressing details I try to include in my worst case scenario, I can never seem to fully anticipate just how truly awful, how really unbearably terrible—

MAN: *(Out of patience.) What do you want?!*

STRANGER: Iwannaseemyconception.

MAN: ...What?

STRANGER: I know, I know, it's crazy. But it's part of my therapy.

WOMAN: Therapy?

STRANGER: Yeah. You see my analyst is this Freudian geneticist who believes that the Oedipal conflict originates in the pre-consciousness of genetic memory. Steinfranck says that the only way to get to the bottom of my pathological narcissism is to trace it back to my prefetal experience. He calls it fertilization trauma...Frankly, I'm pretty skeptical of the whole idea. But what can I do? I've tried just about every kind of therapy there is. I've been through primal, behavioral, confrontational. I've tried Prozac, recovery programs, modern dance. None of them worked.

WOMAN: Are you not well?

STRANGER: Are you kidding? I'm not even close. I've been going through this bout of depression you wouldn't believe. In six years I can only remember being happy once. And I think that was just a chemical imbalance.

WOMAN: But what is it? What's wrong?

STRANGER: Chronic Fatigue Syndrome.

WOMAN: Oh dear. Is that what you have?

STRANGER: Yeah. All my friends have it too. Listen, do you think I could have a glass of water?

MAN: No.

WOMAN: Of course. Let me get it for you.

MAN: Margaret!

WOMAN: Tom, for heaven's sake have a little compassion. Can't you see he's not well? Look, he wants to take his medicine.

STRANGER: Actually they're placebos. But I'm dependent.

MAN: I'll say he's ill. He's nuts. What does he mean he wants to see his conception?

WOMAN: Yes, what *did* you mean by that?

STRANGER: It's Steinfranck's idea. He thinks it might trigger something that could lead to a cure. God I hope he's right. The holidays are coming up.

MAN: Who are you anyway?

STRANGER: Tommy.

MAN: Tommy who?

STRANGER: Tommy Kilroy, your son.

MAN: That does it. *(Man crosses to his duffel bag and begins searching through it.)*

WOMAN: But we don't have a son.

STRANGER: Well no, not yet. But you will.

WOMAN: We will?

STRANGER: The first of December.

> *(Note: At this point the dialogue should begin to accelerate so that the built in Moliere-esque rhyme scheme becomes apparent.)*

WOMAN: But how can that be?

STRANGER: I was three weeks early.

WOMAN: But it doesn't seem possible.

STRANGER: Oh it is. It's inevitable.

WOMAN: My future son here today?

STRANGER: Well the *first* one anyway.

WOMAN: I can hardly believe it.

MAN: Of course not, it's bullshit.

WOMAN: It's miraculous!

MAN: It's ridiculous!

WOMAN: Our son!

MAN: *What* son?!

WOMAN: Didn't you hear what he said Tom?

STRANGER: *(His head in the refrigerator.)* We got anything to eat Mom?

MAN: We don't *have* a son, remember?!

WOMAN: No, but we will in December.

MAN: The *hell* you say.

STRANGER: I haven't eaten all day.

WOMAN: And he's come all this way just to see us!

MAN: Get a grip on yourself Margaret, Jesus.

STRANGER: Any spiced ham or baloney?

MAN: It's a sham, the guy's a phony!

WOMAN: He's our baby, come for a visit!

MAN: He's crazy, don't be an idiot!

STRANGER: Any cheese spread?

MAN: *(Brandishing a Luger from his bag.)* You! Drop the bread!

WOMAN: Tom!

STRANGER: Mom!

MAN: Drop it!

WOMAN: Stop it! Thomas Kilroy you put that down!

MAN: Margaret he's stealing our food.

WOMAN: It's mother's food. And you put down that Luger this instant.

MAN: Margaret for godsake!

WOMAN: You might be able to get away with that kind of behavior in the war, but not here. I will not tolerate gun play in my mother's kitchen. Now give me that thing before someone gets hurt…Come on. Give it to me.

MAN: *(Reluctantly handing it over.)* I want him out of here.

> *(She removes the clip, drops it into her apron, and returns the empty gun to Man.)*

WOMAN: Tommy, you go right ahead and eat whatever you like.

MAN: What?!

STRANGER: Thanks Mom.

MAN: Margaret are you out of your mind? What are you doing, are you crazy?!

WOMAN: No I am not crazy. Now calm down and get a hold of yourself.

STRANGER: Yeah Dad, don't be a jerk.

MAN: Don't call me that!

WOMAN: Tommy don't call your father a jerk.

MAN: No, *Dad!* Don't call me Dad!

STRANGER: We got any mayonnaise Mom?

MAN: And stop calling her Mom!

WOMAN: I'll get it honey.

MAN: And don't call him honey! Margaret for godsake, you can't mean to tell me you actually *believe* all this horseshit?!

WOMAN: Tom! Please! Not in front of the k-i-d.

MAN: *What* k-i-d? He's older than *I* am. And we don't *have* any k-i-dees, remember?

WOMAN: No, but we will.

MAN: Yeah, in the *future.*

WOMAN: Well that's where he's from.

MAN: From the *future?!*

WOMAN: Why not?

MAN: Because it's impossible!

WOMAN: Why?

MAN: Because…how did he get here!

STRANGER: Psychopharmacology.

WOMAN: Psycho what?

STRANGER: Drugs.

WOMAN: Oh.

MAN: Margaret, I'm telling you, this guy is a freeloader. A vagrant. A bum.

WOMAN: Well that may be but he's still our son.

MAN: How can you say that? You never laid eyes on him before?

WOMAN: A mother always knows.

MAN: I don't believe this is happening.

WOMAN: Tommy stop that, you're making a mess.

MAN: Margaret for godsake, think about what you're saying. Just *think* about it. It doesn't make any sense, don't you see?

WOMAN: Not everything in this world makes sense Tom.

STRANGER: Good point Mom.

WOMAN: There are many things in life that we don't understand. And we'll probably *never* understand them. We just have to accept them on faith.

STRANGER: Yeah, like quarks.

WOMAN: Quarks?

STRANGER: Sub-atomic particles.

WOMAN: Oh.

STRANGER: Yeah and gravitons, and positrons and electron spin? Or what about anti-matter? Or artificial intelligence? Or post-modern art? I mean who knows whether these things actually even exist? Not me. I don't understand any of it. I mean the day Buzz Aldrin stuck a flag in the moon that was it for me. Things have gotten just too complicated.

MAN AND WOMAN: The moon?

STRANGER: Yeah, we put men on the moon. Don't ask me how.

MAN: Who did?

STRANGER: We did. The United States.

WOMAN: The United States of America put men on the moon?

STRANGER: Yeah. The Apollo mission. Landed on the Sea of Tranquility. It was weird. They played golf.

WOMAN: Golf?

STRANGER: Yeah. They hit this tee shot. Went like ten miles. Hey Mom we got any mustard?

WOMAN: Spicy or regular?

MAN: Wait a minute, wait a minute, just hold on one second here! Let me see if I got this straight. Are you tryin to tell me that the United States of America took a guy named *Buzz*, sent him all the way to the *moon*, and that when he got there he played golf on an *ocean* and hit a ten-mile *tee shot?!* Is that what you're tellin me?

WOMAN: Was there a tournament?

STRANGER: *(Condescendingly to Man.)* The Sea of Tranquility isn't an ocean, it's a desert. And it's not like they went up there just to play golf. That would be stupid.

WOMAN: *(Taking Tommy's side.)* Of course it would.

STRANGER: Nobody's going to spend billions of dollars to send some guy millions of miles into space just so he can work on his golf game.

WOMAN: Certainly not.

MAN: So what *did* they go up there for?

STRANGER: Rocks.

WOMAN: Rocks?

STRANGER: Moonrocks.

MAN: I'm calling the police.

WOMAN: Tom!

MAN: Moonrocks my foot!

WOMAN: You would call the police on your own son?!

STRANGER: Wouldn't be the first time.

WOMAN: Tom! How can you?!

MAN: No Margaret, don't bother defending him. I don't know who this character is, but he is *not* my son. He's nothing but a two-bit con artist. Don't you see what he's trying to do? He's trying to turn you against me. Well I'm not going to let him get away with it. Now I want this lazy, sponging, good-for-nothin out of my house and I want him out now!

STRANGER: Oh wow. Deja vu.

WOMAN: It's not your house. And I will not allow you to throw our son out on the street.

MAN: He's not our son! Look at him for chrissake! He doesn't even *look* like us.

STRANGER: Everybody always used to say I looked like Uncle Phil.

WOMAN: Yes, of course! No wonder he looked familiar. Look Tom, he looks just like my brother Phil. See? Around the eyes?

MAN: Alright! Alright! Fine! I'm going to put an end to this crap right now. You say you're our son, right? And you say you believe him? Fine. Prove it.

STRANGER: What do you want, a blood test?

MAN: Don't tempt me.

WOMAN: Prove it how?

MAN: Well if he really *is* our son he must know a lot abut us, right?

STRANGER: Oh I get it. You want background. Alright. Let's see…You were both born in Schenectady, New York. Mom has six brothers and sisters and you have three.

WOMAN: Right!

MAN: *(Gruffly dismissive.)* Public record stuff.

STRANGER: …When you were a kid you had to walk five miles to school every day.

MAN: *(Triumphantly.)* Wrong! It was only six blocks! Ah hah!

STRANGER: Figures.

MAN: There. What did I tell ya.

WOMAN: You told *me* it was *twelve* blocks.

MAN: ...Go on.

STRANGER: You met Mom in high school but you didn't start going together until later. Mom didn't like you at first because your hair tonic smelled like fish oil. She didn't want to be seen with a guy all her friends called Tunahead.

WOMAN: That's true! That's absolutely true!... *(Seeing the look on Tom's face.)* Sorry.

MAN: Tunahead?

WOMAN: *(Apologetically.)* Well it stunk Tom.

MAN: Hey it was the same hair tonic *Gable* used. I didn't hear you calling *him* Tunahead.

WOMAN: Well *I* didn't call you that.

MAN: Yeah, who was it? Phyllis?

WOMAN: What difference does it make? The point is he got it right.

MAN: It was Phyllis, wasn't it.

WOMAN: *(Changing the subject, to Stranger.)* What else?

MAN: Funny, fat, Phyllis.

WOMAN: What else?

MAN: I never liked Phyllis.

STRANGER: Alright, here ya go. When you enlisted in the Army you made friends with four guys. Two of them, Tony Pancotti and Butch Conklin got captured in Tunisia. Manny Eisenblatt contracted venereal disease in Algiers. And the fourth one, Benny Bellows, faked amnesia after he fell out of a jeep at Anzio and ran away with a nurse he met at a hospital in Palermo. *(Astonished pause.)*

WOMAN: Is that right?

MAN: ...Lucky guess.

WOMAN: Then it's true! He *is* our son!

STRANGER: Listen, ya think we could get on with the conception. My session only lasts forty-five minutes.

WOMAN: Oh Tom isn't it wonderful?! We're going to have a son! A son named after you! A son you can take fishing!

(At the mention of the word "fishing" the stranger erupts into a violent coughing fit. It's as if something were lodged in his throat.)

WOMAN: ...What's wrong? Did you get something caught in your throat?...Here, here, eat a piece of bread.

(Stranger waves her away as he takes a swig of water.)

STRANGER: No, no, it's fine. I'm alright. It's just that I have this psychogenic reaction to that word.

WOMAN: What word?

MAN: *(Innocently curious.)* What, fishing?

(Stranger erupts into another coughing fit.)

WOMAN: Tom!

MAN: Well how was *I* supposed to know?!

WOMAN: You could've asked without saying the word!...Are you alright?

STRANGER: *(After another swig of water.)* Fine. Fine. It's nothing. Really. It's just that when I was seven years old Dad made me remove this hook from a rainbow trout, and I had this sympathetic nervous reaction. Ever since then I can't hear that word without reliving the trout's torment.

WOMAN: *(Pointedly to Man.)* How awful!

STRANGER: Yeah, it's pretty limiting. Especially in seafood restaurants.

WOMAN: Well then we just won't let you do any...you know, the "F" word...We'll take you to the circus instead.

STRANGER: *(Disgusted at the thought.)* The circus. Gag.

WOMAN: ...You don't *like* the circus?

STRANGER: Nah. All those clowns really bring me down.

WOMAN: Oh...Well what about baseball? You *must* like baseball.

STRANGER: Nah. Baseball is boring. Besides, competition makes me anxious. I mean what's the point? If your team loses you feel lousy, and if they win you only get to feel good for a couple of minutes and then you have to go back to your own lousy, boring life.

MAN: Well what *do* you like?

STRANGER: Oh I don't know. I like *some* things. Talk shows, music videos, computer games...just as long as it's visual.

MAN: *(With horrified apprehension.)* You're not an only child I hope.

WOMAN: *(Excitedly.)* Yes, do you have any brothers and sisters?

STRANGER: Oh yeah, four of them.

WOMAN: *(Ecstatic.)* Four?! Do you hear that Tom? He has four brothers and sisters! Five children! The big family we always dreamed of!

STRANGER: Yeah, and all by Caesarean.

WOMAN: What?

STRANGER: Yeah. And the only one who was under ten pounds was Timmy. And *he* turned out to be gay.

MAN: *(Not understanding.)* ...What?

STRANGER: Yeah, but look, he's still in the closet so don't tell him I told you.

WOMAN: The closet!

STRANGER: Hey it's no big deal alright. It's just the way he is.

WOMAN: But how long has he been in—

STRANGER: All his life. He says he always felt that way. Since he was thirteen.

MAN: Thirteen!

STRANGER: Hey it was obvious. I don't know how you guys missed it.

WOMAN: And he won't come out?

STRANGER: He's afraid to. He's afraid he might lose his job. Look, Ma, don't worry about it. He's fine. Really. He just wants to be allowed to be who he is. *(Pause. Man and Woman are at a loss.)*

WOMAN: *(To Man, searching for the bright side.)* Well…I suppose as long as he's gay.
   (Man shrugs.)

WOMAN: And what about the others? What are *their* names?

STRANGER: Well you got me, Timmy, Billy, Suzie, and Jenny.

WOMAN: Oh of course, *Mother's* name is Jenny.

STRANGER: Yeah. Jenny was born just after Mom Mom died.

WOMAN: Oh no. Mama died?

STRANGER: Yeah, what a relief. She had Alzheimer's. It got so bad the whole
   family had to start wearing name tags around the house. Finally Dad put
   her in a nursing home out in Jersey somewhere and about a year later she
   died of botulism.

WOMAN: Tom!

MAN: What?

WOMAN: You put my mother in a home?!

MAN: No!

STRANGER: Don't lie, you did too.

WOMAN: How *could* you?!

MAN: I didn't! I wouldn't!

STRANGER: Yes you will. You always hated Mom Mom. *(To Woman.)* You know
   what he used to do? He used to take the rubber tips off her cane at night
   so that in the morning when she came downstairs for breakfast,—

MAN: Why you little— *(Furious, he rushes over to the Stranger, grabs him by the
   collar and lifts him up.)*

STRANGER: Mom!

WOMAN: Tom!

MAN: I'll kill him! I'm gonna kill him!

WOMAN: You'll do nothing of the kind! Now put him down! You hear me? Put
   him down this instant!…Now try and get along why can't you.

MAN: Get along with a liar?

STRANGER: It's true.

MAN: It's a lie!

STRANGER: True!

MAN: Lie!

STRANGER: True!

WOMAN: It doesn't matter! Now stop your bickering! Both of you. There's
   nothing we can do about it now at any rate so I don't want to hear another word about it. I want to hear about our children. And what they're
   doing with themselves in the future.

STRANGER: Collecting unemployment mostly.

WOMAN: Tommy you mentioned something about semesters. Are you going to
   some kind of school?

STRANGER: Yeah, college.

WOMAN: College?! Well my goodness. Do you hear that Tom? Your son is going to college! Isn't that exciting?

STRANGER: Not really. After fourteen years it gets to be pretty predictable.

MAN: Fourteen years!

STRANGER: Off and on.

WOMAN: Good Lord Tommy, what are you studying?

STRANGER: Well at the beginning, back in '69 I wasn't studying much of anything. I mean how could I sit in some boring history class when history was being made right outside the window? It was time to get involved. To join the struggle against oppression. To wage war against injustice. I mean we were the Armies of the Night!

WOMAN: So you *quit* school.

STRANGER: Well no, I didn't want to lose my draft deferment. Besides it wasn't long after that that the economy started getting bad, so I figured I'd better get serious and learn how to *do* something. I didn't want to end up like one of those guys with gray ponytails who live in their Volkswagens. So I decided to go into pre-med.

WOMAN: A doctor! Our son is going to be a doctor!

STRANGER: Nah. After a couple of years I had to quit. All that studying was ruining my health. So I switched majors and decided to study law instead.

WOMAN: A lawyer! How wonderful!

STRANGER: Are you kidding? Those people are totally amoral. I mean you're not even supposed to ask the guy if he's guilty. They don't care about justice. All *they* care about is winning. I'm tellin ya, flunkin that bar exam was the best thing that ever happened to me. Really woke me up. After that I went through this intense period of self-evaluation. And I suddenly realized that I had this real problematic relationship with sex and money. I mean I just wasn't *gettin* any, ya know? So finally I said the hell with it and decided to be an artist. I mean that's what I always wanted to be anyway. And look at Picasso. A millionaire at forty and still sexually active at ninety.

WOMAN: So you're going to be an artist?

STRANGER: Nah. I flunked the course.

MAN: Oh my God.

WOMAN: So what will you do now?

STRANGER: I don't know. I just can't seem to find anything I'm good at. So I guess I'll just have to take that job at the Post Office. It's either that or be a banker.

MAN: What's wrong with being a banker?

STRANGER: It's boring.

MAN: It's work. Work is work. If it were all fun and games they wouldn't pay you to do it. Wise up kid. Get a job. Stop freeloadin.

STRANGER: Oh look, don't start in on me alright? I've had a rough trip.

MAN: You don't get anything in this world for nothin pal. Life is hard. And the only way you get anything in it is by the sweat of your brow. You *won't* get it sittin around some fancy ass college.

WOMAN: But Tom, you were just saying how you wanted all your children to have an education.

MAN: Well I didn't realize he was gonna make a career out of it.

WOMAN: Well yes, fourteen years does seem like an awful long time. My goodness Tommy, how do you manage? That must be costing an enormous amount of money.

STRANGER: Oh it is. And don't think I don't appreciate it.

MAN: What?!

STRANGER: Hey Mom, we got anything for dessert?

WOMAN: You haven't finished your sandwich.

MAN: Wait a minute.

STRANGER: Yes I did.

WOMAN: What about that crust?

MAN: Wait a minute.

STRANGER: Aw Mom, crust is boring.

MAN: Margaret, did you hear what he just said?!

WOMAN: Let *me* handle this Tom.

(Assuming that she means the money, Man backs off. She speaks to Stranger severely.)

WOMAN: …Now you listen to me young man. There are children in India who have never even *seen* a crust of bread.

(Man moans "nooo" in exasperation.)

STRANGER: Not anymore. Back in the sixties the United States went in with money and advisors and taught them how to irrigate. India's a food *exporter* now.

WOMAN: You mean there are no more hungry children?

STRANGER: Well there's still the third world.

WOMAN: The third world?

STRANGER: Yeah, *you* know, Africa, Indonesia, Mississippi?

MAN: The *hell* with the third world!

WOMAN: Tom! Shame on you!

STRANGER: Dad's right. People are sick of hearing about it. I mean we had that rock concert, what more can we do?

WOMAN: We can finish our crust.

STRANGER: *Then* can I have dessert?

WOMAN: There's lemon meringue pie in the icebox.

MAN: Margaret didn't you hear what he said?! He spent fourteen years in college and stuck *us* with the bill!

STRANGER: Relax Dad. I was only enrolled for ten. After Billy's accident I dropped out and went to Sri Lanka for about four years to get my head together.

WOMAN: Billy's accident?

MAN: Who paid for *that?*

STRANGER: Yeah, alright. But so what? *You* could afford it. And what about those three years I took off to knock around Europe? *That* didn't cost you anything. Unless you're gonna count that bail money for those trumped up drug charges in Amsterdam.

WOMAN: Our *son* Billy?

MAN: Bail money!

STRANGER: It was a plant. I was framed.

WOMAN: What happened?

MAN: What did *that* cost me?!

STRANGER: I don't know, what's the big deal, it's only money.

MAN: Only money! Did you hear that?! Only money he says! What, you think money grows on trees? I'll give you "only money"! When I was ten years old I had to sell newspapers on the street to put food on the table. My eight-year-old brother was shining shoes down at the train station just so—

STRANGER: Oh God, spare me the boring Depression stories.

WOMAN: What *kind* of accident?

MAN: Boring Depression stories?!!! Did you hear what he just said?!

STRANGER: Look if you didn't wanna spend money you shouldn't have had kids.

MAN: Well if you think I'm going to have *you,* you got another thing coming.

STRANGER: Hey I didn't ask to be born ya know.

MAN: Yeah? Well we can take care of that right now.

STRANGER: *Mom!*

(*Man grabs Stranger by the throat.*)

WOMAN: Tom! Stop it! Stop it I said! Take your hands off him! Take them off this instant!

(*Man releases him.*)

WOMAN: And *keep* them off. And Tommy you stop provoking your father.

STRANGER: He started it.

WOMAN: I don't care who started it, I just want it stopped…Now we are supposed to be a family and it would be nice if just once we could try and act like one…

(*Standing behind her chair she gestures for them to sit in the chairs on either side of her. Grudgingly they do so.*)

WOMAN: Now I want to know what happened to Billy. You said he had an accident.

STRANGER: Yeah, he blew up.

WOMAN: What?!

STRANGER: Well after he got back from his tour of duty in Vietnam he turned into this anti-war activist.

WOMAN: Vietnam?

STRANGER: That's in Southeast Asia.

WOMAN: What was he doing there?

STRANGER: Good question. Anyway, he was making a bomb for this local peace organization when it accidentally went off.

WOMAN: Oh my God, he's not dead is he?

STRANGER: Well no.

WOMAN: Oh thank God.

STRANGER: Not exactly.

MAN AND WOMAN: ...Not exactly?

STRANGER: Well he's kind of in a coma.

WOMAN: Oh no.

STRANGER: Yeah he's been in it for years. It's been a real strain too. I mean the only reason he's still alive is because they've got him hooked up to this artificial life support system. You wouldn't believe how much that stuff costs.

MAN: *(With urgency.)* How much?

STRANGER: Oh thousands.

MAN: *(In severe pain.)* Oh God.

STRANGER: But they say there's still some brain activity so nobody knows what to do.

MAN: *(Unthinkingly, his head in his hands.)* Let him die.

WOMAN: Tom!

STRANGER: Dying's not as easy as it used to be Dad. Except for the uninsured.

WOMAN: You are talking about your son!

MAN: Fine. Let him live. *I'll* die.

STRANGER: Yeah it *is* pretty depressing. I mean Mom and Suzie are the only ones who even still visit him. You know, to cut his hair and trim his nails. But even Suzie's getting a little fed up. If she had *her* way they'd pull the plug and we'd all sit around and chant.

WOMAN: Chant?

STRANGER: Suzie's into alternative belief systems. She got into it after her abortion.

MAN: Abortion!

STRANGER: Yeah. At first she was involved with this Christian love cult that was run by this Korean arms manufacturer. But she quit that after you guys kidnapped her and had her deprogrammed. And then she tried being a charismatic Catholic for a while, but I guess that was just too exhausting. And then last year she moved into this ashram and became an anorexic.

WOMAN: She's living in an ash can?!

STRANGER: No, ash*ram*. It's this place where people go to empty their minds so that they can become one with the universe.

WOMAN: Is it in outer space?

STRANGER: No, it's on Fourteenth Street.

MAN: What's an anorexit?

STRANGER: That's a woman who unconsciously punishes her parents by starving herself to death.

WOMAN: Why would she want to punish us?

STRANGER: Hates ya I guess.

WOMAN: But why?

STRANGER: I don't know. Maybe you made her feel insecure or something.

WOMAN: How did we do that?

STRANGER: I don't know, look, I wouldn't get too hung up about it. *All* kids hate their parents.

MAN: Since when?

STRANGER: Since the mid-sixties.

WOMAN: This is terrible.

MAN: It's a nightmare.

STRANGER: Great pie Mom.

WOMAN: What about Jenny?

STRANGER: *(Reluctantly.)* ...Yeah.

MAN: Yeah what?

STRANGER: Yeah she hates you too.

WOMAN: But why?!

STRANGER: Well she doesn't exactly hate *you*. Just what you stand for that's all.

WOMAN: What I stand for?

STRANGER: Jenny says you're a stooge of the dominant white male culture. She says that your compulsive cleaning and cooking is just a symptom of the guilt you feel about wasting your life in co-dependent servitude.

WOMAN: *(After a moment's confused consideration.)* I don't understand.

STRANGER: *(Quick to empathize.)* Hey me neither. Sounds paradoxical if you ask me. I mean you did the best you could. It's just that raising kids is almost impossible nowadays.

WOMAN: Do *you* have children?

STRANGER: Nah. I had a vasectomy. It was my wife's idea. Carol said it wasn't fair that it was always the woman who was responsible for birth control.

WOMAN: So you're married?

STRANGER: Nah. After she turned thirty-five Carol panicked and decided she wanted kids after all. So she divorced me.

WOMAN: But that's awful!

STRANGER: Yeah. But I guess she had to. It was a matter of self-actualization.

WOMAN: *(On the verge of despair.)* What's happened to our family?

STRANGER: Yeah. Pretty dysfunctional, huh? But it's really not our fault. I mean you have to remember, we were the first generation to have to grow up with the Bomb. You can't imagine what that does to your psyche. I mean do you have any idea what it's like to live knowing that you and everybody around you could be blown up at any second?

MAN: Yeah. *(Pause.)*

STRANGER: Yeah, but do you know what it's like to live in a world where a single madman could bring all of western civilization to the brink of destruction?

MAN: Yeah. *(Pause.)*

STRANGER: Yeah, but do you know what it's like to be young and idealistic and to spend years fighting for peace and justice and then to find out that none of it made any difference?

MAN: I'm beginning to.

STRANGER: It's different with my generation.

WOMAN: Why?

STRANGER: Because *we* were different.

MAN: How?

STRANGER: We were special.

WOMAN: Why?

STRANGER: Because we were.

MAN: How?

STRANGER: Because…because we were non-conformists!

WOMAN: *Who* was?

STRANGER: Everybody! *(Confused pause.)*

MAN: What?

STRANGER: Yeah well you guys were pretty obnoxious too! Thought you were the last word just because you won a war. I mean give us reasons like you guys had and even *we* could've been war heroes. Hitler? Mussolini? Pearl Harbor?! God you guys got *all* the breaks.

MAN: I give up.

WOMAN: But my own children hating me.

STRANGER: Oh it's not that bad Ma. They don't hate you so much any*more*. I mean once you got old and fat it just seemed pointless to—

WOMAN: Fat!

STRANGER: Oh, yeah. After all the kids left home you got real depressed. Menopause I guess. Anyway you got addicted to these diet pills and Dad had to pack you off to a de-tox center for a few months. You got better but once you got back home all you seemed to want to do was eat. Which was perfectly understandable considering how bad Dad's drinking had gotten.

WOMAN: But that's ridiculous. Tom doesn't drink. He's never even—
(She turns to see Man hoisting a flask. He gulps, unaware of their stares.)

STRANGER: He's fallen off the wagon like ten times. After the fire he just stopped trying. Now he buys it wholesale.

WOMAN: What fire?

STRANGER: Oh, about ten years ago Dad torched the house to collect on the insurance.

WOMAN: Our house?

STRANGER: Yeah. He fell way behind on his gambling debts.

WOMAN: Gambling debts!

STRANGER: And then the banking scandal hit and so he had to put back all the cash he embezzled. And then—

WOMAN: Tom!

MAN: What?

WOMAN: You stole money from the bank to gamble with?!

STRANGER: Oh no, that wasn't for gambling. He wanted *that* money to pay the taxes on the property up at the lake.

WOMAN: Our cottage at the lake!

STRANGER: Ten cottages.

WOMAN: Ten cottages?

STRANGER: Yeah. Originally Dad was going to rent them out during trout season and make a bundle? But then the gas shortage hit and people stopped taking vacations. And by the time they started again most of the trout had been wiped out by acid rain and toxic waste so he was stuck. He tried to torch them too but he got caught. Probably would've done time if he hadn't filed for bankruptcy. The judge felt so sorry for him.

MAN: Bankruptcy!

STRANGER: Yeah, that and Mom's cancer treatment. *(He winces over letting this one slip out.)*

WOMAN: Stop it! Stop it, that's enough! I don't want to hear anymore. I can't, it's too awful.

(Man and Woman are in despair. Long silence.)

STRANGER: Look, maybe I shouldn't have *said* anything.

WOMAN: *(Desperate.)* But what about the *good* times? Weren't there any of those? There must have been good times too.

STRANGER: *(Enthusiastically.)* Oh sure, sure.

WOMAN: *(Delighted.)* Well tell us about *those*. Tell us about the good times.

(Pause. Stranger ruminates.)

WOMAN: Well?

STRANGER: I'm thinking, I'm thinking.

WOMAN: Oh dear.

MAN: Oh God.

STRANGER: *(Excitedly.)* Oh there were the reunions!

WOMAN: Reunions?

STRANGER: Yeah. Every year you and Dad go to these reunions. They have parties and banquets and you all get drunk and talk about the good old days.

MAN: *(Hopefully.)* The good old days?

STRANGER: Yeah, you know, the war? The Depression?

WOMAN: *(Crestfallen.)* This is horrible.

MAN: *(Depressed.)* I need a drink. *(He crosses back to his duffel bag, retrieves his flask, sits, and drinks.)*

WOMAN: My son in a coma, my other son in a closet…No. No, I don't believe it. It's not true. It *can't* be true.

STRANGER: I wish it weren't.

WOMAN: *(Determined.)* It isn't! I know it isn't! I refuse to believe that. It's just not possible.

MAN: *(Fatalistically.)* It's no use Margaret.

WOMAN: What?

MAN: It's no use. It's a losing hand.

WOMAN: What are you saying?

MAN: We crapped out.

WOMAN: Thomas Kilroy you stop that! I won't permit that kind of talk.

MAN: It's true. What's the use of pretending?

WOMAN: It's not true. Sure, maybe a few things *will* go wrong. And maybe it *won't* turn out exactly like we planned. But there's still hope.

MAN: I don't see it Margaret.

WOMAN: Tom, we love each other. That's what's important. As long as we have that, we can face anything.

STRANGER: Hey Mom?

WOMAN: *(Not hearing the Stranger.)* I mean we've made it through bad times before. And we'll make it through again.

STRANGER: Hey Mom look, I'm eating my pie crust.

WOMAN: Besides, now that we know these things, we'll be able to change them. It doesn't have to end up like this, don't you see?

STRANGER: *(Intentionally spilling his milk.)* Hey Mom I spilled my milk.

WOMAN: Tom we're just starting out. We can't quit now. We have to at least try.

MAN: *(After a moment's consideration.)* You're right Margaret. You're absolutely right. We *do* have to try. And we *can* change it. We just have to *want* to that's all. I mean forewarned is forearmed, right?

STRANGER: Not really.

MAN: Pipe down you…I mean what are we talkin about here? We're talkin about our life, right?

WOMAN: Right.

MAN: And what happens to us in our life is up to us. It's up to *us* to decide, right?

WOMAN: Right.

MAN: Margaret, I give you my word. From now on no more boozing and no more gambling. I'll never take another drink or place another bet as long as I live.

STRANGER: *(Sarcastically.)* Yeah, sure.

(Man glares at Stranger for a moment. And then:)

MAN: Fishing.

(Stranger erupts into a violent coughing fit.)

MAN: We're gonna do it Margaret. We're gonna turn this thing around. We're gonna prove what people can do when they just take a little personal responsibility.

WOMAN: *(Euphoric.)* We will! I know we will.

(They embrace.)

MAN: I don't know how all this could've happened. But this much I *do* know. It wasn't because these things *had* to happen. It wasn't fate that was to blame. It was ourselves.

STRANGER: *(Ruefully, more to himself.)* You always blamed it on the Dodgers.

MAN: *(With impatient irritation.)* What?

STRANGER: You used to say it all started when the Dodgers moved out of Brooklyn.

(Pause. Man stares at the Stranger in confusion and disbelief. Dazed, he takes a step toward him.)

MAN: The Dodgers moved out of Brooklyn?

STRANGER: Yeah.

MAN: *(Completely forlorn.)* When?

STRANGER: 1958. O'Malley packed up the whole team and moved them to Los Angeles. They're the Los Angeles Dodgers now.

(Man is stunned. His face is stricken with pain and grief. His body sags in agony. A moment or two later he dashes to his duffel bag and begins packing up his things.)

WOMAN: Tom, what are you doing?

MAN: *(With passionate despair.)* It's no use Margaret. It's a stacked deck. Yeah, maybe I *could* quit gamblin. And maybe, *maybe,* I could quit drinkin. But the Dodgers leaving Brooklyn! What could I do about that?! What could *one man* possibly do about that?!... *Tell me Margaret! What?!*

WOMAN: *(After a moment's thought.)* You could write them an angry letter!

MAN: Good-bye Margaret.

WOMAN: But Tom, where are you going?!

MAN: To re-enlist!

(He races out the door. She races out after him and shouts desperately.)

WOMAN: But Tom! Tom, wait!... *Tom?!* *(A moment later she re-enters. She is shattered. She speaks to herself in disbelief.)* He's gone. He's left me.

STRANGER: Ma, believe me, it's the best thing that ever happened to you.

WOMAN: *(On the verge of tears.)* All our plans. All our dreams.

STRANGER: Aw come on Ma, he's not worth it.

WOMAN: And now I'm all alone.

(Stranger sees his chance. Mustering his courage, he tests the waters cautiously.)

STRANGER: You still have me.

WOMAN: *(Confused.)* You?

STRANGER: Why not? He never loved you as much as I did.

WOMAN: He didn't?

STRANGER: *(With passionate urgency.)* Ma, look, I know I didn't turn out exactly like you expected. And I wouldn't blame you if you were even a little disappointed. But it's not my fault! Really! I mean you don't know what it's *like* in the future! You don't know what's going *on* back there. It's gotten so bad it's not even funny. And the worst part is, people pretend that it isn't! I mean no wonder I'm such a wreck. But it'll be different now! Now that I'm back here where it's safe, I'll be able to change!

WOMAN: But Tommy—

STRANGER: No, I will! I promise! I'll be vigorous and decisive! I'll be self-assured again! Like I was when I was young! Like when we used to dance to your Glenn Miller records together. *(Lost in the memory, he takes her in his arms in a dancing position, cheek to cheek.)* Remember?

WOMAN: No...

STRANGER: Because for the first time in thirty years I feel like I could really *do* something! Like I could really make a difference! I mean maybe there really *are* answers!

WOMAN: But Tom is gone.

STRANGER: Forget him! Who needs him?! Don't ya see Ma?! It's a new ball game! A clean slate!

WOMAN: But he's your father.

STRANGER: *(On his hands and knees.)* Ma please! Please don't make me go back there. It's too awful! My life back there is just too dreadful! I'd rather die!

WOMAN: But if you don't have a father—

STRANGER: No I mean it! I'd rather die! I'd rather be dead than have to go back to that dreadful, terrible, miserable... *(Stranger pulls up short. Pause.)* ...What?

WOMAN: Well...I mean...without a father you wouldn't *have* a life, right?

(Stranger considers this for a moment, and then races out the door screaming.)

STRANGER: *Daaad!...Dad I was only kidding!...Come on Dad, can't you take a joke?!...Dad, come back!*

(Blackout.)

END OF PLAY

The Black Branch

by Gary Leon Hill

BIOGRAPHY

Gary Leon Hill is the author of eight plays that have been produced at theatres across the United States. *Food From Trash* won the Actors Theatre of Louisville Great American Playwriting Contest and premiered in the 7th annual Humana Festival of New American Plays in 1983. *The Black Branch* played at Actors Theatre in both the 1984 SHORTS Festival and the 1985 Humana Festival. *Pivot* premiered at the Westside Theatre in New York City in 1986, and *Soundbite* was first produced in the US West Festival at the Denver Center Theatre Company in 1990. *Back To The Blanket* debuted at DCTC in 1991. San Francisco's Magic Theatre has produced both *Say Grace* (1995) and *Watch Your Back* (1993), and his short play about baseball premiered in 1995 as part of *Hitting For The Cycle* in San Francisco.

Hill is the recipient of fellowships from the Rockefeller Foundation, National Endowment for the Arts, Arthur Foundation and New York Foundation for the Arts. He also won the Playwright USA Award from Theatre Communications Group and Home Box Office in 1984 and his play *Back To The Blanket* received an AT&T: OnStage Project grant. Hill has worked as an NEA Artist in Schools and has produced, scripted, photographed and edited seven 16 mm films. The film *Energy And How To Get It* which he made with Robert Frank and Rudy Wurlitzer, was produced with the assistance of a grant from the Corporation from Public Broadcasting.

ORIGINAL PRODUCTION

The Black Branch premiered in the Actors Theatre of Louisville Shorts Festival in 1984, and was remounted for the 1985 Humana Festival of New American Plays. Both productions were directed by Jackson Phippin with the following cast:

Eli Crooner	Delroy Lindo
The Black Branch	Adale O'Brien
Donna Car	Janna Gjesdal
Aide	Dana Mills
Wilmer Allen Norris	Christian Kauffmann
Aunt Hyadle	Sylvia Short

CHARACTERS

ELI CROONER

THE BLACK BRANCH

DONNA CAR

AIDE

WILMER ALLEN NORRIS

AUNT HYADLE (HIGH-ADDLE)

LOCATION

Ash Manor, state-run mental hospital

Office Upstage Center, one partial wall, one medicine cupboard, four-drawer file cabinet, desk, two chairs, waste basket, broom against wall, leather restraints hanging from hook, ticking clock, counter Right with coffee maker and glass pot, an air conditioner framed in Upstage window.

Stage Left of Office, the Tub Room—cast iron bathtub and long white see-through curtain on track which can be pulled to close off tub on three sides.

Downstage Right, the Dayroom, bare of furniture, closet door, two windows—one practical Upstage Right, one special Downstage Right.

Downstage Left, stuffed chair and portable commode.

TIME: July morning.

THE BLACK BRANCH

Eli Crooner, skin and bones black man, head covered with a pink fabric burn mask—holes cut out for eyes, nose, mouth and ears—strikes an oversized cookstove match on the door jamb as he stands from a crouch in the door-frame of the unlit office USC. Dressed in T-shirt, suit vest and baggy wash-pants hung from yellow suspenders, he lights a hand-rolled cigarette. Sotto voce, real reedy, without moving his lips, he croons to the tune of "Going Out Of My Head."

ELI: *(Crooning.)* Well, I think I'm going out of my head.
   Yeh.
   I think I'm going out of my head.
   Hm hm hmm hmm hmm,
   Hm hm hmm hmm hmm—
   (Ping tick tick tick. Overhead light comes on, fluorescent buzz, a cold wash DSR as The Black Branch enters—Caucasian, female, late 40s, built wide, once stunning, her explosion of thick black hair is tangled snakes roping off in all directions now. Arms full of grocery bags and one small bag clenched in her teeth like a dog bone, she moves USR, turns on a second bank of fluorescents, and cuts toward Eli in the doorframe. Hardened feet pound deep into three-inch white wooden clogs as she struts, back bowed, round loaves up and out, dressed in nurse's white. Eli shifts in the doorframe as she sweeps past him into unlit office.)
BLACK BRANCH: Good morning, Eli.
ELI: *(Crooning.)* I want you
   to want me
   I need you so badly
   You can't think of anything
   but you—
   (The Black Branch turns on office overheads, empties her arms on the counter to one side of the coffee maker, and crosses back to Eli in the doorframe. Eli inhales deeply.)
BLACK BRANCH: Stop smoking. *(Snatches cigarette from his lips.)* It'll kill you.
   (Extinguishes his cigarette on her tongue and drops it into the pocket of her service smock. Eli exhales. She pulls a candy from her cleavage—)
BLACK BRANCH: If you live that long.
   (—inserts it into his mouth, turns him at the shoulders, finds his kidneys with her thumbs, and pushes him toward the dayroom. She crosses back to the cof-

fee maker, removes the glass pot from the burner, puts it in a grocery bag, rolls down the top of the bag and smashes it against the counter. Glass shatters. Eli spits. Her candy lifts in a limp arc and hits the floor a couple feet in front of him.)

ELI: *(Crooning.)* Goin' outta my head
Over you.
Outta my head
Over you.
Outta my head
Day and night
Night and day and night
Wrong or right— *(Continues under.)*

(As Eli croons, The Black Branch pulls a stack of 8-1/2 x 11 canary yellow paper from another bag, thumps the loose sheets into a bundle, and places it in the middle of the desk where it will be seen. She steps back to gauge the effect, aims desk lamp at the stack of paper, and turns it on. A yellow pool of light falls onto the paper. In dayroom, Eli slips suspenders off his shoulders and lets his pants drop. Satisfied, The Black Branch takes the bag containing the smashed coffee pot, turns off overhead fluorescents, and exits office, crossing to Eli.)

BLACK BRANCH: *(Pulling up his trousers.)* You keep your pants up, Eli.

ELI: *(Crooning.)* You can't think of a way—

BLACK BRANCH: *(Hitching suspenders over shoulders.)* You have nothing to show.

ELI: *(Crooning.)* —into your heart.
No reason why
My being shy
Should keep us apart.

(The Black Branch stops his singing with a thumb to each kidney, pushes Eli farther into dayroom, and exits DSR. Eli drifts SL, lights a cigarette.)

ELI: *(Crooning.)* No reason why
My being shy
Should keep us apart.

(As Eli sings, Donna Car enters USR behind an aluminum walker—late 20s, big boned, wearing flats, small print cotton wraparound farm dress. She talks to her legs, herself, crossing DSC behind the walker.)

DONNA: Right...left...walker...right...left...walker...right...left... walker...Figure this out...How does it work?

(Eli slips his suspenders off his shoulders, lets trousers drop, crossing into tub room.)

DONNA: First Uncle Ellwell's mother died. He'd no moren put her in the ground then his family started saying it was his fault, his drinking broker heart, that's why she died. *They* say. I say she broker own damn heart. Uncle Ellwell drank cause he wanted to, 'cause he felt bad about Aunt

Hyadle, his wife. And crops. She's like a mother. They were both like parents. But she's been real sick now for two years and it's all she can do to sit in her chair. She can't hardly talk, forgets who she is, won't show her emotions. Plus, she'd wander off if Uncle Ellwell didn't watcher every minute of the day and night and he can't do that. Couldn't. So Uncle Ellwell raised the locks on all their doors up outta Aunt Hyadle's reach. When he leaves now he locks her in for her own good. He did. The day they buried his mother, Uncle Ellwell got real drunk real fast and drank all night. Bartender says all he'd talk about was how his kids blamed him for his mother's death and how bad that made him feel. That night Uncle Ellwell went home and locked all the doors and dropped dead. He was in on the bedroom floor the whole next day. Aunt Hyadle's locked in. She couldn't reach the locks, so she couldn't go for help and she couldn't use the phone 'cause she couldn't remember how. So she just sat there and held his hand until somebody finally missed seeing their dog out and broke in.

(Aide enters DSR and crosses into office.)

DONNA: Neighbor. Her family put her in here. Real family.

AIDE: Your aunt is in her room, Miss… *(Checks chart.)* …Car.

DONNA: *(Out from behind the walker.)* Two chickenshit daughters don't even come see her. Do they?

AIDE: I don't know.

DONNA: They don't. Ask the nurse.

AIDE: It's my second day here.

(Wilmer enters USR—balding, 40, dressy bathrobe with white piping over executive pajamas, shiny slippers.)

WILMER: *(Crosses to Donna.)* I'd come.

DONNA: *(Ties Wilmer's bathrobe.)* She wants to die around people, not locked up alone like Uncle Ellwell did.

(Donna crosses DSL with walker to where Aunt Hyadle snores half slumped in her chair, one bunny slipper in her lap, one on her foot.)

WILMER: *(Sings the Doxology to Donna.)* "Be present at our table, Lord.
Be here and everywhere ignored."

(Aide laughs at Wilmer. He's turned on overhead fluorescents, his attention drawn to the stack of canary memos on the desk.)

AIDE: Morning, Wilmer.

WILMER: *(Crossing into office.)* Here she can die in the lunchroom surrounded by droolers.

AIDE: *(Leafs through memos.)* Where you headed this morning?

WILMER: She can collapse in her food.

AIDE: East or west?

WILMER: I'm driving out to that young one's farm. I'm going to wander forever.

AIDE: Denver or which was it? Kansas City?

WILMER: Which way's Denver?

AIDE: West.

WILMER: Which way's mom?

AIDE: East.

(Clomp clomp clomp—The Black Branch reenters DR, sees Eli who has drifted DL, and crosses to the office door. Donna helps Aunt Hyadle onto commode.)

BLACK BRANCH: Eli's dropped his drawers again.

AIDE: What's that?

BLACK BRANCH: The electric man. Our own Mr. Crooner.

AIDE: He's naked?

BLACK BRANCH: Well, he's down to his dirty underpants again.

AIDE: One thing after another.

BLACK BRANCH: Would you like me to handle it?

AIDE: No, Margaret, I'll get to him.

BLACK BRANCH: That Donna woman and her aunt will pass back through here on their way to the lunchroom.

AIDE: Eli's harmless.

BLACK BRANCH: You don't know.

AIDE: *(Teasing.)* And you don't have to stare.

BLACK BRANCH: *(Entering office.)* There are rules.

AIDE: *(Referring to yellow memos.)* More and more of them.

BLACK BRANCH: We have procedures for dealing with belligerents.

AIDE: You do?

(Wilmer stands, exits office, then offstage R.)

BLACK BRANCH: This institution has procedures for dealing with uncooperative patients, yes it does.

AIDE: I know.

BLACK BRANCH: The procedures are in the rule book.

AIDE: I've been reading that.

BLACK BRANCH: It will simplify your job.

AIDE: I know.

BLACK BRANCH: Goddam woman shouldn't be up here anyway. She belongs in geriatrics.

AIDE: I'd offer you a cup of coffee, but I can't find the pot.

BLACK BRANCH: It's gone?!

AIDE: Some belligerent, perhaps, or maybe the night crew probably left it in the lavatory and didn't clean it out. There's a note here about that somewhere.

BLACK BRANCH: You don't remember? *(Closing space between them.)* Our little accident?

AIDE: Last night?

BLACK BRANCH: *(Dry ice.)* Last night was no accident. *(Warmer.)* I mean yesterday afternoon.

AIDE: Oh the pot. Right.

BLACK BRANCH: *(Eyes wide, plays drama.)* Our faux pas.

AIDE: Did it chip?

BLACK BRANCH: It was all over the floor when I came in this morning.

AIDE: No.

BLACK BRANCH: In pieces.

AIDE: It was just a little chip.

BLACK BRANCH: It must have been a hairline fracture that opened up into something worse.

AIDE: How could—?

BLACK BRANCH: You can't go away with it empty on the heat.

AIDE: I didn't leave it turned on.

BLACK BRANCH: Don't worry.

AIDE: I don't think.

BLACK BRANCH: I swept up the evidence and put the pieces in the dumpster. It won't be traced to us.

AIDE: What do you mean?

BLACK BRANCH: The doctor doesn't have to know.

AIDE: He'll know when I call his office and ask for a new coffee pot.

BLACK BRANCH: Why risk God's wrath?

AIDE: I have to have my coffee.

BLACK BRANCH: You're new here.

AIDE: And I need all the legal drugs.

BLACK BRANCH: We all make mistakes.

AIDE: Last night.

BLACK BRANCH: Our little discretions.

AIDE: I didn't mean—

BLACK BRANCH: *(Cuts him off.)* The doctor likes you. I can tell— *(With the tip of her toe, she slides the wastebasket to one side of where it sits, revealing a hole in the sheetrock.)* —and I can tell the doctor.

AIDE: Shit.

BLACK BRANCH: He counts on me.

AIDE: That I have to fix.

BLACK BRANCH: I have his ear.

AIDE: That's not what it looks like.

BLACK BRANCH: It looks like someone got mad and—

AIDE: I was happy!

BLACK BRANCH: —lost control.

AIDE: We were singing, I was dancing.

BLACK BRANCH: I love it!

AIDE: And I kicked a hole in that cheapass wall.

BLACK BRANCH: You were kicking up your heels.

AIDE: It was an accident.

BLACK BRANCH: A celebration.

AIDE: Because of this job.

BLACK BRANCH: I know how much you need.

AIDE: How lucky I was to get this job.

BLACK BRANCH: How lucky we are to have someone so full of life here finally.

AIDE: First personnel tells me no. They give the job to someone else. Three days later they tell me yes, the job is mine.

BLACK BRANCH: The doctor is unpredictable.

AIDE: What happened?

BLACK BRANCH: The man you replaced—a boy—didn't work out. He would not do his job.

AIDE: I heard it had to do with Eli.

BLACK BRANCH: Now the boy is gone and we have you.

AIDE: Didn't it have something to do with Eli?

BLACK BRANCH: He didn't get along with the staff.

AIDE: What staff?

BLACK BRANCH: How would I know?

AIDE: *(Referring to memos.)* You seem to know what's going on around here.

BLACK BRANCH: I can help.

AIDE: I'll be good at the job.

(She pulls a candy from her cleavage, unwraps it.)

BLACK BRANCH: I know you will. I want to help. That's how I am.

(She inserts her candy into his mouth.)

AIDE: *(Candy in cheek.)* I need this job.

BLACK BRANCH: Because of your wife, I know. So, why risk losing it?

(They hold each other's gaze. She pouts, "lips sealed," eyes big as a baby's. DSL, Aunt Hyadle leans forward from her seat on the commode, fingers wagging toward the floor.)

DONNA: What are you looking at, hon?

HYADLE: Big bugs.

DONNA: I think you're seeing things.

HYADLE: I don't think you are.

(The Black Branch steps back from the Aide.)

HYADLE: *(To Donna who hasn't moved.)* You stepped on one!

(Donna jumps.)

AIDE: *(Shouting out the office door.)* Eli! Crooner! Pull up your pants or I'll—
(To The Black Branch.) What can we do to him?

BLACK BRANCH: Restraints, seclusion, ice packs, cold tub.

AIDE: Pull up your pants or I'll tie you down!

(Eli steps out of his pants and as action continues, he turns around, steps back in and pulls them up, zipper in the seat now, hitching the suspenders over his shoulders.)

HYADLE: I'm not going to let you talk me out of it this time.

(Aide turns back into office as The Black Branch pulls a new coffee pot from a grocery bag.)

BLACK BRANCH: Tah dah!

AIDE: I thought it smashed.

BLACK BRANCH: Identical.

AIDE: You bought one?

BLACK BRANCH: One exactly like the one you broke.

AIDE: How much was it?

BLACK BRANCH: Don't worry what it cost.

AIDE: But I'm going to pay you for it. *(Opens empty wallet.)* Well, in three weeks I'll pay you.

(The Black Branch kisses him on the lips, holding his cheeks with her hands as Wilmer enters USR.)

BLACK BRANCH: I love taking care of you.

AIDE: *(Off balance.)* —they hold that first check three weeks.

WILMER: Hope.

DONNA: *(To Aunt Hyadle.)* Can't go?

BLACK BRANCH: *(Conspiratorially to Aide.)* I'll go fill it up. *(Exits with new coffee pot SR.)*

DONNA: We'll try later.

WILMER: That's something to think about. Hope. *(To Aide.)* What's the book say?

(Aide replaces wastebasket in front of the hole in the sheetrock, ushers Wilmer into office with an upturned palm. Donna helps Aunt Hyadle off the portable toilet and they begin a snail's pace cross DSR and off—Aunt Hyadle behind the walker, Donna talking her through it.)

DONNA: Right…left…walker…right…left…walker… *(Etc.)*

WILMER: The good book.

(Wilmer pulls thick dictionary from Aide's desk, opens it, dives in. Aide leafs through yellow memos.)

WILMER: *(Reading.)* "Hoover, Herbert Clark. Thirty-first President of the United States." That's what I told him.

AIDE: *(Half hearing.)* Told who, Wilmer?

WILMER: The President. I told him we'd have to sit down and talk about this because we can't do it alone. Him *or* me. It's as easy as that. It's going to take sitting down and talking. I told him that.

AIDE: Sit down, Wilmer.

WILMER: *(Sits.)* He didn't have to take it personal.

AIDE: Who?

WILMER: The President.

AIDE: You didn't talk to the President.

WILMER: No. But I told him I would. I made that clear. And when I do, I will speak to the end of the individual. It is over, my friend. The age of the integer, sole figure, Lone Ranger, is no more, Mr. President. A Vietnam migrant with his little son held high on his shoulders, dodging camera-men and police motorcycles to cheer a 19-year-old black man pushing an 88-year-old white woman in a wheelchair as she carries the Olympic torch. That's the picture. That's what I told him.

AIDE: You did?

WILMER: I will. It's gone. Interdependence. Worldwide. That's the current pro-gram. Then, of course, you got to be increasingly careful who you interde-pend *on. (A look to Aide he never sees.)* But—Hoover Dam. I been there.

AIDE: Where's that?

WILMER: Nevada on the Arizona line. Lake Mead. Seventy-two three eighty double clutching.

AIDE: What's seventy-two three eighty?

WILMER: My truck load. Hauling meat. Ten hours and I won't stop. Seventy-two three eighty, I pull that.

AIDE: Ahhh.

WILMER: Two forty-five ten four over and out Al Capone.

AIDE: Seventy-two three eighty-five what?

WILMER: No. Five'll get you sixty-one in Iowa. They fine that five. That's the odd dollar. Costs plenty. It's a road tax. Henry Hendershot.

AIDE: Who's Henry Hendershot?

WILMER: He pulls a load in Texas. Drives out of Texas. Now I got a pair of cowboy boots in the marking room I need. These feet are no good and I'll tell you why. No, I'll tell you. *(Stands in slippers.)* No heel. There's no heel on these. I'm walking flat. Down to earth. Both feet on the ground and they both give me trouble. Maybe I'll soak them.

AIDE: Maybe you should.

WILMER: *(Sits.)* Soak them on up.

AIDE: How far up?

WILMER: That's for you to decide. It's your desk. You tell me. *(Back to dictio-nary.)* "Hop."

(Clomp clomp clomp—he hears The Black Branch reenter.)

WILMER: No. Hooves first. Then hop.

(The Black Branch enters office with a pot full of water as Wilmer continues to read. Wide smile to Aide, she crosses to the coffee maker, ignores Wilmer, spoons coffee into holder, pours water, puts pot on burner.)

WILMER: "To make a short leap or leaps on one foot." This foot, my sore foot. Maybe that did it.

AIDE: What? Hopping?

WILMER: You tell me. You've got the keys— *(A look to The Black Branch.)* For now. I couldn't say. I wouldn't if I could. I know my place.

AIDE: Where's your place?

WILMER: Back with mom. No matter where I go I know enough to come back to mom. Never go too far. *(Pointing.)* There's that much up here.

AIDE: In your head?

WILMER: My atom smasher.

AIDE: Atom smasher?

WILMER: Do you know Einstein?

AIDE: I know of him.

WILMER: Right. It's his computer. My computer is his computer. He doesn't know that much more than me. *(Thumps his temple with index finger.)* Psychology.

BLACK BRANCH: *(Thumps her temple with index finger.)* Kidneys.

(Wilmer extends the Bible toward The Black Branch, aiming the cross at her.)

WILMER: Here, eat this book and be as smart as me.

BLACK BRANCH: *(Stiffening.)* Have *you* eaten it?

WILMER: I don't have to. I'm eating this one. "Hope. A feeling that what is wanted will happen."

BLACK BRANCH: *(To Aide.)* What are you doing?

WILMER: "The object of this."

AIDE: I'm filing.

BLACK BRANCH: My memos?

WILMER: Where's that leave *Bob* Hope? What's *his* out?

BLACK BRANCH: You're filing my memos?

AIDE: Directives, suggestions, comments, remarks—

WILMER: You always got an out.

BLACK BRANCH: They're confidential.

WILMER: But we wouldn't solve anything by going out.

BLACK BRANCH: They're privileged.

WILMER: 'Cause we been there.

AIDE: Been where, Wilmer?

WILMER: On the out. There always is one. That's what there is about the Old Testament, last wills. Those lawyers always leave an out.

BLACK BRANCH: Dear, those memos are between you and me.

WILMER: "A person or thing from which something may be hoped."

BLACK BRANCH: For your eyes only.

WILMER: "To want and expect."

AIDE: They're a big help.

WILMER: "To hope very much."

BLACK BRANCH: They were not written to be filed.

WILMER: Where's Hope?

AIDE: But a lot of these rules aren't in the book.

WILMER: Bob Hope.

BLACK BRANCH: They're a favor to you.

WILMER: Where's he?

BLACK BRANCH: Don't file them.

WILMER: I don't know.

BLACK BRANCH: Don't file them.

WILMER: Neither does he.

AIDE: How am I going to get good at this job if I don't keep up with the changing—

BLACK BRANCH: Anyone can read them if you put them in the file.

AIDE: Not according to this. *(Reads memo.)* "Files are off limits to—"

BLACK BRANCH: They're available to anyone if you put them—

AIDE: No.

BLACK BRANCH: *Any asshole—*

AIDE: Margaret, I think they're important. *(He hands memos to The Black Branch.)* They're a big help to me and besides that, they're feedback from you. *(The Black Branch takes memos.)*

AIDE: That helps me understand you. That helps me help you.

BLACK BRANCH: Help me what?

AIDE: Here— *(Gently peels top memo from stack The Black Branch holds.)* "Somebody left the seat up on the toilet." *(Places memo on desk, peels off next one.)* "Somebody left towels on the floor." *(Next one.)* "Shut off water." *(Next one.)* "Shut off lights when you're not in there." *(Next one.)* "Patients not allowed to be in their rooms with the door closed." *(The Black Branch hands the next memo to Aide, cooperating now.)*

AIDE: "No wearing robes after breakfast." *(The Black Branch points at Wilmer, hands Aide next memo.)*

AIDE: "Belts." *(The Black Branch hands him memo.)*

AIDE: "Ties." *(The Black Branch hands him memo.)*

AIDE: "Disappearing razor blades." *(The Black Branch hands him memo.)*

AIDE: "Unauthorized silverware." *(Next one.)*

AIDE: "Not washing cups." *(Next one.)*

AIDE: "Windows open." *(Next one.)*

AIDE: "Burning churches." *(Faster.)* "Masturbation."

BLACK BRANCH: Yes! *(Hands him memo.)*

AIDE: "Civilian relatives are not allowed on the ward except during legal visiting hours. They cannot come here with unauthorized food. They cannot give care." Who's that?

BLACK BRANCH: That Donna woman's up here every day like she's got nothing better to do than take care of her aunt. She smuggles in bran flakes and fruit and vegetables.

AIDE: That's to help with the constipation.

BLACK BRANCH: She insists on special lunchroom privileges.

AIDE: Because she takes so long to eat.

BLACK BRANCH: That old woman spends 40 minutes trying to cut raw carrots with a butter knife. She drinks beet juice out of the bowl. She should be spoon fed in bed. She'll sit for eight hours staring at her own reflection in the window glass and then want to know who the old lady is. Or where that room is. Or who lives on the third floor. I've told her a hundred times there is no third floor. "Then what about the couple with the dog?"

AIDE: *(Takes memo.)* "No cheeking medication."

(The Black Branch snaps to, hands Aide next memo.)

AIDE: "No holding medication on tongues until the pills turn to goo and then complaining of upset stomach."

BLACK BRANCH: *(Hands Aide memo.)* Her again.

AIDE: "Medication time is strictly 11 A.M." I won't miss that like yesterday. I set the clock.

(The Black Branch hands Aide memo.)

AIDE: "Eli taking his pants off in the dayroom." We talked about that.

(The Black Branch hands Aide memo.)

AIDE: "Eli shouldn't smoke."

(Eli strikes match, lights cigarette, at upstage window.)

BLACK BRANCH: *(Hands Aide memo.)* That's on his chart.

AIDE: "Eli should not have matches."

(The Black Branch hands Aide memo.)

AIDE: "Eli is a pyromaniac."

(The Black Branch hands Aide memo.)

AIDE: "Eli is an arsonist."

WILMER: That was never proved.

AIDE: An arsonist? *(Pulls file from cabinet, starts leafing it.)*

BLACK BRANCH: I know it was never proven.

WILMER: Then it's libel to say it.

BLACK BRANCH: Not if it's true.

WILMER: If it's not true, it's libel.

BLACK BRANCH: It is true. Eli Crooner is an arsonist. He is not allowed to smoke and he is not allowed to have cookstove matches which would be found by mid-morning in the charred remains of the closest smoking church if he were let out there right now.

WILMER: Yer on drugs.

BLACK BRANCH: He would stand across the street and watch it burn.

WILMER: Go void.

BLACK BRANCH: Don't you have reading to do?

WILMER: "To want and expect. To hope very much."

BLACK BRANCH: Have you finished your Bible?

WILMER: Glory the and power the and kingdom the.

BLACK BRANCH: *(Shivers, backs away from Wilmer, closes in on Aide.)* Eli can't have matches. And in his condition he should not be allowed to smoke.

AIDE: *(Reading from Eli's folder.)* Kidney's shot, liver's shot, his lungs are paralyzed, he's asthmatic. That's all there is in his file.

BLACK BRANCH: He shouldn't be smoking.

AIDE: You really care about Eli.

BLACK BRANCH: No. I take care of him, yes. That's my job.

AIDE: That's my job.

BLACK BRANCH: Then do it.

AIDE: There's nothing about his face in the file.

BLACK BRANCH: I want this place run right.

AIDE: Nothing about that mask.

BLACK BRANCH: Just do your job.

AIDE: His burn.

BLACK BRANCH: *(Cuts him off, closing Eli's folder.)* The staff is forbidden from discussing patients in front of other patients. *(Meaning Wilmer.)*

AIDE: What do you know about Eli's wound?

BLACK BRANCH: His *wound?*

AIDE: His face.

BLACK BRANCH: Your wife called.

AIDE: I'm ask— *(Stopped short.)*

BLACK BRANCH: She sounded pissed off about something.

AIDE: *(He readjusts.)* I'm asking you about Eli.

BLACK BRANCH: Maybe how late you got in last night. Or a fishy smell. She was whining. Is Marianne a whiner? Along with everything else? *(Sweeping memos from the desk into the wastebasket.)* I'll go empty this. *(She exits.)*

WILMER: *(As a good-bye to The Black Branch.)* Two forty-five ten four Al Capone.
(Aide is left on one leg at her abrupt departure. The hole in the wall yawns. Wilmer sees it. Aide crosses, stands in front of hole.)

WILMER: *(Shakes head.)* "To trust and rely. Hope against hope. To go on hoping though it seems baseless. Hoper." Well, that's what I mean. that's what I been saying, and it all fits. This one— *(Dictionary.)* —and this one— *(Bible—he slaps them together.)* That's all you need. Two sets of books. In trucking as in life. Two sets of books. *(Puts both books on desk and leans back.)* Now. Whaddya wanna talk about? Sex? Religion? Or home building?
(Eli Crooner appears at office door.)

WILMER: Or home *burning?* That's another case. Ain't that right, Eli?

ELI: I believe so.

WILMER: But that's life. You get it either way. Take it in the ass or take it in the teeth. And if you don't take it, the government takes it. Either end, so— *(Rests his case.)* Two forty-five over and out.

AIDE: Al Capone.

WILMER: If you want.

AIDE: Doesn't Al Capone go along with that?

WILMER: If he wants to. Who am I to say? I'm crazy.

AIDE: And you look like Al Capone.

WILMER: Some say that. I do too. I'll admit it.

AIDE: And the two forty-five?

WILMER: Is what I owe.

AIDE: To who?

WILMER: To the President here. *(Indicates Eli.)* You weren't at the meeting. That's before you came. But we elected Eli President. And I'm Vice-President. And the Vice-President owes the President two forty-five. Ain't that right, Eli?

ELI: Can I open up some windows? Get some air moving through? It's stuffy.

AIDE: You going out of your head, Eli?

ELI: Guess so. Yeah. Out of my head.

AIDE: *(Sings.)* Over you! Out of my head! Over you! Out of my head, day and night—

(Eli cracks up laughing, Aide stops singing.)

AIDE: What's the matter, Eli? Don't you feel like singing this morning?

ELI: *(Wheezing.)* I don't have the air to sing anymore right now. I got no— lungs are flat. I need some— *(Taps breast bone with open hand.)* I need some—

AIDE: Spit it out, Eli! What do you need?

ELI: *(Shares look with Wilmer.)* Not much. Little Bull Durham, a doorway to lean in, matches, metal grounding so I don't short out—

AIDE: You need a bath.

ELI: And some air to breathe.

AIDE: You going to take a bath today, Eli?

ELI: Too charged up today. Too much juice strummin' through me on a full moon. But I do need air.

AIDE: Well, go open the window, for crying out loud. Go ahead.

ELI: Yessir.

AIDE: *(Yelling after him.)* But keep your pants on!

ELI: Yessir.

AIDE: *(Crossing out office after Eli.)* Wait, Jesus Christ, you got them on back-wards, you crazy fucker!

ELI: I know. *(Opens USR window.)*

AIDE: Well, you won't know whether you're shittin' or pissin', will he, Wilmer?

ELI: I took that as a precaution.

AIDE: A precaution to what?

ELI: Against The Black Branch.

AIDE: Black what?

WILMER: *(From office.)* Margaret.

ELI: *(Crossing DSR.)* Turn your clothes around like this, that's protection.

AIDE: *(Following Eli.)* Are you afraid of Margaret, Eli?

ELI: Cautious.

AIDE: Why do you call Margaret The Black Branch?

ELI: Count the joints in her fingers. We have three. She has four.

(Aide throws up a barrage of laughter against this as Eli crosses to downstage dayroom window and Aide moves back into office.)

AIDE: That's the screwiest Goddam thing I ever—He's a funny son-ofabitch, isn't he?

(Wilmer sits stonefaced. Finally:)

WILMER: You think The Black Branch gives a rat's ass about you?

AIDE: What are we talking about now, Wilmer?

WILMER: Or the details of your life she's managed to expunge?

AIDE: Expunge?

WILMER: Squeeze out? That woman is after the reins, the ropes, a drive shaft and a steering wheel. She wants control. Information is power.

AIDE: I don't know what you're talking about.

WILMER: She probes me, I lie. I'm driving toilet paper to Denver, I tell her it's record covers to Des Moines. I'm going to the dayroom, I tell her it's the moon. She, oh, she tried. She was real nice. Too nice. I saw that pasty face roll up with a mouthful of cat bones, I backed off. I still stay wide.

AIDE: *(Defensive.)* Isn't that why your mother had you committed?

WILMER: Eli got caught. Eli got himself involved.

AIDE: You took off with a load for Denver and wound up in Des Moines?

WILMER: Sure, and I'm a borderline schizoid personality fixated with a mother disorder. Isn't that what my files says? But I'm talking about *her*. What's *her* file say? 'Zit say she's a manic depressive with paranoid features?

AIDE: Who? Your mother?

WILMER: Go ahead. Check it. She has no file, that Black Branch. It's gone. Nobody knows spit about her.

AIDE: You been going through the files, Wilmer?

WILMER: Nobody 'cept Eli. Eli is the overall authority on her.

AIDE: Patients are not allowed—

WILMER: Clients.

AIDE: Clients are not allowed to look through these files without written consent from—

WILMER: Clients are not allowed to come into this office, either. But did I invite myself in? Is Eli unwelcome? Can *she* move in and out of here like the Queen Mary? You want to keep your job, you better get with the program. Put down a foot. Draw some lines. Fact, maybe you oughta draw a circle round yourself while you're at it.

(Aide nervously unwraps a candy he's found in his smock pocket.)

WILMER: Could have been anybody took her file. Not me. I am not interested in her details.

(Without thinking where it came from, Aide pops candy into his mouth.)

WILMER: I lost my sweet tooth. It came out in the sugar spill. *(Grins wide.)* Are you going to swallow that? Or chew?

AIDE: *(Candy bulging in his cheek.)* She's been a big help to me.

WILMER: Oh, she'll help you get big all right. She'll enlarge you right outta your job like she did the last one.

AIDE: What are you saying?

WILMER: Starting when?

AIDE: What you just said.

WILMER: Just what I said.

AIDE: What was it?

WILMER: Push playback.

AIDE: Wilmer—

WILMER: Rewind the tape, the tape, the tape.

AIDE: What tape?

WILMER: Your Sony TCS-310 mini cassette recorder, here, purchased under Title Five and activated by a button—there. *(Feels under lip of desk top.)* Tapes here. *(Side compartment of desk.)* Button's there.

AIDE: *(Finds button, suddenly struck.)* Was there a tape going on in here last night?

WILMER: There's a tape going on in here anytime anybody pushes that button.

AIDE: Last night when we were here?

WILMER: And possibly after *we* left.

AIDE: After *you* left.

WILMER: After I left I went down to the marking room and scratched on the door, thinking about those cowboy boots of mine in there I better get on me before my feet fall off. When I came back up here, that door was closed—

AIDE: Did you hear anything?

WILMER: —and the lights were on.

AIDE: Did you hear anything?

WILMER: For awhile.

AIDE: Did you hear anything?

WILMER: In what way?

AIDE: When you came back up here.

WILMER: I heard her say: *(In The Black Branch's voice:)* "You're larger than life." Should be on the tape deck here with the full proceedings. *(Reaches into secret compartment, finds nothing, winks at Aide, smiles.)* Congratulations. You're smarter than I thought.

AIDE: Wilmer—

WILMER: *(Hands up.)* And where you put it is a confidential matter into the likes of which I refuse to intrude.

AIDE: I never knew about a tape recorder until right now.

WILMER: No?

AIDE: No.

WILMER: Ohhhhh.

AIDE: Ohhhhh?

(Wilmer stands, exits office, thinking.)

AIDE: You think Margaret took it? *(Follows Wilmer.)* You think she made a tape last night and now she has it? Wilmer?

(Wilmer ignores Aide, crossing DSL.)

AIDE: Wilmer!

WILMER: *(Finally.)* Maybe.

AIDE: Shit no.

WILMER: Maybe not. *(Turns, sees Eli at open window DSR.)* Maybe Eli. See, old Eli's the only one knows anything about her firsthand. What I know I know from watching from the outside. Eli has been inside. In deep enough to wish he'd never seen it, I think. That's the reason there is tension. You did notice tension between them?

AIDE: She hates him.

WILMER: No. She loves him. And he loves her.

AIDE: Well, he told me—

WILMER: How old are you?

AIDE: Shit, she said—

(Clomp clomp clomp—The Black Branch reenters DSR with wastebasket and shuts Eli's DS window as Wilmer backs Aide into the tub room USL.)

WILMER: Shhh shh sh.

(Donna and Aunt Hyadle enter USR, short move to Eli's USR window.)

DONNA: *(Plays through, under.)* Right…left…walker…right…left… walker…

(The Black Branch moves through dayroom, shuts Eli's US window, drops blinds and crosses into office as Wilmer pulls tub room curtain closed around the tub. The Black Branch turns off overhead fluorescents in the office as Wilmer turns on overhead fluorescents in the tub room. The Black Branch replaces the wastebasket in front of the hole.)

AIDE: What about the fire?

WILMER: I don't know about the fire. I don't think there was a fire. What there was was one night Eli'd had enough, and he took a double edged razor blade and he cut off his penis and put it in a coffee cup like this—

(Same moment—Eli opens blinds at DS window, Donna opens blinds at US window, The Black Branch turns on the desk lamp which throws a yellow pool of light onto a white institutional coffee mug in the center of the desk.)

WILMER: *(Continuous.)* —and handed it to The Black Branch.

(The Black Branch fixes on the coffee mug.)

AIDE: That's crazy!

(Fixated on the cup, The Black Branch fills it with coffee and sits at desk as conversation continues.)

WILMER: *(Continuous.)* Would be for you or me. Made perfect sense to Eli. Put a kink in her plans. He tried to cut his nuts off, too, but she stopped him.

BLACK BRANCH: *(Quietly, to herself, unaware of the others.)* He did it for me.

(Wilmer crosses to DS perimeter of tub room curtain. In dayroom, Eli speaks in low tones, facing DS window.)

ELI: *(Quietly, to himself, his back to her.)* I did not.

BLACK BRANCH: You did it for me.

ELI: Perhaps I did do it *to* you, but I don't wanna hear from anywhere I did it 'cause I care about you or made you a gift.

BLACK BRANCH: You gave it to me.

ELI: To be done witch you, so you'd leave me alone. You took it that way, you took it wrong.

BLACK BRANCH: And now you're afraid of me.

ELI: I'm done witch you.

BLACK BRANCH: My power frightens you.

ELI: Your power over me I give you myself. And when I took it back, I took it all back. You try controlling everybody and everything else because you feel so out of control of yourself. You are. Don't take a moron like me to see that last night.

BLACK BRANCH: You didn't see anything last night.

ELI: I saw you setting up that new aide for a killing of some kind. What do you want dead this time, Margaret?

BLACK BRANCH: I want this place run right.

ELI: Me?

BLACK BRANCH: I want protection.

ELI: From yourself?

BLACK BRANCH: From betrayal. From injury.

ELI: Margaret, you weren't hired here. You were committed. Like me. Like Wilmer.

BLACK BRANCH: My job here is caretaker.

ELI: Taking care of yourself.

BLACK BRANCH: *(Accusing.)* No one else ever did.

ELI: Who'd you ever let?

BLACK BRANCH: What?

ELI: *(Turns toward her.)* Anyone that tried to ever take care of you, you cut down.

(Eli and The Black Branch see each other through "invisible" office wall. Aide leaves tub room as Wilmer pulls curtain back.)

HYADLE: *(At US window.)* Drop it! Just drop it! *(Sheepish, to Donna.)* She's not there, is she?

DONNA: I don't see her, hon.

(Aide enters office, flicks on overhead fluorescents as The Black Branch turns off the desk lamp and Donna and Aunt Hyadle start slow cross to DSL, their "right...left...walker..." playing under.)

BLACK BRANCH: Your wife never got my gift. Why not?

AIDE: What's that?

BLACK BRANCH: I just called Marianne.

AIDE: From where?

BLACK BRANCH: From the phone in the street.

AIDE: That's against the rules.

BLACK BRANCH: I made that rule.

AIDE: You made it?

BLACK BRANCH: That you have to sign out first. I signed out. And I'll sign back *in* right *now* right *here*— *(Writes on a clipboard.)* —because I had to go out to get coffee filters for our new coffee pot! To replace the one that got broken!

AIDE: Leaving the grounds is against the rules. You would like to get me into trouble.

BLACK BRANCH: You're *in* trouble, Mr. You never gave you wife my present to her.

AIDE: You don't even know my wife.

BLACK BRANCH: After last night I feel I do or like I should.

(Wilmer starts slow cross from tub room into dayroom.)

AIDE: Margaret—

BLACK BRANCH: I slept like a baby.

AIDE: You're making more out of it—

BLACK BRANCH: Than you thought I would remember? I remember. What you did, what you said. So don't treat me now like some kind of worthless pathology. You wouldn't have this job if it wasn't for me and you won't keep it without my help. Why didn't you give Marianne my cups?

(Wilmer joins Eli DSR. They huddle, buzz, light crackles. Eli passes Wilmer a tape recorder he has carried in an inside vest pocket.)

AIDE: *(Continuous.)* Your cups?

BLACK BRANCH: With farm scenes on them. Painted cows and pigs and horses and sheep. Marcy made them in crafts class. I won't tell you what they cost. That's none of your business. They're for your wife and I know she will like them.

AIDE: The staff is not allowed to accept gifts from patients.

BLACK BRANCH: They're expensive mugs.

AIDE: You know that.

(Wilmer moves USR.)

BLACK BRANCH: I know your wife is not on the staff and I know she never got my cups. I also know that wife of yours could use a friend, a real one that wouldn't fuck around behind her back, who'd pay the bills and keep up

Blue Cross and do everything else they humanly could to keep her out of a place like this which is, from what she sounds like over the phone, where she belongs. From what I understand, your wife Marianne should be locked up. In here. She can have my bed.

WILMER: *(From dayroom.) Where's the dayroom chairs?*

BLACK BRANCH: *Locked up!*

AIDE: You locked up the dayroom chairs?

BLACK BRANCH: I put them in the closet.

AIDE: Why?

BLACK BRANCH: So they can't be thrown out the windows.

AIDE: Margaret—

BLACK BRANCH: Marianne is waiting. I told her you would call. She's worried.

(They both look at the phone. The Black Branch empties her cup, stands.)

BLACK BRANCH: I'll leave you so you can talk in private.

(She exits. Phone rings. Aide pulls cigarette from pack in his pocket and digs for his lighter, back pants pockets, shirt front, slaps his body for a lighter. Phone rings. He considers it, but exits in direction of The Black Branch USR. Coast clear, Wilmer moves into office, tape recorder under his arm. He puts the recorder in the secret compartment in the desk and answers the phone.)

WILMER: Ash Manor. No, he isn't.

(Donna appears at the office door. Wilmer assumes executive authority.)

WILMER: I guess *I* am. Yes. I will. Good-bye.

DONNA: Excuse me. Can I talk to the nurse?

WILMER: What nurse?

DONNA: The floor nurse.

WILMER: No nurse on this floor.

DONNA: *(Looks at him sideways.)* Sure there is.

WILMER: Am I crazy?

DONNA: I saw her here this morning.

WILMER: What makes you think what you saw here was a nurse?

DONNA: She was wearing nursing clothing, nurses shoes.

WILMER: And she looked like a nurse to you.

DONNA: She *is* a nurse!

WILMER: That one would have you think she was Florence Nightshade.

DONNA: I seen her dispensing medicine.

WILMER: Oh, she'll dispense with your medicine entirely. She'll give you the treatment, too, if you let her. Only that one hasn't got authority. In other words, she hasn't matriculated to the point to where she is anything more or less than a paranoid narcissistic borderline type fixated on her own bazooms. So to speak.

(Eli opens USR dayroom window and drops his trousers.)

DONNA: Who is that man?

WILMER: Her husband. That is Eli the streamer.

DONNA: I've never heard him scream.

WILMER: Stream. He claims he's got electricity streaming through him. And for that he's put in here, stamped crazy. Would Wilhelm Reich have something to say about that.

DONNA: Who's Wilhelm Reich?

WILMER: *(Winks.)* Doctor Orgasm.

DONNA: *(Blushes.)* Does he always go around with his pants down?

WILMER: It gets warm like this, he does. That bother you?

DONNA: Not really, I just—

WILMER: And your Aunt Hyadle can't see, soo— *(Shrugs.)* Lovely woman, your aunt. It's a shame she can't hear either. Eli's got a great voice. He should record. *(Bursts into song.)* "I'd like to hold my head up, and be proud of who I am—"

DONNA: I have to get back to my aunt—

WILMER: "—but they won't let my secret go untold."

DONNA: —but I have to talk to the nurse first—

WILMER: Nurses nurses nurses—

DONNA: —about her medication.

WILMER: —I got eight mentally retarded sisters and they're all nurses! You want to talk about medicine, ask me. I know all about medicine.

DONNA: I think my aunt's being overdosed. She's getting too much.

WILMER: Can you get too much?

DONNA: She's seeing things.

WILMER: Like what?

DONNA: People.

WILMER: Nurses?

DONNA: No. Uncle Ellwell. And a woman in black. And a family folding bedding fulla bugs. And a baby with a doll that's got poisonous hair. She's worried about the baby. She's put soap in the baby's eyes. There's a slice of pie in the cupboard that wouldn't be good for the baby to eat, she says, but Donna could have it. Donna is me.

WILMER: Donna?

DONNA: Yes.

WILMER: I'm Wilmer.

(Extends his hand, they shake.)

WILMER: She's dreaming.

DONNA: This morning she was talking to her Sunday school teacher. He's been dead for 12 years.

(Wilmer lets go of her hand.)

DONNA: What are they giving her, Wilmer?

WILMER: I'd have to check her chart.

DONNA: Will you?

WILMER: I can't.

DONNA: Please.

WILMER: I'm not allowed in the office.

DONNA: But her chart is on the wall right over there.

WILMER: Corporation rules.

DONNA: This office.

WILMER: This is the office I'm not allowed in. I'm only here for the air conditioning. *(Wilmer opens his robe to the air conditioner. Robe flaps, he turns to Donna, robe open.)* Only room on the ward with air conditioning.

DONNA: Look, Wilmer, I don't know what's going on in here— *(Tying his robe belt.)* —but if it was up to me my aunt would be out of here so fast. We'd be up in Antelope County eating right and feeding geese and watering ducks and fixing soup—

WILMER: And killing chickens?

DONNA: And riding the tractor.

WILMER: Sounds great.

DONNA: Now I didn't put her in here, so I can't exactly get her out, but I want to know legally what kind of drugs they're giving her because I have a right to know that and if you don't tell me I'll just march right over here and— *(Crosses to charts on wall.)*

WILMER: Whoa, hold up! Hold up!

DONNA: I am taking care of her if you don't.

WILMER: You can't do that.

DONNA: *(Pulls chart off wall.)* I *can* do this.

WILMER: You can?

DONNA: I will.

WILMER: Let me.

DONNA: *(Hands him the chart and sits.)* Thank you.

(Wilmer reads chart, with one eye to the office door.)

WILMER: She's on Lanoxin for the heart. Furosemide water pills to eliminate her fluids, which takes her potassium, so they give her Slow-K potassium chloride in tablets for that. She gets 325 migs by mouth every 90 minutes aspirin for arthritis and she's got a p.r.n. for Deltazone. Orinase for diabetes. Inderal for high blood pressure. Pilocar eye drops for glaucoma. Maalox antacid. Ex-Lax to soften her stool. Koala-pectin to harden it. Flurazepam to put her to sleep and Ritalin to waker up and ten migs of morphine sulfate to cut down the shouting when they roll her out of bed.

DONNA: That's too much.

WILMER: That was yesterday. Today could be anything.

DONNA: They keep her on the same medication.

WILMER: Why?

DONNA: To stabilize her condition.

WILMER: No stable conditions allowed here. Changes every day.

DONNA: They wouldn't change her medication.

WILMER: Don't they?

DONNA: For no reason.

WILMER: Or, there's a reason.

DONNA: What is it?

WILMER: Polypharmaceuticology's the reason. That's all prescribed drugs on the market—250 thousand 900 and some of them, with more coming all the time. If we didn't try them out, who would? Not to mention generics.

DONNA: No wonder she's hallucinating.

WILMER: She's not hallucinating. She's misperceiving. When she sees something, there's something there. She just mistakes it for what it is. Your aunt's all right. Don't worry. I take everything they got and get and look at me. I was goofy when I got here, I'll be goofy when I go home—hahahahah.

(The Alarm clock goes off.)

WILMER: Speaking of which.

(Donna hurries out office, crossing back to Aunt Hyadle. Wilmer shuts off the clock alarm and leans out office door.)

WILMER: *Medication!*

(He pulls a tray out of the medicine cupboard and places it on the desk. Dixie cups with pills and slightly larger cups of water sit on the tray. The Black Branch chugs full tilt toward the office. Wilmer shuts the bottom half of the office door just as The Black Branch wheels up. She kicks it open and starts in. Wilmer uses the Bible to move her into DSL corner of office and then places a broom on the floor to block her path. She turns, stopped cold. Wilmer smiles. Aide enters with a simple cotton dress on hanger over his shoulder and moves to the office door. He throws a quizzical look at Wilmer who, seeing him, picks broom up and begins to sweep.)

WILMER: *(Sweeping.)* Little pieces of glass all over the floor.

AIDE: Wilmer—

WILMER: Maybe a hairline fracture opened up into something worse. What do you think?

AIDE: I think it's time for your medication.

WILMER: *(Salutes, proud to comply, leans broom against the wall.)* Aye aye, Sarge.

(Wilmer hands tray to Aide, steps out of the office, closes bottom half of Dutch door, faces him. Aide hands Wilmer a Dixie cup. Wilmer downs the pills and drinks water from a second cup.)

DONNA: *(To Aunt Hyadle.)* Can't go? Maybe after you've had something to eat. I brought fruit.

AIDE: Stick out your tongue.

(Wilmer sticks out his tongue, opens wide to prove he's swallowed the pills, smiles, steps to one side. Donna helps Aunt Hyadle off the commode. They start a slow cross SL to SR, "...right...left...walker...")

BLACK BRANCH: I'm not wearing that fucking dress!

AIDE: We'll talk about that later. Come get your medication.

(She doesn't budge. Eli shuffles up, takes his pills, drinks his water, sticks out his tongue, starts toward dayroom.)

AIDE: It's time for your medication.

BLACK BRANCH: You take it. You'll need it.

AIDE: I think you would feel calmer if you took your medication.

BLACK BRANCH: I'm calm.

AIDE: You sound angry.

BLACK BRANCH: *(Mocking.)* "You sound angry."

AIDE: I think you'd feel less angry if you—

BLACK BRANCH: Don't use that doctor-patient bullshit talk on me!

AIDE: Can you hear yourself?

BLACK BRANCH: You're not my doctor.

AIDE: How angry you sound?

BLACK BRANCH: I'm not your patient.

AIDE: Listen to yourself.

BLACK BRANCH: You faggot.

HYADLE: Grace, I'm here.

AIDE: If you refuse your medication, you know what I have to do.

HYADLE: Right here, can't you see me?

BLACK BRANCH: You stupid little prick. You couldn't get hard with both hands.

HYADLE: Grace!

AIDE: Margaret—

BLACK BRANCH: *Don't you call me that!*

DONNA: *(To Wilmer.)* Her sister.

AIDE: If you refuse your medication, I will have to call the doctor.

BLACK BRANCH: Call him.

DONNA: She's been dead nine years.

(She and Hyadle cross off as)

AIDE: I'll call another aide, we'll hold you down—

BLACK BRANCH: And maul me.

AIDE: —and give it to you intravenously.

BLACK BRANCH: Up your ass. I'll leave.

AIDE: This is not a voluntary ward.

BLACK BRANCH: You'll never get your hands on me again.

AIDE: *(Placing hand on The Black Branch from behind.)* The state has determined that for—

(The Black Branch explodes. Pills and cups erupt as she wheels on Aide, driving him into USL corner of office.)

BLACK BRANCH: This isn't the state! This is you and me! You wish I was crazy and out of control so you could pump me fulla drugs, but *I am in control* and I will make you do your job whether you like it or not— *(Backing towards door.)* —because someone has to keep people from hurting each other and hurting themselves and if you can't do that because it's the right thing to do, *what you are paid to do,* you'll do it because *you have no choice! (The Black Branch turns to door. Eli shuts it in her face from the other side.)*

AIDE: *(Offering pills.)* The state has determined that for its protection and for your protection—

BLACK BRANCH: *(Taking pill cup, wadding it, throwing it at Aide.)* The state has not protected me from you and the state *can not* protect you from me!

AIDE: The state—

BLACK BRANCH: Oh shuttup! *(The Black Branch dives for tape recorder in desk compartment.)*

AIDE: *(Seeing recorder.)* Now you listen here!

BLACK BRANCH: *You* listen! *(She punches the play button on the tape recorder.) Everybody listen* what this no-cock little faggot thought he could get away with me last night.

(From the recorder comes Eli's voice singing his version of "Going Out Of My Head.")

TAPE: Cause I can't explain the tears that I've shed
Over you—
(Eli shuffles downstage left. The Black Branch punches rewind, fast forward, play.)

TAPE: Outta my head day and night, night and day and night—
(She punches buttons.)

TAPE: I want you to want me, I need you so badly I can't think of anything but you—
(The Black Branch stabs a flashing glance at Aide, who takes the recorder. She explodes out of office past Wilmer and slams flat into Donna who has hurried in from downstage left.)

DONNA: Nurse! Nurse! Help me my aunt—
(Spun by the collision, not comprehending what Donna wants from her, flaming white hot rage and indignation, The Black Branch shoves Donna down, whirls, charging Eli DSL.)

DONNA: *(Getting up with Wilmer's help.)* My aunt's collapsed in her food.

WILMER: I'll help you, Missy.
(Wilmer exits with Donna DSR as Aide sets tray down, rattled, clumsy, gathering cups, spilling some, then shoving the whole thing into a desk drawer, punching off the recorder as The Black Branch frisks Eli, frantically going through the pockets of his dropped drawers, on her knees.)

BLACK BRANCH: No matches! No tobacco! *(Throws his tobacco and matches out across the floor.)* I want my fucking tape!

ELI: That is your tape, you moron.

BLACK BRANCH: You recorded on *my* tape!?

ELI: Both sides, you maggot.

BLACK BRANCH: You put your pathetic wheezing voice on *my* tape!

ELI: *(Pulling his arms free of her, slipping suspenders over his shoulders.)* All the songs you used to love to hear. Remember, you cow? You pig. You horse. You sheep. *(Eli pulls the wig from her head, holding the black snaky hair high above her patchy skull and pulls a cigarette lighter from his vest pocket.)*

BLACK BRANCH: Give me my hair! *(Pulls up to her feet.)*

ELI: *(Backing away.)* Gimme a kiss.

BLACK BRANCH: Suck your own Goddam tongue, Eli!

ELI: *(Backing SR toward US window.)* Give yer old firebug a kiss and tell me again whose fire that was.

BLACK BRANCH: *Give me my hair!*

ELI: Who set that fire? And who put that fire out?

> *(Aide comes out of office, stops. The Black Branch sees him. Eli flicks the cigarette lighter. It shoots a huge flame.)*

ELI: Who set that fire, Margaret?

> *(Aide pats his pockets. It's his lighter.)*

BLACK BRANCH: *(Quietly.)* You did, Eli.

ELI: You Goddam right I set that fire. And how *big* was that fire?

BLACK BRANCH: It was big, Eli.

ELI: It was *damn* big. And who put that damn big fire out?

AIDE: *(To The Black Branch.)* Margaret?

ELI: *(To Aide.)* Wrong.

> *(Eli pitches the wig out the open window. Aide knocks lighter out of Eli's hand and tackles him with inappropriate, dumb force he instantly regrets. Something cracks.)*

AIDE: Shit, Eli, are you all right?

> *(Eli rattles, trying to breathe. The Black Branch crosses into office, pulling leather straps from wall hook as Aide unlocks closet and pulls out a dayroom chair.)*

BLACK BRANCH: *(Throwing straps at Aide.)* Now you do something!

> *(Aide lifts Eli from floor and sits him in the dayroom chair.)*

AIDE: Sit down in this.

> *(Aide starts tying Eli to the chair as The Black Branch crosses to the tub room where she opens the cold faucet. Water pounds. She crosses DSR to exit.)*

AIDE: *(To The Black Branch.)* Don't leave this ward!

BLACK BRANCH: I'm going to get my hair! *(Exits.)*

AIDE: *(Strapping Eli to the chair.)* You understand why I'm doing this, don't you, Eli?

ELI: I believe so.

AIDE: *(Uncertain himself.)* Why?

ELI: You do it because you're afraid you have to do it. Because of The Black Branch.

AIDE: *(Finished, steps back.)* What is The Black Branch, Eli?

ELI: It is a branch you cannot swing on or sit on or saw off or smoke like you can an Italian cigar or flush down the toilet, though I tried many times. You can't build a fire with it. It won't keep you warm. You can't protect yourself. No birds'll roost or make a nest. There's something sick about it. Something sucks you dry, takes your air. It's a part, it's a character, a role, it acts, behaves, but. There's no person in there. There is just a kind of death. It looks like a branch, like any other twig, but all the other twigs are separated by respect. This branch is like a snake waiting for a bird to perch so it can kill it and eat it. It's a trickster branch, a fake branch. It's a dead, black branch.

(Wilmer enters from SR lunchroom, behind Eli.)

WILMER: Mrs. Ellwell bought the farm.

AIDE: I'll come back for you.

ELI: You take care.

(Aide exits hurriedly DSR. Wilmer stands there. Eli's tobacco and matches lay on the floor.)

WILMER: What are you doing tied up?

ELI: Getting ready for my bath.

WILMER: They finally got your matches.

ELI: My Bull Durham.

WILMER: Yeh.

ELI: Roll yourself a smoke.

WILMER: *(Crosses to tobacco, shakes head no.)* My daddy was buried with 14 cartons of Pall Malls in his casket. He couldn't move his arms or legs. Mama calls them coffin nails. She won't have them in the house.

ELI: Your mama isn't here, Wilmer.

WILMER: *(Tapping his chest with his palm.)* She's here.

ELI: Roll one anyway. Smoke it for me.

(Wilmer picks up the tobacco and matches.)

WILMER: You want to look out the window?

ELI: I believe I would.

(Wilmer turns Eli's chair so he faces DS window. Pause.)

WILMER: *(Finally.)* Why'd you cut off your dick, Eli?

ELI: 'Cause it bit me. Heheh.

WILMER: No.

ELI: Didn't work. Wasn't happy. Just got me in trouble.

WILMER: Didn't it hurt?

ELI: Didn't hurt *me*. I couldn't feel it. *It* screamed a little. Like a mandrake root. Took longer than you'd think. Over thirty minutes clear through. *(Shrugs.)* I gave it to Margaret. She wanted one. Wasn't doing me any good.

WILMER: *(Finally.)* There's other women, Eli.

ELI: Not after awhile there's not. Shit, and how would you know that, Wilmer? *(Wilmer turns his back.)*

ELI: *(Leans in.)* Hadn't been mine since they put me in here anyway. Worse they can get me for's defacing state property.

(He laughs, Wilmer laughs, infectious, can't stop.)

WILMER: *(Laughing.)* Would you do it again?

ELI: *(Laughing.)* No.

(Laughing, Wilmer embraces Eli. Eli clutches Wilmer's robe. Wilmer hugs him, kissing Eli on the head.)

WILMER: *(Finally.)* That's a great tape you made, Eli.

ELI: You like it?

WILMER: *(Tears.)* You sound real good.

ELI: Let me hear it.

WILMER: Okay. *(Wilmer turns Eli's chair to face US and moves into office. He punches the recorder. Eli's voice warbles up.)*

ELI: Turn it up!

(Wilmer does, coming back out into dayroom where he merrily mouths words to song, then pulls tobacco and papers from his robe pockets, makes a face, and goes back into office where he sits at desk and rolls himself a smoke.

The Black Branch enters downstage right wearing wig at an odd angle. Eli's back is to her. A shiver shoots up his spine as The Black Branch crosses to him from behind. Eli starts in on The Lord's Prayer backwards as The Black Branch drags his chair toward the tub room. Tipped back, it rolls on wheels.)

ELI: Glory the and power the and kingdom the is thine
for evil from us deliver
but temptation into us lead
and us against trespass who those forgive we
as trespasses our us forgive and
bread daily our day this us give
heaven in is it as earth on done
be will thy come kingdom
thy name thy be hallowed
heaven in art which father—

(The Black Branch pulls coffee filters from her smock pocket and stuffs them into Eli's mouth, dragging his chair to the bathtub. She draws closed the tub room curtain. Wilmer lights his cigarette with Aide's lighter in office as The Black Branch upends Eli's chair, him strapped to it, head first, into the freezing water. As the tape in the office plays Eli singing "Going Out Of My Head," The Black Branch pushes Eli's head under water.)

BLACK BRANCH: Who put out the fire, Eli?

(Eli comes up, spits filters. The Black Branch pushes him under again.)

BLACK BRANCH: Who put out the fire?

(Aide reenters DSR, crossing to the tub room as The Black Branch pushes Eli's head under water a third time.)

AIDE: *(Throwing curtain open.)* Black Branch!

(Eli rocks up, spits water. Aide rushes in. The Black Branch recoils into the curtain, spinning, spinning. Aide pulls Eli out of the tub room and pushes him in a fast cross DSR and off as Lights Fade To Black. Lights up, Donna gathers Aunt Hyadle's things DSL. Wilmer smokes, a carton of Pall Malls sticking out of his bathrobe pocket.)

WILMER: You're the real caretaker here.

DONNA: I'm what?

WILMER: The real caretaker.

DONNA: Well, her daughters couldn't do it. Not that they had that much to do. Only one of them is married. Neither one's got kids like me, but just they. Wouldn't. They had her in a basement room with no sunlight and no plants, she couldn't hear the birds or see the weather. There was just a bed, no chair, no lamp, no pictures. And they never would talk to her. They'd talk about her in front of her like she wasn't there, go on about how she wet the bed again and how much work that was for them and how she couldn't wipe her own bottom. They wouldn't bathe her, wouldn't take her to the bathroom. They wouldn't bathe their own mother who gave them life. First time I went over she was lying in a bed been wet for hours. She was cold, they wouldn't change her. "Let her lie in her own shit," they said. "She's a cranky old woman. Nothing we do is enough for her." Well, that was right. "She wets the bed for spite," they said. Well, that was wrong. She just had no control over anything. She needed help with everything and she hated that. She hated feeling helpless and in the way and underfoot, and so when she was awake she'd hold it in. Then she'd fall asleep and her body would relax and it'd all just come out. She'd flood the mattress and you'd have to change that and you had to change the pads and the sheets and the blankets and this blue foam mat you had to wash out and squeeze by hand every time. Roll it up tight and squeeze it and roll it and squeeze it. Then put her on her side real easy and make up the bed again. It took a lot of time. And as soon as she'd fall asleep, then she'd flood it again. She wasn't a cranky old woman, Wilmer. She was a helpless little baby and she hated it. It embarrassed her. Sometimes she'd get impacted where she couldn't go at all, sometimes for days, and her little belly would bloat up hard and I would dig her out by hand. You don't help somebody 'cause you want to or it's convenient or you're getting paid to do it. You help somebody who needs help because they need help. And you treat them like a human 'cause they are.

END OF PLAY

Bondage
by David Henry Hwang

BIOGRAPHY
David Henry Hwang won the 1988 Tony, Drama Desk, Outer Critics Circle and John Gassner awards, and the 1991 L.A. Drama Critics Circle Award for his Broadway debut, *M. Butterfly*, which has since been produced in some three-dozen countries around the world. He is the author of *FOB* (1981 Obie Award, Best New Play), *The Dance and The Railroad* (Drama Desk nomination, Guernsey's Best Plays of 1981-82), *Family Devotions* (Drama Desk nomination), *The House of Sleeping Beauties* and *The Sound of a Voice*, all of which were produced at the New York Shakespeare Festival. *Rich Relations* premiered in 1986 at The Second Stage. His one-act play, *Bondage*, premiered in 1992 at the Humana Festival. He wrote the libretto for Philip Glass' opera *The Voyage*, which premiered at the Metropolitan Opera House (October 1992). He previously collaborated with Glass and designer Jerome Sirlin on *1000 Airplanes on the Roof*. Mr. Hwang's screenplay of *M. Butterfly*, starring Jeremy Irons and John Lone, was released by Warner Brothers in 1993. Another film, *Golden Gate*, starring Matt Dillon and Joan Chen, was released in 1993. Born in Los Angeles in 1957, he attended Stanford and the Yale School of Drama.

ORIGINAL PRODUCTION

Bondage was commissioned by Actors Theatre of Louisville and premiered in the 1992 Humana Festival of New American Plays. It was originally directed by Oskar Eustis with the following cast:

Mark . . . . B.D. Wong
Terri . . . . Kathryn Layng

CHARACTERS

TERRI: late-twenties, female.
MARK: early-thirties, male.
TIME: The present.
PLACE: An S & M parlor on the outskirts of Los Angeles.

BONDAGE

A room in a fantasy bondage parlor. Terri, a dominatrix, paces with her whip in hand before Mark, who is chained to the wall. Both their faces are covered by full face masks and hoods to disguise their identities.

MARK: What am I today?

TERRI: Today—you're a man. A Chinese man. But don't bother with that accent crap. I find it demeaning.

MARK: A Chinese man. All right. And who are you?

TERRI: Me? I'm—I'm a blonde woman. Can you remember that?

MARK: I feel…very vulnerable.

TERRI: You should. I pick these roles for a reason, you know. *(She unchains him.)* We'll call you Wong. Mark Wong. And me—I'm Tifanny Walker. *(Pause.)* I've seen you looking at me. From behind the windows of your—engineering laboratory. Behind your—horn rimmed glasses. Why don't you come right out and try to pick me up? Whisper something offensive into my ear. Or aren't you man enough?

MARK: I've been trying to approach you. In my own fashion.

TERRI: How do you expect to get anywhere at that rate? Don't you see the jocks, the football stars, the cowboys who come 'round every day with their tongues hanging out? This is America, you know. If you don't assert yourself, you'll end up at sixty-five worshipping a Polaroid you happened to snap of me at a high school picnic.

MARK: But—you're a blonde. I'm—Chinese. It's not so easy to know where it's OK for me to love you.

TERRI: C'mon, this is the 1990s! I'm no figment of the past. For a Chinese man to love a white woman—what could be wrong about that?

MARK: That's…great! You really feel that way? Then, let me just declare it to your face. I—

TERRI: Of course—

MARK: —love—

TERRI: It's not real likely I'm gonna love you.

(Pause.)

MARK: But…you said—

TERRI: I said I'm not a figment of the past. But I'm also not some crusading figure from the future. It's only 1992, you know. I'm a normal girl. With regular ideas. Regular for a blonde, of course.

MARK: What's that supposed to mean?

TERRI: It means I'm not prejudiced—in principle. Of course I don't notice the color of man's skin. Except—I can't help but notice. I've got eyes, don't I?

(Pause.) I'm sure you're a very nice person…Mark. And I really appreciate your helping me study for the…physics midterm. But I'm just not—what can I say? I'm just not attracted to you.

MARK: Because I'm Chinese.

TERRI: Oh no, oh heavens, no. I would never be prejudiced against an Oriental. They have such…strong family structures…hard working…they hit the books with real gusto…makes my mother green with envy. But, I guess…how excited can I get about a boy who fulfills my mother's fantasies? The reason most mothers admire boys like you is 'cause they didn't bother to marry someone like that themselves. No, I'm looking for a man more like my father—someone I can regret in later life.

MARK: So you're not attracted to me because I'm Chinese. Like I said before.

TERRI: Why are you Orientals so relentlessly logical? *(She backs him around the room.)*

MARK: Well, for your information…it doesn't—it doesn't hurt that you're not in love with me.

TERRI: Why not?

MARK: Because I never said that I loved you, either!

(They stop in their tracks.)

TERRI: You didn't?

MARK: Nope, nope, nope.

TERRI: That's bullshit. I was here, you know. I heard you open yourself up to ridicule and humiliation. I have a very good ear for that kind of thing. *(Cracks her whip.)* So goddamn it—admit it—you said you love me!

MARK: I did not! If I don't tell the truth, you'll be angry with me.

TERRI: I'm already angry with you now for lying! Is this some nasty scheme to maneuver yourself into a no-win situation? God, you masochists make life confusing.

MARK: I came close. I said, "I love—," but then you cut me off.

TERRI: That's my prerogative. I'm the dominatrix.

MARK: I never finished the sentence. Maybe I was going to say, "I love…the smell of fresh-baked apple pie in the afternoon."

TERRI: That's a goddamn lie!

MARK: Can you prove it? You cut me off. In mid-sentence.

TERRI: It does…sound like something I would do. Damn. I'm always too eager to assert my superiority. It's one of the occupational hazards of my profession. *(Pause.)* So I fucked up. I turned total victory into personal embarrassment. God, I'm having a rotten day.

MARK: Terri—

TERRI: Mistress Terri!

MARK: Mistress Terri, I—I didn't mean to upset you. It's OK. I wasn't really going to say I loved apple pie. Now—you can whip me for lying to you. How's that?

TERRI: I'm not about to start taking charity from my submissives, thank you. That's one good way to get laughed out of the profession. *(Pause.)* Sorry, I just—need a moment. Wouldn't it be nice if they'd put coffeemakers in here?

MARK: Look—do what you want. I'm a Mexican man, and you're an Indonesian—whatever.

TERRI: What went wrong—was I just going through the motions?

(Mark kneels behind her, places his hands gently on her shoulders.)

MARK: You feeling OK today?

TERRI: Of course I am! It just...hurts a girl's confidence to stumble like that when I was in my strongest position, with you at your weakest.

MARK: Why were you in such a strong position?

TERRI: Well, I was—a blonde!

MARK: And why was I in such a weak one?

TERRI: Oh, c'mon—you were...an Oriental man. Easy target. It's the kind of role I choose when I feel like phoning in the performance. Shit! Now, look—I'm giving away trade secrets.

MARK: Asian. An Asian man.

TERRI: Sorry. I didn't know political correctness had suddenly arrived at S & M parlors.

MARK: It never hurts to practice good manners. You're saying I wasn't sexy?

TERRI: Well...I mean...a girl likes a little excitement sometimes.

MARK: OK, OK...look, let's just pretend...pretend that I did say "I love you." You know, to get us over this hump.

TERRI: Now, we're pretending something happened in a fantasy when it actually didn't? I think this is getting a little esoteric.

MARK: Terri, look at us! Everything we do is pretend! That's exactly the point! We play out these roles until one of us gets the upper hand!

TERRI: You mean, until *I* get the upper hand.

MARK: Well, in practice, that's how it's always—

TERRI: I like power.

MARK: So do I.

TERRI: You'll never win.

MARK: There's a first time for everything.

TERRI: You're the exception that proves the rule.

MARK: So prove it. C'mon! And—oh—try not to break down again in the middle of the fantasy.

TERRI: Fuck you!

MARK: It sort of—you know—breaks the mood?

TERRI: I'm sorry! I had a very bad morning. I've been working long hours—

MARK: Don't! Don't start talking about your life on my time!

TERRI: OK, you don't need to keep—

MARK: Sometimes, I really wonder why I have to be the one reminding you of the house rules at this late date.

TERRI: I didn't mean to, all right? These aren't the easiest relationships in the world, you know!

MARK: A man comes in, he plops down good money...

TERRI: I'm not in the mood to hear about your financial problems.

MARK: Nor I your personal ones! This is a fantasy palace, so goddamn it, start fantasizing!

TERRI: I have a good mind to take off my mask and show you who I really am.

MARK: You do that, and you know I'll never come here again.

TERRI: Ooooh—scary! What—do you imagine I might actually have some real feelings for you?

MARK: I don't imagine anything but what I pay you to make me imagine! Now, pick up that whip, start barking orders, and let's get back to investigating the burning social issues of our day!

TERRI: *(Practically in tears.)* You little maggot! You said you loved me...Mark Wong!

MARK: Maybe. Why aren't I sexy enough for you?

TERRI: I told you—a girl likes a little excitement.

MARK: Maybe I'm—someone completely different from who you imagine. Someone...with a touch of evil. Who doesn't study for exams.

TERRI: Oh—like you get "A"s regardless? 'Cuz you're such a brain?

MARK: I have a terrible average in school. D-minus.

TERRI: I thought all you people were genetically programmed to score in the high-90s. What are you—a mutant?

MARK: I hang out with a very dangerous element. We smoke in spite of the surgeon general's warning. I own a cheap little motorcycle that I keep tuned in perfect condition. Why don't I take you up to the lake at midnight and show you some tricks with a switchblade? *(He plays with the handle of her whip.)* Don't you find this all...a lot more interesting?

TERRI: I...I'm not sure.

MARK: I'm used to getting what I want.

TERRI: I mean...I wasn't planning on getting involved with someone this greasy.

MARK: I'm not greasy. I'm dangerous! And right now, I've got my eye set on you.

TERRI: You sound like some old movie from the 50s.

MARK: I'm classic. What's so bad about—?

TERRI: Oh, wait! I almost forgot! You're Chinese, aren't you?

MARK: Well, my name *is* Mark Wong, but—

TERRI: Oh, well...I'm certainly not going to go out with a member of the Chinese mafia!

MARK: The Chinese—what? Wait!

TERRI: Of course! Those pathetic imitations of B-movie delinquents, that cheap Hong Kong swagger.

MARK: Did I say anything about the Chinese mafia?

TERRI: You don't have to—you're Chinese, aren't you? What are you going to do now? Rape me? With your friends? 'Cuz I've seen movies, and you Chinatown pipsqueaks never seem to be able to get a white woman of her own free will. And even when you take her by force, it still requires more than one of you to get the job done. Personally, I think it's all just an excuse to feel up your buddies.

MARK: Wait! Stop! Cut! I said I was vaguely bad—

TERRI: Yeah, corrupting the moral fiber of this nation with evil foreign influences—

MARK: Vaguely bad does not make me a hitman for the Tong!

TERRI: Then what are you? A Viet Cong? Mmmm—big improvement. I'm really gonna wanna sleep with you now!

MARK: No—that's even more evil!

TERRI: Imprison our hometown boys neck-high in leech-filled waters—

MARK: No, no! Less evil! Less—

TERRI: Will you make up your goddamn mind? Indecision in a sado-masochist is a sign of poor mental health.

MARK: I'm not a Chinese gangster, not a Viet Cong...

TERRI: Then you're a nerd. Like I said...

MARK: No! I'm...

TERRI: ...we're waiting...

MARK: I'm...I'm neither! (Pause.)

TERRI: You know, buddy, I can't create a fantasy session solely out of negative images.

MARK: Isn't there something in between? Just delinquent enough to be sexy without also being responsible for the deaths of a few hundred thousand U.S. servicemen?

(Terri paces about, dragging her whip behind her.)

TERRI: Look, this is a nice American fantasy parlor. We deal in basic, mainstream images. You want something kinky, maybe you should try one of those specialty houses catering to wealthy European degenerates.

MARK: How about Bruce Lee? Would you find me sexy if I was Bruce Lee?

TERRI: You mean, like, "Hiiii-ya! I wuv you." (Pause.) Any other ideas? Or do you admit no woman could love you, Mark Wong?

(Mark assumes a doggy-position.)

MARK: I'm defeated. I'm humiliated. I'm whipped to the bone.

TERRI: Well, don't complain you didn't get your money's worth. Perhaps now I'll mount you—little pony—you'd like that wouldn't you?

MARK: Wait! You haven't humiliated me completely.

TERRI: I'd be happy to finish the job—just open that zipper.

MARK: I still never said that I loved you, remember?

(Pause.)

TERRI: I think that's an incredibly technical objection this late in the game.

MARK: All's fair in love and bondage! I did you a favor—I ignored your mistake—well, now I'm taking back the loan.

TERRI: You are really asking for it, buddy...

MARK: After all, I'm not a masochist—no matter how this looks. Sure, I let you beat me, treat me as less than a man—

TERRI: When you're lucky...

MARK: But I do not say "I love you!" Not without a fight! To say "I love you" is the ultimate humiliation. A woman like you looks on a declaration of love as an invitation to loot and pillage.

TERRI: I always pry those words from your lips sooner or later and you know it.

MARK: Not today—you won't today!

TERRI: Oh, look—he's putting up his widdle fight. Sometimes I've asked myself, "Why is it so easy to get Mark to say he loves me? Could it be...because deep inside—he actually does?"

MARK: Love you? That's—slanderous!

TERRI: Just trying to make sense of your behavior.

MARK: Well, stop it! I refuse to be made sense of—by you or anyone else! Maybe...maybe you *wish* I was really in love with you, could that be it?

TERRI: Oh, eat me!

MARK: 'Cuz the idea certainly never entered *my* head

TERRI: Oh—even when you scream out your love for me?

MARK: That's what we call—a fantasy...Mistress.

TERRI: Yeah—*your* fantasy.

MARK: The point is, you haven't beaten me down. Not yet. You may even be surprised sometime to see that I've humiliated you. I'll reject *you* for loving me. And maybe, then, I'll mount *you*—pony.

TERRI: *(Bursts out laughing.)* You can't dominate me. I'm a trained professional.

MARK: So? I've been your client more than a year now. Maybe I've picked up a trick or two.

TERRI: I'm at this six hours a day, six days a week. Your time is probably squandered in some less rewarding profession.

MARK: Maybe I've been practicing in my spare time.

TERRI: With your employees at some pathetic office? Tsst! They're paid to humiliate themselves before you. But me, I'm paid to humiliate you. And I still believe in the American work ethic. *(She cracks her whip.)* So—enough talking everything to death! I may love power, but I haven't yet stooped to practicing psychiatry, thank you. OK, you're a—a white man and me—I'm a black woman!

MARK: African-American.

TERRI: Excuse me—are you telling me what I should call myself? Is this another of our rights you're dying to take away?

MARK: Not me. The Rev. Jesse Jackson—He think African-American is the proper—

TERRI: Who?

MARK: Jesse—I'm sorry, is this a joke?

TERRI: You're not laughing, so I guess it's not. Tell me—the way you talk...could you be...a liberal?

MARK: Uh, yes, if you speak in categories, but—

TERRI: Um. Well, then that explains it.

MARK: Explains what?

TERRI: Why I notice you eyeing me up every time I wander towards the bar.

MARK: Let me be frank. I...saw you standing here, and thought to myself, "That looks like a very intelligent woman."

(She laughs.)

MARK: Sorry. Did I—say something?

TERRI: What do they do? Issue you boys a handbook?

MARK: What?

TERRI: You know, for all you white liberals who do your hunting a little off the beaten track?

MARK: Now, look here—

TERRI: 'Cuz you've all got the same line. You always start talking about our "minds," then give us this *look* like we're supposed to be grateful— "Aren't you surprised?" "Ain't I sensitive?" "Wouldn't you like to oil up your body and dance naked to James Brown?"

MARK: I can't believe...you're accusing *me* of—

TERRI: Then again, what else should I have expected at a PLO fundraiser? So many white liberals, a girl can't leave the room without one or two sticking to her backside.

MARK: Listen—all I said was I find you attractive. If you can't deal with that, then maybe...maybe *you're* the one who's prejudiced.

TERRI: White people—whenever they don't get what they want, they always start screaming "reverse racism."

MARK: Would you be so...derisive if I was a black man?

TERRI: You mean, an African-American?

MARK: Your African-American brothers aren't afraid to date white women, are they? No, in fact, I hear they treat them better than they do their own sisters, doesn't that bother you even a bit?

TERRI: And what makes you such an expert on black men? Read a book by some other whitey?

MARK: Hey—I saw "Jungle Fever."

TERRI: For your urban anthropology class?

MARK: Don't get off the subject. Of you and me. And the dilemma I know you're facing. Your own men, they take you for granted, don't they? I think you should be a little more open-minded, unless you wanna end up like the forty percent of black women over thirty who're never even gonna get married in their lifetimes.

(Silence.)

TERRI: Who the fuck do you think you are? Trying to intimidate me into holding your pasty-white hand? Trying to drive a wedge through our community?

MARK: No, I'm just saying, look at the plain, basic—

TERRI: You say you're attracted to my intelligence? I saw you checking out a lot more than my eyes.

MARK: Well, you do seem...sensuous.

TERRI: Ah. Sensuous. I can respect a man who tells the truth.

MARK: That's a...very tight outfit you've got on.

TERRI: Slinky, perhaps?

MARK: And when you talk to me, your lips...

TERRI: They're full and round—without the aid of collagen.

MARK: And—the way you walked across the room...

TERRI: Like a panther? Sleek and sassy. Prowling—

MARK: Through the wild.

TERRI: Don't you mean, the jungle?

MARK: Yes, the...Wait, no! I see where you're going!

TERRI: Big deal, I was sniffing your tracks ten miles back. I'm so wild, right? The hot sun blazing. Drums beating in the distance. Pounding, pounding...

MARK: That's not fair—!

TERRI: Pounding that Zulu beat.

MARK: You're putting words into my mouth...

TERRI: No, I'm just pulling them out, liberal. (She cracks the whip, driving him back.) What good is that handbook now? Did you forget? Forget you're only supposed to talk about my mind? Forget that a liberal must never ever reveal what's really on his?

MARK: I'm sorry. I'm sorry...Mistress!

TERRI: On your knees, Liberal! (She runs the heel of her boot over the length of his body.) You wanted to have a little fun, didn't you? With a wild dark woman whose passions drown out all her inhibitions. (She pushes him onto his back, puts the heel to his lips.) I'll give you passion. Here's your passion.

MARK: I didn't mean to offend you.

TERRI: No, you just couldn't help it. C'mon—suck it. Like the lily-white baby boy you are.

(He fellates her heel.)

TERRI: That statistic about black women never getting married? What'd you do—study up for today's session? You thought you could get the best of me—admit it, naughty man, or I'll have to spank your little butt purple.

MARK: I didn't study—honest!

TERRI: You hold to that story? Then Mama has no choice but to give you what you want—roll over!

(He rolls onto his stomach.)

TERRI: You actually thought you could get ahead of me on current events! *(She whips his rear over the next sequence.)*

MARK: No, I mean—that statistic—it was just—

TERRI: Just *what?*

MARK: Just street knowledge!

TERRI: Street knowledge? Where do you hang out—the Census Bureau? Liar! *(She pokes at his body with the butt of her whip.)* Don't you know you'll never defeat me? This is your game—to play all the races—but me—I've already become all races. You came to the wrong place, sucker. Inside this costume live the intimate experiences of ethnic groups that haven't even been born. *(Pause.)* Get up. I'm left sickened by that little attempt to assert your will. We'll have to come up with something really good for such an infraction.

MARK: Can I—can I become Chinese again?

TERRI: What is your problem? It's not our practice to take requests from the customers.

MARK: I—don't want you to make things easy on me. I want to go back to what you call a position of weakness. I want you to pull the ropes tight!

TERRI: *(Laughs.)* It's a terrible problem with masochists, really. You don't know whether being cruel is actually the ultimate kindness. You wanna be the lowest of the low? Then beg for it.

(He remains in a supplicant position for this ritual, as she casually tends to her chores.)

MARK: I desire to be the lowest of men.

TERRI: Why?

MARK: Because my existence is an embarrassment to all women.

TERRI: And why is that?

MARK: Because my mind is dirty, filled with hateful thoughts against them. Threats my weakling body can never make good on—but I give away my intentions at every turn—my lustful gaze can't help but give offense.

TERRI: Is that why you desire punishment?

MARK: Yes. I desire punishment.

TERRI: But you'll never dominate your mistress, will you? *(Pause.)* Will you?! *(She cracks her whip.)* All right. Have it your way. I think there's an idea brewing in that tiny brain of yours. You saw me stumble earlier tonight— then, you felt a thrill of exhilaration—however short-lived—with your forty percent statistic. All of a sudden, your hopes are raised, aren't they? God, it pisses me off more than anything to see hope in a man's eyes. It's always the final step before rape. *(Pause.)* It's time to nip hope in the bud. You'll be your Chinese man, and me—I'll be an Asian woman, too. *(Pause.)* Have you been staring at me across the office—Mark Wong?

MARK: Who? Me?

TERRI: I don't see anyone else in the room.

MARK: I have to admit—

TERRI: What?

MARK: You are...very attractive.

TERRI: It's good to admit these things. Don't you feel a lot better already? You've been staring at me, haven't you?

MARK: Maybe...

TERRI: No, you don't mean "maybe."

MARK: My eyes can't help but notice...

TERRI: You mean, "Yes, sir, that's my baby." The only other Asian American in this office.

MARK: It does seem like we might have something in common.

TERRI: Like what?

MARK: Like—where'd your parents come from?

TERRI: Mom's from Chicago, Dad's from Stockton.

MARK: Oh.

TERRI: You didn't expect me to say "Hong Kong" or "Hiroshima," did you?

MARK: No, I mean—

TERRI: Because that would be a stereotype. Why—are *you* a foreigner?

MARK: No.

TERRI: I didn't necessarily think so—

MARK: I was born right here in Los Angeles!

TERRI: But when you ask a question like that, I'm not sure.

MARK: Queen of Angels Hospital!

TERRI: Mmmm. What else do you imagine we might have in common?

MARK: Well, do you ever...feel like people are pigeonholing you? Like they assume things?

TERRI: What kinds of things?

MARK: Like you're probably a whiz at math and science? Or else a Viet Cong?

TERRI: No! I was editor of the paper in high school, and the literary journal in college.

MARK: Look, maybe we're getting off on the wrong foot, here.

TERRI: Actually, there *is* one group of people that does categorize me, now that you mention it.

MARK: So you *do* understand.

TERRI: Asian men. *(Pause.)* Asian men who just assume because we shared space in a genetic pond millions of years ago that I'm suddenly their property when I walk into a room. Or an office. *(Pause.)* Now get this straight. I'm not interested in you, OK? In fact, I'm generally not attracted to Asian men. I don't have anything against them personally, I just don't date them as a species.

MARK: Don't you think that's a little prejudiced? That you're not interested in me because of my race? And it's even your own? I met this black girl a few minutes ago—she seemed to support *her* brothers.

TERRI: Well, her brothers are probably a lot cuter than mine. Look, it's a free country. Why don't you do the same? Date a Caucasian woman.

MARK: I tried that too…a couple of women back.

TERRI: I'll tell you why you don't. Because you Asian men are all alike—you're looking for someone who reminds you of your mothers. Who'll smile at the lousiest jokes and spoon rice into your bowl while you just sit and grunt. Well, I'm not about to date any man who reminds me even slightly of my father.

MARK: But a blonde rejected me because I *didn't* remind her of her father.

TERRI: Of course you didn't! You're Asian!

MARK: And now, you won't date me because I *do* remind you of yours?

TERRI: Of course you do! You're Asian!

(Pause.)

MARK: How—how can I win here?

TERRI: It's simple. You can't. Have you ever heard of historical karma? That's the notion that cultures have pasts that eventually catch up with them. For instance, white Americans were evil enough to bring Africans here in chains—now, they should pay for that legacy. Similarly, Asian men have oppressed their women for centuries. Now, they're paying for their crime by being passed over for dates in favor of white men. It's a beautiful way to look at history, when you think about it.

MARK: Why should my love life suffer for crimes I didn't even commit? I'm an American!

TERRI: C'mon—you don't expect me to buck the wheel of destiny, do you? This is the 1990s—every successful Asian woman walks in on the arm of a white man.

MARK: But—but what about Italian men? Or Latinos? Do you like them?

TERRI: I find them attractive enough, yes.

MARK: Well, what about their cultures? Aren't they sexist?

TERRI: Why do you stereotype people like that? If pressed, I would characterize them as macho.

MARK: Macho? And Asian men aren't?

TERRI: No—you're just sexist.

MARK: What's the difference?

TERRI: The—I dunno. Macho is…sexier, that's all. You've never been known as the most assertive of men.

MARK: How can we be not assertive enough and too oppressive all at the same time?

TERRI: It's one of the miracles of your psychology. Is it any wonder no one wants to date you?

MARK: Aaargh! You can't reject me on such faulty reasoning!

TERRI: I can reject you for any reason I want. That's one of the things which makes courtship so exciting. *(Pause.)* It seems obvious now, the way you feel about me, doesn't it?

MARK: It does not!

TERRI: C'mon—whether black, blonde, or Asian—I think the answer is the same. You...what?

MARK: I...find you attractive...

TERRI: Give it up! You feel something—something that's driving you crazy.

MARK: All right! You win! I love you!

TERRI: Really? You do? Why, young man—I had no idea! *(Pause.)* I'm sorry...but I could never return your affections, you being so very unlovable and all. In fact, your feelings offend me. And so I have no choice but to punish you.

MARK: I understand. You win again. *(He heads for the shackles.)*

TERRI: Say it again. Like you mean it.

MARK: You win! I admit it!

TERRI: Not that—the other part!

MARK: You mean, I love you? Mistress Terri, I love you.

TERRI: No! More believable! The last thing anyone wants is an apathetic slave!

MARK: But I *do* love you! More than any woman—

TERRI: Or man?

MARK: Or anything—any creature—any impulse...in my own body—more than any part of my body...that's how much I love you.
(Pause.)

TERRI: You're still not doing it right, damn it!

MARK: I'm screaming it like I always do—I was almost getting poetic, there...

TERRI: Shut up! It's just not good enough. *You're* not good enough. I won't be left unsatisfied. Come here.

MARK: But—

TERRI: You wanna know a secret? It doesn't matter what you say—there's one thing that always makes your words ring false—one thing that lets me know you're itching to oppress me.

MARK: Wha—what do you mean?

TERRI: I don't think you want to hear it. But maybe...maybe I want to tell you anyway.

MARK: Tell me! I can take the punishment.

TERRI: What sickens me most...is that you feel compelled to play these kinds of parlor games with me.

MARK: What—what the hell are you—?!

TERRI: I mean, how can you even talk about love? When you can't approach me like a normal human being? When you have to hide behind masks and take on these ridiculous roles?

MARK: You're patronizing me! Don't! Get those ropes on me!

TERRI: Patronizing? No, I've *been* patronizing you. Today, I can't even keep up the charade! I mean, your entire approach here—it lets me know—

MARK: I don't have to stand for this!

TERRI: That you're afraid of any woman unless you're sure you've got her under control!

MARK: This is totally against all the rules of the house!

TERRI: Rules, schmules! The rules say I'm supposed to grind you under my heel! They leave the details to me—sadism is an art, not a science. So—beg for more! Beg me to tell you about yourself!

(Panicked, Mark heads for the wall, tries to insert his own wrists into the shackles.)

MARK: No! If I'm—If I'm defeated, I must accept my punishment fair and square.

TERRI: You're square all right. Get your arms out of there! Stand like a man! Beg me to tell you who you are.

MARK: If I obey, will you reward me by denying my request?

TERRI: Who knows? Out of generosity, I might suddenly decide to grant it.

MARK: If you're determined to tell me either way, why should I bother to beg?

TERRI: For your own enjoyment.

MARK: I refuse! You've never done something like this before!

TERRI: That's why I'm so good at my job. I don't allow cruelty to drift into routine. Now, beg!

MARK: Please, Mistress Terri…will you…will you tell me who I really am?

TERRI: You want to know—you wanna know bad, don't you?

MARK: No!

TERRI: In the language of sadomasochism, "no" almost always means "yes."

MARK: No, no, no!

TERRI: You are an eager one, aren't you?

MARK: I just don't like you making assumptions about me! Do you think I'm some kind of emotional weakling, coming in here because I can't face the real world of women?

TERRI: That would be a fairly good description of all our clients.

MARK: Maybe I'm a lot more clever than you think! Do you ever go out there? Do you know the opportunities for pain and humiliation that lurk outside these walls?

TERRI: Well, I…I *do* buy groceries, you know.

MARK: The rules out there are set up so we're all bound to lose.

TERRI: And the rules in here are so much better?

MARK: The rules here…protect me from harm. Out there—I walk around with my face exposed. In here, when I'm rejected, beaten down, humiliated—it's not me. I have no identifying features, and so…I'm no longer human. *(Pause.)* And that's why I'm not pathetic to come here. Because someday, I'm going to beat you. And on that day, my skin will become so thick, I'll be impenetrable to harm. I won't need a mask to keep my face hidden. I'll have lost myself in the armor. *(He places his wrists into the wall shackles.)* OK—I bent to your will. You defeated me again. So strap me up. Punish me.

TERRI: But why...why all these fantasies about race?

MARK: Please, enough!

TERRI: I mean, what race *are* you, anyway?

MARK: You know, maybe we should just talk about *your* real life, how would you like that? *(Pause.)*

TERRI: Is that what you want?

MARK: No...

TERRI: Is that a "no" no, or a "yes" no?

MARK: Yes. No. Goddamn it, I paid for my punishment, just give it to me! *(She tosses away her whip, begins to strap him up.)*

MARK: What are you doing?

TERRI: Punishment is, by definition, something the victim does not appreciate. The fact you express such a strong preference for the whip practically compels me not to use it. *(Pause.)* I think I'd prefer...to kill you with kindness. *(She begins kissing the length of his body.)*

MARK: Please! This isn't...what I want!

TERRI: Are you certain? Maybe...I feel something for you. After all, you've made me so very angry. Maybe...you're a white man, I'm a white woman—there's nothing mysterious—no racial considerations whatsoever.

MARK: That's...too easy! There's no reason you wouldn't love me under those conditions.

TERRI: Are you crazy? I can think of a couple dozen off the top of my head. You don't have to be an ethnic minority to have a sucky love life.

MARK: But there's no...natural barrier between us!

TERRI: Baby, you haven't dated many white women as a white man lately. I think it's time to change all that. *(Pause; Terri steps away.)* So— Mark...Walker. Mark Walker—how long has it been? Since anyone's given you a rubdown like that?

MARK: *(After a pause.)* I usually...avoid these kinds of situations...

TERRI: Why are you so afraid?

MARK: My fright is reasonable. Given the conditions out there.

TERRI: What conditions? Do you have, for instance, problems with... interracial love?

MARK: Whatever gave you that idea?

TERRI: Well, you...remind me of a man I see sometimes...who belongs to all races...and none at all. I've never met anyone like him before.

MARK: I'm a white man! Why wouldn't I have problems? The world is changing so fast around me—you can't even tell whose country it is any more. I can't hardly open my mouth without wondering if I'm offending, if I'm secretly revealing to everyone but myself...some hatred, some hidden desire to strike back...breeding within my body. *(Pause.)* If only there were some certainty—whatever it might be—OK, let the feminists rule the place! We'll call it the United States of Amazonia! Or the Japanese! Or the gays! If I could only figure out who's in charge, then I'd know where I stand. But this constant flux—who can endure it? I'd rather crawl into a protected room where I know what to expect—painful though that place may be. *(Pause.)* I mean...we're heading towards the millennium. Last time, people ran fearing the end of the world. They hid their bodies from the storms that would inevitably follow. Casual gestures were taken as signs of betrayal and accusation. Most sensed that the righteous would somehow be separated from the wicked. But no one knew on which side of such a division they themselves might fall.

(Silence.)

TERRI: You want to hear about yourself. You've been begging for it so long—in so many ways.

MARK: How do you know I just said anything truthful? What makes you so sure I'm really a white man?

TERRI: Oh, I'm not. After all these months, I wouldn't even care to guess. When you say you're Egyptian, Italian, Spanish, Mayan—you seem to be the real thing. So what if we just say... *(Pause; she releases him.)* You're a man, and you're frightened, and you've been ill-used in love. You've come to doubt any trace of your own judgment. You cling to the hope that power over a woman will blunt her ability to harm you, while all the time you're tormented by the growing fear that your hunger will never be satisfied with the milk of cruelty. *(Pause.)* I know. I've been in your place.

MARK: You...you've been a man? What are you saying?

TERRI: You tell me. Fight back. Tell me about me. And make me love every second of it.

MARK: All right. Yes.

TERRI: Yes... *Who?*

MARK: Yes, Mistress Terri!

TERRI: Yes—who?

MARK: Yes...whoever you are...a woman who's tried hard to hate men for what they've done to her but who...can't quite convince herself.

(She pushes him to the ground.)

TERRI: Is that what you think? *(Beat.)* Tell me more...

MARK: You went out—into the world...I dunno, after college maybe—I think you went to college...

TERRI: Doesn't matter.

MARK: But the world—it didn't turn out the way you planned...rejection hung in the air all around you—in the workplace, in movies, in the casual joking of the population. The painful struggle...to be accepted as a spirit among others...only to find yourself constantly weighed and measured by those outward bits of yourself so easily grasped, too easily understood. Maybe you were harassed at work—maybe even raped—I don't know.

TERRI: It doesn't matter. The specifics never matter.

MARK: So you found your way here—somehow—back of the Hollywood Star—something—roomfuls of men begging to be punished for the way they act out there—wanting you to even the score—and you decided— that this was a world you could call your own.

TERRI: And so, I learned what it feels like to be a man. To labor breathlessly accumulating power while all the time it's dawning how tiring, what a burden, how utterly numbing—it is actually to possess. The touch of power is cold like metal. It chafes the skin, but you know nothing better to hold to your breast. So you travel down this blind road of hunger— constantly victimizing yourself in the person of others—until you despair of ever again feeling warm or safe—until you forget such possibilities exist. Until they become sentimental relics of a weaker man's delusions. And driven by your need, you slowly destroy yourself. *(She starts to remove her gloves.)* Unless, one day, you choose to try something completely different.

MARK: What are you doing? Wait!

TERRI: It's a new game, Mark. A new ethnic game. The kind you like.

MARK: We can't play—without costumes.

TERRI: Oh, but it's the wildest interracial fantasy of all. It's called...two hearts meeting in a bondage parlor on the outskirts of Encino. With skins— more alike than not. *(She tosses her gloves away.)* Haven't we met before? I'm certain we have. You were the one who came into my chamber wanting to play all the races.

MARK: Why are you doing this to me? I'm the customer here!

TERRI: No, your time is up. Or haven't you kept your eyes on the clock? At least I know I'm not leaving you bored.

MARK: Then...shouldn't I be going?

TERRI: If you like. But I'm certain we've met before. I found it so interesting, so different—your fantasy. And I've always been a good student, a diligent employee. My Daddy raised me to take pride in all of America's service professions. So I started to...try and understand all the races I never thought of as my own. Then, what happened?

MARK: You're asking me?

TERRI: C'mon—let me start you off. I have a box in my closet— *(She runs her bare hands up and down his body as he speaks.)*

MARK: In which you keep all the research you've done...for me. Every clipping, magazine article, ethnic journals, transcripts from Phil Donahue. Blacks against Jews in Crown Heights—your eyes went straight to the headlines. The rise of neo-Naziism in Marseille and Orange County. And then, fur- ther—the mass-murderer in Canada who said, "The feminists made me do it." You became a collector of all the rejection and rage in this world. *(Pause.)* Am I on the right track?

TERRI: Is that what you've been doing?

MARK: And that box—that box is overflowing now. Books are piled high to the hems of your dresses, clippings slide out from beneath the door. And you…you looked at it…maybe this morning…and you realized your box was…full. And so you began to stumble. You started to feel there was nothing more here for you.

TERRI: If you say it, it must be true.

MARK: Is it?

TERRI: *(She starts to unlace her thigh-high boots.)* I'm prepared to turn in my uniform and start again from here.

MARK: You're quitting your job?

TERRI: The masks don't work. The leather is pointless. I'm giving notice as we speak.

MARK: But—what if I'm wrong?

TERRI: I'm afraid I'll have to take that chance.

MARK: No, you can't just—what about your hatred of men? Are you really going to just throw it all away when it's served you so well?

TERRI: I've been a man. I've been a woman. I've been colorful and colorless. And now, I'm tired of hating myself. *(Pause.)*

MARK: And what about me?

TERRI: That's something you'll have to decide.

MARK: I'm not sure I can leave you. Not after all this time.

TERRI: Then stay. And strip. As lovers often do.

(As Terri removes her costume, Mark turns and looks away.)

MARK: I worry when I think about the coming millennium. Because it feels like all labels have to be rewritten, all assumptions re-examined, all associations redefined. The rules that governed behavior in the last era are crumbling, but those of the time to come have yet to be written. And there is a struggle brewing over the shape of these changing words, a struggle that begins here now, in our hearts, in our shuttered rooms, in the lightning decisions that appear from nowhere.

(Terri has stripped off everything but her hood. Beneath her costume she wears a simple bra and panties. Mark turns to look at her.)

MARK: I think you're very beautiful.

TERRI: Even without the metal and leather?

MARK: You look…soft and warm and gentle to the touch.

TERRI: I'm about to remove my hood. I'm giving you fair warning.

MARK: There's…only one thing I never managed to achieve here. I never managed to defeat you.

TERRI: You understand me. Shouldn't I be a lot more frightened? But—the customer is always right. So come over here. This is my final command to you.

MARK: Yes, Mistress Terri.

TERRI: Take off my hood. You want to—admit it.

MARK: Yes. I want to.

TERRI: The moment you remove this hood, I'll be completely exposed, while you remain fully covered. And you'll have your victory by the rules of our engagement, while I—I'll fly off over the combat zone. *(Terri places Mark's left hand on her hood.)* So congratulations. And goodbye.

(With his right hand, Mark undoes his own hood instead. It comes off. He is an Asian man.)

TERRI: You disobeyed me.

MARK: I love you.

(She removes her own hood. She's a Caucasian woman.)

TERRI: I think you're very beautiful, too.

(Mark starts to remove the rest of his costume.)

TERRI: At a moment like this, I can't help but wonder, was it all so terribly necessary? Did we have to wander so far afield to reach a point which comes, when it does at last, so naturally?

MARK: I was afraid. I was an Asian man.

TERRI: And I was a woman, of any description.

MARK: Why are we talking as if those facts were behind us?

TERRI: Well, we have determined to move beyond the world of fantasy...haven't we?

(Mark's costume is off. He stands in simple boxer shorts. They cross the stage towards one another.)

MARK: But tell the truth—would you have dated me? If I'd come to you first like this?

TERRI: Who knows? Anything's possible. This is the 1990s.

(Mark touches her hair. They gaze at each other's faces, as lights fade to black.)

END OF PLAY

21A

by Kevin Kling

Kevin Kling graduated from Gustavus Adolphus College in 1979 and has been a member of The Playwrights' Center in Minneapolis since 1983. He has performed his one person plays, *21A* and *Home and Away*, at The Actors Theatre of Louisville, Westside Arts Theatre and Second Stage Theater (Off-Broadway), Seattle Rep, The Goodman Theater, The Denver Center Theater, Festivals in Sidney and Perth, Australia, Quicksilver Stage, The Jungle and the Guthrie Theatre in Minneapolis. His play *Lloyds' Prayer* received a workshop at the Sundance Institute and premiered at The Actors Theatre of Louisville. Other plays include *The 7 Dwarfs, The Education of Walter Kaufmann, Fear and Loving in Minneapolis* and *The Ice Fishing Play*. Kevin is a recipient of a Heideman Award, a Bush Fellowship, an NEA grant, a McKnight Fellowship, and The Whiting Literary Award. Along with Loren Niemi and Michael Sommers, he is a proud member of the performance trio "Bad Jazz."

ORIGINAL PRODUCTION

21A was originally produced by Quicksilver Stage in Minneapolis, Minnesota. It played in both the 1985 SHORTS Festival and the 1986 Humana Festival of New American Plays. The Actors Theatre of Louisville productions were directed by Frazier Marsh with the following cast:

Ron Huber	Kevin Kling
Gladys	Kevin Kling
Chairman Francis	Kevin Kling
Student	Kevin Kling
Not Dave	Kevin Kling
Captain Twelve Pack	Kevin Kling
Steve	Kevin Kling
Jim Shiply	Kevin Kling

CHARACTERS

RON HUBER: driver of the 21A

GLADYS: in her late 50's, wears a coat, curlers, and cat-eye glasses

CHAIRMAN FRANCIS: in his late teens, wears a dark suit, has a Boston accent

STUDENT: a political science student

NOT DAVE: a man who is not named Dave

CAPTAIN TWELVE PACK: a brand new drunk

*STEVE: a kid, wears thick glasses and second-hand clothes, talks with a lateral lisp

JIM SHIPLY: a nervous passenger with a gun

> *There are actually two Steve's: One that the audience can see, and one that the characters on the bus can see. The character Steve explains this. So that it's clear to the reader, the Steve the audience sees will be typed *STEVE*, and the Steve the characters see will be typed STEVE.

TAPED VOICES: CASHIER; CHAIRMAN STEWART; CUSTOMER.

SETTING: The play takes place on the 21A bus that runs between Minneapolis and St. Paul.

TIME: An autumn morning, the present.

TIME FRAME

21A is a one-person show. All the action takes place in a fifteen minute period of time one autumn morning in the present. The actual show takes longer because the characters go through the same time span one at a time. Bits and pieces of conversation are heard from each character until the end when the total fifteen minutes is complete.

21A

Scene: The play takes place on the 21A bus that runs between Minneapolis and St. Paul. The bus is parked during the action at the beginning of the route. On the bus are a driver's seat, complete with portable cushion, and at least seven other seats for passengers. Also a money box, or till, in the front. Other decorations are optional, such as a steering wheel or overhead ads.

At Rise: The lights fade up on the bus with Ron Huber at the wheel. He is smoking a cigarette and doing a crossword puzzle. There is a five letter word he can't get. Suddenly he turns to a seat.

RON HUBER: Pardon my French but fuck the Twins that's how 'bout 'em. *(He goes back to the puzzle for a second.)* What am I, a goddamn weatherman? I don't know it'll clear up. *(Goes back to the puzzle. Suddenly he look in the rear view mirror, jumps up and runs to the back of the bus.)* Hey! Hey! Git away from there, you kids. Git, I say. This ain't no goddamn toy. Git, I say. *(He returns to his seat.)* Goddamn kids, they play on anything. I get a new gas meter for the house and the next thing I know some neighbor kid is rolling by on the old one. Made a goddamn go-cart outta it. Fifty bucks says I can leave something, anything in my yard and the next day some neighbor kid is selling tickets to it. Shit yeah, you can count on it. What, this route here? Oh, about two years now. I've driven most of the others though, your two, your three, four, seven, twelve, seventeen...I even drove the six for a while. This 21 is a good route though. Ain't a day goes by I don't say, "Shit, I never seen that before." It's a different kind of people, see. Poor? I bet there ain't two bucks on this whole bus. Weary? Some of these people have been through shit a cat wouldn't live through. Crazy? No way. They're just as sane as you or me. Oh, they're a little odd, most of them, you can bet on that. I don't know how they keep from crackin' up. Me? I go up north fishing with my brother-in-law, that would be Ray. Christ, we catch the fish, really knock 'em down. Last year we limited out on Northern and Walleye both. And the beauty of that country...Shit. We were sitting there casting by the shore and I seen four deer come down for a drink. I says, "Lookee there, Ray, I'd give fifty, no a hundred bucks, for my deer rifle right now." See we got another three months before deer season so I just threw a rock. You should meet this guy Ray though. He runs a chicken farm with my sister and two kids, that would be Joe and Bill. But these chickens, you don't eat 'em, see? Ray teaches 'em how to play Tic-Tac-Toe and then sells them to fairs. He makes pretty good money and they're good, too, boy. Shit, I tried all day, never could beat this one. But at these fairs they're in these little boxes, see? And pretty soon some of them chickens start to crack up. Well lookit, one minute they're a chicken on a farm and the next minute they're in a little box, trying to outwit a human. And when they lose just once, *(He makes a raspberry sound with his mouth.)* You might as well start mashing the potatoes. Fichu! Fichu! *(He writes on the crossword puzzle.)* It's a woman's triangular scarf. The way I see it we're all in some kind of box. Sometimes you find your way out, and sometimes you're stuck, like a chicken and then *(Makes the raspberry.)* it don't matter what bus you're on, a two, three, four...six, even. I gotta theory on people who thrive in boxes but that will cost you a cinnamon triangle and a cup of coffee at the Super America. Hey, what is that crunchy shit in them cinnamon triangles, anyhow?...Oh, yeah? *(He stands up and puts out his cigarette.)* Say, lookit, folks. I'm going down to the Super America for a cup of coffee but don't worry, we'll start on time. *(He sets down the crossword and picks up his seat cushion.)* Goddamn kids. *(He exits. Blackout. During the Blackout, traffic sounds are heard. The next section is a taped interlude so the actor has time to change into Gladys. A car rushes by.)*

RON HUBER: Christ, that was close. So like I'm saying you got your two types of people. People who crave the confinement and security that a box offers and people who...don't. Now these box people, like I like to call them, they aren't screwed up necessarily. I think Millard Fillmore was a box person and look at him. Now you can always tell a box person because when they recall the past their eyes wander up and to the right. Your middle child is usually a box person. Now I got a theory on middle children too, but that will run you another cinnamon triangle. Hey. Hey, where are you going?

(Footsteps are heard running off.)

Ah, to hell with you then, I'll buy my own cinnamon triangle.

(Lights up on Gladys. She has curlers in her hair, tucked under a brightly colored scarf. She wears a long coat and carries two large shopping bags in addition to her purse. She goes right for the seats at the front of the bus marked "Handicapped" and sets a bag of groceries on either side of her—taking up a total of three seats. Pause. She smiles, then turns to the unseen Student.)

GLADYS: I know why you're staring, honey. I know that look, I know what you're thinking and I don't blame you a bit. I'd think it too, 'cause I don't miss much in this old world and you're right, this is a lot of food for one cat. But half of it is for my husband. Pot pies for Big Bob, little Friskies for Little Bob. I'll grab something later. But you see how looks are deceiving? I'm 58. What are you? What are you reading? See what I mean? It's like I'm telling Ruby. She worked at the fair this year where you throw a dart at balloons and this little kid comes up to play, well he was too little for darts but Ruby gave him one anyway and before she could turn around he'd thrown it and it stuck in her nose. Well, if you knew Ruby that ain't such an amazing shot, but that dart stuck in her nose and she pulled it out and gave the kid his money back, which I never would have done, but she told this to the Thursday Forum and all the girls laughed until I told Ruby about lockjaw and how it wasn't a laughing matter and when did she have her last tetanus shot? Well, it had been over three years, and everyone stopped laughing and told Ruby she better go in for a shot. Ruby said, "Oh, I'll be all right," but she was awfully quiet for the rest of the night, and I caught her several times wiggling her jaw in the corner. Until the next day she went in for that shot, but I think it was too late. And I told that to Big Bob and he says, "who cares?" and I said you should, Big Bob. See, Big Bob keeps saying he's got cancer, but I think it's gas. But he won't have it checked. And just the other day Ms. Stitt's dog, Tilly, died and they found a tumor the size of Utah in poor Tilly. But Big Bob oughtta know, he's had two heart attacks. He told me once if he had a million dollars guess what he'd buy? And I said "A boat, like Babe Winkleman on that show you're watching," but he said "Nope, I'd buy my health." Well, I started to tell him how no amount of money can buy health cause there's a lot of sick people on the Love Boat—that's my show—and why would they go on a cruise when they could have an operation? Well, I tried to tell Big Bob, but he'd already got back to his show and no amount of talking can pull him out.

(Swings her purse at someone who has boarded the bus and stumbled onto her—it is Captain Twelvepack, unseen at this point.)

GLADYS: Hey, watch where you're stepping, mister. You could've broke my leg. You see my leg there, don't you? How would you like that? Breaking an old lady's leg. You drunks disgust me. Go on! Now get away! Get away! My husband will seek you out and kill you. He'll kill you and I'll watch. He hates disgusting men like you, so it would be no great chore. *You damn drunks make me sick. (Back to the Student.)* Those damn drunks make me sick. I don't have the patience for them, but I used to when I sang. That's right, I was a singer. I almost turned professional, but I didn't. I sang for servicemen and some of them would get so drunk. But there was a war on, so they had a reason. *Not like some people I could point out.* And that's where I met Big Bob and the next day he took me to see the movie "Give Out Sisters" which is still my favorite movie, with the Andrews Sisters, Dan Daily Jr., Grace McDonald and Charles Butterworth as Professor Woof. And we sat through it twice with my knee sweating on Big Bob's hand. Then we went out for a soda and he said I sang better than the Andrews Sisters and I said "Go on" and he said "Way better" and kissed me right there on the lips in public which was a big deal for me because I'd never been kissed before except by relatives and my Uncle Ted, but I'd seen movies so I knew just how I would if I ever got the chance. So, I kissed him and asked right away what it was like. That's the only time I've ever seen Big Bob off guard. But finally he said, "Like saxophones and satin." *(Her first pause.)* Saxophones and satin. *(Pause.)* I melted. Romantic language does that to me. I melt.

(Chairman Francis enters.)

GLADYS: What's that? Huh? Oh, no thanks, honey. Don't waste your time with me. I'm saved every Sunday at 9 a.m. on channel 11. But I appreciate the offer.

(Chairman Francis moves away, Gladys turns back to the student.)

GLADYS: Poor kid, I hope he has another suit. Honestly. I know his plight and it's a tough road. My Uncle Ted used to save people on busses after the accident, but he really was a minister. He married Big Bob and I. I was only seventeen, but I knew Big Bob was for me, so we got married. He'll say he caught me, but don't believe it. It's always up to the woman. And a lot of women were after him, too. Sure they were. See, Big Bob was beautiful. I know you're not supposed to say that about men, but he was. And he'd touch people. Everyone. He'd be talking to you and soon you'd realize he was touching you. And every woman I knew was after that special touch. You bet they were. But I got it. You bet I did. After the wedding reception we were so nervous—you know how that is—but we went to a hotel and I thought everything went just fine, but in the morning Big Bob was still nervous. I thought it was me, so I laid down and cried. Right there. I found out later it's called premature ejaculation and 39 million Americans suffer from it. I also found out they're not the 39 million Americans who are suffering. But I wasn't worried. I figured sooner or later it would go away. And it did.

(Steve appears.)

GLADYS: Oh. Shhhh. Shhhh. Don't stare now. Don't stare. Why, hello, Steve. How are you? I am fine, thank you.

(Steve passes by, she returns her attention to the Student.)

GLADYS: He's retarded. Talks to himself for hours. He thinks that he's talking to another kid, but there's nobody there. Spooky. You know, he can name every city in the world that has a K-Mart. It's amazing. If you're riding the whole route you should ask him to do it. Makes you want to travel. Go ahead. It's okay and his name is Steve. I think he has one of those special brains like he can memorize K-Marts, but he can't tie his shoes. It's like Big Bob. You name a city and he'll tell you what football team plays there.

Or he'll laugh and say there ain't no team from there. Big Bob ain't retarded though. Go ahead and talk to him. I won't say another word. *(Long silence.)* We never had any kids, not that we didn'˙ want them. We did have a Vista cruise station wagon with imitation wood paneling and room in back for kids, and a Kenmore washer-dryer, double load, Spegal 60609—but we were never graced with kids. We made plans even. Big Bob used to say his son would play football and go to college and be better than his old man. I said "I don't care, just so he never says shut up or watches the Three Stooges." Big Bob says "What's wrong with the Three Stooges?" I say "Too violent." Big Bob says "The kid's gotta learn sometime." I say "Wouldn't it be nice if he never did?" Big Bob says "No kid of mine's gonna be ignorant." I say "Just pretend." Big Bob says "Shut up." *(Turns to Captain Twelvepack.)* Hey, leave him alone. He's retarded. You damn drunk. I don't care what he threw at you. Leave him alone. *(Back to the Student.)* Drinking is so important to men. Like the other night Big Bob's watching Monday Night Football and the phone rings. So, I answer it and the man asks "Is Bob around?" and I know it ain't half-time so I say "No, can I take a message?" He says "Tell Bob…Saxophones and satin." And then he leaves a number. So, I wait till half-time and I tell Big Bob a man called and said "Saxophones and satin." Big Bob says "Oh, yeah? I haven't heard that in years." And I'm thinkin' me neither, but the sound of it still sends me. So I ask what's it mean. Big Bob says "Aw, that's army talk, you wouldn't understand." I say "I bet I would." Big Bob smiles and says "Saxophones and satin. That's the great feeling of getting real drunk and then laid. There's nothing like it." *(Pause.)* So, after the game I told Big Bob I wanted a pet. He says, "Why?" "To keep my company," I say. "Okay," says Big Bob, "Don't get a cat. Get a dog. Because a dog is loyal, but a cat don't care about nothing but itself." I say "I like cats." Big Bob gives me his full attention and says "If you die and you're locked in your house, a dog will sit there and starve to death—but a cat will eat you. Now, what do you want?" So, I got a cat and named it Little Bob. I feed Big Bob, but I talk to Little Bob. They hate each other. Like the other night I was making Jello sal— *(Captain Twelvepack bumps into her.)* Look out! I've had enough of you. You don't scare me. You damn drunk. I've lived with your type for 31 years. You disgust me. *(Pause.)* What? How dare you…You'd what?…Ahh, you'd *What?*…*(Smiles.)*…Really? Then what? Oh, yeah?…I am? Oh, no, I couldn't…I really couldn't…Oh, no, behind you. That man has a gun! *Ahh,* Steve let him go! No, Bob look out! *Ahhhhhhhhhhhhh! (Two gunshots are heard as the lights fade quickly to black. During this Blackout noises from the inside of a Super America Service*

Station are heard. The actor is becoming Chairman Francis in this taped interlude.)

CASHIER: OK. Go ahead, pump #5 is clear. Get any gas?

RON HUBER: No, thanks, though.

CASHIER: What can I get you?

RON HUBER: I been looking here...I don't see any of them cinnamon triangles.

CASHIER: These are them, right here. How many do you want?

RON HUBER: Those are round though.

CASHIER: We changed the shape. How many?

RON HUBER: They're the same as the other ones?

CASHIER: Yeah, only round.

RON HUBER: They don't look the same.

CASHIER: Well, they are. How many do you want?

RON HUBER: I know, they don't have the crunchy shit on them.

CASHIER: We stopped putting that on.

RON HUBER: Oh. How come?

CASHIER: Regulations.

RON HUBER: Oh, yeah? Huh.

CASHIER: I can sprinkle some on if you'd like.

RON HUBER: No, that's OK, I finally found out what it was. How come they crunch?

CASHIER: They're toasted. How many?

RON HUBER: Uh...Two. No, them two right there. Yeah.

(Lights up. Gladys' groceries remain where they were, in addition to her purse, which sits on her chair. The lights reveal Chairman Francis. He wear a dark, ill-fitting suit and speaks with a Boston accent. He approaches Gladys, tentatively.)

CHAIRMAN FRANCIS: Good morning. Are you pleased with the status quo? Is your faith serving you well? *(Pause.)* I see. Thank you. *(He approaches Captain Twelvepack.)* Good morning. Are you pleased with the status quo? Is your faith serving you—uh, who, me? Unh-unh, unh-unh, unh-unh. I see. Thank you.

(He approaches the last seat on the bus—where Jim Shiply will sit when we see him. Chairman Francis sits in a seat facing this one and speaks to Jim.)

CHAIRMAN FRANCIS: Do you mind if I sit here? Thank you. Are you pleased with the status quo, is your faith serving you well, do you have a hard time sleeping at night, is the future unclear and do you feel helpless as to its outcome? Of course, you do. Could I ask a minute of your time? It could perhaps give you peace of mind. Thank you. You have heard of the faith of Democratic Progression? Uh, no. Well I am Chairman Francis, and the man out there pursuing the driver of this vehicle is Chairman

Stewart and we are here from Boston as part of our two-year team as missionaries to that particular faith. And what is your name? I see. Then perhaps we may simply call you "Mister Chairman." *(To the entire bus:)* All in favor? *(Raises his hand.)* Aye. Opposed? *(Pause. Back to Jim:)* Very well. Motion carried. Let it come to pass. *(A podium springs out from Chairman Francis' shirt.)* Mr. Chairman, as I speak to you, I see an all too familiar look on your face. A look as if to say, "Before me stands a happy man. A man who is ready, come what may. I wonder how that man achieved this inner peace." Now, Mr. Chairman, you seem like an intelligent man. A man who cares about the world around him. A man who witnesses injustice and evil and is disgusted, but has no recourse. Mr. Chairman, if this disgust remains unchecked it will build up and up with no outlet, no escape, festering and swelling like a giant pus with no relief, Mr. Chairman, no relief. Well this is your lucky day, Mr. Chairman, for I am here to relieve you. "How?" you may ask. Because Mr. Chairman, the church of Democratic Progression believes in change. Mr. Chairman, evil, evil, that dirty little filthy guy, evil is constantly changing, while the church has remained firm and happy sitting on its foundation. Evil loves that, Mr. Chairman. Evil thinks that is a real hoot. Because evil can chip away at that foundation. Evil has its work clearly cut out for it, while the church must stand there and take it. Well, not anymore, Mr. Chairman. Change is what we're all about. Our church is the street, our faith is the people, and our laws are constantly changing. If a law offends us, we pluck it out. If a minister offends us, we pluck him out and elect a new minister who is young and strong and can recognize evil's ever-changing face. We don't believe in miracles, we believe in action. But action takes money. Mr. Chairman, the church of Democratic Progression needs your financial support. Now, Mr. Chairman, how much would you pay to nip evil in the bud? Now I'm not talking about wiping out evil entirely, just your own little personal dark speck. Would you pay forty dollars, Mr. Chairman? Thirty dollars? Twenty dollars, the price of four filthy movies? *No.* Mr. Chairman, for just fifteen dollars a month you can keep a chairman, like myself, on the streets fighting evil on your behalf. What do you say, Mr. Chairman, only fifteen dollars! I see. Then perhaps you would like to purchase a copy of Our Progress for only five dollars. I see. Then perhaps you would like to make a tax-deductible donation for the incumbent minister. I see. Then perhaps you would like to be the incumbent minister. I see. Then perhaps you would care to leave your name and address and another chairman, such as Chairman Stewart, could call on you at a more convenient time. I see. Well I'm sorry I've wasted your time. I will now leave you to sit in your inner torment. *(He moves to the front of the bus and tears off his podium, setting it on the chair in front of where Not Dave will sit.)* Mr. Chairman, I would greatly appreciate it if you would wipe that smirk off your face. Perhaps you think of me as strange or lost. Well I assure you I am not. It's not like I'm following some baldheaded guru who wants to take me camping for the rest of my life. No. Certain unknowns have been revealed to me. See for yourself, Mr. Chairman. Look outside. Look at the wickedness and the violence. Or read the paper, read the paper, Mr. Chairman. I read that paper everyday and it frightens me. And I see my father safe and content in his Easy-Boy recliner lusting after Haley Mills, eating his huge red meat Dagwood Bumstead sandwiches and changing slower than Blondie's girlish figure and *it sickens me.* Well, you can sit there too, Mr. Chairman, you can sit there on your fat foundation. Or you can rise up. You can ride that crest, you can say *enough*—That's it, Mr. Chairman, rise up, that's it, Mr. Chairman, reach in that pocket, that's right, Mr. Chairman, dig deep, that's it, that's…I move we all recognize the man with the large handgun. All in favor, aye. All opposed. Motion carried, let it come to pass. *(He dives behind a seat as the lights go down and we hear two gunshots.)*

(In this blackout the noises continue from the same Super America. The actor is becoming the Student. Again, this is taped.)

CASHIER: OK. Will that be all?

RON HUBER: No, I'll be getting some coffee, but first I need the key to the rest room.

CASHIER: I'm afraid it's already out.

RON HUBER: Well there ain't nobody out there. I already knocked.

CASHIER: Brother, somebody must've walked off with the key.

RON HUBER: What'll I do, I gotta go.

CASHIER: Here use this screwdriver. It works just as good.

RON HUBER: OK. How do I do it?

CASHIER: Push the door in as hard as you can.

RON HUBER: Yeah.

CASHIER: Push the screwdriver next to the bolt.

RON HUBER: OK.

CASHIER: OK. Then with your other hand, jiggle the knob.

RON HUBER: Yeah.

CASHIER: Now, shake the screwdriver in between the latch and the bolt. There's just barely enough room but it fits.

RON HUBER: So now both hands are jiggling.

CASHIER: Uh-huh. Then, when you have the screwdriver wedged just twist it and the door opens.

RON HUBER: That don't sound too hard.

CASHIER: No. And if you can't get in I'll give you the key to the women's.

RON HUBER: I'll get in.

CASHIER: And don't forget to lock it when you're done.

> *(Lights up. Chairman Francis' book is sitting on the chair he last sat in. The lights now reveal the Student. He wears University sweatshirt and holds a few large books. He reads for a few moments, then looks up at Gladys.)*

STUDENT: I'm a student. *(Pause.)* "Political Science."

> *(Two gunshots are heard as lights go quickly to black. This blackout is also in the Super America. The actor is changing into Not Dave.)*

RON HUBER: Hey, lady, over here. Over here. Hey lady, I'm back.

CASHIER: Any problems?

RON HUBER: No. I got a garage door like that at home. Here's your screwdriver back, and the key. It was on the sink.

CASHIER: Thanks. They always leave the key.

RON HUBER: Yeah. Hey, how 'bout that coffee?

CASHIER: Help yourself.

RON HUBER: What are these plastic mugs here?

CASHIER: What? Oh…If you buy coffee in one you can keep the cup.

RON HUBER: Big deal. It costs twice as much as coffee in a styrofoam one.

CASHIER: Yeah, well, you pay sixty nine cents for the first cup and every time you come in you can get a refill for a dime.

RON HUBER: Christ, I'll save a fortune.

CASHIER: And they don't tip over.

> *(Lights up. The Student's book remains on her chair. Lights reveal Not Dave, sitting in a comfortable corduroy coat and a hat. He holds an* Esquire *maga-zine. He sits looking out the window, then suddenly looks to the front of the bus.)*

NOT DAVE: My name isn't Dave. I'm not Dave. *(Addressing the seat next to him now.)* No, I'm not. No. No. No. No. No. No. No. No. No. No. No. No. *(Pause.)* No. No. *(Pause.)* Jim. Bob. Ed. Bill. Roger. Fred. Sam. Mike. Pete. Herman. Jim. Dave. *(Grimaces, pause.)* Abdul. Vito. Horatio. Thucydides. *(Suddenly ducks and then looks to back of bus.)* Hey, look out. *(To chair next to him:)* No. No. No. Look, I'm sick of this. Leave me alone. *Leave me alone!*

> *(Blackout. Two gunshots. Another blackout in the Super America. The actor is becoming Captain Twelvepack.)*

CHAIRMAN STEWART: Uh. Sir. Sir. Are you pleased with the status quo and is your faith serving you well?

RON HUBER: Yeah. What the hell is this?

CHAIRMAN STEWART: My name is Chairman Stewart and with my partner, Chairman Francis, we are serving as missionaries for the faith of Democratic Progression. Could I ask a minute of your time?

RON HUBER: No.

CHAIRMAN STEWART: Well then, perhaps you could leave your name and address and we could contact you at a more convenient time.

RON HUBER: No.

CHAIRMAN STEWART: I see. Thank you very much.

RON HUBER: Hey. Hey, wait, kid. How much area do you and your buddy cover?

CHAIRMAN STEWART: Well, our parish is quite small. Chairman Francis and I must cover the entire five state area.

RON HUBER: So, do you ever get up north?

CHAIRMAN STEWART: Yes. As a matter of fact we will be in the northern sector around August.

RON HUBER: No shit.

CHAIRMAN STEWART: Yes, around August.

RON HUBER: Here, I'll give you the name of a guy who would love to talk to you guys. When you get to Brainerd call this number, and ask for Ray.

CHAIRMAN STEWART: Ray.

RON HUBER: Yeah, Ray. Oh, Ray is gonna shit. Tell him Ron Huber sent you, and don't take no for an answer.

CHAIRMAN STEWART: Yes, yes. Thank you, Chairman Ron. I will be sure to include you in my next speech.

RON HUBER: That's OK. Glad I could help…Ray is gonna shit.

(Lights up. Not Dave's hat and magazine remain on his seat. Captain Twelvepack's voice is heard from off.)

CAPTAIN TWELVEPACK: The siege has ended! Storm the gate!

(Captain Twelvepack enters, trips on the bus steps and crashes into the money till. He wears a tattered old executive's coat and an empty twelve-pack box on his head which covers all but his mouth and one ear which pokes out of the side of the cardboard.)Da-Da-Da! Yield or die at the hand of Captain Twelvepack! *(Pulls himself to his feet.)* I'll take that as a yield. *(Steps on Gladys' feet.)* Out of my way, baseborn slut. Blah blah blah. Bring on this hapless husband. I'll soil his tunic with his own blood. *(Looks to the back of the bus.)* Dave. *(Walks to and sits next to Not Dave.)* Dave, over here. Dave, it's me. God, it's good to see you, Dave, you bastard. How've you been, Dave, ol' pal? *(Pause.)* You are, too, Dave. Yes, you are. Yes, you are. Yes Yes. Yes. Yes. Yes. Yes. Yes. Yes. Yes. Yes. *Goddamn it, Dave, you are, too. (Cries.)* I'm sorry, Dave. I didn't mean it. Now, come on. Guess who I am in here. Come on, guess, Guess. *Guess. (Pause.)* No. No. No. No. No. No. No. No. No. No. *(Laughs.) You're* Dave. No. No. NO. NO. Here, I'll give you a hint. *(Whispers.)* Phil. That's right, it's me all the time. You don't remember me, do you, Dave? Hey, Dave, remember the

time you stole my wife? I never killed you for that, did I, Dave? So, how've you been? Well, I'll tell you—horseshit, Dave, yeah, horseshit. *(Turns to Chairman Francis who stands above him.)* Keep your distance, friar. I have no need of your Saxon god. Now, back off or I'll send you to him in a box. *(Turns back to Not Dave.)* Dave! Yeah, Phil. Right. I'll tell you, Dave, two weeks ago I had a beautiful job, a full-time wife—my wife, how could you do that, Dave? You were my best friend. *(Drops his head.)* I know. I know I deserved it. I know. I know. I know. *(Voice becomes almost inaudibly soft.)* I know. Hey, Dave. If I fall asleep while I'm telling you this, wake me up, Okay? Or they put me in jail. *Jail, Dave.* *(Sits up, confidential to Not Dave.)* I'm on my way to rendezvous with a man named Fat Max. He's laying siege on a cigarette machine on Seventh. The rest of the troops are back at the bridge where I live. *I live under a goddamn bridge, Dave. Free as the wind. I'm a concrete crusader, that's what.* The other guys named me Captain Twelvepack and made me this helmet. How do you like it? I could probably make you one, Dave, yeah, no problem. *(Turns suddenly to back of bus.)* *Hey, watch where you're throwing that apple, you goddamned minion!* *(To Gladys:)* *I don't care if he is retarded, he almost killed my best friend!* *(Back to Not Dave:)* Goddamnit, Dave, I'm not meant for this street life. I should be out in the suburbs, for Christ's sake, in a ranch style home with a basketball hoop and a sprinkler and a dog with a name. I'm like in a panic and these other guys can sense it. They pretend they're real nice, but they smoke all my cigarettes and make me wear this fuckin' hat and I know they're going through my stuff right now. I know they sent me to meet Fat Max so they could go through my stuff, but what am I supposed to say? No, you guys, 'cause you're gonna go through my stuff?—*They'd love that.* They'd pretend I hurt their feelings and then, boy, would I get it. I mean these guys are hard, Dave. One guy called Special Ed—he sleeps on broken glass. And not a scratch. And Tom Cat has part of his cheekbone exposed from an accident—and they use it as the company bottle opener, Dave. But these guys are small potatoes compared to "The Dog." That's what they call him. "The Dog." This is one weird fucking guy, Dave. It's the first night I'm there under this bridge and I ask if it's okay that I stay. They say, "It's okay with us, but you've got to ask The Dog." Okay, I say, who's The Dog? And they point to this hairy guy who's crouched down by part of the trestle. So, I walk over and say "Are you The Dog?" And he looks at me and smiles and there's just two teeth left in his head—and even they're goners, Dave— and he says, "Yes. Please have a seat." So, I do. I mean, here's this grimy, hairy vagabond with the manners of a butler. So, I ask The Dog if I can stay with them and he says "Of course. Of course. If you can manage the responsibility." I say, *"What?"* He says, "See that skyline? Someday that will all be yours." I say, *"What?"* "I hope you're ready because sooner or later we own every building in this city. It's part of our inheritance. As survivors of mankind's ingenuity we are heirs and someday, son, this will all be yours. The older it gets, the closer we get. *(He is now standing above Not Dave.)* Just wait for it to die. Just wait right here where the twelvepack is captain and the bottle is king. Wait right here with rubbish and the scavengers. Wait right here with the roaches and the dogs, the roaches and the dogs, *roaches and dogs, roaches and dogs and dogs and dogs dogs dogs dogs dogs dogs!" (Howls like a mad dog, stops abruptly.)* And then he dropped down and scratched his ear with his foot, Dave. He took this empty twelvepack and he jammed it on my head and said "I christen you *Captain Twelvepack.* Remove this and forfeit your inheritance." And then we drank and drank and drank and I snuck away and coiled myself as tight as I could under that bridge and tried to be invisible and hoped some deranged fucker didn't kill me while I was still awake. *(Silence, he slowly sits back down.)* I can't be like them, Dave. I look at these guys and they know they could be me and have money and teeth. And I look at them and I know that no amount of hardship could give me that soul. I can't have that soul. Shit. *(Pause.)* Hey, I'm making you sweat. You're not doing that just to cheer me up, are you, Dave? You're all right, Dave. Care for a smoke? *(Checks his coat very briefly.)* Oh, I'm all out—You got one? Well, how about you give me change and I'll go get some? Well, how 'bout giving me a buck, I'll get change? Well, how 'bout *loanin'* me a buck? Hey, there's no reason to get uppity, Dave. Conversation is free, shit, sorry I'm alive and now I must depart. *(Stands.)* Keep your sword sharp and your senses dull. And say "Hi" to my wife for me, Dave. I'd tip my hat, but as heir to the city, it would not be wise. *(He moves down the aisle and stumbles again onto Gladys.)* One side, sultry wench. I said, one side. I ought to ravage you on the spot. Have my way with you. *(Pause.)* Good lord…how could I be so blind? Your beauty overwhelms me. I am drawn to you like a magnet. *(Which he is.)* Come away with me and be my queen. Come on. Yes, you can. Yes, you can. Yes. Yes. *(Pause.)* What? A gun? *(Turns to face back of bus.)* Behind me, fair maid. Bullets cannot harm me. Leave this Saxon dog to me. Hold him steady, stable boy. I'll speed his soul to hell! *Da-da-da!!! (He charges the back of the bus as the lights go to black. Two gunshots are heard.)* Dave, I am slain.

(Blackout at the Super America. The actor is changing into Steve.)

CASHIER: May I help you?

CUSTOMER: Yeah, I want a brownie.

RON HUBER: Hey, what's this doing here?

CUSTOMER: Are these things fresh?

CASHIER: We get them fresh every day from Mrs. Moms.

RON HUBER: Lady. What's this doing here?

CASHIER: What? That's cream.

RON HUBER: Yeah, well where's the Coffee Mate?

CASHIER: We ran out so we had to use real cream.

RON HUBER: Christ. First the cinnamon triangles and now this. This place is going to hell. What? What, am I supposed to put that liquid shit in perfectly good coffee?

CASHIER: Look, cream is better than powder. It's more healthy for you.

RON HUBER: You think I come to SA for my health. Now you march to the back and get me some Coffee Mate, young lady. I got a bus waiting.

CASHIER: I told you, we're all out.

RON HUBER: Well, I can't drink it black.

CASHIER: Look, we sell Coffee Mate. You can buy a jar of it in aisle three if you want it that bad.

RON HUBER: What, you want me to buy five gallons of the shit when all I need is four tablespoons? Where's the manager of this place?

CASHIER: I told you we're all out.

RON HUBER: Then find some. I come to SA because I know I won't be surprised like this. I got faith in SA and once one goes *(Makes the raspberry sound.)* the whole franchise is shot, as far as I'm concerned. So you find my Coffee Mate or lose a regular customer.

CASHIER: I'll look in the back.

RON HUBER: Good.

(Lights up. Captain Twelvepack's helmet remains on his chair. Steve enters very slowly, walking with extra care and breathing loudly. He gets to Gladys and pauses for a moment.)

STEVE: Hi, Gladys. *(He continues toward the back of the bus. He reaches his seat and sits.)* Steve told me to stay here and don't move an inch. *(He looks to the seat right next to him, where "Steve" sits. Then he moves one inch.)* There. What do you think of that, Steve? Oh, come on, you big baby. I told you I was sorry. Come on, Steve, talk to me. *(To audience:)* Steve and I aren't talking now 'cause I made him mad. Real mad. We were at the doctor's and got in a big fight. A real big fight and now things look bad for us. Especially Steve. He enjoys his freedom and now it's in jeopardy. We might have to live in confinement for a while and Steve blames me. So we aren't talking. *(To Steve:)* Steve Steve Steve Steve Steve. *(To audience:)* Nope...clammed up. I don't mind. I make friends easily. It's a gift. But Steve holds a grudge. It's his own fault, though. See, Steve is really smart and can look at something and never forget what it looks like. Ever. He can tell you how to build a Piper Cub 'cause he saw the plans once. Or he can tell you the highest elevation of every continent. But he thinks he's really cool 'cause he can name all the cities in the world that have a K-Mart. In alphabetical order. *(To Steve:)* Well, who can't, Steve? *(To audience:)* So, this morning we were at the doctor's office and Steve wanted to show how smart he was 'cause he knows they're thinking about locking us up. So, he starts going through the K-Marts beginning with "A". Well, I read this morning in the paper they're opening a new K-Mart in Burnsville. I'm sitting there nice and quiet and polite the whole time he and the doctor are talking and then Steve starts reciting and gets to the "B's" and ooops—he missed Burnsville. So, I calmly say, "Burnsville." 'cause I didn't want Steve to look bad in front of the doctor. I was only trying to help and Steve said, "What?" And I said, "Burnsville, Steve." And he said, "What about it?" And I said, "There's a K-Mart in Burnsville." Steve goes "Huh uh" and I go "Uh huh" and Steve goes "Huh uh" and I go "Uh huh, I just read it in the paper today." And then Steve really lost his cool and yelled at me to shut up or else. And I go "I was just trying to help, Steve." And Steve goes "That kind of help is gonna get us put away." And then we really had a plate smasher. *(Pause.)* The doctor looked confused at first, but then he called a big dude in white and he broke it up. *(To Steve:)* That is, too, how it went. Uh huh. Uh huh. Uh huh. You did too miss Burnsville. You got problems, pal. (Pause, angry) Take that back, Steve. Take it back or else. *(Watching Steve's movements.)* What are you doing now, Steve? Are you going to eat your lunch? No? You're going to eat that apple? No? You're going to throw that apple? At me? *(Stands and laughs, moving toward Not Dave.)* Oh, Steve, I am shaking in my boots. You better not throw that, Steve, you might hurt your wimpy little arm. C'mon, Steve, you couldn't hit the broadside of a K-Mart! *(Sidesteps the toss and laughs, returning to his seat.)* Ha-ha. Missed me by a mile. Oh, now we're not talking again. See, Steve's good around other people—but I can really tic him off. *(To Steve:)* So...they're sending us away. I wonder where we'll go. St. Peter, maybe. St. Cloud, maybe. Alexandria, maybe. Stillwater, maybe. Shakopee, maybe. Sandstone, maybe. Burnsville, maybe—God, I hope not. I don't know, but after that last outbreak we're going somewhere. *(To audience:)* See, people think Steve has an invisible friend. But I'm not, really. So, when Steve has a big fight with me all they see is Steve going bonkers. They're afraid he'll hurt himself. They've got good reason cause he's tried before. He tried to kill himself when he was little. See, Steve has always been uncoordinated— sorry, Steve, but it's true—and the other kids would torment him. Well, who could blame 'em? So, when it came time to swim, Steve wouldn't go in the water 'cause he knew he'd sink and everyone would laugh. So, the teacher tossed him in. Steve could've stood up easy, but instead he let out all his air and went to the bottom and pretended to pour a cup of tea and drink it. Then he put down the cup and laid down. Right there in the pool. They finally pulled him out, but he was in a coma and stayed that way for days. When he came to, I was there. And I've been with him ever since. See, I won't let him hurt himself. People don't know I help him. They always want to break us up. Even Gladys tried. She's the lady up there with all the cat food. She tried to tell Steve I wasn't here. She tried and tried and tried. Gladys would go "Okay, Steve, you're by yourself now. It's just you and me, honey." And I'd be sitting right there! And I couldn't help but laugh, and when I laugh Steve always laughs. *(To Steve:)* Right, Steve? *(To audience:)* Still ticked. One time Gladys goes "Okay, Steve, close your eyes." And he did. And then she goes "Now when you open them your friend will be gone." Steve said, "No, he won't." But while his eyes were closed I snuck up and hid behind another seat on the bus and when he opened them, I was gone. And boy did he scream bloody murder. And then I jumped up and said "Steve" and we laughed and laughed and— *(To Steve:)* Oh, you smiled, Steve. *Uh huh. Uh huh. Uh huh.* You're such a liar. *(Reaches in pocket.)* I didn't want to have to do this, Steve. Oh no. Not that. Anything but that. Please, no. *(He pulls out a standard sized rubberband from his pocket and stretches it around his head at forehead level. As he opens his mouth and eyes wide, the rubberband creeps toward the crown of his head, taking all his hair with it—finally jerking all the hair up into an instant ponytail. He accompanies this with a slowly building scream that crescendos at the proper moment. Then, he turns back to Steve for his reaction.)* Oh, you smiled. Yes, you did. *Uh huh. Uh huh. Uh huh. Uh huh.* You got problems, pal. *(To audience:)* Now, when we get sent away, they're going to tell Steve I'm not here, maybe. Or they'll make Steve hate me, maybe. Or they'll drug him so he can't see me, maybe. That's okay, we fight a lot these days, anyhow. If they do send me away, Steve, you'll have to behave. I won't be there to talk you out of being stupid. I'm not worried. Stick to things you know. Like Piper Cubs. Okay? I'll miss you, Steve. *(Follows Steve movements with his eyes.)* Steve—don't do that. Let him go! Steve, let him go! *Sssssssssstttttttttttteeeeeeeeevvvvvvvveeeeeeeeee!* *(Blackout. Two gunshots. The last blackout at the Super America. The actor changes into Jim Shiply.)*

CASHIER: *(Taped.)* Here we go. I found two packets, but that's it.

RON HUBER: *(Taped.)* Thanks. Look I'm sorry I made such a ruckus over the Coffee Mate.

CASHIER: It's OK. I understand.

RON HUBER: It's just when your body gets used to something you don't like to throw it out of whack.

CASHIER: Yeah, I know. I'm the same way with hot tamales at a movie.

RON HUBER: Oh, yeah?

CASHIER: Yeah. I don't care how good the show is or who I'm with, if I don't have hot tamales I fidget.

RON HUBER: Yeah. I've heard of that.

CASHIER: I can't explain it.

RON HUBER: No sense trying.

CASHIER: But it limits me.

RON HUBER: Yeah, yeah it does that...

CASHIER: And you like to think you can do anything.

RON HUBER: Yeah. Hey, look I gotta get out of here.

CASHIER: But then you realize you're only human. Excuse me. Clear on number three. Where were we?

RON HUBER: Hey, look I gotta run.

CASHIER: OK, is that is?

RON HUBER: Yeah. That'll do it.

CASHIER: It comes to a dollar thirty-seven.

RON HUBER: Thanks again. I'll be seeing you.

CASHIER: Have a nice day.

RON HUBER: Yeah, you too.

(Two gunshots are heard. Lights come up on Jim Shiply. He has a gun and it's pointed at the seat Steve was in—the Steve the audience saw. There are two bullet holes in the seat. The rubberband sits on the seat, also. Jim Shiply is very nervous.)

JIM SHIPLY: Ah! Look what you made me do, kid. *(He points the gun at the Steve who tried to grab him.)* Sit down. *Sit down. (Jim follows Steve in his seat with the gun.)* OK, thanks. Now it's my turn. Nobody move. Nobody panic. *(He suddenly whirls the gun on the Student.) What!* What do you want?...Well, you don't have to raise your hand, kid. Just speak...Him? *(He points to Captain Twelvepack.)* He can't be dead, I shot over here. *(He points to bullet holes.)* Look he's breathing, see? *(Points back to Twelvepack.)* See that? He's passed out. He's a drunk and he's passed out, that's all. *(Points at the Steve he can see.)* You, kid, calm down. *(Levels the gun on Steve.)* I said, calm down. Thanks, OK, look everybody, nobody is dead yet. But now I'm nervous. That's just something we're going to have to deal with. This is not a robbery. I repeat, this is not a robbery. But I'm going to need all your money. So, starting with the lady in the front, take out all your money and hand it to the person behind you until it all gets back to me. Go. *(During this Jim Shiply moves the gunpoint from one char-*

acter to another. After the Student he says:) I love a quiet bus. *(He continues to point at Not Dave and then Steve. He looks at Steve's hand.)* A dollar seven cents? That's it? That's all the money on this bus? OK. Now I'm mad. That's something else we have to deal with. Somebody is holding out. People must die. First, the kid. *(Points the gun at Steve and then whirls it on the Student.)* What! I told you, you don't have to raise your hand. Well, what is it?…Yeah. I was going to do that. *(Points at Not Dave.)* You. Dave. Reach in his pockets. *(Points to Captain Twelvepack.)* He called you Dave. Why would he call you Dave if that's not your name? Look I've got the gun, your name is Dave, reach in his pockets. *(Jim Shiply stands and goes to Captain Twelvepack. He watches Not Dave reach in the pocket.)* Yuck. What the hell is that? No. No, I've seen enough put it back. *(Goes to the Student.)* OK. What about you? Wait a minute, are you a student? Oh. *(He turns away.)* Forget it then. *(He goes to Chairman Francis.)* You, let's have the collection plate. Nothing? All day? You should have hit a number six. *(He goes to Gladys.)* That leaves you, lady. All of it on pot pies and cat food? All right. I tried. A dollar seven cents, that's it. I tried. Kid. Come here. *(He points the gun at Steve and keeps it trained on him until Steve is right next to the barrel.)* Put the money in the till, and sit down. *(Jim Shiply follows Steve to the till. The sound of money running through a bus till is heard. Jim watches Steve go back to his seat then turns to the till.)* There you go. Drink it down. Nice and easy. There you go. You'll be all right now. *(He puts the gun in his pocket and suddenly turns around.)* That's where your money goes! I watched each one of you get on the bus and forget the till. It's leeches like you that sit in your climate controlled environment and refuse to feed the bus. And when you starve the bus you strangle the flow and it kills the system! Why don't you litter for God's sake? Why don't you eat or drink or smoke? Why don't you parade around with electronic devices while you're at it? Or interfere with the operator? Huh? We can abuse the system right? It won't die. We can afford to lose a route. Sure. We could even lose this route, right? We'd still have a hundred and twenty-two routes left. So big deal. And even if we lost a few more, who cares? So we lose our Saturday service to Rosedale and we drop from second in the nation, behind LA to eighth…behind St. Louis. So what, right? And so we lose convenience fares or Project Mobility. Who cares about the handicapped? And Seniors, they can pay full fare just like the rest of us. Well, not on my bus. Not while I'm abroad. Not while I'm alive…And have a gun. OK. Look. Say it's cold out…Twenty below. And dark…midnight. And I'm lost in a strange part of town. But I have seventy-five cents. Seventy-five cents. *(Goes to Gladys.)* Seventy-five cents will get me home to the ones I love. *(To Chairman*

Francis:) Seventy-five cents buys me a captive audience. *(To the Student:)* Get me an education. *(To Captain Twelvepack.)* A place to sleep. *(To Not Dave:)* It buys me friends when I need them. *(To Steve:)* And gets rid of them when I don't. And my seventy-five cents insures me that next bus will be there when I need it. And if I don't have correct change…I buy a comb. *(He pulls out a handful of combs.)* I will not bother the driver. The driver…If you people had your way this would just be another man out of a job, right? Another man who worked while you slept. A man who was responsible for every action on this bus. The man is a god. Revere him. And take care of your system or it will die. I've got to go now, I'm due on a seventeen. And maybe the next time you get on this bus I won't be here… *(The following lines are done live in the darkness as the actor moves from the back of the bus to the front. Jim's cap ends up on his chair.)* …But maybe I will.

STEVE: Steve. Steve. Over here. He missed me by a mile. Steve, talk to me. Oh, now you're ignoring me. Come on Steve.

CAPTAIN TWELVEPACK: Dave. Dave.

NOT DAVE: What?

CAPTAIN TWELVEPACK: I knew you were Dave.

STUDENT: Pardon me, sir, before you leave, I have a question.

CHAIRMAN FRANCIS: And it came to pass that Prophet Francis was not assassinated and went on to become minister of local bus service.

GLADYS: You robbers make me sick. Those robbers make me sick. Did you see that bullet? It missed me by an inch. I can't wait to tell Little Bob. *(Lights come up as Ron Huber enters.)*

RON HUBER: Whoa…look at that guy. Start mashing the potatoes. Sorry I'm late, folks, they ran out of Coffee Mate at the SA. Can you believe that? Anything happen while I was out? Everybody get their money in the till? All right. *(He sits in the driver's seat and calls out the first stop.)* Lake Street. *(The lights fade to black.)*

END OF PLAY

Fun

by Howard Korder

Howard Korder was born November 24, 1957 in New York City and graduated with a BA in Theater from the State University of New York at Binghamton. His play *Boy's Life* was presented by Lincoln Center in 1988, directed by W.H. Macy and featuring the Atlantic Theatre Company, and received a nomination for the Pulitzer Prize. It is produced frequently at theaters here and around the world. Other plays include *Night Maneuver* (1982); *The Middle Kingdom* (1985); *Lip Service* (1985), his adaptation of which was broadcast by HBO in 1989, winning cable television's Ace Award for best theatrical presentation; *Episode 26* (1985); *Fun* (1987); *Nobody* (1987); *Search and Destroy* (1990) and *The Lights* (1993).

Search and Destroy was commissioned by California's South Coast Repertory, premiering there in 1990 under the direction of David Chambers. He received the Los Angeles Theatre Critics' Award for best new play, and the Joseph Kesselring Prize from the National Arts Club. A production at Yale Repertory Theatre followed, and the play opened on Broadway at Circle in the Square in 1992. A critically acclaimed production of *Search and Destroy* opened at the Royal Court Theatre in London in May 1993 under the direction of Stephen Daldry. A film version, produced by Martin Scorcese, was released in 1995. Korder's play *The Lights* was produced at Lincoln Center Theater in Fall 1993 under the direction of Mark Wing-Davey and received seven Drama Desk nominations and an Obie Award for Playwrighting.

Boys' Life, Fun, Nobody, Search and Destroy, The Lights, Night Maneuver, and *The Pope's Nose* (a collection of short plays) are available in published form from Dramatists Play Service. *The Middle Kingdom, Lip Service* and *Episode 26* are published by Samuel French. *Boys' Life, Fun, Nobody, The Middle Kingdom, Lip Service*, and *Search and Destroy* are also available from Grove Press.

ORIGINAL PRODUCTION

Fun premiered in the 1987 Humana Festival of New American Plays at Actors Theatre of Louisville. It was originally directed by Jon Jory with the following cast:

Casper	Doug Hutchison
Denny	Tim Ransom
Security Guard	Nick Bakay
Waitress	Lili Taylor
Matthew	David Bottrell
Larry	Dana Mills
Workman	Andy Backer

Fun and *Nobody* were later presented as a double bill by the Manhattan Punch Line (Steve Kaplan, Artistic Director; Craig Bowley, Executive Director) in New York City. The production opened on November 6, 1987. It was directed by W.H. Macy. The cast, in order of appearance, was as follows:

Casper	Rick Lawless
Denny	Tim Ransom
Guard	Andrew Winkler
Waitress	Eden Alair
Matthew	Clark Gregg
Larry	Jim McDonnell
Workman	David Jaffe

CHARACTERS

DENNY: a 15-year-old boy   CASPER: his friend, also 15
LARRY: a salesman, late twenties MATTHEW: a movie usher, 19
WAITRESS: 14   WORKMAN: forties
SECURITY GUARD

TIME: The present. An evening in spring.
PLACE: The outskirts of Roberson City, an industrial town in the northeastern United States.

A NOTE ON THE CHARACTERS: In both dress and manner, Denny and Casper should present the image of two normal teenagers, not hard-core punks, metal heads or confirmed sociopaths.

FUN

Casper sitting on the front steps of a house with a boom box playing. Denny enters.

DENNY: Dickwad.

CASPER: Hey Denny.

DENNY: How's it going.

CASPER: I don't know.

DENNY: Uh-huh.

CASPER: You know.

DENNY: Right.

CASPER: How's it going with you.

DENNY: Sucks.

CASPER: Yeah.

DENNY: *(Indicating box.)* Motley *Crüe*.

CASPER: The best.

DENNY: New album?

CASPER: No. *(Pause.)*

DENNY: So what I miss today?

CASPER: Nothing. Exponents.

DENNY: Shit.

CASPER: Little numbers.

DENNY: You take notes?

CASPER: Uh-huh.

DENNY: Thanks.

CASPER: Sure.

DENNY: Thursday, you know? I just couldn't get into it. My head hurt all morning.

CASPER: Yeah, smoke's coming in off the Monsanto plant. *(Pause.)*

DENNY: So you doing anything?

CASPER: Nope.

DENNY: Wanna do something?

CASPER: I don't know. My mom's out, I'm supposed to hang around.

DENNY: Where's she out.

CASPER: On a date.

DENNY: Same dude?

CASPER: No. *(Pause.)* What were you gonna do?

DENNY: Have some fun. I don't know.

CASPER: Well…

DENNY: You wanna?

CASPER: Sure, I don't know. I gotta be back soon.
DENNY: Okay, so let's go. *(They exit.)*

SCENE TWO
The railing of a bridge. Roar of cars. Casper with boom box.

DENNY: This sucks.
CASPER: Yeah.
DENNY: Shit people throw outta cars...
CASPER: It's disgusting.
DENNY: PICK UP YOUR FUCKING GARBAGE, ASSHOLES!
CASPER: WOULD YOU DO THAT AT HOME? *(Pause.)* They got the windows up.
DENNY: They got the AC on. The *cruise* control...they got dinner on the table... *(Mimicking a driver.)* "Thank God *we* don't have to *live* here..."
CASPER: Yup.
DENNY: Fuck *them. (Pause. He looks over the railing.)* I mean lookit that *water.*
CASPER: Okay.
DENNY: You ever look what's in this river?
CASPER: No.
DENNY: You know what I *found* in there once?
CASPER: What.
DENNY: A finger.
CASPER: No.
DENNY: Yes.
CASPER: No way.
DENNY: I did.
CASPER: A whole finger?
DENNY: Most of a finger.
CASPER: Did you pick it *up?*
DENNY: Uh-huh.
CASPER: You didn't.
DENNY: Fuck you, I did.
CASPER: No way.
DENNY: Don't believe me.
CASPER: Whose finger was it?
DENNY: Jesus, the fuck would I know? It wasn't *autographed.*
CASPER: Okay.
DENNY: Some *dead* guy. Some guy jumped off drowned himself in the river.
CASPER: If he drowned himself, how'd he cut off his finger?
DENNY: How?
CASPER: Yeah.
DENNY: Casper, watch out.
CASPER: What?

DENNY: There's something on your neck.

CASPER: Where, get it off!

DENNY: Right…there. *(He flicks Casper's Adam's apple with his finger.)*

CASPER: Ah, shit!

DENNY: You wad.

CASPER: That hurt.

DENNY: *Supposed* to hurt.

CASPER: You could of killed me. You could of broke my wind thing.

DENNY: You'd be dead.

CASPER: I *would* be.

DENNY: Then I could just dump you in the water.

CASPER: *(Feeling his throat.)* I'm practically numb.

DENNY: Bye-bye.

> *(He picks up a stone and throws it in the water. Casper does the same. Pause.)*

CASPER: How far you think we could get on this river?

DENNY: *On* it.

CASPER: Like a raft or something.

DENNY: Who are you, Huckleberry Pinhead?

CASPER: I'm just saying.

DENNY: Jeez, bring your camera, you can get great pictures of old refrigerators. *(Pause.)* So what do you want to do?

CASPER: I don't know. You wanna go to the mall?

DENNY: God, no.

CASPER: You wanna find a party?

DENNY: Who's having a party?

CASPER: I don't know, you wanna see a movie?

DENNY: *What* movie? *(Pause.)*

CASPER: You wanna find some girls? *(Pause.)*

DENNY: Let's check out the mall.

SCENE THREE
> The Mall. A bench with a large potted plant behind it. Muzak playing in the background.

DENNY: This is fucking *stupid*.

CASPER: Yeah.

DENNY: I hate this place. You know how much time we spend in this place?

CASPER: A lot of time.

DENNY: It's like we grew up in here.

CASPER: They got everything, all right. Anything you can think of, it's right in front of you.

DENNY: People dressing themselves up to look at *shoes*. You count the number of shoe stores in this mall? Lookit Thom McCann, and Kinney, and Florsheim, Fayva, National Shoes…

CASPER: Sears.

DENNY: Shoe stores, you hole.

CASPER: They sell shoes at Sears. I got my Ponys there.

DENNY: You know who shops at Sears? Zombies in plaid shirts. They go in there and price band saws.

CASPER: My mother shops at Sears.

DENNY: Mine does too. Is that tasteless or what? She wants me to wear that shit, I told her to go fuck herself.

CASPER: You told her that?

DENNY: I would. I will. Her and my father. Right before I take off.

CASPER: Where you going? *(Pause.)*

DENNY: Check out that car.

CASPER: Excellent car.

DENNY: Gimme *that* car, man.

CASPER: Is that a Camaro?

DENNY: Looks it. Turbo Cammie.

CASPER: How'd they get it in here?

DENNY: They *drove* it.

CASPER: Camaro's a bitching car.

DENNY: Camaro's the best. *(Pause.)* Know what we could do?

CASPER: What?

DENNY: Get in that car, jump start her, tear ass off that platform all through this mall. Mow these fuckers down in their Hush Puppies.

CASPER: Except the girls.

DENNY: Crash it through the plate glass, man, bam through the GNC, bam through the Hickory Farms—

CASPER: Smoked *cheese*—

DENNY: Bam through the Radio Shack, the fucking Waldenbooks—

CASPER: Bam!

DENNY: Then we ditch it in the fountain, right, we break some forty-fours outta Monty Wards, a couple of hunting knives, ammo, and we head upstairs, way up in the mall where no one ever goes, and there is this dude up there, okay, this fat asshole in a control room, all these screens and shit, and he runs the place, he plays all the Muzak and makes the people walk around and smile and buy things only they don't even *know* it, and we shove him down on the counter and blow his fucking brains out.

CASPER: *(Making machine-gun noises.)* Chaka-chaka-chaka!

DENNY: *Except* when we turn around, da-dum...there's like eighty security guards standing there with sawed-offs. *(He makes the sound of a safety clicking.)*

CASPER: We go out the window!

DENNY: There's no *window*.

CASPER: Trapdoor?

DENNY: Forget it.

CASPER: Okay, but behind *them*—

DENNY: Uh-uh. We are on our own. *(Pause.)*

CASPER: What happens?

DENNY: They open up and spray us across the wall. *(Pause.)*

CASPER: *(Solemnly.)* In slo-mo.

DENNY: *Definitely* slo-mo.

   (They do their slo-mo death scenes with sound effects. Pause.)

CASPER: *(Tapping a plant leaf above his head.)* This is rubber or something, you
   know? All this time I thought it was real, but it's not.

   (Pause. A security guard walks by and looks at them.)

GUARD: Evening.

DENNY: How's it going.

GUARD: It's going.

   *(He stands there for a moment, then continues on. Denny and Casper watch
   him go.)*

DENNY: Let's lose this place.

CASPER: Where do you wanna go?

DENNY: I don't know.

CASPER: Okay.

SCENE FOUR

   A "Big Boy's" restaurant. Denny and Casper in a booth with menus.

CASPER: What are you gonna have, Denny?

DENNY: I don't know. Something that's less than three dollars cause that's all I got.

CASPER: I'm gonna have a hamburger.

DENNY: So *have* a hamburger.

CASPER: Only I had a hamburger for lunch.

DENNY: So *don't* have a hamburger. Jesus.

CASPER: But that was a Whopper. This is a Big Boy's burger. I don't know.

DENNY: It's the same cow, wad. *(Pause.)*

CASPER: What are you gonna have, Denny?

DENNY: *Ice* cream, okay? A sundae or something.

CASPER: No, I don't think I want that.

   (The waitress, high school age, enters.)

WAITRESS: Hi.

DENNY: How ya doing.

WAITRESS: Okay.

DENNY: Okay.

WAITRESS: You ready to order?

CASPER: You go first, Denny.

DENNY: Yeah, gimme a chocolate sundae.

WAITRESS: What kind of ice cream?

DENNY: Chocolate.

WAITRESS: You want hot fudge?

DENNY: Yeah, chocolate fudge.

WAITRESS: Sprinkles?

DENNY: Chocolate. Chocolate everything. Make the whole thing chocolate.

WAITRESS: You're into chocolate, huh?

DENNY: I like it, I wouldn't kill somebody for it.

WAITRESS: I would.

DENNY: Yeah?

WAITRESS: When you eat chocolate you're supposed to feel like you're in love.

DENNY: No kidding.

WAITRESS: I read that somewhere.

DENNY: Love is like chocolate, huh?

WAITRESS: That's what it said.

DENNY: Well. Hmm. Yeah. *(Pause. To Casper.)* You know what you want?

CASPER: Ah…oh boy…gimme, um, a stack of blueberry—no, no, give me a hamburger. A well done burger.

WAITRESS: You want that on a platter?

CASPER: Yeah, actually, are the burgers good here?

WAITRESS: They're okay.

CASPER: Compared like to Burger King?

WAITRESS: Well, they're okay. Is that what you want?

CASPER: Yeah, why not. Gimme that. No, actually, miss, can I have a sundae?

WAITRESS: Chocolate?

CASPER: Okay, yeah, chocolate.

WAITRESS: You sure?

CASPER: *(Looking at menu.)* Actually—

DENNY: *(Taking the menu away from Casper.)* He's sure. He's very very sure.

WAITRESS: Okay, two sundaes. *(She exits. Denny looks at Casper.)*

CASPER: What? Should I get something else?

(Denny turns away. Pause. Casper drinks his water and begins chewing the ice cubes.)

CASPER: Who you looking at, Denny?

DENNY: Nobody.

CASPER: You looking at those guys from Saunders? I don't like those guys.

DENNY: I'm not looking at anyone.

CASPER: Remember we bought those Iron Maiden tee's, and they ripped us off right at the bus stop?

DENNY: Uh-huh.

CASPER: I never even got to *wear* mine. How come that stuff always happens to us?

DENNY: Two kinds of people, Casper.

CASPER: Yeah? Which are we?

DENNY: The other ones.

(He looks away again. Casper chews his ice cubes. Pause.)

CASPER: So ask her out, Denny.

DENNY: Ask who.

CASPER: The waitress.

DENNY: Get fucked.

CASPER: I don't know, she's kinda cute.

DENNY: You're cute. *(Pause.)* You think I should?

CASPER: I don't know.

DENNY: You think she's cute?

CASPER: She's kinda cute.

DENNY: You think I should ask her out *tonight?*

CASPER: I don't mind.

DENNY: Where you think I should take her?

CASPER: You could take her to a restaurant.

DENNY: She's *in* a restaurant, you bone.

CASPER: You could go miniature golf.

DENNY: Geez, won't *that* be fun.

CASPER: I don't know, you could go walk on the bridge.

DENNY: What are we gonna do on a bridge?

CASPER: I'm just saying you could go for a walk and wind up on the bridge.
(Pause.)

DENNY: Yeah, we could do that. We could go to the bridge.

CASPER: I don't mind, Denny.

DENNY: Yeah, that would be pretty decent.

CASPER: I gotta get back anyway.

(Waitress enters with two sundaes.)

WAITRESS: Here we go.

CASPER: Wow, check this out.

WAITRESS: You want chocolate, you get chocolate.

DENNY: Great.

WAITRESS: Listen, I gave you nuts, okay? I didn't charge you so don't tell anybody.

DENNY: Okay.

WAITRESS: I mean I just felt like it.

DENNY: Thanks.

(She shrugs. Pause.)

DENNY: So...

WAITRESS: Yeah.

DENNY: You like working here or what?

WAITRESS: It's okay.

DENNY: They make you buy that uniform?

WAITRESS: No, they give it to you.

DENNY: That's good.

WAITRESS: Yeah. *(Pause.)*

DENNY: Umm, how long do you usually work?

WAITRESS: Another half hour. Ten-thirty.

DENNY: No kidding.

WAITRESS: Yeah.

DENNY: Hmm.

> *(Pause. She puts down the check.)*

WAITRESS: Have a good night.

DENNY: Oh yeah, you too.

> *(She exits. Casper begins eating his sundae. Denny picks up his spoon and sticks it in the ice cream.)*

DENNY: Let's go. This place fucking sucks.

> *(He stands, throws some money down, and leaves. Casper watches him and follows after a moment.)*

SCENE FIVE

> *The bridge. Roar of cars. Casper throwing bits of junk into the river. Denny carving on rail post with a house key. Boom box playing.*

CASPER: I don't know, I'm not doing so good in math. Actually I think he's gonna clip me.

DENNY: Fuck him.

CASPER: Yeah. But it's cool cause I'm thinking I could go to trade school.

DENNY: Toolbox U.

CASPER: Yeah, I could learn to do something with my hands.

> *(Denny snorts.)*

CASPER: That's what they teach!

DENNY: "Boys, today we're going to show how to *do* something with your *hands.*"

CASPER: It's only an idea. I gotta do something, don't I? I mean…I don't know. I don't think much is going to happen to me. It's just a feeling I get.

DENNY: Break outta this dump.

CASPER: Yeah, I could always join the army.

DENNY: Right.

CASPER: You wanna join the army, Denny?

DENNY: Sure, we're in the army.

CASPER: We'd fight, wouldn't we? I'd fight, I would. Right?

DENNY: Jesus, Casper, talk about something important.

CASPER: Like what?

> *(Denny says nothing.)*

CASPER: What you doing, Denny?

DENNY: Carving.

CASPER: What's that, a Hitler thing?

DENNY: It's called a swastika.

CASPER: How come you're doing that?

DENNY: Cause I feel like it, Goldberg.

CASPER: My name's not Goldberg.

DENNY: Put another tape on, why dontcha.

CASPER: I don't got another.

DENNY: Then turn on the *radio*.

CASPER: The antenna's broke.

DENNY: Let's go riding.

CASPER: How we gonna–

DENNY: Oh, let's just get wasted!

CASPER: You got proof? I don't think–

(Denny leaps up and screams wordlessly over the bridge. Pause.)

CASPER: You okay, Denny? *(Pause.)* Denny? *(Pause.)*

DENNY: Do you have any shit on you?

CASPER: Geez, I don't.

DENNY: I am going to score some shit.

CASPER: How?

DENNY: I'm going to find a *guy* he owes me a *favor* and we're going to fuck ourselves up. That's what I *want*. that's what's going to *happen*. *(He starts off.)*

CASPER: Where we going, Denny?

DENNY: *(Exiting.)* We're *going* to the *mall*.

(Casper takes the boom box and follows him off.)

SCENE SIX

    *A parking lot outside the movie theater in the mall. A dumpster sits overflow-
ing with garbage, including several large plastic bags of popcorn. Casper, with
boom box, rests on one of the bags. Denny leans against the dumpster.*

CASPER: *(Looking out; after a moment.)* You know, the parking lot looks really
beautiful this time of night. I mean without a lot of cars all over it.

DENNY: It's a poem, Casper.

CASPER: Yeah, I guess so. *(Pause.)* What are we waiting for, Denny?

DENNY: He's gonna come around and meet us.

CASPER: You got any money? I only got like eighty cents.

DENNY: It's cool, I *know* this guy. He owes me.

(Casper starts eating popcorn out of a torn bag.)

DENNY: Don't eat that, it's garbage.

CASPER: It's just popcorn. You can't do anything to popcorn. *(He finds a dis-
carded movie poster.)* Hey, Rambo, remember Rambo? Check out this gun,
Denny. Man, that is *wicked*. *(Imitating a bazooka.)* Ba-doom! Suck on
this, slope, we're coming back!

DENNY: You're the slope.

CASPER: Ba-doom!

(Denny picks up a bag of popcorn and throws it at Casper. He misses.)

CASPER: Missed me! You missed you–

(Denny clubs him with another bag.)

DENNY: Stop acting like a child.

(He drops the bag on Casper's head. Casper "dies." Matthew enters in usher's uniform.)

MATTHEW: Yo, man, don't fuck around with the popcorn.

DENNY: It's in the garbage.

MATTHEW: No, no, my buddy's coming with a van, we're gonna sell it to this porno movie on South Washington. *(He picks some popcorn off the ground.)* That look clean?

DENNY: Yeah.

(Matthew puts it in the bag.)

DENNY: Matt, you know Casper?

MATTHEW: The friendly ghost.

(Casper laughs.)

MATTHEW: How's your brother?

CASPER: I don't have a brother.

MATTHEW: How's your sister?

CASPER: She's okay.

MATTHEW: Oh yeah?

(He laughs. Pause. Casper laughs.)

MATTHEW: Pretty funny, huh? Listen, that's not for free. *(He takes the poster out of Casper's hand. Pause.)*

DENNY: So, Matty.

MATTHEW: Yo.

DENNY: How's college?

MATTHEW: I'm outta there, man.

DENNY: Seriously?

MATTHEW: Waste of my abilities. I'm into venture capital now. Very into the idea of thirty, forty million bucks, my own island, lots of barbed wire, babes, armored Mercedes fleet. I wanna get myself situated before the dark ages start blowing back. Won't be too hard. I got a good growth plan.

DENNY: No kidding.

MATTHEW: Yeah, I'll have that in ten years, tops.

DENNY: That's really excellent.

MATTHEW: It *is* excellent. What can I do for you?

DENNY: We're looking for some shit.

MATTHEW: You check the toilet?

(He looks at Casper. Casper laughs.)

MATTHEW: This man has a sick sense of humor.

(Casper laughs again.)

DENNY: Yeah, well, I thought you could help us out.

MATTHEW: Uh-huh, okay. *(Pause.)*

DENNY: Remember Christmas, I did some drops with you, you said come by I wanted anything.

MATTHEW: Huh.

DENNY: Yeah, up in Port Dickinson, I sat in the car.

MATTHEW: *Christmas.*

DENNY: Yeah. *(Pause.)*

MATTHEW: Okay, so what can I sell you?

DENNY: Well–

MATTHEW: You wanna check out some sess? You want a little marching powder?

DENNY: I thought maybe you could help us out here.

MATTHEW: How you want me to help you? Yo, Friendly, don't sit on the bags. Hmmm? *(Pause.)* You want me to give it to you?

DENNY: You said at Christmas–

MATTHEW: I didn't say I'd *give* it to you. I don't hand out free samples. I'd said I'd sell to you, I don't remember saying anything to you. Most guys, a fifteen-year-old-kid–

DENNY: I'm not fifteen–

MATTHEW: I'm developing a select clientele, you're lucky I–

DENNY: We went up to Port *Dick*inson–

MATTHEW: I don't deal up there.

DENNY: Ah, *shit*, man–

MATTHEW: HEY. You *control* yourself. People are watching a *movie* in there, they don't want to hear about your problems. The world does *not* turn around your navel. No. No, I'm sorry. *(He goes. Silence.)*

CASPER: Denny, you wanna go home? It's getting late, maybe it's time.

(Denny attacks the dumpster, flinging garbage out of it with his hands. Matthew reenters.)

MATTHEW: YO! *(He grabs Denny and bangs him against the dumpster, holding him there.)* The *fuck* is wrong with you? Where'd you grow up, in a cage? Kids, fucking kids, waste my time you don't know *what's* going on. You don't do business this way. Never. This is not how you *conduct* yourself. *(He smacks Denny in the head with the back of his hand.)*

MANAGER: *(Offstage.)* Pauling!

MATTHEW: Yes sir!

MANAGER: *(Offstage.)* You wanna let the people outta the theater?

MATTHEW: Yeah, okay, sorry! *(Pause. To Denny.)* You're furious, right? Look at me. Furious little kid. You gotta do something about that. You can't go spilling it all over the place. Keep it behind your eyes and don't let anyone see it. You know how a killer thinks?

DENNY: How?

MATTHEW: He doesn't get excited. *(Pause.)* All right. I got some dealing up on Chenango later, you meet me there. Ten-twelve Chenango, across from the sausage factory. Maybe I'll have something for you, maybe I won't. I can't make promises. *(Pause.)*

DENNY: When.

MATTHEW: A couple hours. Two, three hours.

DENNY: Okay.

MATTHEW: You wanna check out a movie?

DENNY: Huh?

MATTHEW: A movie, I'll walk you in. There's a midnight show.

DENNY: What's playing?

MATTHEW: *E. T. II.*

DENNY: What else?

MATTHEW: That's it. All six movies.

DENNY: No.

MATTHEW: Suit yourself. Hey, give me your radio. Come on.

CASPER: Why?

MATTHEW: Just give it. An exchange. Let's make a deal here.
   (Casper does not move.)

MATTHEW: No, okay, it's a favor. Overhead. Remember that. *(He starts to exit.
   He stops and turns to Denny.)* How's your father doing?

DENNY: Looking for a job. Waxing the car a lot. Drinking without a glass.

MATTHEW: Huh.

DENNY: Yup.

MATTHEW: Yeah, my Dad was talking about him. Tell him…he says hello.

DENNY: Right.

MATTHEW: Okay, catch you later. *(Matthew exits. Pause.)*

CASPER: I don't know, I kinda liked the first *E. T.*

DENNY: It was a fucking *puppet,* you wad.

CASPER: Yeah, I guess. *(Pause.)* What do you wanna do now, Denny?

DENNY: Go meet Marty.

CASPER: What do you wanna do in the meantime? I got eighty cents. You
   wanna do the Arcade?

DENNY: No.

CASPER: You wanna hang out at the Trailways station?

DENNY: Bunch of alkies waiting for a morning bus.

CASPER: You wanna go to Food World? It's open twenty-four hours. We could
   look at the magazines.
   (Denny just stares at him.)

CASPER: What do you wanna do?

DENNY: I want…to blow up a freight train. I want to hijack a jet. I want
   Madonna to jump off a poster and come sit on my dick. I want them to
   drop every bomb there is and be the only person left alive. I wanna be
   famous, and rich, and I want everybody to be scared of me. That's what I
   wanna do. *(Pause.)*

CASPER: Okay, but what do you wanna do *now?*

SCENE SEVEN

   *A small concrete patio behind a house. Chinese lanterns overhead on a string.
   Card table piled with party rubbish: bottles, potato chip bags, cups, etc. A
   folding chaise lounge, draped by a plastic tablecloth. Portable phonograph
   with a stuck record playing at low volume. A child's Big Wheel tricycle off to
   one side. Denny and Casper standing Center.*

CASPER: You sure this is it, Denny?

DENNY: It's the address he said.

CASPER: There's nobody here. Must of been a party or something, huh?

DENNY: No, it's a car wash. What time did they kick us out of the Food World?

CASPER: I don't know. One-thirty. Around one-thirty. Actually it was more like two.

DENNY: Bastards. Who wants to watch some pimply geek stack oranges anyway. *(He begins looking around.)*

CASPER: Maybe we shouldn't be in this guy's backyard.

DENNY: What are you scared of?

CASPER: I'm not scared.

DENNY: Then don't be. *(He looks at record on the phonograph.)* Jesus, *"Frampton Comes Alive." (He shuts it off.)* Let's have a drink.

CASPER: What if somebody sees us?

DENNY: We're here on business, drain. We got an appointment. Hey, Cutty my man!
    (He picks up a bottle from the table, takes a long swig, and offers it to Casper. Casper shakes his head.)

DENNY: Come on, don't pussy out.
    (Casper takes the bottle without drinking. He sits on the tricycle and slowly pedals it backwards and forwards.)

CASPER: If we join the army, Denny, you think we'd have to—

DENNY: *(Listening to something.)* Quiet!
    (Sound of a woman's laughter from offstage, followed by a man murmuring indistinctly. Laughter from both.)

CASPER: Where are they?
    (Denny points toward the house.)

CASPER: Can they see us?

DENNY: They're not looking at us.
    (More laughter, voices.)

CASPER: Well, *they're* having fun.

DENNY: You know what they're doing?

CASPER: What?

DENNY: What do you *think? (Pause.)*

CASPER: You think so?

DENNY: I bet they're down on the floor.

CASPER: Yeah?

DENNY: With a…with a *ski jacket* under her ass…and her…

CASPER: Her *legs*…

DENNY: …Her legs are open, and she's saying *please*…

CASPER: She's not…

DENNY: Please give it to me, *please*…

CASPER: She's *begging* him…

DENNY: No panties, and he's looking down at her…

CASPER: Oh God…

DENNY: And he says…

CASPER: He says...

DENNY: He says... *(Pause.)* Ah, shit. Who knows what he says. *(He walks over to the bottle and drinks. More laughter.)* Shut the fuck up.

CASPER: Maybe it's just the TV.

DENNY: *(Indicating tricycle.)* Doing that with kids around. That is disgusting.

CASPER: It is.

DENNY: A little kid sees something like that, he doesn't know what to think. He's fucked up for life. And then you know what, *he* has kids...

CASPER: And they're fucked up.

DENNY: And their kids...

CASPER: And *those* kids...

DENNY: Then *they*...

CASPER: It's like a disease.

DENNY: It's like a movie.

CASPER: It's a mess.

DENNY: They probably *are* fucking on the floor.

(More laughter. Pause.)

CASPER: I don't think he's coming, Denny. Or else he already did. Or something.

DENNY: Yah.

(A man's voice comes from beneath the cover of the lawn chair.)

VOICE: Jesus Christ, who shut off the *music?*

(Denny and Casper look at each other. Denny pulls the tablecloth off the chair. Underneath is Larry, dressed in a rumpled suit and tie.)

DENNY: Hi...ah, we...we were supposed to meet—

LARRY: *(As Elmer Fudd.)* Shh. Be verrry quiet, I'm hunting wabbits. *(He gets up, walks to a corner, and starts to urinate.)* This is one of the greatest pleasures known to man. I'm not lying. *(He buttons his fly and turns around.)* Am I right? Now don't *brood* about it.

DENNY: Sure.

LARRY: A *great* pleasure. Pleasure everywhere you look. That's life in a nutshell. And I think you'd probably agree with me, yes? Am I talking English? Hmmm? Am I?

DENNY: Uh-huh.

LARRY: Then why are you *looking* at me like that? Why are you—okay, okay, I know. I've been a bad boy. A bad, bad... *(Pause.)* Where is everybody?

DENNY: They're gone.

LARRY: Gone...where? Home? Did they go home? They can't go home. You can't go home again, didn't they prove that? I mean, scientifically? Look, I'm sorry, don't listen to anything I say. Just tell me—no, but listen to this—did she go? She didn't. She did. Did she?

DENNY: Who?

LARRY: Who, who I'm *saying*. Sandy. Sandra. The beautiful... *(Pause.)* She's gone.

DENNY: Yeah.

LARRY: All right. All right. I'm...sure. *(Pause.)*

DENNY: She left with some guy.

LARRY: Who?

DENNY: Just some guy.

LARRY: *Curse* him. *Kill* him. *Goddamn* that guy. Yeah. *(Pause.)* Hey. Hey, let's have fun. Let's all just do that. Simon says...open up that bottle there. Come on.

(Denny opens a bottle of Scotch.)

LARRY: Simon Says...pour three cups.

(Denny pours three paper cups.)

LARRY: Now drink. *(He drinks his cup.)*

DENNY: You didn't say Simon says.

LARRY: Listen, we're all friends here. Drink up. WAIT. How old are you guys?

DENNY: Nineteen.

LARRY: Nineteen. Great age. Beautiful age.

DENNY: Yeah, I'm nineteen, he's eighteen.

LARRY: Eighteen, a great age.

DENNY: The best.

LARRY: He doesn't *say* much.

DENNY: He likes to think.

LARRY: Who doesn't. What it *is,* man.

CASPER: Hi.

LARRY: So here we *are,* three really *happening* dudes, we're young, we're– *(Pause. He looks at them closely.)* Oh boy. I'm sorry. I can't believe the way I'm acting. Look at you two. Of *course* you are. I can't *believe* it. *(Pause.)* You don't remember me, do you?

DENNY: Ah...

LARRY: You don't, you don't! I can't believe it. I remember *you.* You're Michael and you're, um...Jeffrey.

CASPER: Casper.

LARRY: Casper, sure, sure. *Look* at you guys. You must be what, eighteen, nineteen by now, right?

DENNY: Right.

LARRY: And you don't remember Larry? I'm hurt, I'm hurt!

DENNY: You know, I think...

LARRY: Oh, come on, remember me and Sandy? Remember, I used to come around when you guys lived over on, what, Murray Street, geez, must be ten years.

DENNY: *(With a look to Casper.)* Larry, sure.

LARRY: Oh, fellas, your sister, your sister, I can't apologize eno–you *know* me, I wouldn't...but God she looked great tonight, she really ...she left with some guy, you know that?

DENNY: No.

LARRY: She did, some guy. I had a little drinks, I admit it, but I mean Sandy, ten years, I just *remembered...* *(Pause.)* Yeah. Little Mikey and Jeffy. Little kids. How come you guys grew up, and I'm not any older?

DENNY: I don't know, Larry, it's hard to say.

LARRY: It is, it's hard. It really is. *(Pause.)* Well, fuck it. Let's have some fun. Let's just do that.

DENNY: Okay.

LARRY: I mean what are we here for anyway. The night *beckons*. It's just out there beckoning away, huh? What do you wanna do?

DENNY: Us three?

LARRY: Damn straight. These bozos don't know the meaning of party. What do you want?

DENNY: Ah...

LARRY: You name it. Tell me. *Anything* you want to do.

DENNY: Anything?

LARRY: Anything. My little *buddies. (Pause.)*

DENNY: Well, frankly, Larry...we'd like to get laid.

LARRY: I also would like to get laid.

DENNY: So would we.

LARRY: The question is, how low are your standards?

DENNY: Pretty low.

LARRY: You guys been to Watsonville lately?

DENNY: Yeah.

LARRY: You been on Nanticoke Avenue?

DENNY: Uh-huh.

LARRY: You been in the whorehouse behind the Power Test?

DENNY: No.

LARRY: Then gentlemen, Paradise awaits.

DENNY: Only we don't got any money, Larry.

LARRY: No no. No money. My treat. Mikey and Jeffy. Little buddies. You just tell Sandra I...you say your main man Larry...you tell her...you just let her know.

DENNY: Okay.

LARRY: So...LET'S DO IT!

(He beats his chest. Tarzan-like, grabs a bottle, and runs off. Denny starts to follow.)

CASPER: Denny, I–

DENNY: Shut up. We're finally gonna have some *fun!*

(He exits. Casper gets his boom box and follows.)

SCENE EIGHT

Larry's car. Casper in back. Denny in front with Larry, who is driving very fast. The opening chords of Springsteen's "Born to Run" boom out of the car speakers.

LARRY: BROOOOOOCE! *(He sings along for a few lines, getting the words wrong. He takes a drink from the bottle and passes it to Denny.)* This is

GREAT. Isn't it? Isn't this just GREAT? Gimme a car, man! Gimme a
road! *(Sticking his head out the window.)* BAROOOOOOOOCE!

DENNY: Nice car, Larry.

LARRY: Isn't it? Isn't it *great?* It's the greatest car! I *live* in this car. I mean I *sleep*
in motels but I live in *this car.* And it's not even mine! It isn't! They *give* it
to me! For my *job!* I could wreck it if I want! Just squash it flat! *(He laughs
and takes his hands off the wheel.)* Brooo-ooce! *(He puts his hands back.
Pause.)* It's a great country, fellas. Isn't it a great country?

DENNY: The greatest, Larry.

LARRY: *(Turning the music down slightly.)* No, no, I'm serious. I am. You can say
what you want about it, but here it is, all of it, it's *right here.* The land…
the people…the *garbage.* Our garbage is the best garbage in the world, I
don't *care* what they say I love it. Now you *been* to California, Mikey.

DENNY: No.

LARRY: Oh, we all have to go to California, we have to! Everybody's young in
California, it's not like here. There's *nothing* here, it's all worn out. I
mean…you take a guy like me, huh? Right?

DENNY: Yeah.

LARRY: Let's take a guy who– *(He swerves the wheel suddenly.)* Whoa, that was a
fucking bump, did you see that? You okay there, Jeff?

CASPER: I'm fine.

LARRY: All right, a guy who, let's be honest, I had opportunities, *great* opportunities, and I threw them *away.* I had–I did very well on my SATs, you
know that, very well, the top of the percent–*experts* told me things and I
just did not listen, because *I* thought…I thought I *deserved…* well, fuck
what I *thought.* Here it is, right here. I'm selling industrial tubing out of a
rented car. Is that a disgrace? Is it?

DENNY: Um…

LARRY: I make a lot of money, thank you, I do very well indeed. You march in
there and turn it around, that's business. And there's no reason you can't–
(He swerves again.) Whoa, sorry, sorry–you can't come back home and
feel…something. Just…something. What I'm saying is…hey, guess how
old I am.

DENNY: I don't know, Larry.

LARRY: Guess!

DENNY: You're, ah–

LARRY: No, no, not you. Jeffy, Jeffy!

CASPER: Thirty-five?

LARRY: What? Jesus, no! I'm twenty-nine–twenty-eight. I'm your age. Well,
not–but you know. Rock and *roll!* Hey, remember I took you guys to go-
carts, you, me, and Sandy? You were scared to get on? Does your sister
ever talk about me? So who was that guy? No, don't tell me. *(Pause. They
drive in silence.)*

DENNY: Where we going, Larry?

LARRY: Huh?

DENNY: We're going to Watsonville, right?

LARRY: Oh, we're gonna have fun.

DENNY: Isn't it the other way? *(Pause.)*

LARRY: Right, yeah…Oh, but we're going to the motel first. I need some cash. These ladies don't come cheap. Actually I don't think they come at all. But they fake it pretty good. Huh?

DENNY: Sure.

LARRY: You *know* what I'm saying.

DENNY: Ah, Larry—

LARRY: The sweet spot, boys, it's just like coming home.

DENNY: Larry—

LARRY: Hey, you think they take credit cards? Maybe I could—

CASPER: *(Covering his face.)* WATCH OUT!

LARRY: What the— *(He swerves the car violently and slams the brakes. They plunge forward in their seats as the car stops. Silence.)*

DENNY: Jesus Christ.

LARRY: Son of a bitch.

DENNY: You okay?

CASPER: Uh-huh.

LARRY: Who put that asshole behind a wheel?

DENNY: You were on the wrong side of the *road,* Larry.

LARRY: No I wasn't. Was I?

DENNY: You almost got us killed! *(Pause.)*

LARRY: Ah…yeah…whoo. You know what it is, it's these rented cars. You take your life in your hands, they don't care. I tell you what, let's just, I just need to… *(He takes a drink from the bottle.)* Yeah, yeah, I'm just gonna take a second here and get my bearings, and then we'll—okay, I'm fine. I am. Actually I think I was supposed to be in Albany tonight, I don't know why I… *(He puts his head down and starts sobbing.)* Oh God…what am I doing here…my whole life…I want to be a baby, that's all…I just wanna be a baby… *(He cries some more, then becomes quiet. Pause.)*

DENNY: Larry? You okay? *(He shakes him tentatively. Larry does not stir. Denny leans him against the seat. Larry's head drops back, mouth open.)*

CASPER: Is he dead?

DENNY: He's asleep. Do you believe this guy?

CASPER: He drank too much.

DENNY: He's a fucking *basket* case. No wonder that girl dumped him. God, I don't wanna get old. Yo, wake up! *(No response from Larry.)* Can you drive?

CASPER: I'm not allowed.

DENNY: *Can* you.

CASPER: Not a stick.

DENNY: *(Turning off the tape deck.)* What *is* this shit? *(Pause.)*

CASPER: Are we having fun now, Denny?

(Denny pays him no attention. He is staring hard at Larry.)

CASPER: What you looking at?

DENNY: Nothing much.

CASPER: So? *(Pause.)*

DENNY: You know what we could do?

CASPER: What.

DENNY: We could…just…

CASPER: What?

(Denny reaches over and puts his hand on Larry's exposed throat. He strokes it gently. He looks at Casper, smiling. Casper laughs briefly. Denny puts his thumb and forefinger over Larry's Adam's apple. He presses it slightly. Larry grunts. He wraps his hand around Larry's throat. Larry grunts again without waking. Reaching forward.)

CASPER: Okay, Denny—

(Denny slaps him away with his other hand. He increases the pressure for several seconds. Suddenly Larry coughs and wakes. Denny takes his hand away. Larry looks at them, somewhat dazed. Pause.)

LARRY: What happened?

DENNY: You fell asleep.

LARRY: I did?

DENNY: Yah.

(Pause. Larry clears his throat.)

DENNY: You still wanna go to the motel?

LARRY: Motel?

DENNY: You said for money.

LARRY: Money, right. No problem. And we're going to…

DENNY: Watsonville.

LARRY: Right, Watsonville. *(Remembering.)* Watsonville, yeah! *(Pause.)* What's the car doing in a ditch? *(He looks at them and bursts out laughing. He turns on the tape deck, loud, and floors the pedal. They lurch forward in their seats.)* THIS IS FUCKING GREAT!

SCENE NINE

The upper terrace of a motel off the highway. Denny and Casper in front of a door.

DENNY: You sure this is his room?

CASPER: I thought I saw him go up here.

DENNY: *(Looking along the terrace.)* Christ, this place is built like a *dog* kennel. *(He leans into the door.)* Larry…Hey, Larry…What the fuck is he doing in there?

CASPER: He probably fell asleep.

DENNY: *Larry*…Shit, this isn't his room. Go down the office and ask the guy the room he's in.

CASPER: What should I ask him?

DENNY: Larry's fucking room!

CASPER: Larry *who?*

DENNY: Larry the fuck I don't know what his name is! *(Pause.)*

CASPER: There's nobody down there anyway, Denny. It's too late.

DENNY: *(Pounding on the doorway.)* WAKE UP! *(Pause.)* Where are we.

CASPER: I don't know. Up the Thruway somewhere. I wish I had like another shirt or something. It's getting kind of cold. It's weird, you know, in the daytime, it's hot and then—

DENNY: He said he was going to get us *laid*.

CASPER: Yeah.

DENNY: He was gonna take us and he was gonna *pay* for it! He *promised!*

CASPER: Well, that would of been nice.

DENNY: *Nice?* Don't you *want* it?

CASPER: It just didn't work out.

DENNY: No. Shit. He *promised.* We could be getting ourselves blown right now—

CASPER: I don't—

DENNY: We could! Right now by some *whore* with *big* tits. She'd *have* to, whatever we want!

CASPER: No she wouldn't.

DENNY: Bull*shit* she would, it's her job. I'd say go down on me and she'd do it!

CASPER: Come on, stop.

DENNY: Like a fucking *tootsie* pop…

CASPER: Oh geez…

DENNY: Right on me the whole night! *(Pause.)* Ah, how come I got to feel all this shit when there's nothing I can do about it? I don't wanna *be* like this! I mean why can't I get just ONE FUCKING THING? *(Pause.)*

CASPER: We could…jerk off.

DENNY: What?

CASPER: You know. Like in the Scouts.

DENNY: Are you sick?

CASPER: There's no one around.

DENNY: Me! I'm around! I don't wanna watch you humping your knuckles!

CASPER: I was only saying.

DENNY: Fucking disgusting! *(Pause.)* All right. But don't look at me.

CASPER: Huh?

DENNY: Don't *look* at me! Turn around. Come on, let's just get it over with!
    (They stand with their backs to each other, unzip their pants, and put their hands down their shorts. Denny does not move. Casper begins to masturbate and stops. Pause.)

DENNY: What the fuck am I doing?

CASPER: I don't know, Denny.

(They take their hands out of their pants.)

CASPER: Have you done it yet? With a girl?

DENNY: Yeah.

CASPER: Is it fun?

DENNY: It's a riot. *(Pause.)* Let's get outta here.

CASPER: We don't know where we are.

DENNY: Then it doesn't matter where we go.

CASPER: I guess not.

(Denny looks at Casper. Pause. He takes off his jacket.)

DENNY: Here.

(He throws him the jacket. Casper catches it. Denny exits.)

SCENE TEN

> *A concrete pillar beneath a highway overpass, covered with graffiti. Various kinds of junk shored up against the foot of the pillar, including a cushionless sofa, a broken armchair, and a discarded oven. Sound of steady rain mixed with the rumble of tractor-trailors passing by overhead. Denny and Casper stand with wet hair and rain-splattered clothes. They look out at the rain.*

CASPER: *(After a moment.)* Well, maybe we *shoulda* walked the other way.

DENNY: Great idea.

CASPER: I just thought that gas station looked familiar…I don't know. At least it's dry under here.

DENNY: It's perfect.

CASPER: April showers bring…what do they bring, Denny?

DENNY: Earthworms. Earthworms coming up all over the sidewalks. *(Taking off his wet T-shirt.)* Yach! *(He throws it off to the side, leaving him bare-chested.)*

CASPER: Here, Denny, take your coat back.

DENNY: Uh-uh.

CASPER: Come on, you'll get froze.

DENNY: I don't *want* it. *(Pause.)*

CASPER: You know what the Indians up here used to do? When they were like out in the forest at night? They'd dig a hole in the ground, then they'd lie down and cover themselves with leaves. It kept them warm. Only I don't see any leaves around.

DENNY: You don't see many Indians either.

CASPER: No, you don't.

DENNY: *(Moving to sofa.)* I'm gonna lie down.

CASPER: Smells of piss.

DENNY: All the comforts of home.

(He stretches himself out on the sofa. Casper looks inside the oven and takes

out a pile of old magazines. He sits in the armchair and starts thumbing through them.)

DENNY: What's that?

CASPER: *(Looking at cover.)* Family Circle. December 1979. *(Pause.)*

DENNY: Read me something.

CASPER: Like what?

DENNY: I don't care. Just read it out loud.

(Casper picks a page at random.)

CASPER: *(Speaking haltingly, without punctuation.)* "One-oh-one ideas for Christmas fun holiday time is a time of family joy but today's mother can find her hands full when it comes to keeping the kids...okewped but with a little bit of—"

DENNY: What?

CASPER: "With a little—"

DENNY: Keeping them *what?*

CASPER: Okewped. *(Pause.)* Osapeed?

(Denny takes the magazine from him and looks at it.)

DENNY: Jesus. *Occupied.* Keeping the kids *occupied.*

CASPER: Oh, yeah.

DENNY: Don't you *know* that word?

CASPER: Sure.

DENNY: That's not a hard word! It's right there! Occupied! Can't you read even?

CASPER: Yeah, I can read. I can read fine. I just need some time to...sound out the words. *(Pause.)* Should I do some more?

(Denny shakes his head and lies back down. A truck goes by overhead.)

DENNY: Oh God will you shut UP! Somebody's trying to sleep!

CASPER: They're sixty feet up, Denny. They don't know we're here.

DENNY: But we are. Whether they like it or not. I'm here.

CASPER: Come on, Denny, take your jacket.

DENNY: Casper...are you real?

CASPER: Huh? Ah...I guess so. I'm real. Am I?

(Denny looks at him. Pause.)

DENNY: Yeah. You're lucky.

(Sound of a man whistling in the distance. Denny leans forward and whispers.)

DENNY: Cop?

CASPER: I don't know. *(He looks off.)* Doesn't look it.

DENNY: Alone?

CASPER: Uh-huh.

DENNY: Big dude?

CASPER: It's hard to tell. *(Pause.)* Should we...ask him for directions?

DENNY: *(Not listening.)* Huh?

CASPER: Directions home, Denny. I mean he doesn't look like a—

DENNY: Yeah. Yeah, good idea. You ask him for directions. I'll stash myself here. When he stops I'll yoke him up from the back.

CASPER: What?

DENNY: Like this. *(He demonstrates with his twisted-up T-shirt, miming wrapping it around someone's neck and pulling it taut.)* Right?

CASPER: Aw, Denny.

DENNY: We're not gonna hurt him. We're just gonna do him. We can take a taxi home!

CASPER: No, Denny, why?

DENNY: Because I *want* to, okay? Because I fucking feel like it!

CASPER: Oh boy. Oh no. Oh geez.

DENNY: You gonna help me or not?

(Casper does not answer.)

DENNY: Then get outta here. I'm gonna bag this chump and you're a fucking chickenshit, you are. They won't *take* you in the army. Fuck off! *(Pause.)*

CASPER: What do I have to do.

DENNY: Okay. Okay. Ask him...what time it is. Go in for his wallet while I hold him. Don't act stupid.

(He ducks behind the sofa. Casper sits in the chair and waits. A workman in overalls and raincoat enters. Casper rises.)

CASPER: Excuse me sir, can you tell me what's the time? *(Pause.)*

WORKMAN: It's around five-thirty.

CASPER: Okay, thanks. *(Pause.)* Does this lead back to town?

WORKMAN: Service road to the coal dump. *(Pause.)*

CASPER: Listen...I think you should–

(Denny comes up behind the workman and twists the T-shirt around his neck. The workman lurches forward. Denny tries to drag him back. They stand like this for a few seconds. Then the workman starts inching forward.)

DENNY: His wallet!

(Casper does not move.)

DENNY: The fucking wallet! What are you–

(The workman drops suddenly and tosses Denny over onto the ground. He kicks him twice. He looks at Casper, who remains still. He moves to kick Denny again. Denny cringes. The workman lowers his foot. Pause.)

WORKMAN: Cocksucking little punks. Fence you off in a desert somewhere so you can all beat your own brains out. I worked all my life. You try it!

(He glares at them for a moment and stalks off. Casper watches him go, then comes over to Denny.)

CASPER: You all right, Denny? Let me–

(Denny waves him away.)

CASPER: We gotta go, Denny. He might call the police.

(Denny doesn't move.)

CASPER: Can you walk?

DENNY: *(In an even tone.)* Where were you.

CASPER: I was here. I was standing.

DENNY: Why didn't you do something. *(Pause.)* You're not saying anything.

CASPER: I couldn't. I didn't want to.

DENNY: How come.

CASPER: It's wrong, Denny. It's just wrong to do.

DENNY: The *fuck* made you an expert.

CASPER: *(Coming up to him.)* Oh, I don't know, let's go before–

DENNY: *(Pushing him back.)* Stay...away...from me. Cause I swear to God I wanna kill some fucking thing. *(With a yell he lunges at the oven and yanks at its door until he tears it off. He charges up to the pillar and starts pounding the door against it.)* You, fucker! I want you to die, goddamn you! You fucking concrete...you fucking *highway*...you fucking *bridges*...and *cities* and houses and all the people crawling in 'em, I don't WANT you here! I don't want you in my HEAD! Get OUT! GET OUT GET OUT GET OUT! *(He throws down the door, nearly exhausted. He sees Casper's radio.)* And *this*...this is just *crap*... *(He picks it up and lifts it over his head.)*

CASPER: Don't break it, Denny.

DENNY: WHY NOT!

CASPER: Cause it's mine. Cause I need it. Cause we're friends. Cause... it's not gonna make any difference.

(Pause. Denny feigns tossing the radio against the pillar and throws it sharply at Casper, who catches it. He takes a last swipe at the sofa and collapses onto it. Pause. A police siren sounds in the distance, then fades away.)

DENNY: Jesus, can't I even get arrested.

CASPER: Not this time I guess. *(He picks up the radio and wipes it clean with the edge of his shirt.)* It's getting light. I shoulda been back a while ago. It's a long walk home.

DENNY: Well...at least it's Saturday.

CASPER: It's Friday, Denny. Friday morning.

DENNY: Oh good. *(Pause.)*

CASPER: Hey, we had some fun tonight, didn't we? I mean...all the other stuff aside. We had a little fun.

DENNY: Yeah.

CASPER: Yeah, we had some fun. *(Pause.)* So, Denny...what do you wanna do now? *(Denny looks straight out. He draws in a long, slow breath and holds it. The lights fade to black.)*

END OF PLAY

Watermelon Boats
by Wendy MacLaughlin

Wendy MacLaughlin started writing in mid-life and has been fortunate enough to see every script produced thereafter. Her first full length, *Crown of Thorn*, was produced by The Missouri Repertory Theater and her short play, *Watermelon Boats*, premiered at Actors Theater in Louisville. It then went on to The Edinburgh Festival, several off-Broadway productions and is frequently performed across the country. She won The International Play Award for *Mirror/Mirror*. Her latest play, *Dance With The Wind*, premiered at The Miniature Theater of Chester in the summer of 1995.

ORIGINAL PRODUCTION

Watermelon Boats premiered in the 1979 Humana Festival of New American plays at Actors Theatre of Louisville. It was originally directed by Larry Deckel and Michael Hankins with the following cast:

Kate ....Cynthia Judge
Kitty ....Mary Johantgen

CHARACTERS

KATE: Tan, thin, and healthy. She wears jeans, button down shirt and sweater tied around waist.

KITTY: Rounder, softer, and more feminine. She wears peasant blouse, full skirt and two braids tied with ribbons.

They age from eleven to twenty-one in the course of the play and
change hair styles as indicated in the action.

TIME: The action takes place on the shore of a lake at three different moments over a ten year span.

WATERMELON BOATS

At Rise: Kate and Kitty set on stepladders facing the lake which is located where the audience sits. Both hold watermelon boats, hollowed-out melon rinds with candle masts. All props are imaginary and use of them is mimed.

KITTY: *(Face front.)* How much longer?

KATE: *(Checks watch.)* Twelve seconds. Oh, help, your candle went out. *(Mimes lighting a match on jeans.)*

KITTY: *(Cupping candle.)* Thank heavens you brought more matches.

KATE: Five, four, three, two, one…push them off.

(They each push a boat into the water and watch them sail.)

KITTY: *(Blows a kiss.)* Bon Voyage.

KATE: *(Waves.)* Good luck.

KATE: Aren't they gorgeous?

KITTY: Fabulous.

KATE: Fantastic.

KITTY: The best watermelon boats we've ever made.

KATE: With the candles they look like stars dancing across the water.

KITTY: Sir Galahad sailing out to sea in search of The Holy Grail.

KATE: Mine'll be first across I bet.

KITTY: Why?

KATE: It's smaller. The wind'll pick it up.

KITTY: They look the same to me.

KATE: The secret's in the cutting.

KITTY: *(Preening.)* Kate, notice something?

KATE: No.

KITTY: I'm wearing a bra.

KATE: I'm never going to wear one.

KITTY: My mother says you'll look like a cow if you don't.

KATE: I like cows.

KITTY: Hanging to your knees.

KATE: She just says that to scare you so when you have breasts you'll smash them all down.

KITTY: Ummmm. *(Unbraiding hair.)* Who do you think we'll have for sixth grade?

KATE: Mr. Hawkins, I hope.

KITTY: Me too. He has neat eyes. Every time he looks at me I have to go to the bathroom. Did you know I was born nine months after my brother died?

KATE: Exactly?

KITTY: He died January ninth. I was born October ninth.

KATE: *(Incredulously.)* They did it the day he died?

KITTY: I can't believe boys put that…

KATE: The whole idea is gross.

KITTY: I wonder what it feels like.

KATE: No boy is ever going to do it to me.

KITTY: Never?

KATE: Well maybe if I get married, but I probably won't because of my career.

KITTY: There're still pictures of him all over the house. My father wanted me to be a boy.

KATE: Mine, too.

KITTY: Doesn't that just make you furious? *(Frustrated with her hair.)* Why does Mother braid my hair so tight?

KATE: Here, let me help. *(Unbraids Kitty's hair and mimes brushing.)*

KITTY: Thanks. You've been my best friend since first grade. Isn't it amazing we've been coming to this lake for six years? Am I yours?

KATE: My what?

KITTY: Best friend.

KATE: Sure.

KITTY: Do you have a lot of best friends?

KATE: Some.

KITTY: Don't you think it's weird we're best friends and we're both named Katherine?

KATE: Lucky everyone calls you Kitty and me Kate.

KITTY: Kitty's a funny name.

KATE: Perfect for you.

KITTY: I like Kate better.

KATE: When I'm a great writer everyone'll call me Katherine.

KITTY: Like Katherine Mansfield.

KATE: Who?

KITTY: "I want by understanding myself to understand others." She wrote that in 1922. In her journal.

KATE: Oh…yes.

KITTY: I have total recall. People with high I.Q.'s usually do.

KATE: *(Impressed.)* You know your I.Q.?

KITTY: Ah-huh.

KATE: How?

KITTY: Once I looked it up in Miss Porter's office.

KATE: What's mine?

KITTY: That's not my business.

KATE: But you know it.

KITTY: I might.

KATE: Then tell me.

KITTY: I shouldn't.

KATE: I'll tell Miss Porter if you don't.

KITTY: Weeeeeelllllllll…I don't remember exactly but it's lower than mine.

(Fog horn blows. Kate stops brushing and fixes her hair.)

KITTY: If this fog ruins the race I'll die. I can't even see our boats. Oh there they are. Look, Kate. *(No answer.)* Kate? You're still mad.

KATE: *(Cold.)* I'm not but the rest of the class is furious. We had a chance to win the Drama High School Cup three years in a row.

KITTY: It's just a stupid play. I'm sorry, Kate. I know you wrote it and it's very good but…

KATE: It would have looked good on my college transcript.

KITTY: I'm sorry. I told you to give me sets. I'm good at art. Why'd you make me be that brainless maid.

KATE: Come off it, Kitty. You died to be the maid. The maid got to wear the cute costume.

KITTY: Well no one told me she had any lines.

KATE: Only one.

KITTY: You know I freeze in front of people.

KATE: Four words. Four simple words and you screw them up.

KITTY: My parents must have gone through the floor with embarrassment. God, I wish I had a drink.

KATE: I've told you a million times, every ounce of liquor you drink destroys ten thousand brain cells.

KITTY: Who cares about my brain anyway? Boys certainly don't.

KATE: You really make me mad, you know it? When are you going to grow up? Really, Kitty. When?

KITTY: *(Imitating.)* Really, Kitty. When? You sound exactly like my parents. Grow up, Kitty, be like Kate. Kate has her feet on the ground. Kate has a head on her shoulders. I don't want to be like you. I want to be me. Anyway I can't be you, can I? Boy, am I insecure. Guess it's because I haven't had my period in two months. *(A laugh.)* You don't think I'm pregnant do you?

KATE: Two months isn't very long.

KITTY: I stopped the pill.

KATE: Damn.

KITTY: Who wants to get cancer?

KATE: Who wants to have a baby?

KITTY: I can always get an abortion.

KATE: Don't be crazy.

KITTY: I don't have the vaguest idea who the father might be. Can't imagine any of the imbeciles we know being a father. Can you?

KATE: You've got to stop sleeping around.

KITTY: I can't. I mean, I don't want to.

KATE: Have some respect for yourself.

KITTY: I like it.

KATE: You like being used? That's what they're doing, you know. You might just as well be a urinal.

KITTY: It's not like that. When I'm close to a boy…really close, I feel important. For a time someone needs me. I'm connected to someone, part of the same thing. Afterwards, though, at home in bed…I feel more alone. *(Pause.)* Kate, do you think there might be a real person growing inside of me? A little body with fingers and toes?

KATE: Why do I feel responsible for you?

KITTY: Promise you'll come with me if I have to have an abortion.

KATE: I'd do anything in the world for you but that.

KITTY: You have to.

KATE: I can't. It's wrong.

KITTY: I would for you.

KATE: Abortion is wrong.

KITTY: What'll I do?

KATE: I'm sorry, Kitty. I have to follow my conscience.

KITTY: You're really hard, Kate. You know it?

KATE: If having principles is hard…

KITTY: Even here…in the spring, at the lake. I'm all relaxed but you're still so tight. Thin…brown…

KATE: I wish I could help you.

KITTY: Thin…brown and hard. Year round.

KATE: So be it.

KITTY: Very dull.

KATE: What?

KITTY: Thin…brown and hard. Year round. It's very dull. Booorrrrring.

KATE: *(Tight lipped.)* Sorry.

KITTY: Maybe in your senior year you should let got a little. Maybe…smile at a guy.

KATE: Too disciplined, I guess.

KITTY: Well brought up.

KATE: Probably.

KITTY: Or afraid.

KATE: Afraid?

KITTY: You might spoil the image. Perfect woman. Nobly planned.

KATE: Well, it's late. I have to go.

KITTY: I bet you spend the night thinking of lines you won't cross. Perfect stays on one side looking down her nose at the rest of us screwing it up on the other.

KATE: *(Turns to go.)* Goodnight, Kitty.

KITTY: *(Grabs her arm.)* And you think you're going to be a writer? That's a laugh. Who's going to read you? You don't know the first thing about life. *(Foghorn blows. They change hairstyles.)*

KITTY: *(Shivers.)* Ohhh it's getting cold. *(They put on sweaters.)* Not even a moon. But look, the first star is out. Sometimes I think there're people just like us up there thinking we're a star. Oh God, Kate, promise you won't write that in your first book. Everyone'll think I'm psycho.

KATE: I doubt I'll write one page, much less a book.

KITTY: You're kidding.

KATE: No.

KITTY: You're going to be a famous writer.

KATE: Who says?

KITTY: You've always said.

KATE: Changed my mind.

KITTY: You can't do that.

KATE: Stop staring at me.

KITTY: I counted on you.

KATE: The fog's breaking up. *(Looks out.)*

KITTY: I have a famous friend.

KATE: Swell.

KITTY: You've always known where you were going and how you'd get there.

KATE: That was grade school.

KITTY: High school too.

KATE: Well college is different. Not only harder but there're lots of people out there smarter. And they don't try and please everyone all the time. You were right, Kitty, I do want to be perfect. Remember when you said that?

KITTY: No.

KATE: Five years ago. Here at the lake. At first I was furious. Then I wanted to cry but I couldn't. Know why? I didn't feel enough.

KITTY: That's better than feeling too much, like me.

KATE: You're sensitive.

KITTY: I'm too easily hurt.

KATE: You know what I do when I start to feel something? I come on with my holier-than-thou superior look. Inside I'm dying to experience everything, but I never will because I act like I already have. Oh, Kitty, what if I die without ever feeling anything?

KITTY: Then you won't feel guilty all the time. That's what makes me feel like throwing myself in the lake.

KATE: Right now you wouldn't believe how guilty I feel. If I don't become the world's greatest writer my parents won't be proud of me and you'll be disappointed.

KITTY: But you'll make it. You've got talent.

KATE: I'm not as smart as you.

KITTY: But you're stronger.

KATE: No, Kitty, you are. You wouldn't let me change you.

KITTY: Did you want to?

KATE: I thought you wanted me to.

KITTY: All I want is to get married, be a good mother and have you as my friend.

KATE: You don't need me.

KITTY: You're my friend. My perfect friend. I love you.

KATE: The only thing perfect about me is that.
(Fog horn blows.)

KITTY: *(Climbs ladder.)* From up here you can see our boats. Way out. Sailing together, neck and neck.

KATE: *(Climbs ladder.)* We're not across yet.

KITTY: But we're going to make it.

KATE: The trick is the journey.

KITTY: Isn't it hard to believe we're already twenty-one?

KATE: Seems like only minutes ago we were eleven.

KITTY: *(Extends hand.)* Sometimes I wish we didn't have to get any older.

KATE: *(Takes Kitty's hand.)* Wouldn't it be nice if now could be always?
(They hold hands as the light gets blinding bright before fading to black.)

END OF PLAY

July 7, 1994

by Donald Margulies

This play, at long last, is for Lynn Street.

Donald Margulies was born in Brooklyn, New York in 1954. His plays include *Sight Unseen* (1992 Obie Award for Best New American Play, Dramatist Guild/Hull-Warriner Award, Pulitzer Prize finalist, Drama Desk Award nominee, a Burns Mantle "Best Play"); *The Loman Family Picnic* (Drama Desk Award nominee, a Burns Mantle *"Best Play"*); *Pitching to the Star* (included in *Best American Short Plays 1992-93*); *Found a Peanut; Zimmer;* and *Luna Park* (loosely based on "In Dreams Begin Responsibilities" by Delmore Schwartz). *What's Wrong With This Picture?* was produced on Broadway in 1994, and *The Model Apartment*, for which he received a Drama-Logue Award during its world premiere at Los Angeles Theatre Center, had its New York premiere at Primary Stages in 1995. His one-act play, *July 7, 1994*, which was commissioned by Actors Theatre of Louisville, premiered in ATL's Humana Festival of New American Plays in 1995. His adaptation of Sholem Asch's Yiddish classic, *God of Vengeance*, will debut in 1996 at Long Wharf Theatre. Mr. Margulies's plays have premiered at Manhattan Theatre Club, South Coast Repertory, The New York Shakespeare Festival, and the Jewish Repertory Theatre. He has won grants from CAPS, The New York Foundation for the Arts, The National Endowment for the Arts, and the John Simon Guggenheim Memorial Foundation. A collection of his work, *Sight Unseen and Other Plays*, published by Theatre Communications Group in 1995. Mr. Margulies is a member of New Dramatists and was elected to the council of Dramatists Guild in 1993. He has been a playwright-in-residence four times at the Sundance Institute Playwrights' Lab in Utah and a frequent contributor to the 52nd Street Project. His current projects include new play commissions for South Coast Repertory, the Mark Taper Forum, and Actors Theatre of Louisville. He lives with his wife, Lynn Street, a physician, and their son, Miles, in New Haven, Connecticut, where he is a visiting lecturer in playwriting at the Yale School of Drama.

ORIGINAL PRODUCTION

July 7, 1994 premiered in the 1995 Humana Festival of New American Plays at the Actors Theatre of Louisville. It was directed by Lisa Peterson with the following cast:

Kate . . . . Susan Knight
Mark . . . . Kenneth L. Marks
Señora Soto . . . . Miriam Cruz
Ms. Pike . . . . Myra Taylor
Mr. Caridi . . . . Edward Hyland
Paula . . . . Sandra Daley

CHARACTERS

KATE: a general internist in her late 30s, and
MARK: her husband, an academic, also in his 30s, are both white.

KATE'S PATIENTS

SEÑORA SOTO: in her 40s, is Hispanic;
MS. PIKE: in her 30s, five months pregnant, is black;
MR. CARIDI: in his 40s, is white;
PAULA: in her 30s, very thin, is black.

Special thanks to Lourdes Alvarez.

JULY 7, 1994

The settings are the bedroom and living room of a modest house, and an examination room and waiting area in a community health clinic, both located in a small northeastern city. A television set facing away from the audience is watched by patients in the waiting area.

The play's action takes place on a single day, July 7, 1994.

The play is to be performed without blackouts. As each scene ends the character from the next scene should take his or her place; the transitions should be as seamless as possible, like the way the dissolve is used in film. At the start of each scene, the time of day is projected and soon fades from view.

In the black, a slide is projected: July 7, 1994

When that slide fades out, another is projected: 6:42 A.M.

Kate and Mark are in bed. She is having a dream, whimpering in her sleep. Mark is awakened by the sounds and gently shakes her.

MARK: Kate? Honey?

    (Kate awakens with a slight start.)

KATE: What.

MARK: You were dreaming.

KATE: *(Still sleepy.)* Oh, yeah, I was.

MARK: Do you remember?

KATE: *(Recollecting.)* I was dreaming about Matthew. Oh, God, it was terrible.

MARK: What. Tell me.

KATE: There was a flood.

MARK: Yeah...?

KATE: The house was flooded. There was water everywhere. It left these red water marks on the walls.

MARK: Red water marks? Are you sure it wasn't blood?

KATE: Maybe it *was* blood. Yeah, you're right, it *was* blood. And all the furniture was floating around in it, and all the books. And we were wading through it, you and I, it was kind of fun almost, we were sort of enjoying ourselves, this pool in the living room, and suddenly I got this terrible feeling: Where was Matthew? We forgot about the baby! We'd left him up in the nursery! And the water, the blood, was rising, it was going up the stairs, soon the whole house was gonna be flooded, and I was trying to make it up the stairs to get to him but the current was so strong and I was really panic-stricken, it was awful, I thought I wasn't going to make it up the stairs to save him.

MARK: Did you?

KATE: I don't know; you woke me up.

MARK: Sorry.

KATE: *(Pause.)* Do you have dreams like that?, that Matthew's in distress and you can't reach him?

MARK: Oh, all the time.

KATE: There's some encroaching catastrophe and no matter what you do to protect him, it's no use?

MARK: Sometimes I have these morbid daydreams.

KATE: Really?

MARK: These flashes of dread that something terrible is going to happen to him, something out of my control.

KATE: You really do? You mean it's not just me.

MARK: Oh, no, I imagine him falling down the stairs, cracking his head open in the park, breaking free of my hand and running into traffic...

KATE: What *is* it with us? We weren't always such morbid people.

MARK: We weren't parents before. Oh, God, I just remembered.

KATE: What.

MARK: This dream I had the other night. I was standing, holding Matthew...at the Nicole Simpson murder scene.

KATE: Oh, God! You're kidding.

MARK: No. We were there. Like we beamed-up on Bundy in our pajamas. I was shielding his eyes; I didn't want him to see. I held his face against my shoulder. But *I* could see, very clearly, what was going on. We were invisible; I mean, I saw us standing in that courtyard but they couldn't see us. And it was horrifying. I mean, I saw it all, all the stuff we saw and read about—

KATE: We have to stop watching T.V. Let's get rid of the T.V.

MARK: *(Over "Let's get rid...")* Nicole's standing there barefoot, arguing with him, and O.J.'s completely mad, sweating, shouting...

KATE: You're sure it was O.J.?

MARK: Oh, yeah, and I see he's wearing those gloves, and the fighting escalates, and all of a sudden the knife comes out—it was very fast—and I hear it cut into her throat like, like he's slicing open a melon.

(She winces.)

MARK: And I'm still clutching the baby to me hoping he won't hear or see anything. And then Ron Goldman comes along, he happens up the path to deliver the sunglasses, and stumbles onto this horrible scene going on and he puts up an incredible struggle. I mean, it was fierce. And I'm crying because I'm powerless and it's so upsetting to see. I'm watching these people lose their lives and there's nothing I can do to stop it. Their blood is trickling down the cobblestones like a creek.

(Pause.)

KATE: You know, maybe we really *should* think about getting rid of the T.V. Look what it's doing to our dreams, it's poisoning our dreams.

MARK: I'm not getting rid of that set, we just bought that set.

KATE: Then let's shut it away somehow. Matthew's at that age when kids begin to absorb everything. I don't want him *looking* at some of that stuff. What's it gonna do to *his* dreams?

MARK: What are you gonna do? There's nothing you can do. It's out there. It's not gonna go away. Unless you want to turn him into the bubble-boy or something. I mean, the kid *is* gonna go to school one day, right?

(Pause. Off, Baby Matthew, announcing that he's up calls, "Mom—ma … Dad—dy…" Mark starts to get up.)

MARK: Well, whataya know… I'll go, you go back to sleep; you've got a long day.

KATE: *(over "…a long day.")* No, no, I'll go, you stay… Stay.

(She kisses him, gets out of the bed and exits for the nursery. Mark pulls the cover over his head and tries to go back to sleep.)

Transition

A slide is projected: 9:25 A.M.

As the previous scene ends, Señora Soto, 40s, sad demeanor, comes into the examination room, takes off her blouse, hangs it up, puts on a johnny coat and, with her handbag on her lap, sits and waits. Soon, Kate enters. Kate's Spanish is purposely halting and erratic while Señora Soto's is flawless, even poetic. Sentences that are bracketed and printed in italics are projected as supertitles.

KATE: I'm sorry, Señora Soto, our translator, nuestro translatora, Loida Martinez, ¿conoces Loida Martinez? ¿la mujer que translata aquí?

(Señora shrugs.)

KATE: Well, I thought she was in today but ella es enferma hoy, she's out sick, no aquí, so you're going to have to bear with me, okay? Mi espanol no es muy bien, okay?

(Señora shrugs.) So, this dolor, tell me about this pain. ¿Cuando dolor? *[When do you feel it?]*

SEÑORA: ¿Cuando?

KATE: Sí. Do you feel it… upon exertion? al exertione…?

SEÑORA: No comprendo.

KATE: Sorry. ¿Tienes dificultad caminando?
[Do you have difficulty walking?]
"Shortness of breath"?
(Señora shakes her head in apologetic uncomprehension; Kate demonstrates shortness of breath.)

KATE: ¿Cuantos cuadros puedes caminar?
[How many picture frames can you walk?]
(Señora is utterly confused.)

KATE: Outside, afuera how far caminar antes before you get tired? How do you say, ¿como se dice "tired"? Um... *(She thinks.)* cansado. How many blocks? ¿Cuantos cuadros?

SEÑORA: Oh! ¡¿Cuadras?! ¡¿Cuantas cuadras?!
[Blocks? How many blocks?]

KATE: Sí. Cuadras.

SEÑORA: *(A torrent of words.)* Mi vecindario es bien malo, ¿cuándo camino? *[My neighborhood is so bad, when do I walk?]* Camino a la parada de la guagua y ruego que me dejen en paz. *[I walk to the bus stop and pray to be left in peace.]* Usted debería ver lo que está pasando en las calles. *[You should see what's happening on the streets.]* ¡Las cosas que occurren, debajo de nuestras narices! *[The things that go on, right under our noses!]*

KATE: *(During the above.)* Señora... Slow... Slow... Despacio, por favor...

SEÑORA: *(Continuous.)* Yo recuerdo cuando la gente se protegía. *[I remember when people took care of one another.]* Ahora nadie piensa en nada más que sí mismo. *[Now nobody thinks about anyone but himself.]* Te matan antes de saludarte. *[They'd sooner kill you than say hello.]*

KATE: Señora... En la mañana, in the morning, ¿sí?, ¿lavantas con dolor? *[Do you wake up with pain?]*

SEÑORA: Me despierto con dolor, me acuesto con dolor. *[I wake up with pain, I go to sleep with pain.]*

KATE: Cuando diga "dolor," quiere decir "dolor," ¿o quiere...? *[When you say pain, do you mean "pain," or do you...?]*

SEÑORA: ¡Quiero decir dolor! ¡Dolor! ¡Dolor! *[I mean pain! Pain! Pain!]*

KATE: Okay. The pain, el dolor, ¿es un dolor... "sharp"?
(Señora shrugs; she doesn't understand.)
"Sharp?" ¿Como un... cuch... cuchillo? *[Like a knife.]* Or "heavy"... ¿Como una roca sobre su pecho? *[Like a rock on your chest.]*

SEÑORA: *(Another torrent.)* ¡Me siento como que muero! *[I feel like I'm going to die!]* ¡Como que mi corazón va a explotar en mi pecho y me voy a ahogar en mi propia sangre! *[Like my heart is going to burst inside my chest and I'm going to drown in my own blood!]* ¿Es posible eso? ¿Puede eso pasar, Señora doctora? *[Is that possible? Can that happen, Doctor?]*

KATE: *(Over "Como que mi corazón...")* No comprendo. Más despacio. Por favor. Señora, slow down, por favor. No comprendo cuando habla tan rápido. *[I can't understand when you talk so fast.]*

SEÑORA: Sí. Okay. Sorry.

KATE: Let me listen to your heart, okay?, I need to escuchar su corazón. Okay?
(Señora doesn't understand; Kate indicates the stethoscope.)

KATE: May I?

SEÑORA: Oh. Sí, sí.
(Kate listens to her chest, first the front, then the back.)

KATE: Okay. Respira grande. Big.

(Kate demonstrates; Señora complies.)

KATE: Good. Otra vez. Good, bueno. Again. Bueno. ¿Un otro respira grande? Good. *(Listens carefully.)* ¿Otra vez? Bueno. Gracias. *(Beat.)* ¿Señora, hay una historia de enfermedad de corazón en su familia? *[Is there a history of heart disease in your family?]* Problemas de corazón?

SEÑORA: *(Another torrent.)* Mi mamá perdió una hija, una hijita. *[My mother lost a child, a little girl.]* Un ángel. Mi hermanita. *[An angel. My little sister.]* Y mi santa madre se murió en menos de un año. *[And my sainted mother died in less than a year.]* Se le partió el corazón. *[Her heart was broken.]* El doro fué tam tremendo que su corazón no pudo aguantarlo. *[The pain was so great, her heart could not bear it.]* *(She cries.)* ¡Anhelo a mis hijos! *[I miss my children!]*

KATE: ¿Qué?

SEÑORA: ¡Mis hijos! ¡Mis hijos! ¡Extraño a mis hijos! *[My children! My children! I miss my children!]*

KATE: ¿Dónde están tus hijos? *[Where are your children?]*

SEÑORA: En Puerto Rico.

KATE: ¿Por qué son en Puerto Rico? *[Why are they in Puerto Rico?]*

SEÑORA: Los mandé a vivir con mi abuela. *[I sent them to live with my grandmother.]* Mi abuela los están criando. *[My grandmother is raising them.]* Son pobres pero estan seguros—más seguros de lo que estarían aquí. *[They're poor but they're safe—safer than they would be here.]* La cuidad no es lugar para los niños. *[The city is no place for children.]*

KATE: ¿Tu esposo...? *[Your husband...?]*

(Señora shrugs, speaking volumes.)

KATE: ¿Por que no regresas? *[Why don't you go back?]*

SEÑORA: ¿A Puerto Rico?

KATE: Sí.

SEÑORA: No puedo. *[I can't.]* Lo poco que gano aquí es mucho más de lo que podría ganar allá. *[The little I make here is much more than I could make there.]*

KATE: What do you do? ¿Qué...haces?

SEÑORA: ¿Conoces el Maritime Center? *[Do you know the Maritime Center?]*

KATE: ¿Sí?

SEÑORA: Limpo oficinas. *[I clean offices.]* Todo lo que gano se lo mando a ellos. *[Everything I make I send to them.]* Quiero que vayan a la universidad. *[I want them to go to college.]* Vivo sin nada. *[I live on nothing.]* Alguien tiene que trabajar. *[Somebody has to work.]* Mi abuela está muy vietja ahora. *[My grandmother is very old now.]* No puede trabjar. *[She can't work.]* Si yo volviera, nos moriríamos de hambre. *[If I went back we all would starve.]*

KATE: *(Overlap, calming.)* Señora, Señora... *(Beat.)* Creo que está depresada. *[I think you are depressed.]*

SEÑORA: ¿Comó?

KATE: Depresada. "Down." Abajo, ¿no? "Sad." ¿Como se dice "sad"? *(Thinks.)* ¿Triste?

SEÑORA: ¿Triste? Por supuesto estoy triste. Estoy muy triste. Mi vida es triste. *[Sad? Of course I'm sad. I'm very sad. My life is sad.]* ¿Por qué no estaría triste? *[Why shouldn't I be sad?]* No sería humana si no estuviera triste. *[I wouldn't be human if I weren't sad.]* Sería un animal. Un perro. Un perro en la calle. *[I would be an animal. A dog. A dog in the streets.]*

KATE: Señora, I can give you a drug... Te puedo dar una medicina para... animar tus espíritus. *[I can give you a medicine to raise your ghosts.]*

SEÑORA: *(Confused.)* ¡¿Para qué?!

KATE: To raise your spirits. Una medicina para hacerte menos triste. *[A medicine to make you less... sad.]* Para elevar tu... "mood." A mood elevator. ¿Comprende? Para hacerte contenta. *[To make you happy.]*

SEÑORA: ¿Una droga para que sea contenta? *[A drug to make me happy?]*

KATE: Sí.

SEÑORA: ¿Una píldora? *[A pill?]*

KATE: Sí.

SEÑORA: ¿Para qué? ¿Por qué tomaría una píldora para estar contenta? *[For what? Why would I take a pill to make me happy?]* ¿Me sanaría el corazón? *[Would it heal my heart?]* Mi corazón está deshecho con razón. *[My heart is broken for a reason.]* ¿Cómo querría olvidarme por qué está deshecho mi corazón? *[Why would I want to forget why my heart is broken?]*

KATE: *(Overlap.)* Señora, estoy trantando de ayudarle. *[I'm trying to help you.]*

SEÑORA: *(Continuous.)* Mi corazón está herido. Tengo el corazón herido. *[My heart is broken. I have a broken heart.]*

KATE: I'm trying to help you, ayudarle, to offer some sort of solution.

SEÑORA: *(Continuous.)* ¡Tengo dolor, Señora doctora! *[I have pain, Doctor!]*

KATE: ¿Quiere ir al hospital? *[Do you want to go to the hospital?]*

SEÑORA: ¡¿Hospital?! No, no, ningún hospital.

KATE: *(Continuous.)* ¿Quiere ir al "emergency room"?

SEÑORA: No, no emergency room.

KATE: Señora, if you go to the hospital, they can do a stress test, "un stress test."

SEÑORA: Nada de hospital... *(Makes ad libbed rambling protestations during the following.)*

KATE: Señora, I think you may be depressed. ¿Comprende? Señora? Señora, I think you, I think it's possible depression is causing your symptoms but I'm not sure. Pueden hacer un test para ver cómo responde su corazón al "stress." *[They can give you a test to see how your heart responds to stress.]*

SEÑORA: *(Overlap.)* No, no...

KATE: Then what do you want? What can I do? *(Refers to her chart.)* Señora, veo que doctor Leventhal referió tú a la Clínica Hispánica para "counseling" para depresión. *[I see Dr. Leventhal referred you to the Clinica*

Hispanica for counseling for depression.] ¿Fué a la consultación? *[Did you go for a consultation?]*

SEÑORA: No estoy loca. *[I'm not crazy.]*

KATE: Nobody said you were crazy.

SEÑORA: *(Continuous.)* Mi vida es una miseria. *[My life is miserable.]* ¿Es extraño que tenga un dolor en el corazón? *[Is it any wonder I have a pain in my heart?]* Mire a mi vida. *[Look at my life.]* Mire lo que he perdido. *[Look at what I've lost.]* Mire lo que he tenido que sacrificar. *[Look at what I've had to give up.]* Mire cuán duro trabajo por unos centavos, para nada. *[Look at how hard I work for pennies, for nothing.]* Mire a mi vida. *[Look at my life.]* No necesito un psiquiatra para decirme que mi vida es dura. *[I don't need a psychiatrist to tell me my life is hard.]* Lo sé. *[I know.]*

KATE: Señora, es muy importante. You need to follow up on your appointment at the Clínica Hispánica. Okay? I think the psychiatrist can help you. I am not a psychiatrist. Es muy importante. Okay? But if the pain comes back, si el dolor regresa, I mean very strong, muy fuerte, ¿llamas la clinica? *[Will you call us here at the clinic?]*

SEÑORA: *(Shrugs.)* Los que usted quiera. *[Whatever you want.]*

KATE: It's not what *I* want, it's what you need to do.

SEÑORA: Sí, sí.

KATE: Señora, I'm sorry... Tengo que ver otros pacientes ahora. *[I'm going to have to see other patients now.]* I'm very sorry. I hope you're feeling better.
(Señora nods, turns away from Kate, silently removes the johnny coat, puts her shirt back on. As she goes:)

KATE: I'm sorry.

Transition
A slide is projected: 12:08 P.M.
Kate is now removing stitches from the palm of a woman's hand. Ms. Pike is black, in her thirties, five months pregnant.

MS. PIKE: Ow!

KATE: Sorry.
(Ms. Pike groans in pain.)

KATE: I'm trying not to hurt you, I'm sorry.

MS. PIKE: How many more you got?

KATE: Just a few. *(Pause.) What* happened exactly?

MS. PIKE: Hm?

KATE: *How'd* you hurt your hand?

MS. PIKE: I told you, I don't know, I cut it.

KATE: How?

MS. PIKE: Kitchen.

KATE: Yeah, I know, how?

MS. PIKE: Accident. You know. Damn! Could you not hurt me so much?

KATE: I'm sorry.

MS. PIKE: This gonna take long? 'Cause I got to pick up my daughter.

KATE: I just need to dress it; there's some infection. *(Silence while she attends to her.)* So, have you been following this O.J. thing?

MS. PIKE: Oh, yeah, are you kidding? There's nothing else on. Day and night. I'm really getting sick of it, too: O.J., O.J., O.J....

KATE: So what do you think?

MS. PIKE: What do I think?, you mean did he do it?

KATE: Yeah, do you think he did it?

MS. PIKE: Nah, I think it's all a frame-up.

KATE: You do? Really?

MS. PIKE: Oh, yeah. You can be sure, a famous *white* man, they find *his* wife dead, they ain't gonna be all over *him.*

KATE: Oh, I don't know, a history of abuse? I'm sure the ex-husband is the first one they look for, no matter who he is.

MS. PIKE: *(Over "who he is.")* Oh, I don't know about that.

KATE: Who would want to frame him?

MS. PIKE: You'd be surprised.

KATE: No, who? I mean, it would have to be a pretty elaborate frame-up, don't you think? Dripping his blood, planting the gloves?

MS. PIKE: They got nothing on him.

KATE: You don't think?

MS. PIKE: No way.

KATE: The blood in the Bronco?, the blood at the scene?, the blood in his driveway...?

MS. PIKE: *(Over "in his driveway.")* So what? Did anybody see him do it?

KATE: Well...

MS. PIKE: *(Continuous.)* Did anybody *see* him? No. How do you know it wasn't some mugger who did it? Hm? How do you know it wasn't someone out to get O.J.? You don't know that and neither do I. It could've been some Charles Manson thing. You don't know.

KATE: Do you think the judge is going to allow that evidence?

MS. PIKE: She better not.

KATE: Why?!

MS. PIKE: It's illegal! The cops broke the law when they hopped the wall! They had no right!

KATE: Don't you think they had just cause for entering the premises? The Bronco was on the street.

MS. PIKE: *(Over "The Bronco...")* They didn't have a warrant! They had no warrant! They can't just break into somebody's house...

KATE: But the circumstantial evidence is pretty overwhelming, don't you think? I mean, don't you think there's sufficient cause for him to stand trial?

MS. PIKE: Those L.A. cops, they just want to get themselves one more nigger.

KATE: Why would they want to get O.J. Simpson?

MS. PIKE: Why?! Why?! Honey, what country do *you* live in?

KATE: *(Beat.)* But I think you're confusing the issue; the issue is not about race.

MS. PIKE: Not about race? Sure its about race. Everything's about race. *This* is about race. *(Meaning their exchange.)*

KATE: *(Beat.)* Maybe I'm hopelessly naive.

MS. PIKE: Maybe you are. Maybe you are. *(Beat.)* I don't know, all I know is, if he *did* do it, if he *did,* you can be sure she pushed him.

KATE: Pushed him? How do you mean?

MS. PIKE: *Pushed* him. I bet she got him so mad... her with her sexy clothes, waving her titties around, hanging out with those pretty boy models. I bet she got him plenty mad with her ways.

KATE: What ways?

MS. PIKE: Screwing around. She screwed everything in sight, that girl.

KATE: How do you know?

MS. PIKE: She was a tramp. That's what they say.

KATE: Who says?

MS. PIKE: All the papers. That's what you read. She drove him crazy with jealousy. That was her hold on him. I know women like this. That's how they keep their men. My sister is like this.

KATE: But she was trying to break away. She was finally on her own. It's classic, you know, when battered women—

MS. PIKE: Who said she was battered? You don't know. How do you know that? You don't know what goes on in the privacy of their own home.

KATE: *(Continuous, over the above.)* —break away, when they finally break away, that's when their husbands lose it, that's when they get killed. The cops were called to their house on several occasions, she said she was afraid he was going to kill her.

MS. PIKE: Yeah? If she was so afraid, she should've gotten the hell out of town.

KATE: Oh, come on.—

MS. PIKE: She should've moved.

KATE: *(Continuous, over the above.)* —Take her kids out of school, away from their family and friends? He would've tracked her down anywhere.

MS. PIKE: Ah, she was too busy spending his money to leave. Too busy shopping Beverly Hills.

KATE: Did you hear that 911 tape?

MS. PIKE: Yeah, I heard it.

KATE: And? What did you think about that?

MS. PIKE: What do I think? I think they had a fight. So what? Lots of folks have fights. Doesn't mean he killed her.

KATE: Yeah, but you heard it. That was rage, pure and simple. She was terrified.

MS. PIKE: I heard the reason he was so mad? He walked in on her and some guy going down on him in the living room.

KATE: Where'd you hear that?

MS. PIKE: Waiting in line Stop n Shop, one of those papers. They got sound experts to pick up what he's yelling in the background? He was yelling about her and this guy Keith.

KATE: Who's Keith?

MS. PIKE: *(Shrugs.)* Some guy she was cheating with.

KATE: Wait a second, they were already divorced. She was his ex-wife, she could have sex with whomever she liked. That's not cheating. She was a single woman. And what if she *did* have sex with these guys? Does that mean she deserved to be bludgeoned to death because she was promiscuous?

(Ms. Pike makes a scoffing sound; beat.)

KATE: What are you saying? She deserved it?

(Silence.)

KATE: When your boyfriend hits *you*, do *you* deserve it?

MS. PIKE: What?! Who said my boyfriend hits me?

(Kate looks at her as if to say, You can level with me. Long pause.)

MS. PIKE: It's not the same.

KATE: Why not?

MS. PIKE: Oh, man...

KATE: Why isn't it?

MS. PIKE: 'Cause it's not, okay? *(Beat.)* We got into a fight about the kids, that's all.

KATE: What about the kids?

MS. PIKE: I don't know, he started yelling at them about something. I got worried.

KATE: What were you worried about?

MS. PIKE: I was worried he might hit them.

KATE: Why was he yelling at them?

MS. PIKE: What are all these questions?! They were bad, okay?

KATE: Uh huh. What were they doing that was so bad?

MS. PIKE: Yelling and screaming and stuff. *You* know. Talking back.

KATE: Does he hit the kids? I mean, generally?

MS. PIKE: Sometimes.

KATE: Does he hit them hard?

MS. PIKE: Sometimes he'll smack them around, yeah.

KATE: What do you mean by smack them around?

MS. PIKE: Smack them around, *you* know.

KATE: *Does* he smack them? Or punch them?

MS. PIKE: Yeah, smack them, punch them. Just to scare them, you know?

KATE: Uh huh. And does he?

MS. PIKE: Oh yeah! Sometimes, he'll, *you* know, *use* things.

KATE: *Use* things? What do you mean?

MS. PIKE: Throw things. *You* know, plates, stuff, whatever's there. Once he threw the cat at my son.

KATE: The cat?!

MS. PIKE: *(Continuous.)* Didn't like the way he talked to him?, picked up the cat?, right across the room. I couldn't believe it. You shouldn't've seen: scratches all over his face and stuff.

KATE: Sounds pretty bad.

MS. PIKE: *(Shrugs.)* He got the message, though, my son.

KATE: I don't know... Seems to me there are other ways of getting the message across.

MS. PIKE: You got to do something. I mean, when he hits them, they deserve it. Oh, man, they deserve it alright.

KATE: Why do they deserve it?

MS. PIKE: They're out of control. You should see. They are out of control. They need discipline. They need it. *My* father did it. Otherwise, you know how kids get, they walk all over you. *Some*body's got to take control, show them who's the boss.

KATE: So you were worried he was going to hit the kids, but you say they deserved it? I don't get it.

MS. PIKE: *(Over "get it.")* I was worried he'd get carried away. *You* know.

KATE: Are they his kids?

MS. PIKE: No, no. *This* one's his, though. *(Meaning her pregnancy.)*

KATE: I see. *(Beat.)* So, you got into a fight over the kids, he picked up a knife, started waving it around, and you got cut.

MS. PIKE: It was an accident. He didn't mean it.

KATE: No, you just happened to walk into it.

MS. PIKE: He was mad. He just wanted to scare me.

KATE: "Scare" you? Does he hit you a lot?

MS. PIKE: No! Not a lot. Sometimes. Sometimes he'll, *you* know, give me a punch if I do something he don't like.

KATE: Like what? What could you possibly do to warrant a punch?

MS. PIKE: *(Over "to warrant a punch?")* Could be anything. What I cooked, what I say. He don't like it when I talk back.

KATE: That sounds pretty difficult.

(Ms. Pike shrugs.)

KATE: I mean, you never know when you might set him off.

MS. PIKE: Oh, I have a pretty good idea.

KATE: He just went after you with a knife!

MS. PIKE: *(Shrugs.)* Yeah, well... I interfered—

KATE: You what?!

MS. PIKE: *(Continuous.)* —I shouldn't've.

KATE: Is that what he told you?

MS. PIKE: No, it's the truth. I should've butt out. It was none of my business. He had words with the kids, I should've butt out.

KATE: *(Over "I should've butt out.")* They're your children! Ms. Pike! This man is abusing you and your children!

MS. PIKE: What, you're gonna lecture me now?

KATE: Why would you, why would anyone deserve to be hit?

MS. PIKE: In his eyes I do.

KATE: I'm not talking about his eyes.

MS. PIKE: I mean, the way he sees it, I do something pisses him off, wham.

KATE: Yeah, but do *you* feel you deserve it?

MS. PIKE: I'm used to it by now.

KATE: That's not what I'm asking.

MS. PIKE: It's the way it is. If that's the way it has to be...

KATE: It doesn't have to be that way, there are people you can talk to, you know, agencies.

MS. PIKE: *(Over "agencies.")* Shit...

KATE: *(Continuous.)* I can walk you over to meet someone right here at the clinic, I can introduce you to someone right now.

MS. PIKE: *(Over "...right now.")* What, so they'd tell me to leave him? Tell me to walk out on him? *Then* what? *Then* what happens to me? What happens to my kids? Look, lady, you don't know *me*. You don't know a *damn* thing about my life.

KATE: True enough.

MS. PIKE: I came for you to take our my stitches.

KATE: *(Nods; a beat; while writing a prescription; back to business.)* Here's an antibiotic for that infection. Three times a day with meals for a week. And try to keep that hand dry. *(Rips it off the pad, hands it to her.)*

Transition

> *A slide is projected: 3:53 P.M.*
> *Kate is with Mr. Caridi, an unstable, working-class man in his late 40s.*

KATE: What brings *you* here today, Mr. Caridi?

MR. CARIDI: You.

> *(She good-naturedly rolls her eyes.)*

MR. CARIDI: No, I mean it, I been thinking about you. I *have;* that's the truth.

KATE: *(Over "that's the truth;" keeping her professional cool.)* Mr. Caridi, do you have a complaint?

MR. CARIDI: Only that I don't see you enough.

> *(Another disapproving look from Kate: she is not charmed.)*

MR. CARIDI: What's the matter, I'm embarrassing you? A beautiful girl like you? *Look* at you, you're blushing.

KATE: I am not.

MR. CARIDI: Don't you know you're beautiful?

KATE: Come on, this is really...

MR. CARIDI: *(Over "this is really...")* Doesn't your husband tell you how beautiful you are? Boy, if you were *mine*, if you were *mine*, I'd tell you all the time, all the *time* I'd tell you.

KATE: *(Over "all the time I'd tell you.")* Mr. Caridi, do you have any idea how inappropriate this is? No honestly. Do you? I'm your *doc*tor, Mr. Caridi.

MR. CARIDI: Hey... *(Meaning, "You don't have to tell me.")*

KATE: *(Continuous.)* Do you think you can respect that fact for ten minutes so that I can do my job?

MR. CARIDI: Shoot. *(Meaning, "Go ahead.")*

KATE: Thank you.

MR. CARIDI: *(Beat.)* Can I say one thing, though? You know?, in the beginning I really thought I was gonna have a problem having a lady doctor. But, no, I like it. I really do.

KATE: That's good, Mr. Caridi. I'm glad.

MR. CARIDI: There's something really nice about it, you know? Really refreshing.

KATE: Would you like to tell me what's wrong?

MR. CARIDI: *(Dead serious.)* I really have been thinking about you, you know. I missed you.

KATE: Mr. Caridi, this has got to stop. Okay? Because if you insist on this inappropriate behavior,—

MR. CARIDI: Don't get so worked up!

KATE: —I'm going to have to take you off my patient list and give you to Dr. Leventhal. Do you understand?

MR. CARIDI: Yes, Teacher—I mean, Doctor.

(He cracks himself up; she glares at him.)

MR. CARIDI: That was a joke! Come on! Where's your sense of humor?

KATE: Mr. Caridi, is there a medical reason that brought you here today?

MR. CARIDI: Yeah. What do you think, I make appointments just to see you?

(She says nothing.)

MR. CARIDI: I'm missing O.J. for this! Today's the big day!

KATE: Mr. Caridi, I'm already running twenty minutes late.

MR. CARIDI: Okay, okay, I see you're into being super-serious. I can be super-serious, too. *(He folds his hands like a student.)*

KATE: Well?

MR. CARIDI: I got a few things I care to discuss.

KATE: Alright.

MR. CARIDI: Some personal matters.

KATE: Personal matters or health problems?

MR. CARIDI: Yeah. Health problems. *(Pause.)* You still want me to give up smoking?

KATE: Is that really why you're here? You want to talk about quitting smoking?—

MR. CARIDI: I know, I know.

KATE: *(Continuous.)* —We've talked about this before.

MR. CARIDI: I try. I really do. I just can't. The minute I decide to quit, I can't wait to light up again. Believe me, I'd be so happy to come and see you and tell you I quit. I couldn't wait to see the look on your face when I told you.

KATE: Maybe it's time to think about the patch.

MR. CARIDI: The what?

KATE: The nicotine patch. Remember?

MR. CARIDI: *(Shakes his head, No.)* What's that?

KATE: You wear it on your skin and it releases nicotine into your bloodstream. It takes away the craving.

MR. CARIDI: No kidding.

KATE: Would you like to try it?

MR. CARIDI: Yeah, sure, why not? Does it hurt?

KATE: No, you just wear it on your skin. Like a Band-Aid. Before you go I'll give you a starter kit. And then you'll need to fill this prescription. *(She writes.)* Okay?

MR. CARIDI: Yeah, Doc. Thanks. *(He watches her write in silence, refers to a framed photo.)* That your kid?

KATE: What?

MR. CARIDI: *(Points to the photo.)* The kid.

KATE: Yes. *(Pause.)*

MR. CARIDI: Can I see?

KATE: Mr. Caridi…

MR. CARIDI: Can't I see the picture? I just want to see it. I don't got my glasses. Can I see it up close? I love kids.
(She hesitates, then hands him the frame.)

MR. CARIDI: Thanks.
(He looks at the photo for a long time, which she finds terribly unnerving. She extends her hand.)

KATE: Mr. Caridi?

MR. CARIDI: So: that's your kid.

KATE: Yes. *(Beat.)* May I have it back, please?

MR. CARIDI: That your husband?

KATE: Yes.

MR. CARIDI: Pretty kid. What's his name?

KATE: *(Hesitates.)* Matthew.

MR. CARIDI: Matthew, huh.

KATE: May I please…?

MR. CARIDI: *(Still looking.)* Looks like you, don't he.

KATE: Mr. Caridi, please… Can we get on with this? I've got a whole bunch of patients I've got to see.

(Laughing, he taunts her with the picture frame.)

KATE: Mr. Caridi... Mr. Caridi, please...

(He gives it to her; she puts it back. Pause.)

MR. CARIDI: I wish I had that.

KATE: Had what?

MR. CARIDI: A kid, a family. Maybe if I had a kid... If I didn't have this... disability... Who knows? I might be sitting where you are. Or where your husband sits. You ever think about that? There but for the grace of God?

KATE: All the time. *(Beat.)* Mr. Caridi, have you been taking your lithium?

MR. CARIDI: Why?

KATE: I suspect you haven't.

MR. CARIDI: *(Beat.)* No.

KATE: Why not?

MR. CARIDI: *(Shrugs.)* I hate the way it makes me feel. Makes my mouth taste like shit.

KATE: You can always use a mouthwash if it dries out your mouth. Or chew gum. Mr. Caridi, you've got to be sure to tell your psychiatrist—when's your next appointment?

(He shrugs.)

KATE: Have you been going to your appointments?

MR. CARIDI: I don't like him. Why can't I see you?

KATE: I'm not a psychiatrist. Mr. Caridi, you've got to take your lithium and you've got to take it regularly, do you understand? You have bi-polar *disease—*

MR. CARIDI: Yeah yeah yeah.

KATE: *(Continuous.)* —it's a *disease*, controllable by drugs.

MR. CARIDI: *(Shrugs.)* I got another problem I got to ask you.

KATE: What kind of problem?

MR. CARIDI: It's kind of personal.

KATE: *(Beat.)* Alright.

MR. CARIDI: Kind of confidential.

(She nods, "Okay.")

MR. CARIDI: You're my doctor, right?

KATE: Yes.

MR. CARIDI: I can discuss a personal problem with you, can't I? I mean, that's appropriate, isn't it? Hm? Doctor–patient thing? Like confession, right?

KATE: What's the problem, Mr. Caridi? *(Pause.)*

MR. CARIDI: It's my penis.

KATE: *(Beat.)* Yes?

MR. CARIDI: I don't know, something don't seem right.

KATE: Can you be more specific?

MR. CARIDI: Sometimes... Sometimes I have this burning sensation.

KATE: It's painful when you urinate?

MR. CARIDI: I don't know, I think so. Yeah, it is. And sometimes it gets really big and red and swollen; I think you better take a look, Doc. *(He starts to undo his pants.)*

KATE: Alright, alright, that's it.

MR. CARIDI: *(Feigning shock.)* What!

KATE: I did not tell you to take your pants down.

MR. CARIDI: Don't you want to see what's the matter?!— *(His pants fall to his feet.)*

KATE: Mr. Caridi!

MR. CARIDI: *(Continuous.)* —I tell you I got something wrong with my penis, don't you think you'd better take a look?! What's the matter, you shy? You're a doctor!—you've seen naked men before.

KATE: *(Over "naked men before.")* That's right, I'm not your friend, I'm not your girlfriend, I'm your doctor. Now put your pants back on before I call for help.

MR. CARIDI: *(His pants still around his ankles.)* How do you know there isn't something really wrong with me?!

KATE: You're right, I don't.

MR. CARIDI: *(Continuous.)* —How do you know I don't have cancer or a tumor or something?—

KATE: Mr. Caridi, pull up your pants, Mr. Caridi…

MR. CARIDI: *(Continuous.)* —What kind of doctor *are* you? Aren't you supposed to heal the sick? Aren't you?! You and Hillary Clinton! Phony bitches! All smiles and promises.

KATE: *(Overlap.)* I'm setting up another appointment for you with Dr. Leventhal.

MR. CARIDI: What?! Why?!

KATE: *(Continuous.)* I think Dr. Leventhal should be your primary care physician from now on. I think you need to see a male physician.

MR. CARIDI: Oh, come on! What kind of shit is this? What kind of doctor *are* you, anyway? You're no doctor. Where's your compassion? Doctors are supposed to have compassion.

KATE: Excuse me, I'll go get the patch. *(She leaves.)*

MR. CARIDI: Bitch.

(Pause. He picks up the picture frame to look at again, then impulsively hides it in his newspaper. She returns with the patch.)

KATE: Here, let me show you, all you do is…

(He snatches the patch from her.)

MR. CARIDI: *(As he goes.)* Suck my dick.

Transition

A slide is projected: 6:10 P.M.

Kate is with a woman, Paula, black, 36, frail and sick.

PAULA: *(Brightly, belying its content.)* "Mama, I want to see *Lion King!* I want to see *Lion King!*" I mean, that's all I've been hearing for weeks. "Why can't I see it? Why can't I see it?" You go to *Burger* King, everything is *Lion King*. You go to the store…

KATE: *How* old is she again?

PAULA: Four and a half, be five in October.

KATE: That's what I thought; that's a little young.

PAULA: Right? I mean, isn't that what everybody's saying? "Well, Ka*isha*'s mother let *her* see it. *Trev*or's mother let *him* see it." Well, I was getting real sick and tired hearing whose mother let who see it—I mean, that's all this girl talked about! Day in, day out. I told her, "Lookit, your brother saw it and your sister saw it and they both say you're too young, so forget about it, you're not seeing it, I don't want to hear another word!" Well. To make a long story short… yesterday I get my girlfriend Clarisse drop us off at Showcase in Orange—

KATE: You pushover!

PAULA: *(Continuous.)* —and I take Alexandra to *Lion King*. Yeah.

KATE: And?

PAULA: You see it?

(Kate shakes her head.)

PAULA: *How* old's your boy?

KATE: Just over two.

PAULA: Oh. Well. I don't know who was more upset by it, her or me. You know what happens in it?

KATE: I think so.

PAULA: The father lion dies and Scar makes Simba think it's all his fault?

KATE: Uh huh.

PAULA: Man. Pretty heavy stuff. Well, I'm not sure it was such a great idea. Maybe it was, maybe it wasn't. All I know is, the father dies, right?, and I'm holding my little girl to me, and I'm sobbing my eyes out.

KATE: Oh, Paula…

PAULA: And I mean *sob*bing. Like the dams burst. Whooshh! I totally lose it. I don't know what freaked her out more, me or the stampede. And it's no noisy! It's so loud! It's really scary, it really is, I don't care *what* they say. And I can't stop crying! It's like uncontrollable. Like everything in my life, all the shit, all the disease, everything, is pouring out of my eyes in tears. A flood!, this flood is… And grownups are looking at me funny like "What the fuck *she* on?" and the kids are getting freaked out all around us— "Mommy,–who's–that–crazy–lady?"—and I'm squeezing little Alexandra to me and squeezing her and squeezing her with all my might and wailing and rocking and making an all-around *fool* of myself.

KATE: *(Soothingly.)* No…

PAULA: *(Continuous.)* And then, all of a sudden, it stops. Just like that. Like somebody turned off the water, turned off the faucet, you know? And I'm

sitting there, so wrecked, so wasted... And it's just a stupid cartoon! A kids' movie! I don't know what the hell set me off like that. Man!
(Long pause.)

KATE: Paula... *(Pause.)* The DDI isn't working.

PAULA: Did I tell you?, at the movies?, she had me getting up for *pop*corn, getting up for *Sprite,* getting up to *pee...*

KATE: Paula?

PAULA: *(Beat.)* So put me back on AZT.

KATE: We can't put you back on AZT.

PAULA: *(Over "on AZT.")* Why not?

KATE: It doesn't work that way. It stopped being effective the first time, it's not going to be effective now.

PAULA: *(Over "effective now.")* How do you know?

KATE: It isn't. *(Beat.)* The sputum and blood cultures we took? Both grew out *M. avium intracellulare.*

PAULA: M. what?

KATE: *M. avium intracellulare.* It's a mycobacterium, a kind of a cousin of TB That's one of the reasons you haven't been able to keep the weight back on.

PAULA: That last pneumonia took a long time, too. Remember? I was sick forever—

KATE: This isn't like that.

PAULA: *(Continuous.)* —and I pulled through.

KATE: Yeah, but it's not the same. You were stronger then. You had more resistance. *(Pause.)* Paula, your T-4 count is down to four. That's as low as it goes; it can't *get* any lower than that. *(Pause.)* Paula... With your T-cell count so low...

PAULA: *(Drops eye contact.)* Yeah...?

KATE: Anything can happen. And it will.

PAULA: Uh huh.

KATE: *(Beat.)* Paula?

PAULA: *(Gets up.)* Lookit, I got to go pick up my kids at my mother's. I'm late, I told her I'd get there at six.

KATE: Paula, please sit down?

PAULA: *(Over "sit down;" enraged.)* You kept me waiting twenty minutes out there!—

KATE: Paula...

PAULA: —My time is valuable, too, you know. May not *look* it to you...

KATE: Please.

(Pause; Paula leans against the chair; carefully.)

KATE: I think it's time to give some serious thought. Remember we talked about this? I think it's time to come up with a plan. *(Beat.)* Did you meet with the social worker?

PAULA: Yeah.

KATE: And?

PAULA: *(Shrugs.)* Her perfume made me sick to my stomach.

KATE: Paula, I know it's hard.

PAULA: You don't know shit. You don't know nothing. When was the last time *you* had to worry what was gonna happen to *your* kids? So don't tell me you know.

(Kate nods. Long pause.)

KATE: What did your mother say?

PAULA: My mother don't want them. Can you blame her? I don't. My mother is 54 years old. What does she want a bunch of kids for? She's tired. She's got diabetes, bad circulation. High blood pressure.

KATE: I know.

PAULA: *(Continuous.)* I mean, a couple of days here and there, when I'm in the hospital or whatever, *that* she can handle. But raising kids that ain't even teenagers yet?! Un-uh. She's done. She's had it. And can you *blame* her with what's going on today? Who needs it? She's tired. She raised kids her whole life. *Her* kids, my sister's kids. My little one? Andre? He's a devil. She can't go chasing him around. How she gonna do that? She can't.

KATE: But they're your *chil*dren. Her *grand*children.

PAULA: You don't understand: She don't want no more children. You understand? She don't *want* them.

KATE: Would she come to a family meeting?

PAULA: I'm telling you she don't *want* them. Period.

KATE: *(Over "Period.")* If I arranged a family meeting, if I called her and talked to her myself…

PAULA: You don't get it, do you. Forget about my mother. Forget about her. Make believe she's dead. Make believe I don't *have* a mother. 'Cause she ain't gonna take them.

KATE: All I'm asking is, Paula, can you get her down here for a meeting, that's all I'm asking.

(Paula shrugs.)

KATE: You, me, the social worker, your mother, maybe your girlfriend…

PAULA: Clarisse?

KATE: Yeah, have you considered *her?*

PAULA: Clarisse has got four kids of her own! No man, no job, no money, no nothing. How'm I gonna leave my four kids on her doorstep?

KATE: Isn't there somebody else, a friend or a…

PAULA: *All* my friends got problems of their own. Who do you think my friends are? Rich folks? How my friends gonna raise my kids? I can't ask them that. They got problems feeding them*selves.*

KATE: Paula, what I'm concerned about right now are your *chil*dren, what's going to happen to your *chil*dren.

PAULA: And you think I'm not?

KATE: Of course I don't think that. I'm just trying to—

PAULA: I bet you're sitting there asking yourself what business did she have having all these kids for in the first place?

KATE: No…

PAULA: Well, I had no business doing a lot of the things I did. But the thing is I did 'em. Okay? And this is where we're at. *(Pause.)* You just think I'm selfish.

KATE: I never said that.

PAULA: You do. You think I'm too selfish to think about my kids.

KATE: That's not true. I just think there's no time to fool around.

PAULA: Fool *around?* It look to you like I'm fooling around?

KATE: *(Over "like I'm fooling around"; overly invested.)* You know what I'm saying. This is no time to be passive, Paula, there's not time for that. You *need* a plan. Think about your children. Losing you is going to be hard enough, what if they all get separated from each *oth*er? Hm? Have you thought about that? They'll be shipped all over the place and get tossed around in the child welfare system and maybe get lost forever. Is that what you want for them? You can't let that happen to them, Paula. You've got to plan for it now. Before you get any sicker.

PAULA: You just want to see me dead.

KATE: What?!

PAULA: It's true. You'll be happy when I'm out of your hair forever.

KATE: How can you say that? I've followed you for two and a half years. I care very much about you.

PAULA: *(Over "about you.")* Nah, I'm too much trouble. You'll be happy when I just disappear. One day I will, too, I'll just…poof! and that'll be it. "Bye, bye, Paula. Oh, well, too bad. Next!"

KATE: Paula, let me talk to your mother? *(Pause.)*

PAULA: Look at me. Look at where I'm at. *(She shakes her head.)* My whole life. My whole fucking life: Men. Bad luck with men. Lamar should've just slashed my throat. It've been easier, a lot easier than *this,* that's for sure. A quick knife to the jugular? Sounds good. Sounds good to me. *(Beat.)* Know what it's gonna say on my tombstone? "Fucked over by men." My daddy fucked me over, Lamar finished me off. *(Beat.)* I'm thirty-six years old. Can you believe it? Look at this body, this saggy bag of bones. I look a *hun*dred and thirty-six.

KATE: No…

PAULA: This body used to mean something.

KATE: It still does.

PAULA: *(Shakes her head, then.)* No. No. It was a good body, once. It had value. Now? *(Pause.)* I think back to meeting Lamar? First laying eyes on him? And I think to myself, "Stay away, girl, this man is going to ruin you. This man will make your life hell. This man will poison you and the two of you'll die young and your children'll be cursed forever." *(Beat.)* Did I know, deep down, I was meeting Death himself? Is that what attracted me to him? Did Nicole know when she first laid eyes on that beautiful man? Did she know O.J. was Death and go to him anyway? If Lamar was Death, then let me tell you: Death was hot.

(Kate smiles sadly, puts her hand in Paula's; Paula doesn't reject it.)

Transition
A slide is projected: 9:12 P.M.
Kate finishes writing notes on a chart and packs up for the night. She looks at some framed photos, sees that her framed picture is gone and realizes that it was swiped by Mr. Caridi.

KATE: Sonofabitch.
(Señora appears at the door.)
SEÑORA: ¿Señora doctora?
KATE: Oh, hello.
SEÑORA: Dijo que la llamara. Llamé y me dijeron que podia venir. *[You said to call. I called, they said I could come in.]*
KATE: Sí, sí. Entra. Me voy a casa. I'm going home, terminé por la noche. *[Finished for the night.]* Sólo puedo ver usted por un minuto. *[I can only see you for a minute.]* ¿Qué pasó? *[What happened?]*
SEÑORA: Sentí el dolor otra vez. Volvió el dolor. *[I felt the pain again. The pain came back.]* Dijo que deberia llamar si sentia otra vez el dolor. *[You said I should call if I felt the pain.]*
KATE: Sí. ¿Cuándo paso? *[When did it happen?]*
SEÑORA: Estaba descansador en mi "Lazy Boy." *[I was resting in my Lazy Boy recliner chair.]* Estaba viendo a O.J. Simpson. *[I was watching O.J. Simpson.]* De pronto, me vino una visión. *[Then all of a sudden I had a vision.]*
KATE: ¿Una visión?
SEÑORA: Sí. Mi corazón empezó a latir fuertemente en mi pecho. *[My heart began to pound in my chest.]* La sangre empezó a correr de mi boca *[Blood started pouring out of my mouth]* como un río de sangre *[like a river of blood]* y de los ojos, ye de los oídos y la nariz. *[and out of my eyes, and my ears and my nose.]* La sangre corrio de mi *[Blood gushed out of me]* de alla debajo, de todas partes *[from down there, from everywhere]* llenando el cuarto de sangre. *[filling the room with blood.]* Mi sangre estaba por todo, como un mar. *[My blood was everywhere, like the sea.]* Y pronto los muebles empezaron a bambolear en la sangre *[Soon the furniture started bobbing around in the blood]* el televisor, las sillas, y pronto todo flotó por la ventana. *[the t.v., the chairs, and soon everything floated right out the window!]* ¡Y yo oía a mis hijos llorando! *[And I heard my children crying!]* Ellos estaban en algun otro cuarto, llorando, "Mamá! Mamá!" *[They were in*

another room somewhere, crying, "Mama! Mama!] Yo no los oía pero si los
veía. *[I could hear them but I couldn't see them.* ¡Yo no podía llegar hacia
ellos! *[I couldn't get to them!]* La olas de sangre eran tan grandes. *[The
waves of blood were so strong.]* Que me barraron como una terrible tormen-
ta. *[It tossed me around like a terrible storm.]* ¡Y no podía nadar! ¡Me
ahogué! *[And I couldn't swim! The waves overtook me and I drowned!]* ¡Me
ahogué en mi propia sangre! *[Drowned in my own blood!]* Señora doctora,
¿puede que el dolor haga que se explote el corazón de una madre? *[Can
sorrow make a mother's heart burst open?]* ¿Se puede ahogar uno en su
propia sangre? *[Can you drown in your own blood?]* Creo que es posible. *[I
think it's possible.]* ¡Creo que voy a morir! *[I think I'm going to die!]* ¡Por
favor, no quiero que me lleven de mis hijos! *[Please, I don't want to be
taken from my children!]*

KATE: *(Soothing.)* Señora...

SEÑORA: Ya no puede dormir. *[I can't sleep anymore.]* Tengo conversaciones en
mi mente con mis hijos. *[I have conversations in my head with my children.]* Les hablo toda la noche. *[I talk to them all night.]* Pienso en ellos
todo el día. *[I think about them all day.]* Pienso en ellos ahora mismo. *[I'm
thinking about them now.]* Me duele el corazón. *[My heart aches.]* ¡Creo
que voy a morir! *[I think I am going to die!]* ¡El dolor! ¡El dolor! *[The pain!
The pain!]*

KATE: El dolor es miedo. *[The pain is fear.]*

SEÑORA: ¿Qué?

KATE: El dolor es miedo. Fear. Tienes miedo. *[The pain is fear. You're afraid.]*

SEÑORA: Sí, tengo miedo. Estoy tan asustada. *[Yes, I am afraid. I'm so afraid.]*
Señora doctora, ¿que voy a hacer? *[What am I going to do?]* Ayudame,
Señora doctora. Ayudame. *[Help me, Doctor. Help me.]*

(Kate and Señora are standing at opposite ends of the room in silence.)

Transition

    A slide is projected: 10:05 P.M.

    Mark is seated on a sofa, his bare feet up, reading the New York Times. *Kate
comes in from work.*

KATE: Hi.

MARK: Hi. How are you?

    (Kate kisses him, shrugs, a beat. He senses something is wrong.)

MARK: What.

KATE: *(Shrugs it off.)* Baby sleeping?

MARK: Yeah. He was still flinging himself around the crib a couple of minutes
ago but it's been pretty quiet.

KATE: I'm tempted to go in.

MARK: *(Takes her hand to stop her.)* Don't. Please? You'll wake him.
(Pause. She takes off her shoes, joins him on the sofa.)

KATE: *Frasier* on?

MARK: Rerun.

KATE: Which one?

MARK: He and Niles take his father out to eat? The steakhouse?

KATE: Oh, yeah.

MARK: I turned it off.

KATE: What about *Seinfeld?*

MARK: That was a rerun, too, but I didn't remember seeing it.

KATE: What was it?

MARK: Elaine's in the ladies' room at a movie theater? and find there's no toilet paper and asks the woman in the stall next to hers for some and the woman refuses and they argue but can't see each other and of course it turns out the woman is Jerry's new girlfriend.

KATE: Of course...

MARK: And Elaine has a new boyfriend who she's very defensive about because he's supposedly so good-looking. And Kramer and George and this guy go rock climbing and somehow, I don't know, exactly, I was reading the paper, I think George drops a rope or something and the guy falls and crushes his face.

KATE: *(Winces.)* Ooo.

MARK: Yeah. And then naturally it turns out that Elaine was only interested in him for his looks and has no interest in staying with him if he's disfigured. And also there's this phone sex subplot going on with Kramer where it turns out that the woman he's been calling is Jerry's new girlfriend.

KATE: Was it any good?

MARK: It was alright. *Seinfeld's* getting very, I don't know, there's something very malevolent going on on *Seinfeld.* Something mean-spirited and juvenile.

KATE: Uh huh.

MARK: The attitude toward sex is very screwed up. All this fear and loathing. The women are always portrayed as these alien ciphers good for making out with but there's this underlying ickiness and suspicion. All the women except Elaine all seem to have cooties.

KATE: Mm. Seinfeld seems like a seriously anally-retentive guy.

MARK: Right! I mean, anybody who has fifteen cereal boxes lined up like that... You hungry? There's some tortellini left in the fridge.

KATE: *(Shakes her head, No.)* What happened today?

MARK: You heard that the judge ruled that the evidence was admissible?

KATE: I heard that; I meant what's new with *you?*

MARK: Not much.

KATE: Did you talk to many people today?

MARK: You mean besides a two-year-old and the U.P.S. man?

KATE: That's what I thought. How's the writing coming?

MARK: Maybe I'll be done with this dissertation by the time I'm fifty. Maybe. There's an O.J. update on NBC if you're up for it.

KATE: I'm not.

MARK: Are you okay?

KATE: *(Thinks about elaborating.)* Oh… *(But changes her mind.)* Tell me about our boy. What kind of a day did he have?

MARK: I hear he had a good day.

KATE: Tell me. What did you do tonight?

MARK: Well, we ate tortellini—

KATE: Yeah…

MARK: *(Continuous.)* —which he kept popping into his mouth, it was really quite impressive, he can really put it away. And then we went for a walk.

KATE: Where?

MARK: The construction site and then to the park.

KATE: Oh, a serious walk.

MARK: And we saw the "backhoe" and the crane— "biigg crane" — and we saw bicyclists and doggies and men running — it was a banner day — and an airplane flew overhead and birdies and later he pointed way up high in the sky— "Look, Daddy, hec–coc–ca" and he was right, there was a helicopter. And we went and got some frozen yogurt which he ate with great abandon and got all over himself. And we ran into Pete closing up which was a source of great excitement. And then we got home and I let him play with the hose while I mowed the lawn.

KATE: You mowed? Excellent.

MARK: So he got soaked and ucky and then we went upstairs and got naked and chased each other around for a little while and he peed on the floor— deliberately— "Look, Daddy, pee"—and I got him into the tub where he peed some more and scrubbed my face with the wash cloth—very hard, I had to take it away from him.

KATE: Did you shampoo?

MARK: Not tonight; I couldn't bring myself to. I couldn't take away the wash cloth *and* wash his hair; that would've been too cruel. And then I got him ready for bed.

KATE: What did you read?

MARK: What did we read. Let's see… we read the bulldozer book. And the truck book. And the piggy book. And the potty book—he now says "I want read potty book," you know, he's fascinated, we'd better go get him a potty, quick, this weekend, before the window of opportunity slams shut forever. *(Pause.)* You know how it is when you turn out the light and you're holding him on your lap and you can see his dark eyes shining and you can smell his milky breath and he seems utterly content and starts getting sleepy and his eyes begin to close but he forces himself awake?

KATE: Mm. He's an angel.

MARK: I sat like that with him in my arms for a while and I said, "In the great green room, there was a telephone and a red balloon," and he crinkled up his face in pure pleasure.

KATE: Say it.

MARK: What.

KATE: "In the great green room…"

MARK: "In the great green room
   There was a telephone
   And a red balloon
   And a picture of —
   The cow jumping over the moon."
   (She is weeping, He becomes concerned.)

MARK: Honey? What is it?
   (She shakes her head dismissively.)

MARK: Bad day?

KATE: That's the thing: it was completely typical; it just got to me today.

MARK: You want to tell me?

KATE: Just finish the story.

MARK: What?

KATE: Finish. Go ahead.
   (He hesitates.)

KATE: Please? I want to hear your voice.

MARK: *(Beat.)* "Goodnight room
   Goodnight moon
   Goodnight cow jumping over the moon
   Goodnight light
   And the red balloon
   Goodnight bears
   And goodnight chairs
   Goodnight kittens
   And goodnight mittens"
   (Pause; She is weeping.)

MARK: "Goodnight clocks
   And goodnight socks
   Goodnight little house
   And goodnight mouse
   Goodnight comb
   And goodnight brush
   Goodnight nobody
   Goodnight mush
   And goodnight to the old lady whispering 'hush.'
   Goodnight stars

Goodnight air
Goodnight noises everywhere."
(During the above, he holds her as lights fade.)

END OF PLAY

Stones and Bones

by Marion McClinton

Marion McClinton is a company member with both the Penumbra Theatre Company and New Dramatists. His directing credits include *East Texas Hot Links* at the New York Shakespeare Festival, *A Midsummer Night's Dream* at La Jolla Playhouse, *I Am a Man* at the Goodman Theatre and *Stones and Bones* at Actors Theatre of Louisville. *Stones and Bones* premiered in the 1994 Humana Festival of New American Plays and was the co-winner of that year's Heideman Award for best play submitted to the National Ten-Minute Play Contest. His other awards and fellowships include: a Playwrights Horizons Revson Commission Grant, a TCG and Pew Charitable Trust National Theatre Artists Residency at Center Stage, a Bush Fellowship and the 1992 Kesselring Award for his play *Police Boys*, which premiered at Playwrights Horizons in New York.

ORIGINAL PRODUCTION

Stones and Bones premiered in the 1994 Humana Festival of New American Plays at Actors Theatre of Louisville. It was directed by Marion McClinton with the following cast:

Mister Bones ....Timothy D. Stickney
Sistuh Stones ....Stacy Highsmith
Bone..Terry E. Bellamy
Stony..Fanni Green

CHARACTERS

MISTER BONES: a young black man
SISTUH STONES: a young black woman
BONE: a black man
STONY: a black woman

TIME: The ever present now.

SETTING

Very minimal. Should be all done with light and sound. No furniture, no props, nothing save the imagination of the artists is necessary. This will make the piece very stylized, but that is the way it should be. Mister Bones and Sistuh Stones are dressed in the primary colors of hip-hop fashion, but they wear a minstrel's black face in all its blatant big-lipped caricature. If they have dreads, it should look more pickaninny than Bob Marley, but MOVE is an option for the look as well. They should be very colorful, like cartoons, and they should be trying to fight through the image of the role they have been designated to play. Stony and Bone are buppies to the max. Both groups of couples are on stage the entire play. It should not be played for the psychological subtext, but rather the effect they have on each other. They can notice each other as seems fit.

STONES AND BONES

There will be no other stage direction until the end of the play except for this: Music starts. Lights Up.

MISTER BONES: Yo, baby.

SISTUH STONES: Hello.

MISTER BONES: Yo baby, yo baby, yo baby, yo.

SISTUH STONES: Shit.

MISTER BONES: What's up, you fine cutie, honeybear-looking thing you.

SISTUH STONES: Uh huh.

MISTER BONES: Where you going on with this fine motherfucking day, and shit? Man, fine as this motherfucking day is with all that sunshine and shit, the bitch ain't no kind of ways finer than your sweet motherfucking ass, I know that. What I don't know is if you're wearing the sunshine, or if that sunshine is wearing you. You know what I'm saying?

SISTUH STONES: Yeah.

MISTER BONES: So fuck all the dumb shit, you know what I'm saying?

SISTUH STONES: I wish we would.

MISTER BONES: Yeah, move over and let me sit next to your fine motherfucking ass. I'm the number one nigger, ain't a motherfucker bigger, make your body all a quiver, and find your soul's motherfucking trigger. I'm the true, for real dope motherfucker on time with all the hype rhymes, you know what I'm saying?

SISTUH STONES: Look...I just changed my seat...okay?

MISTER BONES: Yeah...so?

SISTUH STONES: I would rather not have to move again. There's too much ignorance perpetrating itself on this bus, and not enough seats to go around...you hear what I'm saying? *(Pause.)*

MISTER BONES: You saying I'm a counterfeit motherfucker? Is that what you saying?

SISTUH STONES: As a three dollar bill with Whoopi Goldberg's picture on it...my brother.

MISTER BONES: Oh, it's like that now, huh? You just gonna front my manhood all off and shit like I'm some kind of bust-out punk?

SISTUH STONES: Yeah, well, you know what they say?

MISTER BONES: No, what do they say?

SISTUH STONES: If your shit is to the curb, you gonna wind up in the gutter.

MISTER BONES: Yeah? Well, fuck you, bitch!

SISTUH STONES: Not in this life, junior.

(Mister Bones leaves. A moment. Mister Bones returns.)

MISTER BONES: So, you busy tonight or what?

SISTUH STONES: I can't believe you...

MISTER BONES: Believe it, baby. I'm for real.

SISTUH STONES: This goes beyond all normal boundaries of stupidity into something truly weird.

MISTER BONES: Whatever...so you busy tonight?

SISTUH STONES: Nigger, drop dead.

MISTER BONES: So what about tomorrow?

SISTUH STONES: Nigger, I wouldn't accept a glass of ice water from you if I was on a roasting spit in hell for a thousand motherfucking years! A thousand years, you hear me!

MISTER BONES: That's all right, baby. I'm a nineties nigger. I'll just wait for the next millennium to make its way by here. You worth waiting a thousand years for. Shit, the devil will quench his motherfucking thirst before I'm done waiting on you. Shit, baby, I'm a nineties nigger. I ain't got nothing promised me but time. You know what I'm saying?

BONE: Something wrong?

STONY: You tell me?

BONE: What?

STONY: Can't you talk?

BONE: I don't know what you're talking about.

STONY: You are a lie and a half. I can smell the truth stinking all over your tongue. Tell me the truth, and get your taste back. *(Pause.)*

BONE: How do you know? I thought I was...I don't know...

STONY: Careful! (God, I hope you were careful.) I have danced with you inside of my heart with my soul, Bone. Who did you think I was? Come on...speak. You were always such a good talker. So good with words. Tell me something true, Bone.

MISTER BONES: Miss me much, baby?

SISTUH STONES: You...shit.

MISTER BONES: Where you been?

SISTUH STONES: I'm mourning my life.

MISTER BONES: I knew your ass missed me. You missed me, didn't you?

SISTUH STONES: I'm sorry, brother...

MISTER BONES: Mister Bones.

SISTUH STONES: Whatever...you put too much pressure on somebody. Hard to remain a lady if I listen to you, do what you want me to do. Understand. You need to chill down. You too psychotic about it.

MISTER BONES: Why I gotta be all of that? I just think you and me could be fantastic together. I see you, and I see my whole life stretched out before me, and I get excited. I don't usually get excited about my future, so I gotta grab that motherfucking ring when it swings on by, you know what I'm saying? I talk shit, but I ain't a not-about-shit-Motherfucker...shit...I want the motherfucking finer things in life my own damn self, and you, sweet honey in the rock, is one of them kind of things.

SISTUH STONES: That's exactly what I feel like when I talk to brothers like you, Mister Bones. Some kind of thing for some coonshow nigger who think he got some kind of rap that got something to say to me. All you rough-neck gangstuh brothers been hitting on me so hard I'm a serious TKO behind all that mess you talk. You all done hit on me until your words got tired, and your mouth got sore. I ain't even here anymore.

MISTER BONES: Look, I walk through the world like I got some kind of right of way in it. I'm loud because nobody gives enough of a shit about nothing to do with me to pay attention to whatever I'm saying. I ain't like y'all sis-tuhs. Y'all done bought that white girl chickenshit about being victims so long lately you become addicted to victimization. I don't tear you down. You do a good enough job of that your own damn self. To tell you the truth, I hate to look at it. Breaks my motherfucking heart.

SISTUH STONES: You might not be trying to tear me down, but you sure as shit ain't trying to build me up. Ask me what's on my mind outside of do I want to do the nasty with you. You hate to look at it? Good. I wish you would quit looking here, and take your twenty-twenty somewheres else. I need a mate, not a date…you know?

BONE: So you wanna know anything else?

STONY: No.

BONE: About whether they married, or have children, or anything?

STONY: No.

BONE: Their age, weight, height, the color of their eyes, whether they remind me of you or not?

STONY: If they got children, and are married, and unsatisfied with their life, then I know what about them reminds you of me.

BONE: I still want us to be together.

STONY: I don't believe this chickenshit bullshit.

BONE: Look, I don't take them out, never fucked them through the night, and ignore you in our own bed, I don't buy them things, I don't call them every chance I get in the day free and clear, I never said anything about them being better lovers, or finer women than you, or that being unhappy with you was the reason I was with them. You know what I'm saying? I didn't, don't, and won't love them period. It's me! OK? I'm just wrong! I'm all of everything you was afraid I was gonna be! I'm wrong, down and dirty, no good to the motherfucking bone! OK! I don't know why! What else you want me to say? How many more ways can I say it?

STONY: There is one thing you could tell me. Something you neglected to mention.

BONE: What, Stony, damn?

STONY: Whether or not these bitches are white. You can talk about that.

MISTER BONES: Well…this is where I hang. The motherfucking crib in all its glory.

SISTUH STONES: Yeah. Charming.

MISTER BONES: So you like?

SISTUH STONES: It's all right.

MISTER BONES: I tried calling you, you know, all afternoon and shit, and like you weren't never around, or nothing.

SISTUH STONES: Yeah? So?

MISTER BONES: Look, this shit ain't easy for me either, you know what I'm saying? It's hard to get next to somebody on the real tip. This shit hurts my gut it's so bugging, you know what I'm saying? I'm trying to touch another like motherfucking human being and shit. I mean, like fuck the dumb shit, you picked up on me, and I want to deliver. Not just that physical thing, but I mean I want to thaw out your soul, raise you up, I mean, I don't even know why you even are up here with my black ass this minute, you know…

SISTUH STONES: Just be all right with me being here, that's all you gotta do, and I'll be cool with it.

MISTER BONES: No, fuck that, I gotta know! Why here, why with me, why…any of it, why?

SISTUH STONES: You need something? All right…because you brush your teeth three times a day, put some deodorant under those funky armpits, and every other word out of your mouth ain't "bitch" or "ho." *(Pause.)* Because you said I was beautiful, and meant it. Said it sweetly, and smiled with a smile looked like it was full of French champagne when you said it.

MISTER BONES: I ain't that kind of motherfucker. I wish I was, but…

SISTUH STONES: I don't need to hear it from your lips, baby. I know all of that already. Besides I didn't come up here to talk to you anyways. You promised me something else, some other kind of time. I'm here for that. I don't want to talk about it anymore. I want to taste all that sweet champagne you got behind your lips. I want to drink my fill. *(Pause.)*

MISTER BONES: You better go home, honeybaby. You know too much, and you too thirsty.

SISTUH STONES: What…you kidding me, right? A round-the-way fellow with the funky fuck of the ages up inside of your pants? I thought…

MISTER BONES: I ain't got that much champagne in me. I'll call you tomorrow.

SISTUH STONES: Jesus will have come back, and gone by then. I can't wait that long.

MISTER BONES: I'm scared, Sistuh Stones.

SISTUH STONES: I knows the feeling, Mister Bones. We sitting chin deep in some blackfaced, shit-stomping, low down blues, baby, and we can't get up out of it without each other. *(Pause.)* This shit is supposed to be scary.

STONY: You know…

BONE: No, what?

STONY: When I'm breathing, when my heart is flying all around up in my mouth screaming, all I can do is think about it...

BONE: Think about what?

STONY: You touching them with your smile all wide open, slipping all of that champagne that be all mine by right of birth, all turned around, turned out, and your smile.

BONE: Enough, baby. You gonna lose your mind behind all of this. I just better go.

STONY: Yeah, well enough is never enough...I ain't thinking about that. That what is stealing my sleep away from me all through the night. Something else.

BONE: What, Stony.

STONY: If I could take my nose, and cut it, pull my flesh from off of my bones and put on a skin made of peaches like it was a new winter coat, if I could look at you like you were a criminal all the time, cross to the other side of the street every time I see you coming my way, never wait on you first when it's your turn in line, never sit next to you on the bus even if it's the only seat, make you forget you had a mama that always looked old, and a daddy that always seemed broken, if I could make you forget the manhood that supposed to be in between your legs, make you dream in black and white, and turn the black to gray, if it were true that I had more fun, and knew what Clairol knows, and make you feel it's all right and cool with me if you take every last bit of black that was passed down to you from every African hanging from your family tree, trash it like it wasn't never there, and wasn't never anything worth keeping no how. If I can get you to change how you talk, if I can refine all the loudness from out of your soul...if I didn't know nothing about nothing worth knowing about you...If I was white would I stop intimidating you so you could hold me through the night, clutched to your chest? Would you be scared of me then? Would you stop being scared of yourself then? *(Silence.)*

BONE: I don't know. *(Beat.)*

STONY: Oh.

SISTUH STONES: God dammit...that was the best...I hoped you was something special...

STONY: Okay.

MISTER BONES: Shit, baby, I knew I could rock your world.

BONE: I do know it wouldn't change anything. I been trying to fuck myself into a new life. I ain't got that much juice in me.

SISTUH STONES: This shit is frightening, ain't it?

STONY: Well.

BONE: I don't recognize my own voice anymore.

MISTER BONES: Seem like I know myself so well when I'm inside of you.

STONY: I know you.

SISTUH STONES: I know.

MISTER BONES: Just gonna get better and better.

BONE: I don't know.

SISTUH STONES: Ain't nobody else supposed to make me feel like you do. Maybe that's it.

STONY: Maybe you just plain can't...

BONE: Love you? Maybe I never did.

MISTER BONES: Shit, baby, you with the jam master blaster of ceremonies hisself.

STONY: You love me. Probably always will. It'll be the only thing that will keep you alive in the end. But until you can love yourself and we can take each other in hand, neither of us will ever live.

MISTER BONES: We gonna be getting busy, and swapping spit full of Dom Perignon, and being happy forever and a day. For ever and ever and ever...

MISTER BONES AND SISTUH STONES: ...and ever, forever, and ever, and ever, and ever...until death do us part...amen.

(Lights go down to Black as Mister Bones and Sistuh Stones are in an embrace, and Stony and Bone are far apart, as we hear the sound of lovemaking, mingled with the sound of crying tears.)

END OF PLAY

Tone Clusters

by Joyce Carol Oates

Joyce Carol Oates is the author of twenty novels, and many volumes of short stories, poems, essays, and plays. She has received awards from the Guggenheim Foundation, the American Academy and the Lotus Club, and she received a National Book Award in 1970 for her novel, *them*. Her novel *Because It Is Bitter, And Because It Is My Heart* was nominated for the 1990 National Book Award, and *Black Water* (1992) was a finalist for the Pulitzer Prize and the National Book Critics Circle Award. *What I Lived For* (1994) was also a Pulitzer finalist.

For many years her short stories have been included in the annual Best American Short Stories and the O. Henry Prize stories collections, and she has twice been the recipient of the O. Henry Special Award for Continuing Achievement. *Heat: And Other Stories*, her collection of short stories was published in 1991 to critical acclaim. She is a member of the American Academy and Institute of Arts and Letters.

Most recently, in 1990, she was awarded the Rea Award for the Short Story, given to honor a living U.S. writer who has made a significant contribution to the short story as an art form. In naming Joyce Carol Oates the 1990 winner, the jury for the Rea Award cited: "One of the magical things about Joyce Carol Oates is her ability to constantly reinvent not only the psychological space she inhabits, but herself as well, as part of her fiction. She can operate, as a writer, out of a combination of bewilderment and immediate intuitive understanding–turning to fiction what impinges on her life, wherever she chooses to live it."

Her plays have been produced by Actors Theatre of Louisville, Ensemble Studio Theatre, Circle Repertory Theatre, American Place Theatre, The Guthrie Theatre, Long Wharf Theatre, Philadelphia Festival Theatre, McCarter Theatre, Sharon Stage and Georgia Repertory Theatre. Her play *Tone Clusters* premiered at Actors Theatre of Louisville in 1990 and was co-winner of the Heideman Award for best new play submitted to the National One-Act Play Contest. Many of her other plays have been published in *Twelve Plays* by Joyce Carol Oates and *The Perfectionist and Other Plays*. *The Interview* was included in *Best American Short Plays* 1993-94.

Born in Lockport, New York, she was educated at Syracuse University and the University of Wisconsin. Joyce Carol Oates is married and lives in Princeton, New Jersey, where she is the Roger S. Berlind Distinguished Professor in the Humanities at Princeton University.

ORIGINAL PRODUCTION

In Darkest America, two plays by Joyce Carol Oates, premiered at the 14th Annual Humana Festival of New American Plays at Actors Theatre of Louisville in 1990.

Tone Clusters was directed by Steven Albrezzi with the following cast:

Voice	William McNulty
Frank Gulick	Peter Michael Goetz
Emily Gulick	Adale O'Brien
Stage Manager	Jay McManigal

CHARACTERS

FRANK GULICK: 53 years old
EMILY GULICK: 51 years old
VOICE: Male, indeterminate age

TIME: The present

SETTING: These are white Americans of no unusual distinction, nor are they in any self-evident way "representative."

Tone Clusters is not intended to be a realistic work, thus any inclination toward the establishment of character should be resisted. Its primary effect should be visual (the dominance of the screen at center stage, the play of lights of sharply contrasting degrees of intensity) and audio (the *Voice*, the employment of music–*tone clusters* of Henry Cowell and/or Charles Ives, and electronic music, etc.) The mood is one of fragmentation, confusion, yet, at times strong emotion. A fractured narrative emerges which the audience will have no difficulty piecing together even as–and this is the tragi-comedy of the piece–the characters Mr. and Mrs. Gulick deny it.

In structure, *Tone Clusters* suggests an interview, but a stylized interview in which questions and answers are frequently askew. Voices trail off into silence or may be mocked or extended by strands of music. The *Voice* is sometimes overamplified and booming; sometimes marred by static; sometimes clear, in an ebullient tone, like that of a talk-show host. The *Voice* has no identity but must be male. It should not be represented by any actual presence on the stage or within view of the audience. At all times, the *Voice* is in control; the principals on the stage are dominated by their interrogator and by the screen which is seemingly floating in the air above them, at center stage. Indeed the screen emerges as a character.

The piece is divided into nine uneven segments. When one ends, the lights dim, then come up again immediately. (After the ninth segment lights go out completely and darkness is extended for some seconds to indicate that the piece is ended: it ends on an abrupt cut off of lights and images on screens.) By degree the Gulicks become somewhat accustomed to the experience of being interviewed and filmed, but never wholly accustomed; they are always slightly disoriented, awkward, confused, inclined to speak slowly and methodically or too quickly, *unprofessionally*, often with inappropriate emotion (fervor, enthusiasm, hope, sudden rage) or no emotion at all (like *computer voices*). The Gulicks may at times speak in unison (as if one were an echo of the other); they may mimic the qualities of tone cluster music or electronic music (I conceive of their voices, and that of the *Voice*, as music of a kind); should the director wish, there may be some clear-cut relationship between subject and emotion or emphasis—but the piece should do no more than approach *realism*, and then withdraw. The actors must conceive of themselves as elements in a dramatic structure, not as *human characters* wishing to establish rapport with an audience.

Tone Clusters is about the absolute mystery—the *not-knowing*—at the core of our human experience. That the mystery is being exploited by a television documentary underscores its tragi-comic nature.

TONE CLUSTERS

Lights Up. Initially very strong, near-blinding. On a bare stage, middle-aged Frank and Emily Gulick sit ill-at-ease in comfortable modish cushioned swivel chairs, trying not to squint or grimace in the lights [which may be represented as the lights of a camera crew provided the human figures involved can be kept shadowy, even indistinct]. They wear clip-on microphones to which they are unaccustomed. They are dressed up for the occasion, and clearly nervous: They continually touch their faces, or clasp their hands firmly in their laps, or fuss with fingernails, buttons, the microphone cords, their hair. The nervous mannerisms continue throughout the piece but should never be too distracting and never comic.

Surrounding the Gulicks, dominating their human presence, are TV monitors and/or slide screens upon which, during the course of the play, disparate images, words, formless flashes of light are projected. Even when the Gulicks own images appear on the screens they are upstaged by it: They glance at it furtively, with a kind of awe.

The monitors always show the stage as we see it: the Gulicks seated, glancing uneasily up at the screen. Thus there is a screen-within-a-screen.

The employment of music is entirely at the director's discretion. The opening might be accompanied by classical tone cluster piano pieces—Henry Cowell's "Advertisement" for instance. The music should never be intrusive. The ninth scene might well be completely empty of music. There should certainly be no "film-music effect." [The Gulicks do not hear the music.]

The Voice too in its modulations is at the discretion of the director. In a way, I would like Tone Clusters to be aleatory, but that might prove too radical for practicality. Certainly at the start the Voice is booming and commanding. There should be intermittent audio trouble [Whistling, Static, etc.]; the Voice, wholly in control, can exude any number of effects throughout the play—pomposity, charity, condescension, bemusement, false chattiness, false pedantry, false sympathy, mild incredulity [like that of a television MC], affectless "computer talk." The Gulicks are entirely intimidated by the Voice and try very hard to answer its questions.

Screen shifts from its initial image to words: In a Case of Murder— large black letters on white.

VOICE: In a case of murder (taking murder as an abstraction)   there is always a sense of the inevitable once the identity of the murderer is established. Beforehand there   is   a   sense   of disharmony.

And humankind fears and loathes disharmony, Mr. and Mrs. Gulick of Lakepointe, New Jersey would you comment?

FRANK: ...Yes I would say,   I think that

EMILY: What is that again, exactly?   I...

FRANK: My wife and I, we...

EMILY: Disharmony...?

FRANK: I don't like disharmony.   I mean, all the family, we are a law-abiding family.

VOICE: A religious family   I believe?

FRANK: Oh yes.   Yes,
We go to church every

EMILY: We almost never miss a,   a Sunday
For a while,   I helped with Sunday School classes
The children,   the children don't always go but they believe, our daughter Judith for instance she   and Carl

FRANK: oh yes yessir.

EMILY: and Dennis,   they do believe they were raised to   believe in God and, and Jesus Christ

FRANK: We raised them that way because   we were raised that way,

EMILY: there *is* a God whether you agree with Him or not.

VOICE: *Religion* may be defined as   a sort of adhesive matter invisibly holding together   nation-states, nationalities, tribes, families   for   the   good   of those   so   held together,   would you comment?

FRANK: Oh,   oh yes.

EMILY: For the good of...

FRANK: Yes I would say so,   I think so.

EMILY: My husband and I, we were married in church, in

FRANK: In the Lutheran Church.

EMILY: In Penns Neck.

FRANK: In New Jersey.

EMILY: All our children,

BOTH: they believe.

EMILY: God sees into the human heart.

VOICE: Mr. and Mrs. Gulick   from your experience would you   theorize for our audience: is the Universe *predestined*   in every particular   or   is man capable   of   acts of   *freedom*?

BOTH: ...

EMILY: ...I would say,   that is hard to say.

FRANK: Yes. I believe that man is free.

EMILY: If you mean like, I guess   choosing good and evil?   Yes

FRANK: I would have to say   yes. You would have to say   mankind is free.

FRANK: Like moving my hand. *(Moves hand.)*

EMILY: If nobody is free   it wouldn't be right would it   to punish anybody?

FRANK: There is always   Hell.
I believe in Hell.
EMILY: Anybody at all
FRANK: Though I am not free to, to   fly up in the air am I? *(Laughs.)* because
   Well I'm not built right for that am I? *(Laughs.)*
VOICE: Man is free.   Thus man is   responsible for his acts.
EMILY: Except, oh   sometime if,   maybe for instance if
   A baby born without
FRANK: Oh one of those *AIDS* babies
EMILY: Poor thing
FRANK: *crack* babies
   Or if you were captured   by some enemy, y'know and tortured
   Some people never have a chance,
EMILY: But God sees into the human heart,
   God knows who to forgive   and who not.
   (Lights down.)

SCENE 2
   Screen shows a suburban street of lower-income homes; the Gulicks stare at the
   screen and their answers are initially distracted.

VOICE: Here we have Cedar Street   in Lakepointe, New Jersey   neatly kept
   homes (as you can see) American suburb   low crime rate, single-family
   homes suburb of Newark, New Jersey   population 12,000 the neighbor-
   hood of Mr. and Mrs. Frank Gulick the parents of   Carl Gulick. Will you
   introduce yourselves to our audience please?
   (House lights come up.)
FRANK: ...Go on, you first
EMILY: I, I don't know what to say
FRANK: My name is   Frank Gulick, I   I am fifty-three years old   that's our
   house there   2368 Cedar Street
EMILY: My name is Emily Gulick, fifty-one years old,
VOICE: How employed,   would you care to say? Mr. Gulick?
FRANK: I work for the post office,   I'm a supervisor for
EMILY: He has worked for the post office, for twenty-five years
FRANK: ...The Terhune Avenue Branch.
VOICE: And how long have you resided   in your attractive home   on Cedar
   Street?
   (House lights begin to fade down.)
FRANK: ...Oh I guess, how long   if this is
   this is 1990?
EMILY: (oh just think: 1990!)
FRANK: we moved there in, uh   Judith wasn't born yet so

EMILY: Oh there was our thirtieth anniversary a year ago,
FRANK: wedding
    no that was two years ago
EMILY: was it?
FRANK: or three, I   twenty-seven years, this is 1990
EMILY: Yes: Judith is twenty-six,   now I'm a grandmother
FRANK: Carl is twenty-two
EMILY: Denny is seventeen, he's a senior in high school
    no none of them are living at home now
FRANK: not now
EMILY: Right now poor Denny is staying with my sister in
VOICE: Frank and Emily Gulick you have been happy here   in Lakepointe rais-
    ing your family like any American couple   with your hopes and aspirations
    until recently?
FRANK: …Yes, oh yes.
EMILY: Oh for a long time we *were*
FRANK: oh yes.
EMILY: It's so strange to,   to think of
    The years go by so
VOICE: You have a   happy family life like so many millions   of Americans
EMILY: Until this, this terrible thing
FRANK: *Innocent until proven guilty*—that's a laugh!
EMILY: Oh it's a, a terrible thing
FRANK: Never any hint beforehand of   the meanness of people's hearts.
    I mean the neighbors.
EMILY: Oh now don't start that, this isn't the
FRANK: Oh God you just try to comprehend
EMILY: this isn't the place, I
FRANK: Like last night: this carload of kids
    drunk, beer-drinking foul language in the night
EMILY: oh don't, my hands are
FRANK: Yes but you know it's the parents set them going   And telephone calls
    our number is changed now, but
EMILY: my hands are shaking so
    we are both on medication   the doctor says,
FRANK: oh you would not believe, you would not believe the hatred like Nazi
    Germany
EMILY: Denny had to drop out of school,   he loved school he is an honor student
FRANK: everybody turned against us
EMILY: My sister in Yonkers, he's staying with
FRANK: Oh he'll never be the same   boy again, none of us will.
VOICE: In the development of   human identity there's the element of chance,
    and there is genetic determinism.
    Would you comment please?

FRANK: The thing is,   you try your best.

EMILY: oh dear God yes.

FRANK: Your best.

EMILY: You give all that's in your heart

FRANK: you
   can't do more than that can you?

EMILY: Yes but there is certain to be   justice.
   There *is* a, a sense of things.

FRANK: Sometimes there is a chance, the way they turn out
   but also   what they *are*.

EMILY: Your own babies

VOICE: Frank Gulick and Mary   what is your assessment of
   American civilization   today?

EMILY: ...It's Emily.

FRANK: My wife's name is,

EMILY: It's
   Emily.

VOICE: Frank and *Emily*   Gulick.

FRANK: ...The state of the   civilization?

EMILY: It's so big,

FRANK: We are here to tell our side of,

EMILY: ...I don't know: it's a,   a Democracy

FRANK: the truth is,   do you want the truth?
   the truth is where we live
   Lakepointe it's changing too

EMILY: it has changed

FRANK: yes but it's all over, it's
   terrible, just terrible

EMILY: Now we are grandparents we fear for

FRANK: Yes what you read and see on TV

EMILY: You don't know what to think,

FRANK: Look: in this country   half the crimes
   are committed by the,   by half the population against the other half.
   (Laughs.) You have your law-abiding citizens,

EMILY: taxpayers

FRANK: and you have the rest of them.
   Say you went downtown into a city like   Newark, some night

EMILY: you'd be crazy if you got out of your car

FRANK: you'd be dead.   That's what.

VOICE: Is it possible,   probable   or in your assessment *im*probable that the
   slaying of   fourteen-year-old   Edith Kaminsky   on February 12, 1990 is
   related to
   the social malaise   of which you speak?

FRANK: ...*ma-lezz?*

EMILY: ...oh it's hard to,   I would say yes

FRANK: ...whoever did it, he

EMILY: Oh it's terrible the things that
    keep happening

FRANK: If only the police would arrest the right person,

VOICE: Frank and Emily Gulick   you remain adamant in your belief   in your
    faith in your twenty-two-year old son   Carl
    that he is innocent   in the death of   fourteen-year-old Edith Kaminsky
    on February 12, 1990?

EMILY: Oh yes,

FRANK: oh yes that is the single thing we are convinced of.

EMILY: On this earth.

BOTH: With God as our witness,

FRANK: yes

EMILY: Yes.

FRANK: The single thing.
    (Lights down.)

SCENE 3

*Lights up. Screen shows violent movement: urban scenes, police patrol cars, a
fire burning out of control, men being arrested and herded into vans; a body
lying in the street. The Gulicks stare at the screen.*

VOICE: Of today's pressing political issues   the rise in violent crime most con-
    cerns American citizens Number one political issue of   Mr. and Mrs.
    Gulick tell our viewers your opinion?

FRANK: In this state
    the state of New Jersey

EMILY: Oh it's everywhere

FRANK: there's capital punishment supposedly

EMILY: But the lawyers   the lawyers get them off,

FRANK: you bet
    There's public defenders the taxpayer pays

EMILY: Oh, it's   it's out of control
    (like that what is it *acid rain*)

FRANK: It can fall on you anywhere,

EMILY: the sun is too hot too:

BOTH: (the *greenhouse effect*)

FRANK: It's a welfare state by any other name

EMILY: Y'know who pays:

BOTH: the taxpayer

FRANK: The same God damn criminal, you pay for him   then he

That's the joke of it *(Laughs.)*
the same criminal who slits your throat *(Laughs.)*
He's the one you pay bail for to get out.
But it sure isn't funny. *(Laughs.)*

EMILY: Oh God.

FRANK: It sure isn't funny.

VOICE: Many Americans have come to believe   this past decade   that capital
punishment is one of the answers: would you comment please?

FRANK: Oh in cases of actual, proven   murder

EMILY: Those drug dealers

FRANK: Yes *I* would have to say, definitely   yes

EMILY: I would say so yes

FRANK: You always hear them say   opponents of the death penalty
"The death penalty doesn't stop crime"

EMILY: Oh that's what they say!

FRANK: Yes but *I* say, once a man is dead he sure isn't gonna commit any more
crimes, is he. *(Laughs.)*

VOICE: The death penalty *is* a deterrent to crime   in those cases
when the criminal has been   executed

FRANK: But you have to find the right,
the actual murderer.

EMILY: Not some poor innocent   some poor innocent.*
[*_Innocent_ is an adjective here, not a noun.]
(Lights down.)

SCENE 4

*Lights up. Screen shows a grainy magnified snapshot of a boy about ten.
Quick jump to a snapshot of the same boy a few years older. Throughout this
scene images of Carl Gulick appear and disappear on the screen though not in
strict relationship to what is being said, nor in chronological order. Carl
Gulick in his late teens and early twenties is muscular but need not have any
other outstanding characteristics: he may look like any American boy at all.*

VOICE: Carl Gulick, twenty-two years old   the second-born child of Frank and
Emily Gulick   of Lakepointe, New Jersey   How would you describe your
son, Frank and Emily

FRANK: D'you mean how he looks or...?

EMILY: He's a shy boy, he's shy   Not backward just

FRANK: He's about my height I guess   brown hair, eyes

EMILY: Oh! no I think   he's much taller Frank
he's been taller than you   for years

FRANK: Well that depends on how we're both standing.
How we're both   standing

Well in one newspaper it said six feet one inch, in the other
six feet three inches, that's the kind of
EMILY: accuracy
FRANK: reliability of the news media
you can expect!
EMILY: And oh that terrible picture of,
in the paper
that face he was making   the police carrying him against his will   laying
their hands on him
FRANK: handcuffs
EMILY: Oh that isn't *him*
BOTH: that isn't our son
(Gulicks respond dazedly to snapshots flashed on screen.)
EMILY: Oh! that's Carl   age I guess about
FRANK: four?
EMILY: that's at the beach one summer
FRANK: only nine or ten, he was big for
EMILY: With his sister Judith
FRANK: that's my brother George
EMILY: That's
FRANK: he loved Boy Scouts,
EMILY: but
Oh when you are the actual parents it's a different
FRANK: Oh it is so different!
from something just on TV
VOICE: In times of disruption   of fracture   it is believed that human behavior
moves   in unchartable leaps   History is a formal record of such   leaps
but in large-scale demographical   terms
in which the   individual   is   lost
Frank and Emily Gulick it's said your son   Carl charged in the savage
slaying of   fourteen-year-old shows no sign of   remorse   that is to say,
awareness of the act: thus the question we pose to you Can guilt reside in
those   devoid of *memory*
EMILY: …Oh the main thing is,
he is innocent.
FRANK: …Stake my life on it.
EMILY: He has always been   cheerful, optimistic
FRANK: a good boy, of course he has not
forgotten
BOTH: He is innocent.
EMILY: How could our son *forget* when he has nothing to
BOTH: *forget*
FRANK: He took that lie detector test voluntarily didn't he

EMILY: Oh there he is   weight-lifting, I don't remember
      who took that picture?
FRANK: When you are the actual parents you see them every day,
      you don't form judgments.
VOICE: And how is your son employed, Mr. and Mrs. Kaminsky?
      Excuse me: *Gulick.*
FRANK: Up until Christmas he was working in
      This butcher shop in East Orange
EMILY: …it isn't easy, at that age
FRANK: Before that, loading and unloading
EMILY: at Sears at the mall
FRANK: No: that was before, that was before the other
EMILY: No: the job at Sears was
FRANK: …Carl was working for that Italian, y'know that
EMILY: the lawn service
FRANK: Was that before? or after
      Oh in this butcher shop   his employer
EMILY: yes there were hard feelings, on both sides
FRANK: Look: you can't believe a single thing   in the newspaper or TV
EMILY: it's not that they lie
FRANK: Oh yes they lie
EMILY: not that they lie, they just   get everything wrong
FRANK: Oh the do lie!   And it's printed and you can't stop them.
EMILY: In this meat shop, I never wanted him to work there
FRANK: In this shop there was pressure on him
      to join the union.
EMILY: Then the other side, his employer
      did not want him to join.
      He's a sensitive boy,   his stomach and nerves
      He lost his appetite for weeks, he'd say "oh if you could see
      some of the things I see"   "the insides of things"
      and so much blood
VOICE: There was always a loving   relationship in the household?
EMILY: …When they took him away he said,   he was so brave
      he said Momma I'll be back soon
      I'll be right back,   I am innocent he said
      I don't know how she came to be in   our house
      I don't know,   I don't know he said
      I looked into my son's eyes and saw   truth shining
      His eyes have always been   dark green,
      like mine.
VOICE: On the afternoon of   February 12 you have told police that
      no one was home   in your house?

EMILY: I, I was…I had a doctor's appointment,
   My husband was working, he doesn't get home until
FRANK: Whoever did it,   and brought her body in
EMILY: No: they say she was   they say it,   it happened there
FRANK: No I don't buy that,   He brought her in carried her
   whoever that was,
   I believe he tried   other houses
   seeing who was home and who   wasn't
   and then he
EMILY: Oh it was like lightning striking
VOICE: Your son Dennis   was at Lakepointe High School attending a meeting
   of the yearbook staff,   your son Carl has told police he
   was   riding   his motor scooter
   in the park,
FRANK: They dragged him like   an animal
   put their hands on him like
   Like Nazi Germany,
EMILY: it couldn't be any worse
FRANK: And that judge
   it's a misuse of power, it's
EMILY: I just don't understand.
VOICE: Your son Carl on and after   February 12 did not exhibit (in your pres-
   ence)   any unusual sign of emotion?
   agitation? guilt?
EMILY: Every day in a house,   a household
   is like the other days.   Oh you never step back, never *see*.
   Like I told them, the   police,   everybody. *He did not.*
   (Lights down.)

SCENE 5

   Lights up. Screen shows snapshots, photographs of the murdered girl Kaminsky.
   Like Carl Gulick, she is anyone of that age: white: neither strikingly beautiful
   nor unattractive.

VOICE: Sometime in the evening of February 12 of this year forensic reports
   say   fourteen-year-old Edith Kaminsky daughter of   neighbors 2361
   Cedar Street, Lakepointe, New Jersey   multiple stab wounds, sexual
   assault   strangulation
   An arrest has been made but   legally or otherwise, the absolute identity of
   the murderer has yet to be
EMILY: Oh it's so unjust,
FRANK: the power of a single man
   That judge

EMILY: Carl's birthday is next week
   Oh God he'll be in that terrible   cold place
FRANK: *segregated* they call it
   How can a judge refuse to set bail
EMILY: oh I would borrow a million dollars if I could
FRANK: Is this America or   Russia?
EMILY: I can't stop crying
FRANK: ...we are both under medication you see but
EMILY: Oh it's true he wasn't himself   sometimes.
FRANK: But that day when it happened, that wasn't one of the times.
VOICE: You hold out for the possibility that   the true murderer   carried Edith
   Kaminsky into your house, into your basement
   thus meaning to throw suspicion on your son?
FRANK: Our boy is guiltless that's the main thing, I will never doubt that.
EMILY: Our body is innocent...   What did I say?
FRANK: Why the hell do they make so much of
   Carl lifting weights, his   muscles
   He is not a freak.
EMILY: There's lots of them   and women too, today like that,
FRANK: He has other interests he used to collect stamps   play baseball
EMILY: Oh there's so much misunderstanding
FRANK: actual lies
   Because the police do not know who the murderer *is*
   of course they will blame   anyone they can.
   (Lights down.)

SCENE 6
   *Lights up. Screen shows the exterior of the Gulick house seen from various
   angles; then, the interior [the basement, evidently, and the storage area where
   the young girl's body was found.*

VOICE: If, as believed, *premeditated* acts arise   out of a mysterious sequence of
   neuron discharges   (in the brain) out of what source   do
   unpremeditated acts   arise?
EMILY: Nobody was down in,   in the basement
until the police came.   The storage space is behind the water heater,   but
FRANK: My God if my son is   so shiftless   like people are saying just look: he
   helped me paint the house last summer
EMILY: Yes Carl and Denny both,
FRANK: Why are they telling such   lies, our neighbors?   We have never wished
   them harm,
EMILY: I believed a certain neighbor was my friend, her and I, we we'd go shop-
   ping together   took my car
   Oh my heart is broken

FRANK: It's robin's-egg blue,   the paint turned out brighter than
  when it dried, a little brighter than we'd expected
EMILY: *I* think it's pretty
FRANK: Well. We'll have to sell the house, there's no choice
  the legal costs   Mr. Filco our attorney has said
EMILY: He told us
FRANK: he's going to fight all the way, he believes Carl is   innocent
EMILY: My heart is broken.
FRANK: *My* heart isn't,
  I'm going to fight this all the way
EMILY: A tragedy like this,   you learn fast who is your friend and who is your
  enemy
FRANK: Nobody's your friend.
VOICE: The Gulick's and Kaminsky's were   well acquainted?
EMILY: We lived on Cedar first,   when they moved in I don't remember:
  my mind isn't right these days
FRANK: Oh yes   we knew them
EMILY: I'd have said Mrs. Kaminsky   was my friend, but
  that's how people are
FRANK: Yes
EMILY: Carl knew her,   Edith
  I mean, we all did
FRANK: but now well,
EMILY: just neighbors
  Now they're our declared enemies, the Kaminsky's
FRANK: well,   so be it.
EMILY: Oh! that poor girl   if only she hadn't,
  I mean, there's no telling who   she was with, walking home
  walking home from school I guess
FRANK: Well she'd been missing overnight,
EMILY: yes overnight
FRANK: Of course we were aware
FRANK: The Kaminsky's came around ringing doorbells,
EMILY: then the police,
FRANK: then
  they got a search party going,   Carl helped them out
EMILY: Everybody said how much he helped
FRANK: he kept at it for hours
  They walked miles and miles,
  he's been out of work for a while,
EMILY: he'd been looking
  in the *help wanted* ads but
FRANK: …He doesn't like to use the telephone.

EMILY: People laugh at him he says,

FRANK: I told him no he was imagining it.

EMILY: This neighborhood:

FRANK: you would not believe it.

EMILY: Call themselves Christians

FRANK: Well, some are Jews

EMILY: Well it's still white isn't it a white neighborhood, you expect better.

VOICE: The murder weapon has yet to be found?

FRANK: One of the neighbors had to offer an opinion, something sarcastic I guess
Oh don't go into *that*

FRANK: the color of the paint on our house
So Carl said, You don't like it, wear sunglasses.

EMILY: But,
he was smiling.

VOICE: A young man with a sense of humor.

FRANK: Whoever hid that poor girl's
body
in the storage space of our,
basement well clearly it
obviously it was to deceive
to cast blame on our son.

EMILY: Yes if there were fingerprints down there,

BOTH: that handprint they found on the wall

FRANK: well for God's sake it was from when Carl
was down there

BOTH: helping them

FRANK: He cooperated with them,

EMILY: Frank wasn't home,

FRANK: Carl led them downstairs

EMILY: Why they came to our house, I don't know.
Who was saying things I don't know,
it was like everybody had gone crazy
casting blame on all sides

VOICE: Mr. and Mrs. Gulick it's said that from your son's room
Lakepointe police officers confiscated comic books, military magazines,
pornographic magazines a cache of more than one dozen
knives including switchblades plus
a U.S. Army bayonet (World War II)
Nazi memorabilia including a *souvenir* S.S. helmet (manufactured in
Taiwan)
a pink plastic skull with light bulbs in eyes
a naked Barbie doll, badly scratched
numerous pictures of naked women

and women in magazines,
their eyes   breasts   crotches   cut out with a scissors
Do you have any comment   Mr. and Mrs. Gulick?
FRANK: Mainly they were hobbies,
EMILY: I guess I don't,
FRANK: we didn't know about
EMILY: Well   he wouldn't allow me in his room, to vacuum or anything
FRANK: You know how boys are.
EMILY: Didn't want his mother
FRANK: poking her nose in
EMILY: So… *(Emily upsets glass of water.)*
VOICE: Police forensic findings (bloodstains, hairs, semen)   and the DNA *fin-gerprinting* constitute a tissue of circumstance   linking your son to the murder but cannot rise   to revelation?
EMILY: Mr. Filco says   it's all pieced together
Circumstantial evidence, he says.
FRANK: *I* call it bullshit. *(Laughs.)*
EMILY: Oh Frank
FRANK: *I* call it bullshit. *(Laughs.)*
VOICE: Eye witnesses seem to   disagree,   two parties report having seen Carl Gulick and   Edith Kaminsky   walking together in the afternoon, but a third party   a neighbor   claims to have seen the girl in the company of a stranger   at approximately 4:15 p.m.
And Carl Gulick insists he was riding his motor scooter all that afternoon.
FRANK: He is a boy
EMILY: not capable of lying.
FRANK: Look: I would discipline him sometimes,
EMILY: you have to, with boys
FRANK: Oh yes you have to, otherwise
EMILY: He was always a good eater
FRANK: He's a quiet boy
EMILY: you can't guess his thoughts
FRANK: But he loved his mother and father
EMILY: always well behaved at home.
That ugly picture of him in the paper,
FRANK: that wasn't him.
EMILY: You can't believe the cruelty in the human heart.
FRANK: Giving interviews
EMILY: telling such cruel lies
FRANK: his own teachers from high school
VOICE: Mr. and Mrs. Gulick you had no suspicion no awareness   you had no sense of   the fact that   the battered and mutilated body of fourteen-year-old Edith Kaminsky

VOICE: was hidden in your basement   in a storage space
     wrapped in plastic garbage bags
     for approximately   forty hours,
     no   consciousness of   any disharmony   in
     your household?
EMILY: Last week at my sister's where we were staying,
     we had to leave   this terrible place
     in Yonkers I was crying,   I could not stop   crying
     downstairs in the kitchen   three in the morning
     I was standing by a window and there was suddenly   it looked like snow!
     it was moonlight moving in the window and there came a shadow I guess
     like an eclipse?   was there an eclipse?
     Oh I felt so, I felt   my heart stopped   Oh but I, I wasn't scared
     I was thinking   I was seeing how the world is
     how the universe *is*
     it's so hard to say, I feel like a   a fool
     I was gifted by this, by   seeing   how the world *is* not
     how you see it   with your eyes, or talk   talk about it
     I mean names you give to,   parts of it   No I mean how it *is*
     when there is nobody there.
VOICE: A subliminal conviction of disharmony may be nullified by   a tran-
     scendental leap of consciousness;   to a "higher plane"
     of celestial harmony,
     would you comment   Mr. and Mrs. Gulick?
EMILY: Then Sunday night it was,
FRANK: this last week
EMILY: they came again
FRANK: threw trash on our lawn
EMILY: screamed
     Murderers! they were drunk, yelling   in the night *Murderers!*
FRANK: There was the false report that Carl was released on   bail
     that he was home with us,
EMILY: Oh dear God if only that was true
FRANK: I've lost fifteen pounds since February
EMILY: Oh Frank has worked so hard   on that lawn,
     it's his pride and joy and in the neighborhood everybody knows, they
     compliment him,   and now
     Yes he squats right out there, he pulls out crabgrass by hand
     Dumping such ugly nasty disgusting things
     Then in the A&P a woman followed me   up and down the aisles I could
     hear people   *That's her, that's the mother of the murderer*   I could hear
     them   everywhere in the store *Is that her,   is that the mother of the murde*
     er? they were saying   Lived in this neighborhood, in this town   for so

many years we thought we were welcome here and now
Aren't you ashamed to show your face! a voice screamed
What can I do with my face, can I hide it forever?
FRANK: And all this when our boy is innocent.
VOICE: Perceiving the inviolate nature of the Universe apart from human
suffering rendered you happy, Mrs. Gulick is this so?
for some precious moments?
EMILY: Oh yes, I was crying but
not because of
no I was crying because
I was happy I think.
(Lights down.)

SCENE 7
*Lights up. Screen shows neurological X-rays, medical diagrams, charts as of
EEG and CAT-scan tests.*

VOICE: Is it possible that in terms of fracture, of evolutionary unease or, perhaps, at any time human behavior mimics that of minute particles of
light? The atom is primarily emptiness the neutron dense-packed
The circuitry of the human brain circadian rhythms can be tracked but
never, it's said comprehended. And then in descent from *identity*
(memory?) to tissue to cells to cell-particles electrical impulses axon-
synapse-dendrite and beyond, be-
neath
to sub-atomic bits
Where is *Carl Gulick?*
*(Gulicks turn to each other in bewilderment. Screen flashes images: kitchen
interior; weight-lifting paraphernalia; a shelf of trophies; photographs; domes-
tic scenes, etc.)*
VOICE: Mr. and Mrs. Gulick you did not notice anything unusual in your
son's behavior on the night of February 12 or the following day, to the
best of your recollection?
EMILY: ...Oh we've told the police this so many many times
FRANK: Oh you forget what you remember,
EMILY: That night, before we knew there was anyone missing I mean, in the
neighborhood anyone we knew
FRANK: I can't remember.
EMILY: Yes but Carl had supper with us like always
FRANK: No I think, he was napping up in his room
EMILY: he was at the table with us:
FRANK: I remember he came down around nine o'clock, but he did eat.
EMILY: Him and Denny, they were at the table with us

FRANK: We've told the police this so many times, it's I don't know any longer

EMILY: I'm sure it was Denny too.   Both our sons. We had meatloaf   ketchup baked on top, it's the boys' favorite dish just about   isn't it?

FRANK: Oh anything with hamburger and ketchup!

EMILY: Of course he was at the table with us,   he had his usual appetite.

FRANK: ...he was upstairs, said he had a touch of flu

EMILY: Oh no he was there.

FRANK: It's hard to speak of your own flesh and blood,   as if   they are other people
it's
hard   without giving false testimony against your will.

VOICE: Is the intrusion of the *extra-ordinary*   into the dimension of the *ordinary*   an indication that such Aristotelian categories are invalid?   If one day fails to resemble the preceding   what does it resemble?

FRANK: ...He has sworn to us, we are his parents
He did not touch a hair of that poor child's head   let alone the rest.
Anybody who knew him, they'd know

EMILY: Oh those trophies!   he was so proud
one of them is from the, I guess the Lakepointe YMCA there's some from the New Jersey competition   at Atlantic City two years ago?

FRANK: no, he was in high school
the first was, Carl was only fifteen years old

EMILY: Our little muscle-man!

VOICE: Considering the evidence of thousands of years of human culture of language   art   religion   the judicial system   *The family unit*   athletics hobbies   fraternal organizations   charitable impulses   gods of all species is   it   possible   that humankind   desires
not   to   know
its   place   in
the
food
cycle?

EMILY: One day he said   he wasn't going back to school,
my heart was broken.

FRANK: Only half his senior year ahead
but you can't argue,   not with

EMILY: oh his temper!   he takes after,
oh I don't know who

FRANK: we always have gotten along together
in this household   haven't we

EMILY: yes but the teachers would laugh at him he said
girls laughed at him he said   stared and pointed at him he said

and there was this pack of   oh we're not prejudiced against Negroes,   it's just that
the edge of the Lakepointe school district
well

FRANK: Carl got in fights sometimes
in the school cafeteria and   I guess the park?

EMILY: the park isn't safe for law-abiding people these days
they see the color of your skin,   they'll attack
some of them are just like animals   yes they *are*

FRANK: Actually our son was attacked first   it isn't like he got   into fights by himself

EMILY: Who his friends are now, I don't remember

FRANK: He is a quiet boy, keeps to himself

EMILY: he wanted to work
he was looking for work

FRANK: Well: our daughter Judith was misquoted about that

EMILY: also about Carl having a bad temper   she never said that
the reporter for the paper twisted her words
Mr. Filco says   we might sue

FRANK: Look: our son never raised a hand against anybody let alone against

EMILY: He loves his mother and father,   he respects us

FRANK: He is a religious boy at heart

EMILY: He looked me in the eyes he said Momma you believe me don't you?
and I said Oh yes Oh yes   he's just my baby

FRANK: nobody knows him

EMILY: nobody knows him the way we do

FRANK: who would it be, if they did?
I ask you.

(House lights come up, TV screen shows video rewind. Sounds of audio rewind. Screen shows Gulicks on stage.)

VOICE: Frank and Mary Gulick we're very sorry something happened to the tape we're going to have to reshoot   Let's go back just to, we're showing an interior   Carl's room   the trophies I'll say, I'll be repeating
Are you ready?

(House lights out, all tech returns to normal.)

VOICE: Well Mr. and Mrs. Gulick your son has quite a collection of trophies!

FRANK: ...I,   I don't remember what I

EMILY: ...yes he,

FRANK: Carl was proud of   he had other hobbies though

EMILY: Oh he was so funny, didn't want his mother poking through his room
he said

FRANK: Yes but that's   how boys are

EMILY: That judge refuses to set bail, which I don't understand

FRANK: Is this the United States or   is this the Soviet Union?

EMILY: we are willing to sell our house to stand up for what is

VOICE: You were speaking of your son Carl having quit school,
     his senior year?   and then?

EMILY: …He had a hard time, the teachers   were down on him.

FRANK: I don't know why,

EMILY: we were never told
     And now in the newspapers

FRANK: the kinds of lies they are saying

EMILY: that he got into fights, that he was

FRANK: that kind of thinking is all a distortion

EMILY: He was always a quiet boy

FRANK: but he had his own friends

EMILY: they came over to the house sometime, I don't remember   who

FRANK: there was that one boy what was his name

EMILY: Oh Frank   Carl hasn't seen him in years
     he had friends in grade school

FRANK: Look: in the newspaper there were false statements

EMILY: Mr. Filco says   we might sue

FRANK: Oh no: he says we can't,   we have to prove *malice*

EMILY: Newspapers and TV are filled with lies

FRANK: Look: our son Carl never raised a hand against anybody let alone
     against

EMILY: He loves his mother and father,

FRANK: He respects us

VOICE: Frank and,   it's Emily isn't it   Frank and Emily Gulick
     that is very moving.
     (Lights down.)

SCENE 9
     Lights up. Screen shows Gulicks in theater.

VOICE: The discovery of radioactive elements   in the late nineteenth century
     enabled scientists to set back the estimated age of the Earth to several bil-
     lion years,   and the discovery in more recent decades   that the Universe
     is expanding,   this that there is a point in Time when the Universe   was
     tightly compressed   smaller than your tiniest fingernail!
     thus that the age of the Universe is many billions of years
     uncountable
     Yet   humankind resides in Time,   God bless us.
     Frank and Emily Gulick as we wind down *our*   time together.
     What are your plans for the future?

FRANK: …Oh that is, that's hard to   that's hard to answer.

EMILY: It depends I guess on

FRANK: Mr. Filco had advised

EMILY: I guess it's,
next is the grand jury

FRANK: Yes: the grand jury.
Mr. Filco cannot be present for the session   to protect our boy I don't
understand the law, just the prosecutor is there
swaying the jurors' minds
Oh I try to understand but I can't,

EMILY: he says we should be prepared
we should be prepared for a trial

VOICE: You are ready for the trial   to clear your son's name?

FRANK: Oh yes...

EMILY: yes that is a way of,   of putting it
Yes.   To clear Carl's name.

FRANK: ...Oh yes you have to be realistic.

EMILY: Yes but before that   the true murderer of Edith Kaminsky
might come forward.
If the true murderer is watching this   *Please come forward.*

FRANK: ...Well we both believe Carl is protecting someone, some friend
another boy

EMILY: the one who really   committed that terrible crime

FRANK: So all we can do is pray.   Pray Carl will come   to h is senses   give
police the other boy's name, or I believe this: if it's a friend of Carl's
he must have some decency   in his heart

VOICE: Your faith   in your son remains unshaken?

EMILY: You would have had to see his   toes,
his tiny baby toes in his bath.
His curly hair,   splashing in the bath.
His yellow rompers or no: I guess that was Denny

FRANK: If your own flesh and blood looks you in the eye,
you believe

EMILY: Oh yes.

VOICE: Human personality, it might be theorized, is a phenomenon of memory yet memory   built up from cells, and   atoms   does not *exist:*   thus
memory   like mind   like personality
is but a fiction?

EMILY: Oh   remembering backward is so hard!
oh it's,

FRANK: it pulls your brain in two.

EMILY: This medication the doctor gave me, my mouth   my mouth is so dry
In the middle of the night I wake up drenched in

FRANK: You don't know who you are   until a thing like this happens,
then you don't know.

EMILY: It tears your brain in two, trying to remember,
like even looking at the pictures
Oh you are lost
FRANK: in Time you are lost
EMILY: You fall and fall,
...ever since the, the butcher shop
he wasn't always himself but
who he was then, I don't know.
It's so hard, remembering why.
FRANK: Yes my wife means thinking backward the way the way the police
make you, so many questions you start forgetting right away it comes
out crazy.
Like now, right here I don't remember anything up to now I mean, I
can't swear to it: the first time, you see, we just lived. We lived in our
house. I am a, I am a post office employee I guess I said that? well, we
live in our, our house. I mean it was the first time through. Just living.
Like the TV, the picture's always on, if nobody's watching it you know?
So, the people we were then, I guess I'm trying to say
those actual people me and her the ones you see *here* aren't them.
(Laughs.)
I guess that sounds crazy,
VOICE: We have here the heartbeat of parental love and faith, it's a beautiful
thing Frank and Molly Gulick, please comment?
FRANK: We are that boy's father and mother.
We know that our son is not a murderer and a, a rapist
EMILY: We know, if that girl came to harm there is some reason for it to be
revealed, but
EMILY: They never found the knife, for one thing
FRANK: or whatever it was
EMILY: They never found the knife, the murderer could tell them where it's
buried, or whatever it was.
Oh he could help us so if he just would.
VOICE: And your plans for the future, Mr. and Mrs. Gulick of Lakepointe, NJ?
FRANK: ...Well.
I guess, I guess we don't have any.
(Long silence, to the point of awkwardness.)
VOICE: ...Plans for the future, Mr. and Mrs. Gulick of Lakepointe, NJ?
FRANK: The thing is, you discover you need to be protected from your own
thoughts sometimes, but who is there to do it?
EMILY: God didn't make any of us strong enough I guess.
FRANK: Look: one day in a family like this, it's like the next day and the day
before.
EMILY: You could say it *is* the next day, I mean the same the same day.
FRANK: Until one day it isn't
(Lights out.)

END OF PLAY

Devotees in the Garden of Love
by Suzan-Lori Parks

Suzan-Lori Parks is a playwright and screenwriter whose plays include *The Death of the Last Black Man in the Whole Entire World, The Sinners Place, Devotees in the Garden of Love, Betting on the Dust Commander, Imperceptible Mutabilities in the Third Kingdom* (which won a 1990 Obie award for Best New American Play), and *The America Play* which recently received its world premiere at The Yale Repertory Theatre, moved to the Joseph Papp Public Theatre, and received a simultaneous production at Boston's American Repertory Theatre. Her newest play, *Venus,* is scheduled for production at Yale and The Public in their 1995-6 seasons. Parks' productions for radio include *Pickling, Third Kingdom* and *Locomotive.*

She is a member of New Dramatists, an Associate Artist at Yale Rep and has received grants from the Rockefeller Foundation, the Ford Foundation, the Whiting Foundation, New York Foundation for the Arts, The Kennedy Center Fund for New American Plays, The W. Alton Jones Foundation, and is a two-time playwriting fellow of the National Endowment for the Arts. In 1989 the *New York Times* named her "the year's most promising new playwright." Her plays have been published in numerous anthologies most notably *The Bedford Introduction to Drama* (St. Martin's Press), *The Best of Off-Broadway* (Mentor Books) and *Moonmarked and Touched by Sun* (TCG). The text of *The America Play* appeared in the March 1994 issue of *American Theatre Magazine.* A collection of her plays and essays *The America Play and Other Works* is available from Theatre Communications Books. Ms. Parks is a playwriting professor at the Yale School of Drama and has recently completed *Girl 6,* an original screenplay for Spike Lee.

ORIGINAL PRODUCTION

Devotees in the Garden of Love was commissioned by Actors Theatre of Louisville and premiered in the 1992 Humana Festival of New American Plays. It was originally directed by Oskar Eustis with the following cast:

Lily ....Margarette Robinson
George..Esther Scott
Madame Odelia Pandahr ....Sandra Sydney

CHARACTERS

    THE LOVERS:

        LILY

        GEORGE; later PATTY

    MADAME ODELIA PANDAHR: a Panderer

TIME AND PLACE: Once upon uh time way up there in uh garden in thuh middle of nowhere.

DEVOTEES IN THE
GARDEN OF LOVE

A.

A garden on a hilltop. In the middle of nowhere. Lily, a teeny tiny older woman in a wedding dress, sits in an old-time wheelchair. George, a much larger, much younger woman in a wedding dress, sits on a camp stool practicing conversation.

LILY: Ooooohlukater. Huh. Thuh huzzy.

GEORGE: Oooooh. *Mon nom? Ah, Monsieur, je m'appelle*–George. Jooooorrrrge.

LILY: Who does she think she is. Bein down there.

GEORGE: *Et vous? Comment vous appelez-vous?*

LILY: Down there amongst thuh action.

GEORGE: *Monsieur Amour? Oooh là là, Monsieur Amour! "Monsieur Amour"–très romantique, n'est-ce pas?*

LILY: Down there amongst thuh action where she do not belong.

GEORGE: *L'amour est très romantique. La romance est la nature de l'amour. Et vous, Monsieur Amour, vous êtes le roi d'amour.*

LILY: In my day uh woman spoke of her table. And that was all.

GEORGE: *Est-ce que vous êtes le roi d'amour?*

LILY: We did things thuh old-fashioned way. In my day. Thuh old-fashioned way was even "old-fashioned" back then. I go way back. Huh. Who thuh hell is she pretendin tuh be way down there in thuh thick of it.

GEORGE: *Vous êtes le roi d'amour, et je serai votre reine.*

LILY: Upstart, George girl. At high noon.

GEORGE: *Oooh là là Monsieur Amour! Oui oui! Oui oui!*

LILY: Look at that upstart! George! Uh upstart. In white even. At high noon. Huh. Thuh huzzy. Huh. Thuh upstart.

GEORGE: Starting up?! Not without my say so they dont!

LILY: Huh?

GEORGE: Start up?! Not without my say so!

LILY: Upstart. Uh huzzy.

GEORGE: Oh.

LILY: See?

GEORGE: *Oui oui! Oui oui!*

LILY: See?!

GEORGE: *Oui.* I see. In my heart. Madame Odelia Pandahr says that because all the eyes of the world are on the heart of the bride-who'll-be's heart thuh bride-who'll-be's heart thus turns inward, is given to reflection and in that way becomes an eye itself. Seeing inward to examine her most deepest thoughts and feelings and seeing outward too tuh give her form and grace thatll guide her in her most natural selection, that is, her choice of suitors.

LILY: Drop that lorgnette girl and use thuh bo-nocks. See?

GEORGE: *Oui!*

LILY: BO-NOCKS!

GEORGE: Oh.

LILY: HIGH NOON!

GEORGE: High noon?

LILY: HIGH NOON!

GEORGE: High noon.

LILY: Not your time! My time! High noon my time my time! George girl get over here and–ooooooooooh! Thuh huzzy. Right *in* thuh thick of it.

GEORGE: Thuh woman?

LILY: Thuh huzzy.

GEORGE: In white?

LILY: In white.

GEORGE: Mama Lily?

LILY: Right in thuh thick of it.

GEORGE: Mama Lily thats Madame Odelia Pandahr Mama. Oooh hooo, Madame! *C'est moi!* Jooooooooorge! Oooh hoo! Oooh hooo!

LILY: Gimmieuhminute. Wheremy specs. —. Huh. Huh. —. Well.

GEORGE: Madame Odelia Pandahr ssgonna be monitoring thuh situation play by play.

LILY: Play by play.

GEORGE: Madame Odelia Pandahr says that thuh ultimate battle of love requires uh good go between. In thuh old days Madame Odelia Pandahr says they had matchmakers and messengers—

LILY: Them old days was my days.

GEORGE: Madame Odelia Pandahr says that our new days require thuh kind of reportage that she's doing. "Reportage." Ha! Madame Odelia Pandahr, you know, she's French.

LILY: I guess they just do things different.

GEORGE: They do. *Enchanté de faire votre connaissance, Mon-sieur.*

LILY: Look. They all lookin at us. Look.

GEORGE: You think they can see us way up here?

LILY: They all lookin our way.

GEORGE: Oooooh! *Bonjour! Bonjour! Bonjour! Bonjour!*

LILY: Honey?

GEORGE: Huh?

LILY: Theyre waitin for your signal.

GEORGE: Thuh hankie?

LILY: Thuh hankie.

GEORGE: *Oui oui! Oui oui!*

LILY: Let it drop like we talked uhbout.

GEORGE: Madame Odelia Pandahr says that uh hankie should be dropped—

LILY: Go on then.

GEORGE: *Comme ça!*

(*The battle begins.*)

LILY: Thatll do. (*Pause.*) And it's begun. (*Pause.*) See? See?

GEORGE: You may, now, Sir, return my handkerchief to my hand now Sir.

LILY: See?

GEORGE: In my heart. Madame Odelia Pandahr says that—

LILY: Out there. Look.

GEORGE: In my heart—

LILY: Take uh look see through this. Go on. Lookie. Use your right eye. Put your hand over your left. Thats it. Figet thuh focus. Thats it. Now look-see. See!? See?!

GEORGE: Uh—

LILY: Try these. Go on. Both eyes on um. I used this pair tuh watch your daddy triumph over his rival. Ah—ooooooooooooooooh!

GEORGE: *Oooh là là!*

LILY: KERBLAM! Sweet Bejesus! Scuze my French! Sweet Bejesus answer my prayers looks like ThatOne done sunked ThisOnes battleship rockum sockum rockum sockum—ONE O'CLOCK love of uh girl! ONE O'CLOCK!

GEORGE: One o'clock.

LILY: My time!

GEORGE: Your time.

LILY: Off lookin at nothin at 19:45. They say love makes yuh blind. Only ever made me sweat. In my day my motherud say 16:15 and there wernt no question that it was 16:15 her time. Thuh time helpin tuh tell you where you are oughta be where you oughta be lookin and whatcha oughta be lookin at. Frenchiz in uh different time zone. Seems tuh me. Must be. Huh. All that *français*. Dont belong on uh field uh battle. Tuck it outa sight. For now. We got our own lingo and what we cant say with our own—hometown lingo just wont get said. For thuh time being. Go on. Tuck thuh *français* away—WOOOOOOOOOOOH! And there it all is. Raging. TWO O'CLOCK LOVE OF UH GIRL! KERBLAM! See?! SEE?!

GEORGE: Oooooooh—

LILY: Impressive. Impressed?

GEORGE: Rockets red blare at 2 oclock, Mama Lily. Makes my heart sing.

LILY: Thats my girl!

GEORGE: Our word is "Devotion." My match was made in heaven.

LILY: Thats my George!

GEORGE: We will hold fast unto thuh death. We will not come all asunder. We wont flinch.

LILY: Thats my George! Lookie lookie lookie: Bombs bursting in air at 10:25. Just like thuh ditty.

GEORGE: Oooooooooooh!

LILY: KERBLAM! Direct hit! Makes it all worthwhile.

GEORGE: Mama?

LILY: AH-AH-AH-AH-AH-AH-AH-AH. RAT-TA-TAT-TAT.

GEORGE: Mama Lily? At 9 o'clock? —My time. I think I see an instance of uh bodily harm.

LILY: You crossed your legs before you held your head up. First steps you took you took with uh board on your head balanced there as an insurance of premiere posture. Preschool charm school with all the trimmings we couldnt afford it so, thats my girl, thats my George, bless your sweet heart, sweetheart I taught you your basics. How tuh lay uh table. How tuh greet uh guest. Thuh importance of uh centerpiece. How tuh fix uh "mess." Thuh difference between "mess" and "messy."

GEORGE: "Mess" means food and should be plentiful. "Messy" means sloppy and should be scarce.

LILY: How, if you went tuh uh party and arrived early, how not tuh go in and catch thuh hostess unawares but tuh walk up and down thuh sidewalk until 20 minutes after thuh affair had begun.

GEORGE: The importance of being fashionably late.

LILY: Every affair is uh battle—

GEORGE AND LILY: And every battle ssgot tuh have uh battle-*plan.*

LILY: Even learned you uh little bit uh fan work. Then it was off tuh Madame Odelia Pandahrs. On full scholarship!

GEORGE: *C'était magnifique!* —It was wonderful!

LILY: My George finishes Madame Odelia Pandahrs Finishing Academy at thuh top of her class! Planning dinner parties for uh hundred and forty! Knowed thuh places for settings I'll never lay eyes on. Didnt have them places back then. *Au courant* we calls her. Thats my George. Thats my girl.

GEORGE: 9 o'clock. Mama Lily. Looks like weve got ourselves uh premiere example of uh decapitation.

LILY: So it is. So it is.

GEORGE: Major dismemberment at 9:05.

LILY: So it is. So it is.

GEORGE: Blood. Blood. Blood. Dust. Ashes. Thick smoke. —Carnage.

LILY: Conclusion, Miss George?

GEORGE: In conclusion, Mama Lily, I'd say that the fighting is well underway.

LILY: Further?

GEORGE: Further, Mama Lily? If I'd go further I'd say "fierce."

LILY: Prognosis, Miss George?

GEORGE: Prognosis, Mama Lily? Well—looks like I just may be married in thuh mornin, Mama.

LILY: Makes my heart sing.

GEORGE: *Mon coeur est plein d'amour!*

LILY: Hold off until thuh peace talks please love of uh girl.

GEORGE: They may not be peacing by morning though. My match by morning may not be made. Madame Odelia Pandahr says there arent 2 suitors alive more well matched than ThisOne and ThatOne. While any other suitor in thuh area of conflict would be smote right down for dead ThisOne has uh move which ThatOne counters and ThatOne has uh counter to which ThisOne always gives reply. From what Madame Odelia Pandahr says ThisOne and ThatOne are even steven one for one move for move uh perfect match.

LILY: Keep your eyes stuckd inside them bo-nocks my sweet thing. Down theres where thuh action is.

GEORGE: It could be uh protracted engagement down there. I may be sittin uhround protractedly engaged up here. —. But I think thingsll wrap theirselves up nicely.

LILY: And how come?

GEORGE: How come cuz thuh cause of Love thats how come. L-O-V-E. ThatOne could start uh charge on ThisOne and ThisOne would rally back. Cuz thuh cause of Love. ThisOne may sever thuh arms and legs off uh all uh ThatOnes troops and those maimed and mismangled arms and legs would riiiise up uhgain and return to their trunks like uh child coming home for supper when thus triangle bell was rung. Cuz thuh cause of Love. Guns with them knives on thuh ends may run through lines and lines of thuh faithful piercing through and through and through and fingers and toes may travel to foreign countries where we aint never been, Mama Lily, puss green-slimed bile and contagion may grow from thuh wounds of thuh wounded seep intuh thuh ground and kill and kill and kill and kill and kill and kill and kill and kill and kill and thuh cannons may roar thuh wind may moan thuh sky may shake and spit fire and crack open and swallow um all up but itll all end nicely. Our word is "devotion." My match was made in heaven. We will hold fast. Unto thuh death. We will not come out all asunder. We wont flinch. How come? Cuz thuh cause of Love.

LILY: Seems all quiet now. Must be taking uh lunchtime. Nobody down theres movin. Huh. In my day things were just as interesting. Dont think twice uhbout that. Thuh lucky ones were pursued. Thuh unlucky ones had tuh make do. Ssallways been like that. My suitor fought for me and its only right that you oughta be so sought after. If I havent given you you nothin else at least I've made sure uh that. George? GEORGE!? Where you gone off to? Thuh gettin was just gettin good. Theys takin uh break we kin sit here in watch em lick their wounds. Shoot. Uh dogs lickin on that one. Werent no dogs uhllowed on thuh field uh battle in my day. Everythings gone tuh pot. De-volution. Huh. Where you been?

GEORGE: Had tuh get my hope chest.

LILY: Had tuh get your hope chest. Thats my George.

GEORGE: As uh bride-who'll-be I'm waiting at thuh ready. Ready for uh inspection. As bride I expect my groomll inspect me. Maybe you could inspection my wares while theyre getting reinforcements.

LILY: Could do. Go on—lounge uhround like you didn't know it was coming. Lounge girl, go on. Madame Odelia Pandahr didn't cover lounging?

GEORGE: Given thuh ensuing conflict she questioned its ethical nature.

LILY: Huh. —. Sit on thuh grass pick daisies look right on off intuh thuh 3 o'clock. Smoke uh cigarette. Sing.

GEORGE: Sing?

LILY: La de de la de dah and et cetera.

GEORGE: La de de la de dah la de de la de dah.

LILY: La de de la de dah la de de la de dah ssjust uh normal day who knows what may be up next.

GEORGE: La de de la de dah la de dah dah le deee—

LILY: SPEC-SHUN!

GEORGE: YES, MAAM.

LILY: Gimmie gimmie gimmie. Bring it over here lets see whatcha got. 2 tablecloths: Irish linen. 1 tablecloth: fancy lace. Napkins tuh match. Place settings for—40—42—.

GEORGE: Some may break.

LILY: Thats my George! Thats thuh battleplan! Ah ha: uh brown sac uh peppermint candies. For fresh breath?

GEORGE: For fresh breath.

LILY: Reason bein?

GEORGE: Reason bein cuz after battle my suitor may be uh little in need of refreshin. Madame Odelia Pandahr says that theres only one thing staler than thuh mouth of uh suitor—ha—and thats thuh mouth of thuh one that lost thuh fight. Ha ha ha ha. Aaah.

LILY: Yummy. Dont mind if I inspect thuh taste of thuh brown sacked mints for fresh breath do you Miss George. Uh set of informal nap-pi-kans. Everyday *serviettes*. Matchin everyday tablecloth. Plenty of sheets: hand-sewn. Doilies hand done. Extra bedsprings for thuh—wedding night. Bloomers xtra large hand sewn. Only one pair. Practicin economy. Brassieres galore tuh match. Why you got so many uh these things I will never know. You only got 2 tits girl.

GEORGE: Uh war brides gotta point thuh way.

LILY: Didnt we pack you uh pair of white elbow-length gloves?

GEORGE: Uh huhnn. Madame Odelia Pandahr borrowed um. She said ThisOne and ThatOne needed em. You know, tuh slap each others faces with and throw down and challenge.

LILY: Throwin down thuh gauntlet! Thats thuh old style! Ah! And thuh silver! 84 piece set. Stole it one by one from—well they aint never gonna know now is they. They aint noticed yet and they aint never gonna know cause we aint never gonna tell. Nicely polished. Shinin like thuh lake. In my day thuh first vision uh future battle bride envisioned was her table. Her place settings was thuh place holders for her company. Who would come tuh dine throughout her generations. Seein thuh vision of her table was thuh most important thing. Guess it aint like that now. Now you got—technology. Huh. Lets see now: uh few jewels for adornment. And your bridehead: intact. Intact, Miss?

GEORGE: I aint touched it. Seal on thuh jar iduhnt broke izit?

LILY: Hmmmmm. Hmmmmmmmmm. HMMMMMMMMMMM. HMMMMMMMMMMMMMMMMM. Huh. Nope. Ha! Makes my heart sing, Miss George. Love of uh girl. Ha ha ha ha ha—whasszis? *(A TV!)*

GEORGE: Madame Odelia Pandahr says todays battle bride oughta be ade-quately accoutrementalized by thuh modern age.

LILY: Thuh modern age.

GEORGE: Madame Odelia Pandahr says there iduhnt nothing like watchin thuh conflict play by play like.

LILY: We got thuh spy glass. We got thuh bo-nocks. I used these bo-nocks when I watched your Daddy triumph over his rival.

GEORGE: Madame Odelia Pandahrs even featured this year. We may be sittin up here on thuh sidelines so tuh speak but Madame Odelia Pandahrs down there representing thuh modern age. Shes gonna be in charge of thuh regular broadcasts.

LILY: My day we had messengers. Skinny mens and womens who earned uh cent or two by running up and down thuh hillside. In my year I had me uh particular favorite. Nothin but bones by thuh time it was all through. That messenger came rippin up here at all hours. In thuh dead uh night!

In thuh crack uh dawn! Would report—you know—thuh important stuff. Who said what, reenact. ThissuhBodys troops last gasp or show me how one uh Thatuh-Bodys troopers kept walkin for hours with uh flag run through their guts and how thuh run through flag had pinned uhnother tuh his back so he was walking for two—with one piggy back, you know. Like uh shishkebob. That messengers speciality was thuh death throes. Kept us in stitches up here showing us who dropped dead and how. And they was droppin dead down there like flies drop so that messenger kept busy. Runned up here tuh tell me thuh news. Whuduhnt nothing but bones by battles end. Last time that messenger runned up here just his bones was doin thuh runnin and thuh stuff that holded thuh bones tugether was all used up as fuel tuh get them bones up thuh hill. We didnt bury thuh messenger. Gave him uh higher honor. My corset is from that messengers bones, you know. In my day we didnt waste.

GEORGE: Madame Odelia Pandahr says that uh unit like this can do double duty: keep us up here abreast of thuh action and after thuh wedding serve as uh device for entertainment.

LILY: Enter-whut?

GEORGE: Entertainment. Fun.

LILY: Oh. Serves uh double duty do it?

GEORGE: So she claims. Just pull thuh knob. And: presto.

LILY: Just pull thuh knob. Huh. Pres-to.

GEORGE: And enjoy.

LILY: Huh. Pres-to.

B.

At the Front. Madame Odelia Pandahr, the panderer, in a wedding dress with microphone in hand, broadcasts live.

ODELIA PANDAHR: Rat uh tat tat and kerblam kerblooey. As someone said long ago: "Thems fighting words." That adage today has well proven true. There is only one way to describe the scene here the scene that began shortly over 5 days ago and seems well intended to last at least through the night. What began as what could be characterized as a border skir-mish, a simple tribal dispute, has erupted into a battle of major conse-quence. High high up above me is the encampment of the bride-who'll-be who has been keeping watch on his situation. The actual area of our attention is not high high up but right down here right down here in, so to speak, "the thick of it." In the area just behind me through this thick veil of deadly deadly smoke you can just make out the shapes of the 2 opposing camps and of course we are speaking of the camps of ThisOne and the camps of ThatOne. The two suitors vying for the hand of Miss

George the beautiful most sought after bride-who'll-be who watches now from high above us with her mother, Ms. Mother Lily, from that far high hilltop. There is one word that, I guess you could say, sums up this brilliant display this passionate parade of severed arms and legs, genitals and fingertips, buttocks and heads, the splatterment the dismemberment, the quest for an embrace for the bride-who'll-be which has, for many, ended in an embrace of eternity, and that one word I think we could say that one word is "Devotion." This is Ms. Odelia Pandahr. At the front.

C.

In the garden.

GEORGE: Dont run from me Mama.

LILY: Aint runnin.

GEORGE: Dont roll from me.

LILY: Mmon uh roll.

GEORGE: Gimmie.

LILY: Not thuh place settings George honey.

GEORGE: Gimmie.

LILY: I got my wheels dug in George.

GEORGE: Sseither them knives and forks and spoons and butter knives and salad tongs and pickle prongs and lobster tools sseither thems or my brassiere and they aint getting my brassiere.

LILY: In my day we went without.

GEORGE: She aint gettin it.

LILY: In my day thuh table was of most importance.

GEORGE: Uh bride like me ssgotta point thuh way and I intend tuh point thuh way so gimmie. Gimmmmmmmmmmmie!

LILY: You kin give her thuh model of your dream home.

GEORGE: Ssalready been gived.

LILY: Thuh nap-pi-kans. *Serviettes,* love of uh girl?

GEORGE: Mopped up thuh sap of thuh wounded.

LILY: —bloomers?

GEORGE: Turned intuh flags.

LILY: They had tuh know who was who huh?

GEORGE: Gimmie.

LILY: In my day thuh first thing thuh very first thing uh bride-tuh-be envisioned was her table. Thuh shape or size, thuh dimensions of her table were not thuh question. Uh table could be round and of uh cherry wood or square and of oak. Thuh one I always seed was oblong, I was uh little fancy for uh war bride. Oblong and of pine. But thuh materials and dimensions were not really thuh center of thuh envisioning. No. You could have uh table and uh chair—traditional style—or just on uh blanket on thuh ground. Outdoors. Thats uh picnic. Thuh first thing was always her table. And when she had seen it she told her mother and her dear mother tooked it as uh sign that she would be—you know—uh bride. Uh bride with uh groom in all. Like on thuh cake top. On her table with thuh cloth stretched out she would see places for those who would come to mess with her, you know—

GEORGE: Eat.

LILY: In her envisioning she'd see how many there would be and where and what theyd all eat. (You could always tell thuh eats by thuh forks and knives and so on she saw laid out.) What tuh drink. If there was tuh be coffee or tea. And desserts. Thuh first vision was always thuh table. You girls dont see tables these days but I still see mines sometimes—not that I actually ever had no guests like that—but sometimes I still kin see it. Rows and rows of flatwear spiralin out like they was all holdin uh place for me. Holdin my place.

GEORGE: She can take thuh cake top. She can take thuh hope chest itself.

LILY: How uhbout that book. Your *French Love Words and French Love Phrases?*

GEORGE: Uh uhnn.

LILY: Oh.

GEORGE: Ssunder my gown.

LILY: Oh.

GEORGE: Keepin my gut in.

LILY: Oh. Lets lay low. Maybe she wont want nothin.

(Enter Odelia Pandahr.)

ODELIA PANDAHR: Madame Mother Lily. And thuh most fought over Mademoiselle Miss George.

LILY: Delighted, Maam.

GEORGE: *Enchanté de faire votre connaissance, Madame Pandahr.*

ODELIA PANDAHR: —. *Votre fille est si charmante, Madame Mama Lily.*

LILY: *Oui oui! Oui oui!* Well, —I dont—speak thuh language—.

GEORGE: You think they can see me way up here?

ODELIA PANDAHR: Of course they can, dear girl. The eyes of the heart can see across continents and through stone, Mademoiselle George! Your every breath your every whisper your every tear wink and sigh.

GEORGE AND LILY: Aaaaah!

ODELIA PANDAHR: ThisOne thanks you for the great gift of the tatted dishtowels. They have been reshaped and put into service as shifts for the war captured. ThatOne is beholden to you for your gracious coughing up of the salad plates which have been split pie shape stood on end and now instead of serving salad serve as an impediment to the advancing shoeless enemy. You both no doubt have seen the most effective translation of the bridal bloomers? Ripped in 2 and dipped in dye theyve created *voilà:* the bright green flag of ThatOne and at 11 o'clock the dark deep green of ThisOne. It is only an extravagance of your devotion which offered up the bloomers and now allows the troops to distinguish themselves. Of your jewlery, most gracious Miss George, both ThisOne and ThatOne have made great use. Both have pinned the baubles to their respective bodies an act which literally transfixes them. Pinned by desire, they are spurred on to new deeds of devotion. Your jewels, George, also make the boys real shiny— easier for my crew to track their night-time skirmish activities.

GEORGE: Skirmish.

ODELIA PANDAHR: Itll be upgraded to "conflict" any day now.

GEORGE: Skirmish.

ODELIA PANDAHR: We wont fail you Miss George. I know youve got yourself set for the big win and we will not fail you. With but a few more of your very dear contributions, my dear Mademoiselle, I'll not only personally insure an upgrade but will promise promise promise that youll be wed. To thuh Victor. By sunset tomorrow. So gimmie.

GEORGE: Uh uhnn.

ODELIA PANDAHR: Ive schooled you in all aspects of Devotion Mademoiselle George. Pouting was not one of those aspects.

GEORGE: We dont got nothing else.

ODELIA PANDAHR: And neither was hoarding. What will you be donating today, Mademoiselle?

GEORGE: —.

ODELIA PANDAHR: Cough up.

LILY: What do they require, Maam?

ODELIA PANDAHR: With more ammo ThatOne claims he'll have the whole skir-mish—conflict—wrapped up by sunrise.

LILY: Ammo?

ODELIA PANDAHR: A melted down butterknife makes one hell of uh bullet, Mother Lily.

LILY: In my day—

ODELIA PANDAHR: All ThisOne wants is a decent silver serving spoon. The medic says itll make a nice new kneecap. If you object tuh thuh weapons question ThatOnes troops need their teeth filled.

LILY: Thuh table.

GEORGE: We got thuh cake top.

ODELIA PANDAHR: Useless.

GEORGE: Dont suppose youd take thuh Tee Vee.

ODELIA PANDAHR: Weve got plenty.

GEORGE: You kin take thuh hope chest itself.

ODELIA PANDAHR: The morgue officerll come and pick that up this evening. Seems weve had a problem with animals exhuming and consuming the— well thats not a subject for a young ladys ears. *(Pause.)* SILVER. Cough up.

LILY: Thuh table.

GEORGE: How uhbout my brassiere. My last one howboutit.

ODELIA PANDAHR: A bride must point the way, Miss George!

GEORGE: Ssall we got.

ODELIA PANDAHR: Unfortunately brassieres are not what theyre requesting right now but well but well but well it will most likely come in handy so go ahead and take it off. Keep it in the ready and I'll keep you posted. Anything could happen at this point! You know how skirmis-flicts are. You know.

GEORGE: We know.

ODELIA PANDAHR: Your generosity will not go unnoticed, Miss George. Perhaps I can even finagle a citation of some sort for you. For both of you. Would you like that? Hmmmmm? What the troops need right now is something that will unquestionably smack of "Devotion." Smack of Devotion clear as day. Dont you think?

LILY: How uhbout my chair.

ODELIA PANDAHR: Weve got plenty.

GEORGE: Im gonna look all wrong. Be pointin at down 6 o'clock instead of out at 9. You say they can see me from here. How they gonna know whats what?

ODELIA PANDAHR: Mama Lily. Surely you can help.

LILY: Uh table is—

ODELIA PANDAHR: Uhround your neck.

LILY: Oh.

ODELIA PANDAHR: May I? Thanks. Their eyes have been under such a—such a strain. These will do just the trick.

LILY: My bo-nocks. I watched your father triumph with them bo-nocks. They still got his winnin image in um somewheres.

ODELIA PANDAHR: I'll be on the 11 o'clock update. I'm sure youll tune in.

LILY: Sure.

ODELIA PANDAHR: *Enchanté, Madame. Enchanté Mademoiselle George.*

GEORGE: *Enchanté! Enchanté! Oui oui! Oui oui!*

ODELIA PANDAHR: *Au revoir, Mademoiselle. (Exits.)*

GEORGE: Oh. *Au revoir, Madame. (Pause.)* Just turn thuh knob. And enjoy. *(George turns on the TV.)*

LILY: Huh. Presto.

D.

The Front. Odelia Pandahr broadcasts live.

ODELIA PANDAHR: At this hour there is silence. Silence from the guns and swords which only hours ago smote with such deathly volume. Silence from brave troops who only hours ago charged out with the whoops of battle in their throats. Many of those throats are cut now. At this hour. And the cries which spurred them on just hours ago have fled out through their wounds to find refuge in the silence. What began some years ago as a skirmish, what some years ago was upgraded to a conflict now has all the trappings of war. Last week the destruction of ThisOnes troops seemed imminent as the forces of ThatOne marched on and captured the enemy command post. Reports from the field claimed that ThisOne remained defiant vowing that the body could and would continue to fight—headless yes headless if necessary and that it did. What many of us believed and reported to you to be a "headless hen" certain to succumb with the sunset has become a very different bird altogether—striking again and again with an unbelievable fierceness and very much redefining this battle. For the Victor: comfort in the lap of the bride-who'll-be, and the bride-who'll-be is of course the most beautiful and most sought after Miss George who with her mother, Mother Lily, sits high above us on the hilltop just behind me, waiting and watching, watching and waiting. So for the Victor, comfort in the lap of the beloved and for the vanquished, for those who do not triumph, there is only comfort in the lap of the earth, here in this valley. They have renamed this valley "Miss George's Valley" after, of course, their beloved. Several minutes from now, when the troops rise and resume their positions, the wind will awake and unfurl the flags and the echo of Love will once again resound throughout Miss George's Valley. An echo like no other an echo that will not die and fall and forget and be forgotten. An echo that can only be called— "Devotion." This is Ms. Odelia Pan—

E.

The Garden. Lily and George watch TV.

GEORGE: Turn it off. *(Pause.)* Zit off?
LILY: Ssoff. *(Pause.)* Turn thuh knob. Hhhh. Presto.
GEORGE: Presto. *(Pause.)*
LILY: Ssdark. *(Pause.)*
GEORGE: Ssdark. *(Pause.)*

LILY: Ssquiet. *(Pause.)*

GEORGE: Ssquiet. *(Pause.)* Zit off?

LILY: Ssoff. Love of uh girl.

GEORGE: Guess theys all dead. Or dying.

LILY: Or restin.

GEORGE: Ssquiet.

LILY: Uh huhnn. Ssquiet. *(Pause.)*

GEORGE: How come you called me George?

LILY: In my day we had rules. For thuh battle. Rule Number One: No night fightin. Maybe theys observin Rule Number One.

GEORGE: How come you gived me George? As uh name?

LILY: Maybe theys lickin their wounded. I kin just hear thuh sound of uh tongue on riddled flesh. Or maybe its uh dinner break. Maybe what I hear is lips slurpin soup. Whisperin over thuh broth. So quiet. So quiet.

GEORGE: I'm thuh only one I know named George. Seems like thuh name went out uh fashion when you used it on me.

LILY: In my day—. Hhhh. Well. We iduhnt anywhere near them days nowuh-days now is we. Hhh. Clear outa sight. Un-seed. I sure do miss my bo-nocks, George.

GEORGE: Call me somethin pretty. Somethin with uh lift at thuh end, K, Mama Lily? Somethin like—oh Idunno—. Patty? Patty got uh French ring to it dont it?

LILY: George iz all we had.

GEORGE: Patty. Patty. Patty-Patty.

LILY: George iz all we got now, George. Huh. "Patty." "Patty." Huh. Idunno. Gimmieuhminute.

GEORGE: Pattyssgot uh happy ending tuh it.

LILY: Huh. Love of uh girl. Love of uh girl. "Patty." Huh. Gimmie-uhminute.

GEORGE: So quiet down there. HELLO? Huh. Just thuh echo. I waved my handkerchief at um this noon. Then I dropped it. No one came runnin. My etiquettes up here goin tuh waste. *French Love Words and French Phrases.* Huh. *(Pause.)* Quiz me.

LILY: Huh?

GEORGE: Quiz me. Quiz me before I forget.

LILY: Okay. Our lingo first. Tuh warm up. Suitor: "My sweetest flower of the morning, when your eyes open it is the dawn and when they close the sun cannot resist and sets with you. My sweetest flower, you have dropped your handkerchief." Bride-who'll-be?

GEORGE: "As the sun itself returns to its house after providing light unto the entire world, so may you, kind Sir, return my scented cloth unto my scented hand."

LILY: Uh—. More like this: "After providing light unto the entire world which wakes first for you then proceeds upon its course, so may you, kind Sir," and et cetera.

GEORGE: Oh.

LILY: Lets try uhnother, K? Suitor: "In my hand I hold a diamond in my heart I hold your image. You are infinitely more beautiful fair and precious than this most precious stone. Oh my heart would be the most basest and plainest of rocks if ever you did not move me." Bride-who'll-be?

GEORGE: "The earth moves—as do its consorts, the planets. Daily engaged in their revolving. By its very nature, Lover, Love itself revolves, revolves to bring you back, Lover, to me." *(Pause.)*

LILY: Uh uhnn.

GEORGE: Oh. Gimmieuhhint.

LILY: "My image—"

GEORGE: Oh oh oh. "My image—which you keep with such care in your heart, my image, fair as it may be is not so nearly as fair as—"

LILY: Uh uhnn. "My image, Sir, is merely a—"

GEORGE: "My image, Sir, is merely—a reflection in that safe keeping mirror of your heart."

LILY: Good.

GEORGE: "As gardens should be judged by their caretakers so should my image be judged by your care. Base rocks are bulwarks to the great ocean but they too sand in time. And time itself is a round thing, a round thing that—that—that—"

LILY: Thatll do. Now. —. Uh—*en français?*

GEORGE: *En français?*

LILY: Uh huhnn. Go on.

GEORGE: *Oui oui! Oui oui!* Uh—. *Monsieur.* —. Uh—*Monsieur*—. Uh—. Gimmieuhminute.

(Enter Odelia Pandahr.)

ODELIA PANDAHR: Madame Mama Lily and the most fought over Mademoiselle Miss George! I arrive today triumphant gather round gather round! I bring you: Yes! The Victor! The Victor, Miss George, the true suitor who has won through the truest test your hand! The Victor, Miss George, smiter of the victim! Stand back stand back! Now! Wait right here!

LILY: "Patty." "Patty." We'll call ya "Patty," Patty. Patty?

PATTY: How I look? Wedable?

LILY: Patty. Love of uh girl.

PATTY: I look all right?

LILY: Like uh happy ending.

PATTY: Huh. Thatll do. Whats our word? Our words "Devotion." We will hold
    fast. Unto thuh death. We will not come all asunder. We wont flinch. I'll
    see him and he'll see me. We will exchange words of love and fall fall fall
    into eachothers arms—.

LILY: Thats my girl. Here they come honey. —. Suck in your gut.

ODELIA PANDAHR: May I present to you Madame Mother Lily and beautiful
    most fought over bride-who'll-be Mademoiselle Miss George: The Victor!

PATTY: Thuh Victor!

LILY: Thuh Victor!

ODELIA PANDAHR: *Voilà!*

PATTY: *Voilà!*

LILY: *Voilà!*

    (*Odelia Pandahr uncovers a head on a platter.*)

PATTY: Oh.

LILY: Presto.

PATTY: Wheres thuh rest of im, Madame?

ODELIA PANDAHR: He's full of love for you, Mademoiselle George. His lips are
    pursed in a kiss. His eyes only for your fair image, Mademoiselle. I
    recounted to him the story of your waiting. The history of the gifts you
    gave. The story of the tears you shed for him. The tale of your devotion.
    The way you wrung your hands. There is only one word for such a show
    of bravest bravery,—

PATTY: Wheres thuh rest of im?

ODELIA PANDAHR: There is only one word for such a show of bravest bravery,
    Mademoiselle George—

PATTY: Patty.

ODELIA PANDAHR: Patty?

LILY: Presto.

ODELIA PANDAHR: —Patty—. There is just one word for such valorous valor
    just one word for such faithful faith just one word, Mademoiselle George for—

PATTY: Patty.

LILY: Patty.

ODELIA PANDAHR: Patty?

PATTY: Patty.

LILY: Turn it off.

ODELIA PANDAHR: Now your suitor, Mademoiselle—Patty, may be just a
    head—a head kept alive by a wealth of technology, the fruits of our mod-
    ern age. Your suitor may be just a—head—uh head-stone of thuh former
    self but as we are schooled in Madame Odelia Pandahrs, the head is the
    place where sit thuh lofty—the lofty-most thoughts. Weve, you could say,
    done away with thuh base. We would do away with this base but then of

course your handsome and devoted suitor would have difficulty standing you understand.

LILY: Turn it off. Turn it off Patty.

PATTY: Patty. Pattysgot uh happy ending to it. Arent him and me supposed tuh fall into eachothers arms?

ODELIA PANDAHR: It is true that in the rage of battle suitors ThisOne and ThatOne were thick as tigers around an old gum tree. Even steven blow for blow a perfect match! They always did look uh bit uhlike, Mademoiselle—Patty. There has been a bit of debate down in your valley as to just which one this is. Some say ThisOne some say ThatOne. There is talk of the two opposing camps taking up arms to settle the matter. But that is not our affair now is it. I myself think well I myself know this to be ThatOne. I am after all his mother.

LILY: Turn it off. Turn it off. Zit off?

ODELIA PANDAHR: PATTY! Patty!? ThatOne looks as if uhbout to speak!

LILY: Speak?!

ODELIA PANDAHR: Words of love!!

PATTY: Love?!!

ODELIA PANDAHR: Lean in close, love of uh girl. LEAN IN CLOSE. Some need a little prodding I understand. Ive seen it all. LEAN. IN. CLOSE. —. See? See? Thuh lips twitch. Oh—sssssssssh! Hear? Hear? —. —. Now hows that? Uh happy ending!

PATTY: Oh. Oh. Mama? Oooh. Mama? He said: "Be Mine."

LILY: Oh! "Be mine!"

F.

At the Front. Patty with a microphone.

PATTY: Once upon uh time way up there in uh garden in thuh middle of nowhere there were 2 who got married. After thuh marriage thuh boy it seemed soon forgot his home-town lingo. To woo her he had used thuh words "be mine." Now "be mine" is fine for uh woo but it iduhnt enough tuh build anything longlasting and stable on. Sheud ask him tuh say something. Sheud plead with him tuh say anything. He'd just say "be mine" and although they were in love that "be mine" got rather old rather quick. Soon even his "be mine" dried up. And she realized that he had forgotten his home-town lingo. And she realized that he couldnt pick it up again. So she did what she had to do. She left her wordless husband and went journeying. Abroad. To Gay Paree. And lived over there amongst them. For 12 long years. Full of her new words and phrases she then came home to him. Where he waited. She took off her traveling cloak and did what any anybody would do, that is, she taught him French. It was rough going at first, but he was eager. And soon they could make decent conversation. They became close. In their way. Made a go of it. Raised uh family. Thuh usual. He told his war stories *en français.* She opened up uh finishing academy and they prospered. And they lived that way. Lived happily ever after and stuff like that. Talking back and forth. This is Ms. Patty. At thuh Front.

END OF PLAY

The Love Talker
by Deborah Pryor

Deborah Pryor has had productions of her plays at Ensemble Studio Theatre, Arena Stage, the Hudson Guild Theatre, the Actors Theatre of Louisville Humana Festival for New Plays and Virginia Stage Company. She is a recipient of an NEA Playwriting Fellowship grant (1986). *Briar Patch* garnered the Charles MacArthur Award for Outstanding New Play in 1990 and the Nicoll Fellowship in Screenwriting in 1989. She also received the Mary Roberts Rinehart Award for *Burrhead* in 1987, an Honorable Mention in the FDG/CBS New Plays Program Award for *Wetter Than Water* in 1985 and was a runner-up in the Arnold Weissberger Competition for *Briar Patch*, 1988. The playwright has been published in *The Best Short Plays of 1988, (The Love Talker),* and *Burrhead* and *Wetter Than Water* were published in the Theatre Communications Groups' *Plays-in-Process* in 1984 and 1987. She received an M.F.A. in Playwriting from the University of Iowa and was a literary intern at Arena Stage Theatre in Washington, D.C. She is a member of the Playwrights' Unit in Washington, D.C. and joined New Dramatists in 1990.

ORIGINAL PRODUCTION

The Love Talker was originally directed by Jon Jory at Actors Theatre of Louisville for the 1987 Humana Festival of New American Plays. The cast included:

The Red Head	Janet Zarish
Gowdie Blackmun	Lili Taylor
Bun Blackmun	Suzanna Hay
The Love Talker	Steve Hofvendahl

CHARACTERS

GOWDIE BLACKMUN: a 14 year old girl
BUN BLACKMUN: her sister, 20 years old
THE RED HEAD
THE LOVE TALKER

SETTING: An old house in the Clinch Mountains, Virginia.

TIME: The present, the longest day of the year.

THE LOVE TALKER

*The lights go up on a very old house surrounded by woods. Beyond the house is
a ridge of mountain where the sky shows through the trees. Woods close in on a
small yard with a hollow tree stump rooted near the house.*

*At the very edge of the yard, almost in the woods, stands the Red Head. She is
female, but her age is difficult to pin down. She may look childish one
moment, older the next. Her hair is tangled and wild. She wears a long dark
covering, a cloak or blanket. She is compelling to look at, but not pretty. There
are things not quite human revealed in her body and mannerisms. These
things should be very subtle and not dawn on us easily.*

*From the first moment she's seen, she's turned toward the house, pointing at it.
She stands patiently a moment. The light goes out on her, pointing.*

*The light in the yard comes up to the brightness of a mid-summer evening.
The great room of the house is old and the walls and floor have settled cock-
eyed. There's a big cupboard and a little bed next to the wall. The front door is
low, wide and deep. Into the lintel wood above it are carved a row of crosses.
The door knob has been painted red. The windows all have red thread or
yarn tacked from top to bottom of the sills. There is another door leading out
to other rooms. This is not a cabin, but a very old house. Some of its furnishings are heirlooms gone to seed, some crude homemade pieces. There's a table,
a half-churn, some chairs and a little stool. Nobody is in the house.*

*Gowdie Blackmun stumbles into the yard from the woods. She is a 14-year-
old girl wearing a dirty work dress and boots. She drags an empty burlap sack
after her and carries a shorthandled mattock, half pick axe, half hoe, over her
shoulder.*

*She wanders disorientedly into the yard, dropping the sack and mattock
behind her in a trail. She comes to a stop in front of the hollow stump, stands
staring down into it a moment, looking at herself, then splashes the rainwater
in her face. She squats on the ground, reaches for a stick and starts drawing in
the dirt.*

*Bun Blackmun enters the yard from a path. She is 20 years old, wears a work
dress and is carrying a half-full milk pail. Gowdie stands up, staring at her
drawing, drops her stick absently.*

BUN: You just back? Looka this. One pail. Three cows and this is the grand
prize. They all got blue tits, too. The old people used to say it means
Something's been sucking them dry. Lucy and June both tried to kick me
when I's milking but I ducked and they got each other. Now they're all
mad. How 'bout that? A shed fulla steaming cows with blue tits and not
enough milk to wash your foot in. *(Realizes Gowdie's not listening.)*
Gowdie?

(Gowdie looks up at Bun for the first time.)

GOWDIE: Huh?

BUN: Gotta listen right the first time. Blink once and I'm gone. Got your work done?

GOWDIE: I guess.

BUN: Well it's late to be just trailing back. Which field were you?

GOWDIE: Back digging them osh taters like you told me. *(They both look at the empty burlap sack.)* I spilt'em.

BUN: Uh huh.

GOWDIE: I had a dragging weight full, but coming back I tripped...and I spilt'em. They all rolled down a hill.

BUN: All of them.

GOWDIE: *(Laughs despite herself.)* Into gopher holes. Plugged 'em right up.

BUN: What are you snickling at? Have you lost your sense?

GOWDIE: *(Sober.)* I'll pick them up tomorrow, Bun.

BUN: I reckon you will. I don't want you coming back so late again, you hear? I was starting to bother. The sun went from the ash to the poplar. If it wasn't St. John's you'da been walking in pitchy black.

GOWDIE: *How* long? From the ash–

BUN: To the poplar. *(She sees the drawing.)* Is this yours?

(Gowdie starts to dart into a run but Bun grabs her and makes her stand and look at it.)

BUN: What do you call that? *(Bun grabs the drawing stick and switches Gowdie's legs.)* Stand still. Stand still!

GOWDIE: Ow! God dang, Bun!

BUN: If you'da spoke something nasty as that, you'd had Boraxo bubbles coming outta your mouth a week, you know it? DO YOU KNOW IT?

GOWDIE: I know it! *(Inspects her legs.)* You nigh laid me open.

BUN: *(Scuffing drawing out.)* I don't want no more art work on the yard. Where'd you get a low idea like that?

(Gowdie stares at the ground.)

BUN: Get on inside. *(Bun picks up the sack and mattock. She looks at the clean blade.)* Them's awful high class potatoes you been diggin that ain't touched dirt.

GOWDIE: *(Under her breath.)* Maybe I licked it clean.

BUN: Don't give me sass. If you wasn't diggin osh taters, what was you doing?

GOWDIE: I'll pick'em up tomorrow.

BUN: I smell fish so bad they must be hanging in the trees. Go on, get.

(Gowdie goes in the house, toys with one of the red threads at a window.)

Well. We ain't got no taters so we ain't got no mash so we ain't got no supper. Nothing but resurrection pie.

(Bun sets the mattock against the side of the house and brings the milk pail inside.)

GOWDIE: I ain't hungry.

BUN: You gonna break your health, digging all them imaginary potatoes and not eating.

GOWDIE: *(Goes eagerly to a cupboard.)* I'll make you something. I'll make you sweet sop. *(Gowdie takes a loaf of bread and cuts it into chunks.)*

BUN: *(Dips a finger in the milk pail.)* If them cows get sick, won't that be a mess? I know what Grandaddy'd done if he's seen them looking like that. Woulda set up all night with a rifle on his lap.

(Gowdie brings the plate over to Bun and pours syrup over the bread. Bun reaches out and grabs the tail of Gowdie's dress. She picks burrs off the material, silently holds up a palmful to Gowdie.)

GOWDIE: *(After a frozen hesitation.)* Stickers?

BUN: Like hotel labels on a suitcase. Where you been, girl?

GOWDIE: No place.

BUN: It's written on you clear as paint. Them brambles and that clean hoe. They're dancing around and singing a song to me. Did you go off the road?

GOWDIE: Why would I?

BUN: Did you go off the road?

GOWDIE: It were just a rabbit. I didn't reckon there's anything so terrible following a rabbit a little ways.

BUN: I told you, don't go in them woods for nothing. Not a rabbit, not a ladybug, not St. Joseph flying on a broomstick.

GOWDIE: I never meant it. I was just walking along to the patch. And I seen this little brown rabbit run across the road in front of me. And he stopped and turned his head like he was saying, Come on behind me.

BUN: So you followed this white-tail til almost sundown, that what you want me to swallow?

GOWDIE: He went in the woods, I went in the woods. He'd hop a step and I'd follow. Then we come to the end of that old fallow cornfield. And I lost him.

BUN: Gowdie, do you get what I say when I talk or do you just hear my teeth clacking? I mean it! Keep outta them woods.

(Gowdie pauses, looking at Bun uncertainly.)

GOWDIE: When I looked up, in the middle of the field there was this little springhouse sitting where I never seen one before. White with a little pointy roof.

BUN: *(Deadly quiet.)* Don't make things up. Don't you dare make things up.

GOWDIE: There wasn't no door at all but a board loose, so I squeezed in. It was dark at first and all I could tell was water bubbling from the spring in the very middle. Then my eyes brighted and I could tell there was stuff on the walls.

BUN: Like what stuff?

GOWDIE: Pictures of men and women. Seemed like.

BUN: You ain't sure? It dark at noon or something?

GOWDIE: Men and women. Drawed with something like a piece of char from a fire. Covered ground to ceiling.

BUN: Were these ladies and gentlemen doing anything like what you was drawing in the yard?

(Gowdie gives no answer for a moment.)

GOWDIE: At first they was hard to look at. It give me a funny feeling. Like wet fish slipping down my back. I felt the air hugging me. And all them folks doing like animals up on the walls was winking and saying, Come up here with us. I don't know how long I was sitting and I heard this plop in the spring, so I looked down in it. And when I caught sight of myself, the me in the water looked like it knew more than I did and waiting for me to catch up.

BUN: Hush.

GOWDIE: Then the springhouse just weren't there no more and I was on my knees in the middle of the field and the sun going down.

BUN: *(Slaps Gowdie.)* Hush! *(Bun goes to the front door, looks out of it suspiciously.)* Don't talk no more. Forget it all, right down to the rabbit.

GOWDIE: How can I? It's in my head like a picture on the wall.

BUN: Right down to the *rabbit. (Bun goes out the door to her room. Gowdie sits at the table alone.)*

GOWDIE: *(Low, to herself.)* It weren't so bad.

(Gowdie sulks a moment, dips her finger in a sugar bowl and eats sugar. She gets up to take the sugar bowl with her to her bed. But she looks up to see a man standing at the threshold of the open door: the Love Talker. He is barefooted and drenching wet, his hair matted in clumps. Long pond grasses are stuck to him. He stands dripping, looking at her. She drops the sugar bowl and it spills across the floor. The Love Talker stoops down, reaches over the threshold and presses a finger in the sugar. He sucks it off his finger, smiling at her. Then he stands up and disappears from the door. Gowdie is frozen a moment, then runs to the door. She stoops and wipes at the drips. Glancing at Bun's door, she runs out into the yard, sees nothing, then runs a little ways into the woods. The man is nowhere to be seen. A strange, watery, rushing noise is heard. The Red Head appears in the woods.)

GOWDIE: Did you see...anybody?

(The Red Head smiles at Gowdie. She moves her mouth as though speaking, but all that's heard is the rushing, bubbly sound of water. As Gowdie comes closer.)

GOWDIE: What? What?

(The Red Head beckons Gowdie closer. Her voice is heard, gradually getting louder above the watery sound.)

RED HEAD: Don't be afraid. The blood of fifty bulls, the sap of an old vine, the sharp edge of the new moon is in you. Your enemy will crush like a brown leaf in your hand.

(Gowdie keeps going closer to the Red Head. Bun comes back into the great room with an old cardboard box. She sees the mess of sugar and starts out the door at a bolt.)

BUN: Girl!

(The Red Head suddenly disappears. Gowdie runs back toward the house. Bun catches her.)

BUN: I'll frail you til you look like a candy cane if I catch you going in them woods again.

(Bun pushes Gowdie inside the door. Gowdie stoops and tries to clean up the sugar.)

BUN: What happened?

(Gowdie says nothing for a long moment.)

GOWDIE: Nothing. I had a clumsy fit.

(Bun goes to the cardboard box, starts taking out ash-wood crosses, red ribbons, bunches of dried yellow flowers. Gowdie inspects it.)

GOWDIE: I never seen these.

BUN: Grandma's old charms. *(Bun starts hanging up the ash crosses and ribbons around the room: the walls, the door, the bedposts.)*

GOWDIE: You gonna hang the house with this mess?

BUN: *(Reciting as she places charms.)*

Cold steel they cannot stand,

Crosses made of ash,

Rowan berry, red thread,

Nor knife in door may pass.

Grandma taught me that before I was three. Don't you undo a one of them. No telling what you been calling up. *(Bun takes a red ribbon and hangs it around Gowdie's neck.)* You shouldn't a gone in. You understand me? Whatever your little white house looked like, it wasn't what it seemed. Just tricks and glamor.

GOWDIE: It was such a calling thing.

BUN: I just bet it was. Calling, wiggling its hips and looking pretty. *(Gowdie angrily takes the ribbon off and throws it on the floor. When Bun speaks, her voice is softer.)* Come here. Come on, I'll comb your hair. I heard you can comb bad thoughts right out of a person's head. They come out in little blue crackles. I'll show you.

(Bun pulls a stool into the open doorway. Gowdie finally comes and sits on it. Bun combs her hair; an old, pleasurable ritual.)

GOWDIE: *(After a silence.)* What do you reckon they're like? Them things that made that little house?

BUN: The kinds of things that would wait all day for the chance to hurt you. It's jam on bread to'em. Get you out in the woods to step on the stray sod so you couldn't find your way in bright sunlight three yards from your house. There's the little girl without no clothes who walks beside you from the thorn at the gate to the big oak and sinks in the ground. If she can't lead you off the side of the mountain in the dark before then. The thing in the orchard that you can't see, but you can feel it in the trees, hating you. Up on the old cut where it goes through the hollow, there's something like a old man, only brown-leathery and haired all over, following you ten paces behind and stopping when you stop. It got in Grandaddy's car once. He booted the thing out. That's what I say, boot 'em all out.

GOWDIE: *(Under her breath.)* I don't know if I would.

BUN: I beg your pardon?

GOWDIE: Said maybe I wouldn't boot 'em all out.

BUN: I'm glad your Grandma ain't alive to hear that talk. She and her sister went to this granny that lived over the ridge to get their fates told. And the granny touched spit on Grandma's eyes and not on her sister's. And they were walking home and sister looks off the road and says, Ooooooo, ain't it pretty! And Grandma says, What is, fool? That little chair, setting in the woods. I'm gonna go get it and take it home. So Grandma has to charge after her and gets there just in time to see her sister sitting down on a big nest of brownie spiders like it was the peartest little chair in the world. They had to hold her in bed for a month. That granny'd set your Grandma's eyes so she could see it was a trick. Them People couldn't never pull a thing over on her from that day on..

GOWDIE: I ain't a idiot. I ain't gonna sit down in a spider's nest.

BUN: Tricks and glamor. Food-stealing, empty-handed-jealous baby-switchers. They can take one look at you and know what's written on your last page. *(Bun stops combing.)* It ain't good to even speak of them. *(Bun closes the door. The gloaming is over and the house is dark.)*

GOWDIE: Did Mama ever see one?

BUN: God knows what she saw.

GOWDIE: Did she, yes or no?

BUN: No more talking now. Time for bed. *(Bun lights a kerosene lamp. She takes a big knife from the cupboard and lays it on the floor in front of the front door with the edge facing out.)* Don't you worry. This is a safe house as long as you keep the door shut and your mind orderly. Maybe you better come in with me.

GOWDIE: I ain't no baby.

BUN: Then wear this. *(She picks up the red ribbon Gowdie threw off and hands it to her.)*

GOWDIE: Did you ever see that springhouse?

BUN: Once.

GOWDIE: You never said!

BUN: There weren't nothing to say. I was twelve, I seen it in the woods and I said to Hell with it.

GOWDIE: How could you not go in, Bun?

BUN: Don't mistake it, maidy. They are not your friends. Forget what you see today and you'll be happy. And say your prayers so the lights comes back quick.

GOWDIE: *(A revelation.)* Bun's jealous!

BUN: Of what?

GOWDIE: Of what's in the springhouse.

(Bun stares at her angrily. Gowdie smiles at her with a look of wonder. Bun furiously pinches Gowdie's arm and hurls the red ribbon in her face.)

BUN: WEAR IT!

(Bun goes in her room and slams the door. Gowdie tries on the charm again, reluctantly. She takes off her dress and has on a homemade shift underneath it. She takes her boots off. She sets the lamp by her bed and turns the wick down dimly. All during this process she says, over and over:)

GOWDIE: Truely the light is sweet and a pleasant thing it is for the eyes to behold the sun. Truely the light is sweet and a pleasant thing it is for the eyes to behold the sun...

(She sits on the bed. Her reciting trails off. She toys with the charms on the bedposts, then flips them off onto the floor. She sits breathless, waiting. Nothing happens. She gets up and listens at Bun's door. Then she takes down the ash crosses. She gets scissors from the cupboard and cuts the red thread in the windows. She takes a chunk of bread and fills a basin with milk and places them on the table. She takes the knife away from the door and opens the door wide. Each of these steps is taken with trepidation. After each charm is removed, she waits tensely for what might happen. Last, she takes the ribbon off her neck, slowly, and drops it on the floor. She jumps in bed and lies there, shut-eyed and listening. A whipporwill calls close by. The Love Talker appears in the door. He walks in, goes to the table, tips up the basin and drinks the milk. He eats the bread. Then he climbs over the footboard of Gowdie's bed, hunkers down, sitting on her feet, and watches her. She lies frozen, eyes closed. The Love Talker reaches out and touches Gowdie's forehead with his finger. She opens her eyes. He smiles at her.)

LOVE TALKER: I have good news for you, Gowdie Blackmun.

(He reaches to turn down the lamp. The lights go out. The lights come up on the house, early the next morning. The lowing of cows can be heard, far off. Gowdie is alone, asleep in her bed. She bolts upright, takes a moment to realize she's awake. She gets out of bed, glances at Bun's door, and goes outside. From behind the house she drags a washtub and some rags. The tub has some water in it. She takes the tub into the woods, sets it down and kneels to wash her face. She frowns at her face in the water. She stands in the basin and starts washing with the rag. She scrubs herself roughly, but then lets the rag glide up her leg, between her legs. The Red Head has appeared from the woods behind her. She watches unseen awhile.)

RED HEAD: Pretty stuff, lookie at it. All hunched up and grabbing the nightie. *(Holds out a friendly hand.)* All done? Come out of the little sea.

(Gowdie takes the Red Head's hand and steps out. The Red Head sniffs Gowdie's neck.)

RED HEAD: Good work. Very clean, so it is. Let's make friends, okay? *(Leans in close to Gowdie.)* Don't you talk?

GOWDIE: Can you tell dreams?

RED HEAD: I'm very good at that. I'm good at just that very thing.

GOWDIE: It was last night. I lost it, after how you do when you wake up. But it been coming back to me.

RED HEAD: Like a fish flipping out of the pure air into you lap. Shhh! I see it! I caught your dreamfish. There's you in bed, froze for listening. A bird called. And Something come in the door. This weight, heavy and warm as sun through a window pressed itself on you. He pushed gifts and riches into your hands you'd never seen before. He squeezed hot birthday present through your blood veins. He poured the running oil of gladness over your head, in your eyes, down your throat and between your breasts. And when the weight of all them presents was on you, he called you to come out of the old skin. And at first you wouldn't. You held on to the bed post.

GOWDIE: It seemed it might be bad. Floating thataway. I might not come back at all.

RED HEAD: But you let him drag your soul right up from the bed and when he dropped it, you fell for miles back onto the mattress. But not back into the little girl. She'd shrunk like a curl of ash. You were humming like something lightening'd stuck alive.

GOWDIE: That was the dream.

RED HEAD: It wasn't no dream. Lookie. *(The Red Head motions Gowdie to look in the basin of water.)* He says: you're prettier than the apple tree in the west corner of the yard. *(Gowdie touches her face as she looks at her reflection.)* He says: look for him again.

GOWDIE: You know him?

RED HEAD: *(Holding up two twined fingers.)* That's us. Snug as a snake curled round an egg. He'll be back. He's got more for you. He'll put something in you like a heartbeat that'll make the trees try and touch you. He'll give you everything. Do you know what I mean?

GOWDIE: Sure.

RED HEAD: You opened the door. Your fortune was, you opened the door. There ain't no taking a welcome back. *(The Red Head kisses Gowdie's feet.)* No taking back. *(The Red Head takes the thorn wreath off her head and shows it to Gowdie.)* My present.

GOWDIE: White thorn.

RED HEAD: Yes. Pretty-pretty. Pleasure and pain twisted together.

(The Red Head suddenly jams the wreath on Gowdie's head. Gowdie screams in pain. The Red Head runs away.)

GOWDIE: Owww! *(Gowdie stumbles blindly through the woods trying to pry the thing off.)* Son of a bitch! *(She sits on the ground wrestling with it. In the house, Bun enters from her bedroom. She stands and listens.)*

BUN: I either lost my mind or them cows is out. Gowdie—? *(She looks at Gowdie's bed, sees she's not there.)* No. *(She sees the cut threads, the ash crosses thrown down, the bowl of milk.)* No. No ma'am! Like the old days. The goddamn old days! *(Bun rushes out of the house and finds Gowdie in the woods. She is now looking at herself in the basin, tugging at the wreath. Bun runs at her, knocks her over and sits on top of her.)* Who give you the crown, Miss America?

GOWDIE: Get off!

BUN: Let me tell you 'bout my morning so far. Someone's been rearranging the furniture and sending the cows on vacation.

GOWDIE: Lemme go, Bun!

BUN: What you done? What you let in?

GOWDIE: Don't sit on me, Bun. You scaring me.

(Bun pulls her up by the wrists.)

BUN: Ain't no call to be scared of me, maidy. Just tell me. What you let in our house?

GOWDIE: I thought it was a dream. There was this man. A nice man.

BUN: Girl, you never let in no man and he wasn't nice.

GOWDIE: *(Whispers.)* Bun! He came straight to me. Climbed in my bed and knew my name—

(Bun pounces on Gowdie and shakes her.)

BUN: You know how bad a thing it is you done? You got no right opening our house like that! You ain't the only one living in it!

GOWDIE: He weren't bad. He said I was like the apple tree in the corner of the yard. He said I was grown and I'd be mistress of my own house. He talked pretty.

BUN: A pretty thing? Jumped down offa that springhouse wall?

GOWDIE: You wouldn't even go in. How do you know?

BUN: I know his voice sure enough.

GOWDIE: How? HOW? You don't know nothing!

BUN: Mama let him in. When you was a baby. I hid in my room and sat up all night holding you in my lap, listening to her laugh and him trying to get in, pressing on my door like the wind bellying a sail. You put us in danger. You got to slam the door in his face.

GOWDIE: But I called him.

BUN: Come in the house.

(Gowdie runs from her.)

GOWDIE: No!

BUN: Do you hear what I say?

GOWDIE: *(Flitting away from her, laughing.)* No! Not today.

BUN: Where you think you're going?

GOWDIE: Off the path! *(Gowdie laughs, running off into the woods. Bun starts after her, stops. She looks around at the trees.)*

BUN: You picked the wrong little sister.

(The lights go down on her. The lights come back up on the house, sunset light. Bun is sitting in the house, wearing the red ribbon around her neck. She is working the dasher in a little churn by her chair. As she churns, she looks over a worn, handwritten book in her lap. Turns pages, reading.) The old people in the woods. To know their shapes. *(Turns page.)* Charms. Said spells. Hurts. *(She stops at this page.)* Hurts. To destroy, steal their power. To steal their power, steal their name. This hurt they say the workingest, the best, the hardest to use. First, catch it. *(She puts down the book, thinks a moment. The door to her room swings open a little. She gets up and shuts it. She sits back down, watching. The front door opens, slowly. She closes it. Both doors open. She runs at them both, slamming them hard. It's still a second. Bun slaps at something near her ankle, as though something had brushed it. She pushes at something touching her farther and farther up her legs.)* Stop it. *(Something unseen touches her more and more intimately. She tries to get away from it. It runs her onto Gowdie's bed.)* STOP IT RIGHT NOW! *(She grabs a pair of big iron shears from a corner, opens them in the form of a cross and lays them under the bed and sits on it. The touches stop.)* I know you're still there. Waiting at the edges.

(The front door starts to open. She runs to shut it, but this time, Gowdie walks in. Her shift is muddy and torn. She has a dirty face, hands and legs. She still wears the wreath.)

BUN: Where you been all day, driving me to death worrying?

GOWDIE: I been here and I been there. *(Gowdie peeks in the churn, dips a finger in and licks the cream.)*

BUN: You dirty as an animal. Roaming around with your eyes looking like they glazed over with powder sugar icing. Where you been? You give up speech? That what he tells you? He telling you to hate me?

GOWDIE: No, Bun, don't speak that. I'll tell you where I been. I been finding him. He's all over the woods, only hidden.

(Bun shies away from her.)

BUN: Don't tell me nothing.

GOWDIE: So I draw him with water on the flat rocks in the creek. I carve his face in the trees. I'm making him seeable.

BUN: Quit it!

GOWDIE: Then a shadow'll move under a oak. There he is! And I'm nothing but sky-blue eyes looking at him, the hair on my head starts flowing to him up-breeze and I got come-to-me hands growing outta my pockets like the two I was born with ain't enough. Then he touches my eyes blind, sends my standing bones useless and folds his grape and cedar dark around me.

BUN: He don't take you no place but a trick.

GOWDIE: He makes it so I can feel the roots of the trees growing down into the earth like it was a dark sky. Then he makes it all tilt so the earth sky and the root trees are on top and the airy ones are below. And I can see both, tilting and twirling, dark sky chasing light sky, never catching each other. He lets me see this. He said he's gonna give me everything.

BUN: You want to be like your mama?

GOWDIE: I don't even remember my mama.

BUN: I do. Real good. When daddy died, her eyes got dark. She holed up in the back room, rocking, facing the window, sputtering down like candle fat before the light goes out. And she called Something.

GOWDIE: She do it like this? *(She stands in the open door.)* Stand in the window with the curtains blowing across her face. Watching for the stir in the leaves. Saying, come on out. Come closer.

(Bun yanks Gowdie away from the door.)

BUN: He killed her. He turned her mind til she went milkwhite from wanting him. *I* was the one took care of you!

GOWDIE: You making it up.

BUN: She drew things on the walls I had to scrub off every day, 'cause if you looked at them too long they made you crazy. Went up on the ridge, cutting stumps and branches into such god-awful shapes I couldn't even name'em to you. I'd be walking down the road and there'd be one grinning through the leaves at me. Or up where you can see the sunset, there'd be something funny about a branch over my head and it'd turn out to be something nasty she'd done to it. I hacked down every one I found and I burned it. You know what I think? I think you and Mama got you the same boyfriend. I recognize the goat smell.

(Gowdie splashes the dasher down in the church angrily.)

GOWDIE: Making it UP!

BUN: Mama's in the dirt. Don't you be going dark on me too. Don't end up creeping through the woods at night and forgetting your own human name. What does he do that could make it worth that?

GOWDIE: *(Whispers teasingly.)* What's he do? What's he do?

BUN: I ain't sharing this house! It tries to get in my room. It holds me so I can't move and it gives me dreams. Gowdie, please!

GOWDIE: Poor Bun. Her house got a hole knocked in it. The vines are slipping in, curling up the walls, strangling the cups and pitchers, squeezing the boards til they crack. What's she gonna do when she can't tell her house from the woods? Maybe it was the weight of something good buckling in your door and pressing you in the bed.

BUN: There's ways to drive him off. We'll blast him away, every bit, even that bruisy fist he got squeezed around your brain. It ain't too late. Shut the door on him!

(Gowdie takes Bun's hands and kisses each.)

GOWDIE: Bunny. Fall half-way down a well for me. Then I will.

(She gives Bun a little slap or sudden playful pinch. A noise has begun to stir outside. It goes around and around the house, making the walls creak as if they were being squeezed. It is a windy, rushing noise, getting louder. The cream in the little churn bubbles up and over the top onto the floor. Gowdie looks at everything delightedly. Bun grabs a towel and tries to staunch the flow of cream from the churn. If the front door is closed, it now bams open. Bun runs to her room and comes back out with a quilt.)

BUN: I ain't staying where he is. *(Bun runs out of the house into the dark woods and crouches down.)* Father father father, deliver against all wild things, all runners in darkness and tricking spirits, night-whisperers, dream-pressers, things there but not to be seen–! *(She can't go on. The noise is much louder–unbearable to her. She presses her hands to her ears and hides under the quilt. The noise suddenly stops. Gowdie slowly walks toward the open front door.)*

GOWDIE: Come in. Come in. Let me ride in your hand. Let one hand drop me and the other hand catch.

(The lights go out on her as she stands in the doorway. The lights come up on the woods, dawn. Bun, camouflaged by her quilt and the underbrush, is asleep on the ground. The Red Head is wandering slowly through the woods, bent close to the ground. She doesn't see Bun. Every once in a while she catches something and eats it.)

RED HEAD: Squirm squirm. I gotcha. Ha!

(She slaps at something and swallows it . Bun wakes up, cautiously peeks out and watches.)

RED HEAD: Dig dig dig dig dig. Pop! *(Pops something in her mouth.)* Ha!

(Bun crouches motionlessly, then runs and tackles the Red Head. The Red Head screams and struggles wildly to get free.)

RED HEAD: Let gooooooo!

(Bun holds onto her and grabs a handful of the Red Head's hair.)

BUN: Ain't this interesting? Now what could this scrawny thing be? Not big enough for a human. Not pretty enough for a animal. You're slipping, Red, letting somebody sneak up on you like that.

RED HEAD: Lemme go. I just live down the mountain. My mama'll be looking for me.

BUN: They ain't a mama on earth looking for you. You're caught, doll baby. You done stepped in it like cow squat.

(The Red Head lunges and tries to tear at Bun's face, but Bun holds her.)

BUN: Oh don't leave now. Seems to me we got a little business to settle, me seeing one of you 'fore you seen me. I get a prize, don't I? I been thinking what's the worst hook I could stick into you nightcrawlers. It's names, ain't it? Them names you guard like stolen sin.

RED HEAD: No no no no. Nevernevernevernever names!

BUN: That's just what I want, then. A name. That bastard's. That love talker.

RED HEAD: Uh-uh! No!

(The Red Head struggles more wildly than ever to get away. Bun yanks her head back by the hair.)

BUN: You got to. I caught you and you got to give me what I want. Ain't it a shame? WHAT IS IT?

RED HEAD: Got something better. Listen. I give you rich things. Sparkles. You like sparkles?

BUN: What, magnolia seeds for rubies? Godspeed petals for sapphires? Tricks and glamor, gone like pouring water on sugar.

(The Red Head takes a ring off her finger and pushes it frantically at Bun.)

RED HEAD: Put this on! Never wrinkles, never old!

BUN: Tell me his NAME!

(Bun slams the Red Head's head on the ground. The Red Head shuts her eyes and mumbles something in Bun's ear.) Better not be no trick.

RED HEAD: Done it, done it. Lemme go.

BUN: Not til you tell me how it works.

(The Red Head hesitates. Bun starts to slam her head down again.)

RED HEAD: Catch his eye unblinking and say the name to him in triple. In his ear.

BUN: Look him in the eye and say the name three times? And then it's done? He's gone? Not just shooed away til the next big moon, but blasted to flinders? Evaporated?

RED HEAD: Yes! Yes! What you think?

BUN: And what's gonna keep him in whispering distance while all this is going on?

RED HEAD: If he comes near to you and you have his eye, he can't leave til you say it—or not.

BUN: Don't fret yourself. He comes close enough, I'll say it.

RED HEAD: Listen. I know something. *(Whispers.)* He wants you. He told me. More than her.

(Bun is struck speechless a moment. The Red Head smiles knowingly. Bun's face hardens and she suddenly wrenches the Red Head's arm behind her.)

BUN: Well tell him I'm looking for him. I'd like a date. And if he's too scared to try his luck, he better stay away from me and my sister. Got it?

RED HEAD: Loose!

(Bun lets the Red Head up. She scrambles away.)

RED HEAD: Gonna get what you asking for, fool!

BUN: *(Laughs.)* Oh, I'm shaking! I'm peeing right down my leg!

(The Red Head furiously throws a pine cone at Bun. This only makes her laugh more. The Red Head disappears into the woods. Bun picks up her quilt

and walks back to the house. Part of the time she is lost from view, gathering wild flowers as she goes through the woods. When she reaches the yard, she strews a trail of flowers up to the front door and right up to the bed where Gowdie is asleep. Without waking her, Bun gently draws back the coverlet from Gowdie and hikes up the hem of Gowdie's shift until she's satisfied with the picture. She sits down away from the open door.)

Bait's on the hook, fish. Come and taste it.

(A breeze blows through the door, stirring the flowers. Gowdie moves in her sleep, but doesn't wake. The Love Talker appears at the front door. He stays outside the threshold and his features are not clearly seen. All he may be is a shadow. He wavers at the door.)

BUN: Come kiss her good morning. You ain't shy.

(At Bun's voice, he sinks back quickly from the door.)

BUN: Come on. You dead salt thirsty and she right here like a pitcher of November water.

LOVE TALKER: *(In a soft voice.)* Bunny. You ain't bound to use what you got. There's all kinds of possibilities.

BUN: Look at her. That skin all hot and pink from sleeping. Come on in. I'll give you a possibility. *(Bun moves slowly closer, gets near Gowdie's bed.)*

LOVE TALKER: You wouldn't be mean to me. Be nice. Find out what Mama was laughing about on the other side of the door.

BUN: Come close enough for me to tell the color of your tricking eyes.

LOVE TALKER: Bun. I know you. I know who you are. You hold your hands over your eyes when you dream.

BUN: Come here and get it, you bastard!

(Bun pulls the him of Gowdie's shift up higher and higher. Gowdie wakes. She looks immediately at the open door.)

GOWDIE: Come in. The door's wide. You lurking in it like cedar smoke. Teaser.

(Gowdie runs to the door and the Love Talker sinks back from her. Gowdie freezes. She looks from the Love Talker to Bun. She tries to bolt, but Bun catches her and holds her in front of the door.)

BUN: All yours. For just three steps forward.

(The Love Talker wavers closer and closer to the door.)

GOWDIE: Come in! Why won't you come in?

(Gowdie struggles to get free from Bun. Bun wrestles her onto the bed. She pins Gowdie and clamps a hand over her mouth.)

BUN: Come get your sweetheart. She thinks you can do anything.

LOVE TALKER: Bun wouldn't use the name. If she was good to me, I'd do anything she wanted. I make her so happy she sprout leaves from her fingers.

BUN: Run and beg, boy. Come closer or stay away, They both suit me fine.

(He starts to scratch on the doorjamb, while his voice remains sweet.)

LOVE TALKER: Bun. Be nice. *(He motions around the room at the charms.)* Look at all the magic you got. I must be all you think about.

(Bun furiously rushes at him, but he steps back.)

LOVE TALKER: Bunny bunny bunny. One way or the other.

(He vanishes from the door completely. Gowdie runs up to it, looks out, sees nothing.)

GOWDIE: What you done?

BUN: Your loverboy's circuit ride's been cut. Big sister knows his name and you ain't his girl no more.

GOWDIE: Liar!

BUN: Then where is he? So gooey with love he nearly melts out on the floor for you. Where's he now?

GOWDIE: You're just dead green jealous. He don't leave just 'cause you flap your apron at him. *(Gowdie darts out the door.)*

BUN: Come back in this house!

(Bun runs out in the yard after her, but Gowdie has disappeared into the woods. Bun lets her go. In the woods. Gowdie runs in, flops down, stretches out on her back under the trees. She laughs.)

GOWDIE: Shoo you away with her apron! Maybe she been practicing. Scooping up storms in her tassie cup. Sopping up creeks with her mess rag. Pushing back the dark like a window curtain. *(Laughs at the idea.)* You'll come. You'll bend down to me like a tree. *(She reaches her arms up. There is a long, still silence. She sits up suddenly.)* Won't you?

(There is a distant rumbling of dry thunder. The lights go down on her. In the yard, Bun turns from the woods. She starts back to the house. She passes the tree stump and looks at her reflection in the water. She hits the reflection with her fist. Bun goes to sit in the front door and watches the woods. The daylight fades. Bun still sits in the door. It's dark. Bun rests her head against the jamb, asleep. Gowdie reappears in the woods. She is dirtier, her clothes torn. Her movements are odd and weightless. She looks sick. She moves slowly into the yard, looking at the back of her hand.)

GOWDIE: So white. With little blue rivers. He won't come near to me. I tried and tried. I'm a leaf-slider. I'm a soft-flapper in the trees. I'm Nothing brushing by. *(She looks at Bun, asleep in the door.)* Gonna have your way. Gonna get your doors closed and have your way!

(Bun wakes and sees Gowdie. She goes to her.)

BUN: Come here to me. Come to Bun. It's alright.

(Gowdie lets herself be led into the house. She looks amazed at the back of her hand.)

GOWDIE: A snowfield! And little blue rivers pouring me out. *(She touches Bun's face.)* Feel how cold. Feel.

BUN: Shh. You home now. He gonna leave you alone.

GOWDIE: Why you want to be thisaway?

(Bun sits Gowdie at the table. She puts a plate in front of her.)

BUN: Get you some food. Get you washed up. Then you sleep long and heavy and wake up like my old girl.

(Gowdie violently knocks her plate off onto the floor.)

GOWDIE: Ain't hungry and I ain't your old girl.

(Bun replaces the plate firmly.)

BUN: He's not coming back to you.

GOWDIE: He is!

(She starts to knock the plate off again, but Bun catches her hand.)

BUN: Well, let's see. Maybe he'll stand dying for you, think so? *(Bun opens the door and dog-whistles loudly.)* Come on, boy! You were gonna knock my door in, don't be shy now!

(Gowdie starts to cry. Bun closes the door and goes to comfort her.)

BUN: You'll forget all about him.

(Gowdie tries to hit Bun.)

GOWDIE: No!

BUN: Don't you strike at me.

GOWDIE: I won't. I won't hit. I won't do anything bad. Please. Let him in. I won't run away again. I promise. *(Whisper.)* Listen, listen. I'd share. I would. You let him in, he forget every mean thing you done. He give you double sweet, overflowing, sopping out over the rim–!

BUN: NO.

(Gowdie suddenly flails out and beats on Bun in a rage, then stops herself, appalled.)

GOWDIE: I didn't mean it. I didn't mean it. Bun, Don't be mad. *(She kneels and hugs Bun. Sings softly.)*

Bun, Bun, I'm her slave,

She's the Queen and I'm her knave.

BUN: Will you stop wanting him? Will you stop looking for him?

(Gowdie starts to nod yes, then explodes.)

GOWDIE: NO! *(Gowdie tries to run for the door but Bun holds her.)*

BUN: Alright, then!

(Bun drags and wrestles Gowdie over to the foot of the bed. She grabs a rope hanging on a peg on the wall and ties Gowdie standing up to the bedposts by her wrists. Gowdie tries to bite and kick her.)

BUN: Cut out that kicking! *(As though to Love Talker.)* I'm gonna find you. You'll come or I'll know you for a coward. Then you watch out, slippery boy. I'll say your name so loud it'll blow you back to Hell butt forward. *(She finishes tying Gowdie to the posts. She lifts Gowdie's face up.)* They switched on me. They stole my pretty little girl and stuck me with a monkey-faced changling with old eyes. I want my baby back.

GOWDIE: She ain't coming back. She's dead.

(Bun pushes angrily away from the bed and opens the front door. She looks out at the dark woods.)

BUN: I'll be what you like, brother. I'll be the half-dressed bait in your woods. Then I'll lie you into eye-shot and pour your name in your ear like poison. *(Bun takes her work shoes off. She opens buttons on the front of her dress. She hikes her skirt up. She loosens her hair so it floats and swims around her face.)* Tell me, Gowdie. Have I got it?

(Gowdie is silent, swaying weakly in her ropes. Bun starts out the door.)

GOWDIE: Sister. Be careful you don't take a wrong step.

(Bun hesitates in the door, then goes out. Gowdie slowly, silently twists her wrists in the ropes. The lights dim down on her. The lights go up on Bun walking through the yard and into the woods.)

BUN: *(Stops, listening.)* I'm coming to your house. Stepping underneath your mistletoe. See? *(She listens. Nothing.)* Come on. Want me to do like mama? Sway myself. Feel the air telling my shape, hugging around me. You so far away. Ain't you jealous of the air touching me all over? If you was here...if you was here, it would be you. *(She stands with her eyes closed. She sways luxuriously. She kisses the air. Suddenly she stops, opens her eyes.)* Come on. Come on now. *(She moves away from the spot where she was, almost in a panic. Before she gets very far, she stops short as though she's bumped into an invisible wall that spins her in another direction. At this moment, the woods around her black out, leaving her in a tight little circle of light. She laughs uneasily at herself and starts off in another direction. The same force stops her, twirls her in another direction.)* That's silly. I know where I am. I know just where I am. *(She is totally disoriented, runs in all different directions but can't get farther than a few feet before she's twirled about again. She sinks down in panic. Breathlessly fast.)* Father-father-father, deliver against all wild things, all runners in darkness and tricking sprits, night-whisperers, dream-pressers, things there but not to be seen, crawlers in the leaf mold, the rager with dark blood on its face, the love talker that touches the brain with cold and burns the body, from these deliver me. All creation is in your power and all these dangers you made to. *(She stops, frowns.)* These you made...too.

(She looks up to see the Love Talker at the very edge of the light. He can barely be seen and his eyes are averted down. They remain frozen in the light. The lights come up on the house. Gowdie is still swaying and creaking in her ropes. The Red Head appears in the door. She scratches a fingernail playfully down the wood of the door. Gowdie raises her head.)

RED HEAD: My, my. We doesn't look so good.

GOWDIE: She gone to get him. She got his name. Lookit me.

RED HEAD: It's pitiful. Be able to see the grass through your head soon, poor pretty. *She* done this.

GOWDIE: Can't he stop her?

RED HEAD: Oh, he made to try. He think if he can put a hand on her, she pop open like a touch-me-not pod. What if she don't pop, cold bitch? What if she blasts him and sends him to smithereen? Where's you, then? Long as she's breathing, she's saying "no." She'll no you into a ghost.

GOWDIE: She been my own mama.

RED HEAD: What day she gonna let you have him?

(Gowdie says nothing, twisting the rope slowly.)

RED HEAD: What day?

GOWDIE: Never.

RED HEAD: He didn't promise pretty. He promised you everything. *(Starts untying Gowdie's ropes.)* How can a little mind hold it? Like dipping a tea cup in a river, it'll knock it from your hands. Better not try and know it. Better just step in and let it float you down. A darkness cracking with light and a brightness muffled up in a coat of dark. One hand drops, the other hand catches. One hand catches, the other hand drops. It's all for you.

GOWDIE: He said he had good news.

RED HEAD: That is the good news, creature. Him or her. You got to choose.

GOWDIE: What if I can't?

RED HEAD: There's no such a thing.

GOWDIE: What if I choose against him?

(The Red Head pushes Gowdie swiftly down on her back, folds her hands over her chest like a corpse and closes Gowdie's eyes.)

RED HEAD: You wouldn't like it at all. *(The Red Head remains sitting crouched on top of Gowdie. She bends down close.)* Let's make friends. Okay?

(The Red Head leads Gowdie by the hand out of the house to the hollow stump. She stands facing Gowdie across it. She dips her hand into the stump and it comes out dripping red. She presses her hand to Gowdie's chest, leaving a bloody hand print.)

RED HEAD: Do something about it.

(The Red Head walks backwards until she's out of sight. Gowdie follows her into the woods. Bun, still trapped in the circle of light, stands and faces the Love Talker. He stays in the shadows.)

BUN: I knew you wouldn't let me down. Come closer.

(The Love Talker keeps his eyes down and doesn't move.)

BUN: Look at me. Tied up with tissue and ribbons for you. I got something to whisper to you. Come on.

(He steps into the circle of light. His eyes are still down.)

BUN: Show me your eyes. You ain't made of run-and-hide. You made of shimmy-up-and-try.

(He puts a hand out toward her. He raises his eyes and looks at her. Bun keeps her eyes on him.)

LOVE TALKER: You turning your back to me so many times I know it better than your face. Holding your heart like a velvet jewelry box. Open it up and I'll cover you with all them dangerous pretties you never spent.

(He moves closer to her. Bun leans in and whispers his name in his ear moving her head back swiftly and keeping her eyes on his.)

BUN: Once.

LOVE TALKER: Back in the old days. When you heard Mama singing and the window sash rumbled up. You laid the baby on the pillow and pressed your ear against the door so hard you could hear the swirls in the wood. You listened. And when Mama screamed, you screamed with her. I heard you. In the whispery, little girl voice, you screamed. Dirty girl. Bunching up the sheets and falling through the sky so fast your nerves got tails like comets. Come with me. I'll set you a dinner of smooth arms and round legs and wet hair at the back of the neck. I'll pour slow syrup on it all and then throw in the match and make you dead and alive and nowhere.

(She leans in to whisper the name again, pulling back quick to keep eye contact with him.)

BUN: *(Grimly.)* Two times.

LOVE TALKER: Bunny. I'll give you joy and pain flipping like the sides of a penny. I'll take you off that straight path and set your feet dancing on a ground of witch burrs. All places will be yours. I'll make you someone you hardly know and when you catch a sight of your dirty, smiling face in a still stream, you'll scare yourself. But it'll be all of you. Jump. It ain't the jaggedy end of the world. There's all sorts of possibilities.

BUN: Three times. *(She leans in to say his name the final time. She gets closer and closer to his face. She kisses him. The kiss is deep and for a moment, she is lost in it, then hurtles back from him.)* NO!

(The Love Talker freed, laughing, quickly vanishes into the shadows. Bun wipes the kiss off her mouth.)

BUN: You son of a salt bitch! I still know your name.

(A low rushing, keening noise has begun. Bun starts hurriedly back to the house, grabbing the mattock from the yard. She spits on it, places it in the doorway: a charm. She tries to put the charms back up. She crouches on the bed, trying to tie the red threads in the window back up. Gowdie enters the yard from the woods. The Red Head appears up on the ridge in her black cloak. She watches Gowdie walk to the house. The Red Head crouches, covers her face with her hood and puts her hands on her head. Gowdie reaches the front door. She stoops and picks up the mattock. Bun sees her and freezes. The low, rushing noise goes round and round the house. Gowdie starts into the room and toward Bun, then hesitates.)

BUN: Why you stopping?

GOWDIE: *(Whispered.)* Bunny.

BUN: Why you stopping? I been your mama. You be my sweet thing again. My baby.

(Gowdie stands still, tentative, the mattock held looser in her hand.)

BUN: Til we dressed in white and lay down in the earth side by side, safe.

(Gowdie holds the mattock firmly and advances to Bun. Bun pushes the bed out and tries to hide between it and the wall. Gowdie kneels on the bed, swings the mattock up and brings it down in one hard stroke between the bed and the wall. There is no sound from Bun. The keening noise stops. Gowdie watches a stream of blood run slowly out from under the bed. The Red Head stands up, uncovering her head. The Love Talker appears in the door. Gowdie turns to look at him over her shoulder. The lights fade quickly out.)

END OF PLAY

The Value of Names

by Jeffrey Sweet

Jeffrey Sweet's other plays include *Porch, American Enterprise* (winner of several awards and grants), *With and Without, Responsible Parties, The Unreasonable Man* and *Stops Along The Way,* as well as the book for the musical *What About Luv?* (Outer Critics Circle Award winner) and the book and lyrics for *I Sent a Letter to My Love,* both of which played off-Broadway. He is also the author of two books on the theater, *Something Wonderful Right Away* and *The Dramatist's Toolkit,* co-edits the *Best Plays* Annual, and has written many hours of TV, including the prize-winning adaptation of Hugh Whitemore's *Pack of Lies.* He has lectured on playwriting at many universities and theatrical institutions. *The Value of Names* was written while he was a member of the New York Writers Bloc, with whose other alumni, Jane Anderson and Donald Margulies, he is pleased to cohabit in this volume.

ORIGINAL PRODUCTION

The Value of Names premiered in the 1982 SHORTS Festival at Actors Theatre of Louisville and was also presented in the 1983 Humana Festival of New American Plays. It was originally directed by Emily Mann with the following cast:

Norma . . . . Robin Groves
Benny . . . . Larry Block
Leo . . . . Frederic Major

CHARACTERS
   NORMA
   BENNY
   LEO

SETTING: The play takes place on a patio high up in the hills over Malibu.

THE VALUE OF NAMES

The set is a patio high up in the hills over Malibu. Upstage is Benny Silverman's house. It is the house of someone very comfortably off. The patio may be entered either through a door from the house or through a gate that leads directly from the road.

At rise, Benny has an easel set up and is painting the view from his patio. He is in his late sixties or early seventies and appears to be in fine health. Norma is in her early twenties. A few seconds of quiet, then he speaks—

BENNY: Does it sound too Jewish?

NORMA: *(To audience.)* No, hold on. First, a couple of things you should know: It's 1981. A patio up in the hills overlooking Malibu. Over there, the Pacific Ocean. Next to me, my father. On the whole, I have less trouble with the Pacific.

BENNY: *(As in "Are you finished?")* OK?

NORMA: Sure. Go ahead.

BENNY: Does it sound too Jewish?

NORMA: Pop—

BENNY: You're changing your name. Stands to reason there's something about the one you've got you don't like. Or maybe find inconvenient.

NORMA: *(To audience.)* I should have known he'd take it like this.

BENNY: Could put you at a disadvantage. A name like Silverman. Some parts—the casting directors won't even look at you. I know. Say, for instance, they do a new version of *The Bells of St. Mary's*. Casting people see the name Norma Silverman, what are they going to say? "Nope, don't call her. A person obviously without nun potential. Get me an O'Hara or a Kelly. Get away with this Silverman." And there goes your chance to play Ingrid Bergman. Of course, Bergman, too, is a name that's a little suspect.

NORMA: Pop—

BENNY: But then, one look at her, that question's laid to rest. Even if she did play Golda Meir once. One look at that nose of hers. That was not a Jewish nose. But then—thanks to the magic of science—who can tell from a nose?

NORMA: Of course.

BENNY: I could show you Horowitzes and Steins and Margulieses with noses on them look like they belong to Smiths. Very funny seeing a Smith nose on a Horowitz. Or a Horowitz nose on a Smith, although this is rarer.

NORMA: They don't transplant noses.

BENNY: You want to know why?

NORMA: *(With a sidelong look to the audience.)* OK, why?

BENNY: Run the risk of the body rejecting. Sure, it's a big problem. Heart transplant, kidney transplant—the body sometimes says, "No, thank you. Take it away." A case like that, all that happens is maybe someone dies. But a nose transplant—could you imagine the humiliation if that happened? Walking down the street, maybe you hiccup, a slight tearing sensation, and suddenly there's a draft in the middle of your face. You look down on the pavement, see two dainty nostrils staring up at Heaven.

NORMA: Are you finished?

BENNY: Are you?

NORMA: With what?

BENNY: This nonsense. This changing-your-name nonsense.

NORMA: It's not nonsense. I'm going to do it.

BENNY: Fine. So do it. So what do you want from me?

NORMA: I don't want from you. I just thought I should tell you.

BENNY: OK, you've told me. So what do you want me to say? You want me to say congratulations? Like you're having a baby—congratulations? You're having a new name—how wonderful! And who's the father of this new name? I know who the father of the old name is. I see him sometimes on the Late Show.

NORMA: OK, Pop.

BENNY: It's not OK. But never mind, we won't talk about it.

NORMA: Fat chance.

BENNY: So what else is new? A sex change?

NORMA: It doesn't have anything to do with Jewish or not Jewish.

BENNY: What *has* it to do with?

NORMA: You.

BENNY: Oh. *I'm* the *to-do-with?*

NORMA: Here we go.

BENNY: *I'm* the reason you're changing your name?

NORMA: Do you want me to explain now? Or shall I give you a little room for a tirade?

BENNY: What tirade?

NORMA: The tirade you're gearing up for.

BENNY: Who, me?

NORMA: I wish you'd understand.

BENNY: What's to understand? You're changing your name. You're changing your name because it's my name. This makes me feel instantly terrific and wonderful. It makes me feel how glad I am to have my daughter's love and respect. How fulfilling it is to be a parent. How worth it all it's all been. Would you like a little coffee?

NORMA: Look, every time I've ever done anything, every time I've ever been reviewed, they always put in that I'm your daughter. My name is not

Norma Silverman. My name is Norma Silverman Benny Silverman's daughter.

BENNY: So what are you trying to do—convince people you're the product of a virgin birth?

NORMA: I'm very proud of being your daughter. But I would like, for once, when I get on a stage, for them to see me. Not just see you in me. There's a comparison implied there. "Is she as good as?"

BENNY: Aren't you?

NORMA: I don't think I should have to fight that. You really don't want to understand, do you?

BENNY: Who put you up to this?

NORMA: What?

BENNY: This is your mother's idea, isn't it?

NORMA: No.

BENNY: I recognize the style.

NORMA: What do you mean?

BENNY: Right after the divorce, she got her driver's license changed back to her maiden name. Sarah Teitel. And her checking account and her magazine subscriptions and all the rest. Sarah Teitel. Didn't want to be known by her married name any more, thank you very much. Oh no. Said she wouldn't use it ever again. You know what I did? I made the alimony checks out to *Mrs. Benny Silverman*. Would have loved to see her face when she had to endorse them.

NORMA: She didn't have anything to do with this.

BENNY: Maybe not, but she didn't tell you no.

NORMA: Actually, she told me you'd probably scream your head off, but she understood.

BENNY: That's generous of her.

NORMA: She respected my decision. Because that's what it was, Pop—my decision. She didn't enter into it. It's something I decided to do by myself, for myself. It's what I wanted.

BENNY: Fine—you wanted, you got.

NORMA: You know something—if you look at it the right way, it's a compliment.

BENNY: It is?

NORMA: If you look at it the right way.

BENNY: Let's hear this right way.

NORMA: Never mind.

BENNY: No compliment?

NORMA: Help.

BENNY: First it's out with the name, then it's good-bye compliment. Beats me why I should give you a cup of coffee.

NORMA: I don't want a cup of coffee.

BENNY: I can understand that. If I were you, I'd have enough trouble sleeping at night.

NORMA: *(Referring to the painting.)* I like it.

BENNY: Do you know anything about art?

NORMA: Do I have to know something about art to like it?

BENNY: If you knew something about art, you'd be able to appreciate the shadings, the nuances—all the really subtle reasons why this is lousy.

NORMA: One of the things I love about you is this terrifically graceful way you have of accepting compliments.

BENNY: I like my compliments honest.

NORMA: What's not honest? I said I like it. I *do* like it. I didn't say that it's good.

BENNY: Oh, so you *don't* think it's good.

NORMA: Obviously I'm not entitled to think it's good *or* bad. I'm not even entitled to like it. So what *am* I entitled to? Statements of verifiable fact only? OK, a statement of verifiable fact: You are painting a painting, and it's sitting on an easel.

BENNY: Thank you, I'm flattered.

NORMA: And what would be so terrible if I liked it?

BENNY: Anybody can like. To like doesn't take any great skill, any great powers of discernment.

NORMA: I see. Only people with certifiably elevated taste are entitled to like something.

BENNY: Do you know what Monet or Chagall would say if they saw this?

NORMA: What?

BENNY: "Benny, stick to your acting."

NORMA: So why don't you?

BENNY: I like it.

NORMA: *You* like it?

BENNY: Yeah.

NORMA: I thought you said it's lousy.

BENNY: It *is* lousy.

NORMA: It's lousy but you like it.

BENNY: It's *because* I know that it's lousy I can like it.

NORMA: Come again?

BENNY: I don't pretend it's good. I don't delude myself. All I can say is that standing here, doing this, I enjoy myself. It doesn't have to be good for me to enjoy myself.

NORMA: Someone should make you a ride in an amusement park.

BENNY: You really like it?

NORMA: Yes. ·

BENNY: When I finish, it's yours. I hope you treat it better than other things I've given you. Like my name.

NORMA: OK, Pop—

BENNY: *(Referring to a play script near her.)* I've read this script of yours.

NORMA: I didn't write it.

BENNY: Well, you're going to be in it.

NORMA: That still doesn't make it mine.

BENNY: It makes you associated with it.

NORMA: As in guilt by association?

BENNY: Who said anything about guilt?

NORMA: Your tone does. You don't like the play.

BENNY: It's OK for what it is. Are you really going to take off your clothes?

NORMA: Not clothes. Just my top.

BENNY: Your top isn't clothes?

NORMA: I'm not taking off my clothes, plural. I'm taking off a piece of clothing, singular.

BENNY: A piece of clothing singular, that covers up parts of you, plural.

NORMA: It's not a big deal. A lot of plays these days call for it.

BENNY: That excuses everything.

NORMA: I didn't realize there was anything to excuse.

BENNY: It's your business.

NORMA: It is, you know.

BENNY: You knew what was in the script before you signed the contract?

NORMA: Of course.

BENNY: It's your business. It's not my ass people will be looking at.

NORMA: It's not my ass either.

BENNY: Just your boobies.

NORMA: That's right.

BENNY: I never had to do that. Of course, who would pay to see my boobies? Or my ass, for that matter?

NORMA: Who knows, somebody might.

BENNY: Nobody I'd want to meet.

NORMA: I knew you were going to pick up on that. Out of everything in the script, that was the one element you were going to bring up.

BENNY: You like this play?

NORMA: I like it very much. I like my part very much. I feel very lucky to have landed it.

BENNY: All right.

NORMA: It's my business?

BENNY: Who else's?

NORMA: Not yours?

BENNY: Never.

NORMA: Well, I'm glad we got that settled.

BENNY: There was never any issue.

NORMA: Could have fooled me.

BENNY: And your mother?

NORMA: What about her?

BENNY: She doesn't have any opinion?

NORMA: All she wanted to know was if it's in—

BENNY AND NORMA: *(Together.)* —good taste.

BENNY: Of course, I'm used to a different kind of play. The kind with ideas and metaphors.

NORMA: I think this play is metaphoric.

BENNY: There is nothing metaphoric about an attractive young woman with her top off.

NORMA: That moment you keep harping on is about vulnerability.

BENNY: In your mind it may be about vulnerability. Maybe in the playwright's mind. In the audience's mind it will be about tits. The women out there will be thinking, "Gee, I couldn't do that. Well, maybe I could do that. But how many Margaritas would it take?" Meanwhile, the guys in the audience will be thinking—Well, you *know* what they'll be thinking. And their wives will know what they're thinking. And the women will look at their husbands like they're saying, "Yeah, and what are you gawking at?" And the guys will go, "Hey, I'm not gawking." And the women'll go, "Oh, yeah, right." And the guys will go, "Hey, but it's OK: this isn't tits, this is art. I'm having a catharsis here. Swear to God." You're up there acting your heart out, in the meantime, they've forgotten your character's *name*.

NORMA: Could be the audience is more sophisticated than you think.

BENNY: Don't believe me then.

NORMA: It's not a question of my believing you or not. I believe that you see things the way you see things. I just don't. But things have changed in the theater since you got started. I know it's hard to believe, Dad, but Clifford Odets is dead and gone.

BENNY: Clifford Odets? He was dead and gone even before he was dead.

NORMA: Maybe you'd like to recommend a good hotel.

BENNY: Hotel, for what?

NORMA: To stay in.

BENNY: You don't like the bed in your room?

NORMA: The bed's fine.

BENNY: I should hope so. The mattress was rated a "best buy" from *Consumer's Union*. What are you talking about a hotel? What have I got a house with three bedrooms for, so that you can pay money to strangers to sleep someplace?

NORMA: Look, the next few weeks aren't going to be easy for me. It's a new script, and what's undoubtedly going to happen is that, after I've finally memorized the lines, they're all going to be changed on me during rehearsal.

BENNY: That goes with the territory.

NORMA: What I'm concerned about is what goes with *this* territory.

BENNY: A nice view of the Pacific where occasionally a whale swims by, spouts off.

NORMA: And you.

BENNY: I don't swim any more.

NORMA: You do your share of spouting off.

BENNY: That's me—Benny the whale.

(Benny laughs and goes back to his painting.)

NORMA: *(To audience.)* I was fifteen-years-old, pushing a shopping cart at the A&P, when I found out what he'd been through. There were two people standing in line ahead of me, so I checked out the magazine rack to see what I could waste a few minutes with. And there was a caricature of my father grinning out at me from the cover of *TV Guide*. At the bottom it said, "Benny Silverman of *Rich But Happy*." That was the name of the situation comedy he played a crazy neighbor on—*Rich But Happy*. So, of course I'm eager to see what it has to say about him. Maybe he'll mention me or Mom, though at that point they'd been divorced already ten years or so. So I'm standing in line at the A&P, smiling, reading about how he's buddies with all the technicians on the set, about a practical joke he played on the producer once, about how the younger actors on the show revere him as a comic genius, and so forth and so on. And then there was this classic *TV Guide* transitional sentence. Something about—"But Benny Silverman still has vivid memories of the black days when his chief concern was not fine-tuning a laugh but fighting for the right to practice his craft." This was followed by how he was named in front of the House Committee on Un-American Activities. And how he had been subpoenaed to appear, and how he did appear but did not cooperate. And then, years of not being able to find work. I was in the middle of this when it was my turn at the checkout counter. I paid for the groceries, and I took them home and dumped them on the kitchen table. And I asked my mother whether it had been by planning or oversight that nobody had ever told me a word about it.

BENNY: Planning. I asked her not to.

NORMA: Why?

BENNY: It happened before you were born. It had nothing to do with you. Why should you be bothered by it?

NORMA: You expected me never to find out?

BENNY: What did it matter whether you found out or not?

NORMA: If it didn't matter, why keep it from me?

BENNY: You were a kid. Your mother and I figured, between homework and puberty, you had enough to handle. What did you need to know about something that took place years before you were even conceived?

NORMA: It might have helped me to understand you better.

BENNY: Understand what?

NORMA: Why you are what you are. Why you do what you do.

BENNY: You expect to understand all that? Nothing like modest ambitions.

NORMA: I had to go to the library, for God's sake. I had to look up your name in indexes. I had to *read* about you.

BENNY: Well, at least some good came of it. It was always murder to get you to crack a book.

NORMA: Can I ask you something?

BENNY: No. What is it?

NORMA: There was another book I found, on political theater. And there was a picture. A photo of The Labor Players—

BENNY: *(Correcting.)* The *New* Labor Players.

NORMA: Maybe seven or eight of you in the picture. And standing next to you is Leo Greshen, and your arm is around his shoulder.

BENNY: That was a fake arm. They touched that arm into the picture.

NORMA: He was a friend of yours.

BENNY: He gave that appearance for a while.

NORMA: So what did he say?

BENNY: Look it up. The transcript's public, it's easy to find.

NORMA: I don't mean his testimony. I mean what did he say to you?

BENNY: Why you want to dig into this is beyond—

NORMA: Did he call you afterwards? Try to explain?

BENNY: Not afterwards, before. Squealer's etiquette. Sort of like an arsonist calling up ahead of time. "Hello, I'm going to burn your house down. Thought you might like to know." Only instead—"Hello, I'm going to burn your career down." "Thanks a lot, Leo. Hope to return the favor someday."

NORMA: But he was a friend. Didn't he give you reasons?

BENNY: Oh, everybody knew the reasons why. He had the prospect of directing his first picture, and he didn't want this to blow it for him.

NORMA: He said this to you? That was why he was going to testify?

BENNY: Did you know "testify" and "testimony" come from the same Latin root as "testes" as in "balls?" I'm not making this up. In Rome, if you wanted to make a big point that something you said was true, when you said it, you'd grab your balls. Which is why I don't think what he said to the Committee really qualifies as testimony. How could it? The man had no balls to grab.

NORMA: I shouldn't have had to find out that way—reading it in a book.

BENNY: "Find out." You talk as if you'd uncovered something shameful.

NORMA: Being ashamed of something is one reason why someone may keep something secret.

BENNY: I was not ashamed. I *am* not ashamed. Perhaps I had a very good reason for not telling you.

NORMA: Such as what?

BENNY: To protect you.

NORMA: To protect me from something you weren't ashamed of. Sure, that makes sense.

BENNY: Do you remember the Epsteins?

NORMA: The Epsteins?

BENNY: The Epsteins, the Epsteins.

NORMA: Why?

BENNY: Do you?

NORMA: I think so.

BENNY: They lived in your Aunt Bertha's building

NORMA: All right, yes, I remember the Epsteins. So?

BENNY: All right. One night, your mother and I were at the Epsteins'. Ten-thirty, eleven o'clock, their daughter Becky comes in. She's coming home from a date with someone her parents don't approve of, which is to say someone who isn't Jewish. An argument starts. Didn't they tell Becky not to see him? She doesn't care what they told her. She has a mind of her own, her own life to lead, she'll make her own decisions, etc. If she wants to go out with him she'll go out with him, and it's just too damn bad if her parents don't like it. And it keeps going like this, back and forth, more and more heat and passion and arm waving. Finally, her mother cries out, "This is what I survived Buchenwald for? For a daughter with a mouth like this?" I shudder to think how much time that girl probably ended up spending on a psychiatrist's couch.

NORMA: So you think they shouldn't have told her?

BENNY: I think it's not right to bludgeon other people with your suffering.

NORMA: There's a difference between bludgeoning and telling.

BENNY: There's a difference between everything and everything else. You can draw distinctions till you're blue in the face.

NORMA: Don't dance away from me like that. We're talking about something here.

BENNY: All right, so I was a little over-protective. When did this become a felony? But what did you learn that was so valuable? That some son-of-a-bitch, in order to save his own ass, got up in front of some other sons-of-bitches and said he'd seen me a handful of times in the same room with another group of sons-of-bitches.

NORMA: And you didn't work for years after that.

BENNY: This was all way before you were born. Do you ever remember going to bed hungry because I couldn't provide? No. So it didn't touch you. So why are you complaining? Are you complaining because you didn't have pain? Or are you complaining because the pain you did have isn't the pain you wanted to have? Maybe you can give Becky Epstein a call, see if she wants to trade. Or maybe she'll give you the name of her shrink. You can go lie on his couch and complain about how awful I was that I didn't lift up my shirt and show you ancient scars.

NORMA: Just because I didn't know about it doesn't mean that it hasn't touched me.

BENNY: Enough already. Are we going to go over all this again? *(A beat.)* So, what name now? So when I look in the program I know which one is you.

NORMA: Norma Teitel.

BENNY: Teitel?

(Norma nods.)

BENNY: I should have guessed. You sure this wasn't your mother's idea? *(A beat.)*

NORMA: Hey, are you glad I'm here?

BENNY: How could you doubt?

(They both smile. During Norma's following speech, Benny hauls his easel and canvas and paint into the house. He is back on the patio at the conclusion of the speech.)

NORMA: *(To audience.)* And you know something? We get along OK for a little over a week. And the play's coming along well, too. And then our director has a stroke. They take him off to the hospital, where they tell us the prognosis is, thank God, good. But that leaves us without a director. The producers call a hiatus for a couple of days so they can put their heads together and come up with a new director. And then I get a call and they tell me who they've decided on. And that their offer has been made and accepted. I tell them I have some problems with their choice. I explain why. They say they hope I will stay with the show, but that I have to decide quickly. "Think about it seriously," they say. I promise I will. And then I tell Pop.

BENNY: Do you tell me because you want my advice?

NORMA: I tell you because I think you should know. I mean, it's partially for your sake I'd be doing it. If I did it.

BENNY: Quitting?

NORMA: Yes.

BENNY: Well, it *is* your decision.

NORMA: I know.

BENNY: I will only say one thing, and this is not to in any way influence your decision, but—if you were to stay with the play, I wouldn't be able to go to it.

NORMA: You hate him that much?

BENNY: I used to go see his stuff. And when it was good work, I'd be angry. And when it was bad or flopped, I'd get satisfaction. And then I thought to myself, "What am I doing to myself? I mean, this is stupid. I've got myself to the point where I'm happy about bad work and miserable about successes." I was letting the guy twist me into knots, plus a percentage of my ticket money was going into his pocket so that I was paying for him to do this to me. So I stopped. I don't go to see his stuff, I don't go to see the stuff of some of the others. And do you know something? The world doesn't end because I miss a play or a movie.

NORMA: So there are people whose work you won't go to see.

BENNY: I think that's what I said.

NORMA: Because of their political beliefs?

BENNY: Because of the way they *expressed* these beliefs.

NORMA: I guess you wouldn't work with them either.

BENNY: No, I wouldn't.

NORMA: When you were on *Rich But Happy,* did the issue ever come up? Was there ever a time when the producer wanted to hire one of these guys that you wouldn't work with?

BENNY: No, they knew not to do that.

NORMA: They knew there were certain people you didn't want hired.

BENNY: They were sensitive to the way I felt.

NORMA: Was there a list?

BENNY: What?

NORMA: Of people you wouldn't work with. Did you write up a list? *(A beat.)*

BENNY: Cute.

NORMA: Well, I'm your daughter.

BENNY: What you're describing is not the same.

NORMA: You weren't hired, and you turned around and saw to it that other people weren't hired.

BENNY: There's a difference. There's a distinction.

NORMA: I'm sure there is.

BENNY: To anybody with a pair of eyes in her head.

NORMA: Explain the distinction to me.

BENNY: I don't have to defend myself to you.

NORMA: All right.

BENNY: What—do you think I should forget? Would you expect me to work with, for instance, a Nazi?

NORMA: Nazi?

BENNY: You know from Nazis, don't you? They're the guys who had the franchise on swastikas before the Hell's Angels. Let's say I'm in a movie, OK? I'm going to do a scene with this guy. While we're waiting to shoot, we're sitting around, we're kibitzing. I tell an anecdote. He laughs and says, "You know that reminds me of something funny that happened when I was in the SS."

NORMA: Right.

BENNY: So according to you what I should say back is "Hey, Fritz, want me to cue you on your lines?"

NORMA: Why is it whenever you get mad, you reach for a Nazi?

BENNY: What are you talking about, "reach for a Nazi"?

NORMA: You do, you know.

BENNY: You make it sound like a soft drink. "Worked up a thirst? Reach for a nice, refreshing Nazi!"

NORMA: It's like a conversational preemptive strike. Whenever you don't agree with me, it always comes around to Nazis or anti-Semitism. First is my name too Jewish. Then it's Becky Epstein and the Holocaust. And now, even this, in come the jackboots again.

BENNY: "Even this?" What *this* are you saying "even this" about?

NORMA: McCarthyism, the blacklist—

BENNY: And you don't think that was anti-Semitism? Look at who was on the Committee. Martin Dies. Harold Velde. Karl Mundt.

NORMA: Oh come on, everybody with a German name isn't an anti-Semite. Besides which, there are a lot of people on the Committee who weren't German.

BENNY: That's right, Nixon isn't German. And we all know what a warm feeling he has for people of—how would he put it?—Hebraic persuasion? And as for the guys he and his buddies went after—

NORMA: All Jews, right?

BENNY: Let's just say you wouldn't have had trouble raising a minyan. Oh, and the fun the Committee had with the Jewish names! You can't tell from reading the transcripts—how they punched them, mispronounced them, tried to make them sound sinister and alien. "Carnovsky, Papirofsky, Ruskin." Ever hear anything so suspicious in your life? And did they have a field day with the ones who had *changed* their names! "You call yourself 'Holliday' but your real name, the name you were born with is what? 'Tuvim.'" As if they were talking to a criminal trying to hide something. You're going to tell me that wasn't anti-Semitism?

NORMA: That's not my point.

BENNY: Oh, I know what your point is.

NORMA: I never said you should work with Nazis.

BENNY: So, it's OK with you if I don't? I mean, you won't disapprove if I turn down a contract to co-star with Dr. Mengele?

NORMA: There *is* a difference between Mengele and Nixon.

BENNY: You're absolutely right—one murdered Jews, the other only made it hard for them to eat.

NORMA: OK, go ahead, twist everything.

BENNY: And you weren't twisting? That comment about my having a list?

NORMA: I was just raising what I thought was an interesting question.

BENNY: I was kept from working because some of the views I used to have suddenly weren't popular any more. If I prefer not to work with people who kept me from working or gave support to people who kept me from working, I think I'm within my rights. *(He exits into the house.)*

NORMA: Pop...

(She follows him off, hoping to calm him down. A second after she exits, Leo

enters. Like Benny, he is in his late sixties, early seventies. He looks around the patio. He knows he is trespassing, but he is mentally prepared to face whoever might come out and face him. He is casing the place when Norma returns to the patio. Initially, due to where he stands, she doesn't see him.)

LEO: Miss Teitel?

(Startled, she turns to look at him.)

NORMA: You're Leo Greshen.

LEO: *(With a smile.)* Guilty. I thought, rather than ring the doorbell, I'd just come around. I hope you don't mind.

NORMA: They told you.

LEO: Our beloved producers? Yes. At first, I couldn't figure it out. They said your father was somebody I used to now and that that was the reason why. And I kept thinking, "Teitel. When did I ever know a guy named Teitel?"

NORMA: My mother's name.

LEO: You changed it from Silverman?

NORMA: Yes.

LEO: Benny must love that. Why?

NORMA: Personal reasons.

LEO: You and he have a falling out?

NORMA: No.

LEO: OK.

NORMA: This is his house. I'm staying here.

LEO: Point taken.

NORMA: I shouldn't have said anything to them.

LEO: Them meaning our producers?

NORMA: I shouldn't have told them.

LEO: What then? Just walked out without warning?

NORMA: Of course not. I haven't decided to leave. All I said to them was that I was thinking about it. It didn't occur to me that they'd tell you.

LEO: Not to mention my popping up unannounced.

NORMA: There's the telephone.

LEO: True, but I've heard that the view here is terrific.

NORMA: Yes, well, there it is.

LEO: Very pretty.

NORMA: The blue part is the Pacific.

LEO: Somehow I never could live in LA. Oh, I usually have a good time here. But I'm really a lazy bastard at heart, and this climate would probably aggravate that. Too easy to forget that time is passing when there's basically only one season. You're from the East, too, aren't you?

NORMA: New York.

LEO: Sure, you know what I mean. Every three months, you've got another season kicking you in the ass, telling you that the meter's ticking. One moment you're trying to find your sandals, the next you're digging galoshes out from the closet. Keeps you alert. *(A beat.)* Is he here?

NORMA: Inside. Probably taking a nap.

LEO: Ah. *(A beat.)* Did he ask you to drop out?

NORMA: No.

LEO: But he's not terribly happy about it. About the idea of you working with me.

NORMA: Did you think he would be?

LEO: How is he anyway?

NORMA: Fine.

LEO: He's a talented man, your father. We did a lot of work together.

NORMA: I know.

LEO: He told you?

NORMA: Not really. I did some reading.

LEO: Reading?

NORMA: Yes.

LEO: What did he do—hand you a bibliography and tell you there'd be a quiz?

NORMA: There are certain things he just never talks about.

LEO: And I'm one of those things. Right. *(A beat.)* You know, there were once these two guys named Stalin and Trotsky. They were both bigwigs in the Russian revolution.

NORMA: You don't have to patronize me, Mr. Greshen. I do know who Stalin and Trotsky were.

LEO: In my experience, that puts you firmly in the minority of the people your age. Their idea of history is when the Beatles first appeared on Ed Sullivan. Anyway, as you apparently know, after Lenin died, Stalin took over and tossed Trotsky out of Russia. Parenthetically, Trotsky was later murdered with a pickax. One of these days Brian de Palma will make a movie about this. Anyway, if you were an earnest young student of history while Stalin was in power—at Moscow U., say, or Petrograd Prep—you would have searched in vain to find any mention of Trotsky's part in the revolution in the state-approved texts. In the jargon of the time, he became a non-person.

NORMA: Your point is?

LEO: Your father has the making of a fine Stalinist historian. Never talks about me at all, hunh?

NORMA: A little—recently, when I asked him. But not very much. The subject's painful for him, I guess.

LEO: Believe it or not, there was a time when he didn't hate my guts. But I don't imagine that was in your reading.

NORMA: You were both members of the New Labor Players.

LEO: Actually, I was one of the founders. A fellow named Mort Kessler was one of the other actors. He also wrote a lot of stuff. That's how he got started as a writer. Anyway, one day he brought in this piece—it was about St.

Peter and about how two or three fat-cats con their way past him into Heaven. *(Remembering title.) Capitalist Heaven*—That's what we called it! Well, of course, as capitalists always did in our subtle little plays, they set up an exploitive society—turned the poor cherubim into wage slaves in the harp factory, clipped their wings, etc. Anyway, we didn't have a St. Peter, and somebody knew your father. They had seen him do imitations or something at a party. So I met him. He was working in the garment district. I suggested he might have more fun earning next-to-nothing with us than earning almost-next-to-nothing hauling around big rolls of fabric. He believed me. And that's how he became an actor. He was a terrific St. Peter. Who would have guessed he would end up in a swanky place like this? Talk about *Capitalist Heaven. (A beat.)*

NORMA: Did you want to see him?

LEO: I came to see you.

NORMA: Yes, but this is his house. You must have known there was a reasonable chance of running into him.

LEO: I'm not afraid of that.

NORMA: I didn't say you were.

LEO: I'd like you to stay with the show.

NORMA: Have you seen any of my work?

LEO: The producers seem to think you're good.

NORMA: But you've never seen me do anything?

LEO: Nope.

NORMA: If I were to leave, it wouldn't be difficult for you to find someone else.

LEO: That's true.

NORMA: There are lots of good actresses.

LEO: A dozen or so at least.

NORMA: It might be easier for you.

LEO: Thank you for your concern, but I think I could bear up. I long ago accepted the fact that Mother Teresa would beat me in a popularity contest.

NORMA: I don't see why it would be worth it to you.

LEO: Why is your understanding so important?

NORMA: Because, if I were to stay, I'd like to know on what basis.

LEO: That you do your job. What other basis is there? You fulfill a contract that was negotiated in good faith. Or don't you think you can play the part?

NORMA: I can play it.

LEO: It's not unheard of for an actor to come up with a convenient excuse to leave if he thinks he's out of his depth.

NORMA: I can play the part.

LEO: I believe you. Now, as for me, you acknowledge that I probably can do that job I've been hired for. True?

NORMA: Yes.

LEO: Then isn't that all we need be concerned about?

NORMA: I should just do my work and go on about my business.

LEO: It's called a professional attitude.

NORMA: You wouldn't be trying to prove something to my father?

LEO: What would I be trying to prove?

NORMA: You can't tell me the fact that I'm his daughter doesn't enter into this somewhere. Let's face it, I'm being kind of difficult here. And it's not as if I have any real reputation or name that you should have to put up with it.

LEO: Wait a second. Do you want me to fire you?

NORMA: I didn't say that.

LEO: What do you want?

NORMA: Mr. Greshen, I happen to believe I'm good at what I do. I happen also to have a well-known father who's also an actor.

LEO: That can be an advantage.

NORMA: It's an advantage I don't want. Whatever my career is, wherever it goes, I want it to be on the basis of what I do myself. One of the real kicks of getting this part was that they hired me without knowing who my dad is. I mean, they hired *me*.

LEO: I understand.

NORMA: Well, now I get the feeling that it's because of him you want me to stay.

LEO: Isn't it because of him you're thinking of leaving?

NORMA: Those are two separate issues.

LEO: I don't think so.

NORMA: But it *is* because of him you want me to stay. At least partially.

LEO: If you've got to know, it's because I don't like being walked out on. All right? *(A beat.)* Jesus, even if I *didn't* know you're Benny's daughter, I'd probably guess. You're a lot like him, Miss Teitel. By the way, that's a compliment.

(Benny enters. At first, Norma sees him and Leo doesn't. Then Leo senses his presence and turns around.)

BENNY: Very difficult to nap. All this back and forth outside my window.

LEO: Hello, Benny.

BENNY: She's right, you know.

LEO: Oh?

BENNY: If you think you're going to prove something to me—

LEO: No?

BENNY: You proved all that you had to prove to me a long time ago. That fabulous phone call.

LEO: The book is closed, hunh?

BENNY: That's the way it is.

LEO: You know, I've got an Aunt Sadie, still has my Cousin Ernie's baby shoes.

A friend of mine, he saves matchbooks from restaurants. But you—you collect old injuries.

BENNY: A shame, isn't it?

LEO: I think so.

BENNY: A shame and a waste. You feel sorry for me.

LEO: I do.

BENNY: I am touched by your concern.

LEO: I can tell.

BENNY: No, really. It comes a little late. But what's thirty years in the grand scheme of things?

LEO: I've always been concerned.

BENNY: "'I weep for you,' the Walrus said, 'I deeply sympathize.'" You know, I believe him. I believe his tears are genuine. I have my doubts about the Carpenter, but the Walrus is a feeling man. Or as feeling as a Walrus can be. You, too, Leo.

LEO: Same old Benny.

BENNY: Some people are born walrus, some people achieve walrus, and some have walrus thrust upon them. You can't blame the people who are *born* walrus. After all, that's all they know. But the ones who *choose* it—

LEO: It's all nice and simple for you, isn't it?

BENNY: Why don't I throw you off my patio?

LEO: Maybe you don't want to.

BENNY: Why wouldn't I want to?

LEO: It's been almost thirty years.

BENNY: You say that as if there's a statute of limitations.

LEO: *Are* you going to throw me off your patio?

BENNY: I'm thinking about it. *(A beat.)* You want a beer?

LEO: Couldn't hurt.

BENNY: *(To Norma.)* You want to bring this bastard a beer?

NORMA: What about you?

BENNY: Why not?

(Norma exits. Leo sits. Benny picks up a bowl of chips, offers him some. Leo takes a few. Benny grabs some chips for himself and sits. For a while, they sit and munch chips in silence. Then—)

LEO: She looks like her mother.

BENNY: We're divorced.

LEO: I heard. I'm sorry.

BENNY: She isn't. She's a very happy divorcee. She's told me so herself. *(A beat.)* So you're coming back to the theater. What happened? The movies go sour on you?

LEO: The movies are going fine. As a matter of a fact, in a couple months I start a new one.

BENNY: But you're directing this play.

LEO: I wasn't aware of any rule that if you do one you can't do the other.

(Norma returns with two beers. She hands one to Leo during the following. He nods thanks.)

LEO: No, the producers were in a bind. They needed a director. They talked to my agent. The timing worked out OK. I read the script.

(Norma now hands Benny his beer.)

BENNY: You like it?

LEO: It's a little lighter than I usually do, but I thought it might be fun to direct.

BENNY: Fun to look at my daughter's chest?

(Norma wishes the ground would open up.)

LEO: Hunh?

BENNY: The scene she takes her top off.

LEO: Oh that.

BENNY: Yes, that.

LEO: I told the playwright I want to cut that. I don't like naked actors on the stage. Distracts from the play.

BENNY: Oh.

LEO: You don't agree?

(Benny shrugs, but he sends a pointed look in Norma's direction.)

NORMA: I think I'm going to take a drive.

BENNY: Where to?

NORMA: Nowhere in particular. Just a drive. Things to think about.

BENNY: I see.

NORMA: Besides, you probably want to be alone, right?

BENNY: *(Not replying to her line.)* Will you be gone long?

NORMA: I don't know.

LEO: I'm glad I had a chance to meet you, Miss Teitel.

NORMA: Mr. Greshen. *(She exits.)*

LEO: You should let her do the play, Benny. It's a good part. People will notice. She'll be on her way.

(Benny laughs.)

LEO: What?

BENNY: Good thing you didn't say that in front of her.

LEO: What?

BENNY: About my *letting* her. She would have laughed in your face.

LEO: Is that so?

BENNY: The idea that I have anything to do with what she decides.

LEO: Not a thing, hunh?

BENNY: Do you think I *let* her go into acting?

LEO: No?

BENNY: If you knew how hard I tried to keep her out of this business. And you can see how successful I was.

LEO: She never consults you.

BENNY: Who's around to consult? This is the first time we've actually laid eyes on each other in almost two years. She's in New York, I'm here.

LEO: And the telephone hasn't been invented.

BENNY: Why should she care about my opinion?

LEO: *(Anticipating Benny saying this—)* You're just her father.

BENNY: What do you think? She does your show, I'm going to cut her out of my will?

LEO: Apart from everything else, whether or not the show does well, I think she'd find it a valuable experience.

BENNY: You want me to tell her that? You want me to put in a good word for you, Leo? *(A beat.)*

LEO: When's the last time *you* did a play?

BENNY: Half dozen years ago.

LEO: Which?

BENNY: *Front Page.*

LEO: Who'd you play?

BENNY: Pincus.

LEO: Remind me.

BENNY: The little schmuck with the message from the Governor.

LEO: Bet you were good.

BENNY: Me? I was terrific.

LEO: Not a big part, though.

BENNY: It was one of those all-star casts. Limited run.

LEO: Ah.

BENNY: I did it for the fun of it.

LEO: Was it fun?

BENNY: Sure.

LEO: So why not anything since?

BENNY: Wasn't *that* much fun.

LEO: Oh.

BENNY: Besides, nobody's sent me a script I really wanted to do in a long time. God, the things they call musicals these days! Most of them seem to be about some kid screaming how he wants to be a star. I've also been sent a lot of plays about people dying. You think they're tying to tell me something? Sometimes you get an adventurous blend of the two—about celebrities who die. From what I can tell, nobody's writing about anything anymore but show business and cancer. As if there were a difference.

LEO: You don't think you're overstating the case?

BENNY: Not by much, no.

LEO: You could always revive *Capitalist Heaven.*

BENNY: At least that was about something.

LEO: Yeah, about twenty-five minutes.

BENNY: You didn't think so at the time.

LEO: At the time was at the time.

BENNY: What a way with words you have!

LEO: We were talking about you doing a play.

BENNY: Why should I haul my ass down to some drafty theater eight times a week? It's not like I need the money.

LEO: That I noticed. *(Referring to the house.)* Is the inside as nice as the outside?

BENNY: You'll have to take my word. *(A beat.)*

LEO: When did you start painting?

BENNY: How do you know I'm painting?

LEO: I could pretend to be Sherlock Holmes and say it's the smudge of blue on the side of your thumb.

BENNY: Did Norma tell you?

LEO: Nobody told me. I saw.

BENNY: Saw what?

LEO: One of your paintings.

BENNY: Where?

LEO: I was at someone's house. There was a picture on the wall. A view from this patio.

BENNY: I paint it a lot. Monet had water lilies and haystacks. Silverman's got smog.

LEO: Anyway, I told him I liked it, and he said you painted it.

BENNY: He?

LEO: Mort Kessler.

BENNY: I didn't know you and Morty were in touch.

LEO: More than in touch.

BENNY: Oh?

LEO: We get together whenever I'm out here. Or he gives me a call when he's east. Sure.

BENNY: From what happened I wouldn't say it was all that sure.

LEO: Oh, we patched all that up a long time ago.

BENNY: Patched it up?

LEO: There was a fund-raiser. Somebody did a dinner in their home, for the farm workers, I think. One of those, I don't know. As it happened, Morty and I found ourselves seated near each other. He pretended I wasn't there for a while. Then I remember some woman walked by with impossibly blonde hair. Well, the lady I was with made some comment like, "Do you believe that hair?" And Morty said, "Hey, I happen to know her mother was a natural fluorescent." I laughed. He looked at me. You can't ignore a man who laughs at your joke, right? And we started talking, and before the evening was over we were friends again.

BENNY: He never said.

LEO: Probably thought it would upset you.

BENNY: Why should it upset me who he chooses for friends? Just surprises me a little, that's all.

LEO: Like I said, we patched it up.

BENNY: He always did have a forgiving streak. You know, a couple weeks ago, I even heard him say something nice about his third wife.

LEO: He didn't forgive me. I didn't ask him to forgive me. I don't ask anybody to forgive me.

BENNY: He may have done it without your asking. Without your permission. He's got a sneaky side.

LEO: I don't think so. I don't think forgiving had anything to do with anything. I think he just put it aside. Somewhere along the line, he must have weighed things in the balance—

BENNY: And put it aside.

LEO: Yeah.

BENNY: First he weighed it, then he patched it, then he put it aside. Where? In storage?

LEO: In the past, where it belongs.

BENNY: Well, he never told me.

LEO: He knows you had strong feelings.

BENNY: I still do.

LEO: I guessed as much. But I suppose you're entitled.

BENNY: Thank you. *(A beat.)*

LEO: So, how are you feeling?

BENNY: How am I feeling about what?

LEO: The question is health, Benny, not opinions.

BENNY: I'm feeling fine.

LEO: You've recovered.

BENNY: What am I supposed to have recovered from?

LEO: Morty said something about you in the hospital.

BENNY: Oh, that. Nothing dramatic. Just a little prostate trouble.

LEO: How much is a little?

BENNY: It got to the point where it was taking more time for me to pee than to prepare my taxes. The doctor kind of thought maybe we should do something about that. So did my accountant.

LEO: So you went to the hospital. How was that?

BENNY: Not too terrible actually.

LEO: Did they knock you out?

BENNY: No. They gave me a spinal. That just anesthetizes you from about the navel down. The upper part stays wide awake. As a matter of fact, they asked me did I want to watch?

LEO: And?

BENNY: I took a pass.

LEO: If you could take a pass, you wouldn't have needed the operation.

BENNY: Anyway, I said no, thanks, my idea of entertainment was not to watch them drill for oil in my privates. So they put up a sheet to block the view, and they called in a Roto Rooter man. A few hours, and that was it.

LEO: So it was all right.

BENNY: All right? What are you talking about? Better than all right! Fantastic! Really, Leo, you should give it a try.

LEO: I mean it healed nicely. No complications.

BENNY: Such an interest you take! What—you want to make an on-site inspection?

LEO: Maybe some other time.

BENNY: Nope, you had your chance. For awhile there I had to avoid orange juice, grapefruit juice, pineapples—

LEO: Why?

BENNY: Citric acid, you know. Stings like crazy.

LEO: Right.

BENNY: But it's fine now.

LEO: Well, that's good news.

BENNY: Jesus.

LEO: What?

BENNY: I remember when we used to talk about girls and the revolution. Now—

LEO: You want to talk about girls, I'll be glad to talk about girls.

BENNY: Morty keeps you posted on my health.

LEO: He doesn't hand me bulletins or anything, but I like to keep track of the old gang.

BENNY: You heard about George.

LEO: I saw it in the *Times*. Christ, every morning, opening the goddamned *Times* to find out who I've survived.

BENNY: I know.

LEO: You went to the funeral?

BENNY: They didn't have a formal funeral. There was a kind of memorial thing.

LEO: What was that like?

BENNY: Sort of fun actually. Everybody got up, told stories.

LEO: *(Laughing.)* Oh?

BENNY: No, the clean ones.

LEO: Must have been a short memorial.

BENNY: They read some from his file. You know, he got the stuff the FBI kept on him under the Freedom of Information thing.

LEO: Sounds like a lot of laughs.

BENNY: Did you ever hear about when he was in the army?

LEO: I know that he was in the army—

BENNY: About when he was in the hospital in the army?

LEO: Wait a second? About the FBI agent?

BENNY: Came to question the other guys in the ward about him—

LEO: I've heard it, yeah.

BENNY: Didn't recognize him. Gave a testimonial to his own—

LEO: Yeah, I heard it.

BENNY: They asked him his name—

BENNY AND LEO: Jake Barnes.

BENNY: You heard it.

LEO: I heard it.

BENNY: You ever send for your file?

LEO: What for?

BENNY: To see what they said about you.

LEO: What for?

BENNY: I sent for mine.

LEO: To see what *they* said about you?

BENNY: What are you smiling about?

LEO: You remember the end of the second part of *Faust?*

BENNY: It doesn't spring to my lips, no.

LEO: Goethe.

BENNY: All of a sudden this is *GE College Bowl.*

LEO: He talks about "the Eternal Feminine." The last line is something about constantly pursuing "the Eternal Feminine."

BENNY: So?

LEO: So, instead of "the Eternal Feminine," for you it's the Eternal *They. They* do this, *they* keep you from doing that. Always *they.*

BENNY: Not always, Leo. Sometimes it's *you.*

LEO: So you sent for your file.

BENNY: I sent for my file.

LEO: Anything interesting?

BENNY: Great nostalgia value. Lists of the petitions I signed, the magazines I subscribed to. Some bastard even showed up at one of the benefits I performed at. "Subject performed allegedly humorous routine—"

LEO: "Allegedly humorous." He said that.

BENNY: Fucking critics, they're everywhere. You remember—just after Sarah and I got married, I had to go out of town on that tour?

LEO: *Native Son,* wasn't it?

BENNY: Probably. Anyway, Sarah was doing real well in radio then, so she didn't go out with me. So we wrote each other a lot. Some of it was kind of personal stuff.

LEO: You mean love letters?

BENNY: Well, yeah, I guess you could call them that. Anyway, I'd lost the originals a long time ago in one of our moves. But, like I say, I had the FBI send me my file, and they must have kept a mail cover on us, because there they were—all those letters I'd lost. A lot of them, anyway.

LEO: They Xeroxed your letters?

BENNY: Xeroxed? In nineteen forty—

LEO: Right.

BENNY: No, someone actually typed them up. Probably anchored them with a book or something so they'd lie flat, be easier to type from. You know Sarah's handwriting—probably had to hire a cryptographer to decipher. Sarah and I were waiting for the final divorce papers when I got that file from the Feds. *(A beat.)* I almost sent her copies.

LEO: *(Gently.)* Almost?

BENNY: What purpose would it have served? It was all over between us by then.

LEO: Benny, what happened?

BENNY: Well—

LEO: The two of you—I've never seen a couple like—
(Benny suddenly realizes how close he's gotten to the old friendship. He forces himself to pull back.)

BENNY: No, I'm not going to talk about that.

LEO: If there's something you want to—

BENNY: Not with you. *(A beat.)*

LEO: OK.

BENNY: Anyway, I get some satisfaction out of knowing that the S.O.B. who typed that all up is probably dead now.

LEO: Or maybe having a prostrate operation of his own.

BENNY: He should only have it done without a spinal. *(A beat.)* How's your beer?

LEO: Fine. *(A beat.)* I was given an honorary degree, you know. Last spring.

BENNY: In what—communications?

LEO: A doctor of letters, actually. Avery College, New Hampshire. For my body of work. That's how they phrased it. Sounds cadaverous, doesn't it? "Here lies Leo Greshen's body of work." I had to laugh when I was told. But I said sure. Sure, I'd be honored to be honored. And, generous fellow, that I am, I say I'll throw in a seminar on directing or some damn thing. They couldn't be happier. I'm met at the airport. I have dinner with a bunch of deans and professors and nice faculty wives, faculty husbands, whatever. Some nice stroking. Springtime in New Hampshire. Who could object to that? So I'm scheduled to speak to this media studies class. The guy who runs the class introduces me. My pictures, the plays I've directed, blah, blah, blah, and would you please welcome. Applause. All very nice. He asks me questions. I answer. I make jokes. He tosses in a quip or two like a regular Dick Cavett. Everything's bopping along well. About forty-five minutes of this, he says he's going to open the floor to questions. Four or five hands shoot up. I see this one intent kid off to the side, near the window. Skinny kid with eyes like lasers. I look at him and I know he's going to ask it. I just know it. But my friend, the would-be Dick Cavett, calls on some girl who asks me how it was to work with so-and-so, and I tell an amusing story and everybody laughs in the right place except for the kid with the laser eyes. I've barely finished my amusing story when his hand shoots up again. The professor again chooses another hand. Bearded kid wants to know if I story-board when I'm in pre-production. I tell another amusing story. Soon as I'm finished with that one, again that kid's hand shoots up. Again my host chooses another hand, but I interrupt him. I say, "Wait a second. There's a young man over there by the window seems to have something urgent to ask. Yes, son, what is it?" Yes, son, I'm thinking, go ahead and prove how brave and liberal you are. Nail me in front of all your nice classmates and your nice teacher on this nice campus in New Hampshire. "Yes, son," I say, "what's your question?" He doesn't disappoint. No sooner has he said the magic words "House Committee on Un-American Activities" than my friend the professor interrupts, says that we are not here to discuss that. "We are here to discuss Mr. Greshen's art, Mr. Greshen's craft. We are here to learn what we can from Mr. Greshen's years of experience in the theater and film. Politics has nothing to do with it." And he asks if there are any other questions. I answer two more, and my friend the professor wraps it up by thanking me on behalf of the class for my generosity and candor. Applause. My host and I go the faculty lounge. He buys me a drink and tells me that he's sorry about the boy's rudeness. Apparently that boy has a habit of stirring things up. And that was why my friend hadn't wanted to call on him. He was trying to protect me. Seems like this kid had circulated a petition calling on the college to rescind the honorary degree. That it would not redound to the school's credit to honor a stoolie. This was not quite how my friend put it, but that was the gist of it. So there was a ceremony, I got my degree, shook a lot of nice hands and went home. And all through this I was thinking of how I should have answered the little bastard.

BENNY: And what would you have said?

LEO: That he hadn't earned the right to ask me that question. He hadn't earned the right to brandish his moral indignation in my face.

BENNY: That's a nice snappy reply. Maybe you'll have another opportunity to use it.

LEO: Oh, I don't lack for opportunity. Even after all these years, it knocks with regularity. I'm constantly being offered forums for public confession. Really, it's very touching to know how many people are concerned about my moral rehabilitation. So eager to help me get this awful weight off my shoulders. This one woman—from some French film journal—for some reason I agreed to be interviewed for an article she was writing on my films. Turned out to be structuralist bullshit. Anyway, in the middle of it—here we go again. To be fair, we'd had a bottle of wine and we were getting along. Anyway, I informed her as affably as possible that I really didn't want to get into that subject. And she leaned forward and took my arm with that easy familiarity that a shared bottle of wine can encourage, she took my arm and looked into my eyes and said, "But Leo…" Not "Monsieur Greshen" but "Leo," right? "But Leo," she said, "you will feel—how do you say it?—the relief, no?"

BENNY: And you don't think you'd feel relief?

LEO: Benny, please. To step into a mess of dog shit once—that's something that can happen to anybody. To intentionally step into the same dog shit again—

BENNY: What dog shit is that?

LEO: Look, I've been through this before. "Leo, get up, get it off your chest. You'll feel better, swear to God." All I had to do was submit to a nice dirty ritual of public cleansing. Did you read the Navasky book?

BENNY: I glanced at it.

LEO: Well, I think a lot of it is double-talk. But he got that part right. The ritual part. Get up in front of the Committee, admit your errors. Prove how repentant you are—*demonstrate* your sincerity by naming a few names, you'll emerge redeemed, rehabilitated. Decent American folks will be happy to shake you by the hand, slap your back, let you do your work. Now, though, different political truths are operative, as the saying goes. Now I'm told that I bought the moral equivalent of a pig in a poke. I got myself the wrong brand of cleansing and rehabilitation. There's a new improved formula. Yes, there is! This season, if I want to be cleaner than clean, I'm supposed to get up and say I done wrong when I said I done wrong before. I'm supposed to do a *mea culpa* over my other *mea culpa*. Only instead of doing it in front of a mob of congressional Neanderthals, I'm supposed to confess to someone like Navasky or that French structuralist or that kid at Avery College. And after I choke out my apology, Navasky, on behalf of his enlightened readers, will dispense absolution. "Go and sin no more." In my book, it's the same damn ritual of public cleansing, only some labels have been changed to conform to the spirit of blacklist chic. Well, like I say, I stepped into that shit once. I'm not doing it again. Not even for you, Benny. And believe me, you're about the only reason I'd think of doing it.

BENNY: Sounds like you've got this all thought out.

LEO: It's not like I haven't had the time.

BENNY: Just one problem, Leo. When you called me up that night, you didn't call me because you thought you were right. You called me because you felt lousy about what you were going to do.

LEO: Benny, I never claimed to feel good about it.

BENNY: But you did it.

LEO: Only a fool fights the drop.

BENNY: You want to translate?

LEO: You've seen enough cowboy movies. If the bad guys have got the drop on you, it's crazy to draw on them. You're only going to get gunned down. Can't fight if you're dead.

BENNY: So now we're cowboys?

LEO: Thank you for taking what I have to say seriously.

BENNY: Seriously, OK: Leo, not only did you not fight the drop, you helped the bad guys gun down some good guys. What would the kids in the balcony say if Roy Rogers shot Gabby Hayes?

LEO: Bad guys, good guys—

BENNY: It's your analogy.

LEO: I said nothing about good guys.

BENNY: Oh, I see: there were no good guys?

LEO: Present company excepted, of course.

BENNY: No good guys. Well, that makes it nice and convenient, doesn't it? If everybody's equally scummy, then the highest virtue is survival. That must make you pretty goddamn virtuous. You should write a book about your philosophy, Leo. Really. I've got the title for you: *Charles Darwin Goes to the Theater.*

LEO: Being a victim doesn't automatically entitle you to a white hat, Benny. It's that old liberal impulse—romanticize the persecuted.

BENNY: What the hell would you know about liberal impulses?

LEO: Hey, I've got my share of them.

BENNY: You—a liberal? Don't make me laugh.

LEO: I sure wouldn't want to do that, Benny—make you laugh.

BENNY: Maybe you're a checkbook liberal. You send in contributions to those ads with pictures of kids starving in South America, a couple bucks to the ACLU—

LEO: More than a couple of bucks, but never mind—

BENNY: More than a couple? Well, hey, that changes my opinion completely.

LEO: I'll tell you where I part company with a lot of them, though. I won't romanticize. Just because someone's a martyr doesn't make him wise and good and pure. Sure, I sent in money to Joan Little's defense fund, but that doesn't mean I'd trust her to baby-sit my grandchildren.

BENNY: The guys the Committee went after weren't accused of murder, just of having believed in something unpopular. And the ones who wouldn't buckle under—out with the garbage.

LEO: Which is exactly what they did to each other when they were members of the Party. Those bastards were always browbeating each other, excommunicating each other for not embracing "the correct revolutionary line." Do you remember when the Party endorsed Henry Wallace for President? Lenny Steinkempf got up in a meeting, said he thought it was a crappy idea. So what did the Party do? They threw him the fuck out. And after *they* threw him out, his *wife* Elaine, being a loyal party member, *she* threw him out. As far as I was concerned, facing the Committee was an exercise in *déjà vu.* Believe me, Nixon and Mundt could have taken lessons from some of those old Commies. I wasn't about to put my dick on the block for any of those guys. Why should I keep faith with them when they couldn't keep faith with themselves?

BENNY: The point wasn't to keep faith with *them.* Leo, don't you remember anything about how or why we put together the New Labor Players?

LEO: Oh, for Christ's sake!

BENNY: For Christ's sake what?

LEO: *(Laughing.)* Benny, you aren't seriously going to hit me with the New Labor Players?

BENNY: And why not?

LEO: All that agit-prop bullshit, the slogans, screaming our lungs raw—

BENNY: Worthless?

LEO: Not worthless, exactly—

BENNY: Then *what,* exactly?

LEO: All we ever did was play to people who felt exactly like we did. Invigorating—sure. Fun—absolutely. And a great way to meet girls. But don't try to tell me we ever accomplished any great social good. I doubt that we ever changed anybody's mind about anything.

BENNY: That's how you measure it?

LEO: You measure it differently?

BENNY: Seems to me there's some value in letting people know—because they laughed or maybe cheered at the same time as a bunch of other people— letting them know they aren't alone. That there are other people who feel like they do.

LEO: Maybe we should have broken out some red pom-poms while we were at it.

BENNY: Pom-poms?

LEO: Hey, if you're going to cheerlead, you should have pom-poms. "Give ma a P, give me an R, give me an O, give me an L!"

BENNY: Leo—

LEO: "Whattaya got? Proletariat! Whattaya got? Class struggle! Whattaya got? Dialectical materialism! Rah, rah, rah!"

BENNY: Some terrific joke, Leo. Very funny.

LEO: What's funny is you telling me this stuff.

BENNY: What's funny about that?

LEO: You think I don't know my own spiel when I hear it?

BENNY: Your spiel?

LEO: Of course my spiel. "Class consciousness is the first step. Through theater we give dramatic form to our lives and hopes and so create our identity and the identity of our community." You like it? I've got another three or four hours of this. Rousing stuff, hunh? *(A beat.)*

BENNY: Yeah, I thought so.

LEO: Oh, I convinced myself pretty good, too. But I'm not a twenty-two-year-old kid any more, and neither are you. And I'm not going to let you get away with pretending that *Capitalist Heaven* and the rest of it was any great golden age of drama. Face it, Benny, it was amateur night.

BENNY: I'm not talking about how sophisticated or how professional. Leo, what I'm saying is that when we started, all right, we may not have had much polish or technical expertise, but we did have a sense of purpose. There was a *reason* I started acting. There was a *reason* Mort Kessler started-ed writing. There was a *reason* you started directing. And then came a point you gave up your reason so you could keep on directing.

LEO: Maybe directing *was* my reason.

BENNY: What—directing anything?

LEO: Of course not.

BENNY: You say of course not, but I don't take it for granted that there are things you wouldn't direct. Before the Committee—yes. But after?

LEO: So all of a sudden I'm a whore. Of course, it isn't whoring to do some dumb-ass sitcom. What was it called—*Rich and Happy?*

BENNY: *Rich But Happy.*

LEO: I stand corrected. Truly edifying, uplifting stuff. My God, in the old days, if somebody had told you that's what you'd end up doing! *Rich But Happy.* I mean, back then just the *title* would have made you gag!

BENNY: I had to live.

LEO: So did I, Benny. So did I.

BENNY: But if I did crap—and God knows I'm not holding up *Rich But Happy* as an example of high culture—but if I did crap, I didn't destroy other people to do it.

LEO: I don't happen to think that the work I did after that *was* crap. As a matter of fact, a lot of it was damn good.

BENNY: If you do say so yourself.

LEO: You're going to tell me that it wasn't? Oh, I know this riff. If a guy's politics aren't approved, aren't correct, then he can't be any good as an artist. I bet you're one of those people who think God took away Frank Sinatra's voice as a punishment for voting Republican.

BENNY: I'm not talking party affiliation—

LEO: I know what you're talking about: In order to be an artist, you've got to be a certified good guy.

BENNY: Being a *mensch* enters into it, yes.

LEO: And if he isn't, you feel cheated. Short-changed. Well, if art by bastards upsets you so much, you should drop everything right now, go into your library and toss out anything you have by Robert Frost. Now there was a world-class shit! And how about Ezra Pound! And let's not bring up Wagner!

BENNY: I don't have any Wagner in my house.

LEO: No? Well now *there's* a brave stand! My hat's off to you, Benny! Keep those doors guarded. Be vigilant! Hey, you can't be *too* careful. I mean, you never know when somebody might try to sneak the fucking *Ring Cycle* into your house without your knowing it, right?

BENNY: This I'm enjoying—you linking arms with Wagner!

LEO: Tell me something, if you found out that Charles Dickens shtupped ten-year-old boys, would that make him any less of a writer?

BENNY: Well, it sure as hell would make a difference in how I read *Oliver Twist.*

LEO: Whatever you or anybody else thinks about me as a person, I did good work, Benny. Not just before. After, too.

BENNY: I wouldn't know about after. I didn't see most of it.

LEO: Well, you missed some good stuff. If you don't want to take my word for it, you can take it from the critics. You can look on my fucking mantle in New York at the prizes and the plaques—

BENNY: I'm sure they would blind me.

LEO: They mean something, Benny, even if it's fashionable to sneer at them. They mean that a lot of people thought that the work was good.

BENNY: And that's important to you.

LEO: Yes, it is.

BENNY: You like having the good opinion of others.

LEO: Is that a crime?

BENNY: No, I don't think it's a crime. I like it, too. I'm just sorry to have to tell you that you haven't got *my* good opinion, Leo.

LEO: And I'm sorry to have to tell you I don't give a damn.

BENNY: Then why are you here?

LEO: Because I don't want your goddamn daughter walking out of my goddamn play.

BENNY: Fine, you told her that. So why are you still here?

LEO: Because I'm a masochistic idiot!

BENNY: What, you expected me to throw my arms open?

LEO: No.

BENNY: Then what?

LEO: Damn it, Benny—thirty years! It's been more than thirty years! We're going to start *dying* soon! *(A beat.)* While there's still a chance. *(A beat.)*

BENNY: Leo, you got a car?

LEO: Yeah. Why?

BENNY: Let's say for the sake of argument there's someplace you want to go. So you go to your car, put the key in the ignition—nothing. It isn't working. But there's this place you want to go. You want to go there real bad. You take a look in my garage, what do you know?—I've got a car. A car in good working condition. It's got a few years on it, but it runs fine. We're talking about a respected make. So you ask me, can you take my car? I say no, I'm sorry, I've made plans, I need it. You tell me about this place you want to go, how important it is to you to get there. I say I'm sorry, but no, I can't let you have my car. What do you do? You take it anyway. Now what do you figure I do in a situation like this? Call the cops, of course. Give them your description and the license number, they take off after you. What happens if they catch you? You end up being charged with grand theft auto. All right, you didn't steal my car. But there *was* someplace you wanted to go, and the only vehicle you could get your hands on was something else that belonged to me.

(Norma has entered during the above. Neither Benny nor Leo betrays any notice of her presence. Which is not to say that they don't know she's there.)

BENNY: Something that belonged to me, something that belonged to Morty, something that belonged to a few other guys. I don't know how you did it with them, but I get the famous phone call. You call and tell me what you're going to do. You cry about the pressure. You tell me how much getting to this place you want to go means to you. You want me to tell you, "Sure, Leo, go ahead. Take it for a drive. Barter it for the good opinion of a bunch of cynical shits. Buy yourself a license to work." But it doesn't play that way. I say no. And the next day, you go into that committee room, and you use it anyway. The difference between that and you taking my car—my car you can return. *(A beat.)* Leo, I'm not Morty Kessler. I won't put it aside. I'm sorry. *(A beat.)* Norma, Mr. Greshen dropped by to ask you about his show. Why don't you tell him what you've decided? *(A beat. Norma doesn't respond.)* Norma? *(A beat.)*

LEO: Miss Teitel, I would appreciate it if you would call me later.

(Norma nods. Leo exits. A beat.)

NORMA: OK, I think I've got it now.

BENNY: What is that?

NORMA: Why you didn't throw him out before. All these years, you've been thinking, working up what you would say if you ever met him again—

BENNY: Who wanted to meet him again?

NORMA: I'm saying *if.*

BENNY: I did my best to make sure that wouldn't happen.

NORMA: I'm sure you did.

BENNY: I gave up my favorite Chinese restaurant. A place I knew he sometimes ate. Never went back. Last thing I wanted was to see him.

NORMA: Last thing, hunh?

BENNY: If you'll have the stenographer read back the transcript, I think you'll see that's what I said.

NORMA: I know you said it—

BENNY: But you—with your years of wisdom and experience—you see the deeper truth, is that it?

NORMA: Maybe *at first* you didn't want to meet him again—

BENNY: Oh boy, here we go—

NORMA: Maybe in the beginning—

BENNY: I can see where all this is heading. I didn't, but really underneath it all, I did.

NORMA: After all, you had the speech ready. What good is a speech if you don't give it?

BENNY: And there it is, folks—my soul naked and quivering.

NORMA: Then why did you come out in the first place? If you knew who I was talking to—

BENNY: This isn't a Chinese restaurant. This is my patio. I won't stop coming here.

NORMA: That's not what I'm saying.

BENNY: Oh, you grant me the right to step out on it if and when I please?

NORMA: Sure, and it pleased you to do it then because he was out here.

BENNY: I should hide inside?

NORMA: Nobody said anything about hiding.

BENNY: What about Leo? It sure pleased *him* to barge in here uninvited.

NORMA: We're not talking about him.

BENNY: No? Oh, I see, *you're* setting the agenda here. The topics of discussion. Sorry, Mr. Chairman.

NORMA: Mr. Chairman?

BENNY: Mr. Silverman, you aren't being cooperative. If you would please answer the question. Did you or did you not know that the American Committee for Spanish Freedom was a Communist front organization?

NORMA: Pop—

BENNY: And just exactly who was present that night in Mr. Kessler's house?

NORMA: If you can't tell the difference between me and the Committee—

BENNY: The tone is similar, believe me.

NORMA: You're misunderstanding—

BENNY: I don't know what you think you're accusing me of—

NORMA: I'm not accusing you—

BENNY: No?

NORMA: I'm not disagreeing with anything you said to him.

BENNY: Then what? That I said it at all?

NORMA: Never mind.

BENNY: What—are you afraid I lost you your job?

NORMA: No.

BENNY: That's it, isn't it?

NORMA: The job isn't yours to lose.

BENNY: Right. Your decision.

NORMA: That's what he said.

BENNY: And you can take it from me, he's a man to be trusted. Yes, sir.

NORMA: I just hope you got what you wanted.

BENNY: And what might that be?

NORMA: I don't know. Satisfaction?

BENNY: No way to get satisfaction.

NORMA: Then why do it?

BENNY: Sometimes you do a thing because you've got the right to do it. Or don't you think I have the right?

NORMA: Of course you've got the right. And I've got the right to do some things, too.

BENNY: Like to judge me, my behavior? Well, I beg to differ, kiddo. You haven't earned it.

NORMA: Oh, so it's like with the painting. I don't have the proper background, so I can't appreciate it. Because I didn't suffer through the blacklist, I can't have an opinion.

BENNY: Have any opinion you want, but don't expect me to get all worked up about it.

NORMA: No, of course not. Who the hell am I, anyway? If I happen to think that walking around spitting battery acid at the world is no kind of a life—

BENNY: I don't have to listen to this.

NORMA: Pop, he did a shitty thing to you. No argument. But after all of these years, to let it keep eating at you, to let it take over your life—

BENNY: "A shitty thing." Your command of the language—"A shitty thing." Like maybe he stole a girl from me or got drunk and peed in my swimming pool. It goes beyond. You think something happens and that's it, it's over with? That it's gone and remote because you can stick a date to it and a lot of calendars have been tossed out in the meantime? All those books you've read, all that time in the library, you still don't understand a thing. *(A beat.)* I was an actor. Basic to being an actor is the fact that you can't do it by yourself. It's not like plumbing or fixing shoes or painting a picture. You've got to do it *with* other people in the *presence* of other people. If someone does something to cut you off from them, you're not an actor any more. I don't care what you call yourself or what you put on your resume, you're not. You can't grow, you can't develop. You're not allowed to be what you could. You aren't even allowed to be who you are. You're an exile. Not just from your profession, your business. You're an exile from yourself. That's what Leo did to me when he said my name. This charming fellow with all of his stories and his reasons. Sorry, yes. I'm sure he is. But that's what he did.

NORMA: And that's what you want me to do to myself. Because you couldn't work, you want me to refuse to work. Doesn't what you were saying apply to me as well? About needing other people to be an actor? You were entitled to work. Aren't I entitled, too? Or am I supposed to give up my entitlement because I'm your daughter?

BENNY: But with *him*.

NORMA: Since when do you have to like everybody you work with?

BENNY: Fine, you want the part, you keep the part. It's your decision.

NORMA: Pop—

BENNY: No, I think it's a terrific career move. And as far as your not liking him goes, I'll bet you get past that. I'll bet you two get along great. After all, so much in common: he steals my name, you throw it away.

NORMA: What do you want? You want me to blacklist myself?

BENNY: I want you to go ahead and do what you're going to do and spare me the hypocrisy of pretending that you give a good goddamn about what I want.

(Benny exits. A beat. Norma turns to the audience.)

NORMA: That afternoon, I move to a motel. We go back into rehearsal a couple days later, a couple weeks later we open. True to his word, Pop doesn't come to the opening. The next day, I drive over to see him.

(Benny enters with brushes and paint, goes to the easel. He begins to work. A beat.)

BENNY: The reviews?

NORMA: Mostly good.

BENNY: What about for you?

NORMA: Also good.

BENNY: Congratulations.

(Norma takes out a program.)

NORMA: Something I want to show you.

BENNY: What is it?

NORMA: The program.

BENNY: What about it?

(Norma opens it to a specific page, hands it to him.)

NORMA: Here.

BENNY: Your bio? I'm familiar with your credits.

NORMA: I added a line to the end.

(A beat. Benny looks at it, reads.)

BENNY: "Norma Teitel is the daughter of actor Benny Silverman." *(He hands the program back to her.)* It's not enough.

(A beat. She stands there as he goes back to painting. The lights fade on them.)

END OF PLAY

Fireworks
by Megan Terry

BIOGRAPHY

Megan Terry is an internationally recognized playwright of more than 60 plays and musical theatre pieces; plays produced nationally and internationally; Playwright-in-Residence and Literary Manager for the Omaha Magic Theatre 1970-present; also performs, composes and photographs for the artist-run company; photographer and co-editor of *Right Brain Vacation Photos–New Plays and Production Photographs from the Omaha Magic Theatre*, 1972-1992; Nebraska Arts Council Artist-in-the-Schools, 1982-present; lectured, conducted workshops and artist-in-residence at major universities throughout the country including: University of Iowa Playwright's Workshop, Hill Professor of Fine Arts–University of Minnesota-Duluth, Dancy Lectures–University of Montevallo, Alabama, and Bingham Professor of Humanities, University of Louisville; performer in touring productions of *Body Leaks* and *Sound Fields;* founding member of the Open Theatre, NYC, and New York Theatre Strategy. Fellowships include: National Endowment for the Arts, Guggenheim, Rockefeller, Yale; awards: lifetime member College of Fellows of the American Theatre, investiture April 1994; "Playwright's Center/McKnight National Residency Artist," 1993; "Nebraska Artist of the Year," 1992; Dramatists Guild for "Recognition of her work as a writer of conscience and controversy and many lasting contributions to the theatre;" American Theatre Association Silver Medal for "Distinguished Contribution to and Service in the American Theatre;" Obie Best Play–*Approaching Simone;* committees: National Endowment for the Arts Theatre Panel, Opera Music, Overview Panel, Rockefeller, Bush, NE Committee for the Humanities.

Megan Terry, a major playwright for The Open Theatre in the 1960s and 70s, now writes for and works with The Omaha Magic Theatre in Nebraska. She wrote *Fireworks* in 1979 on a commission from Actors Theatre of Louisville.

ORIGINAL PRODUCTION

Fireworks premiered in the 1979 Humana Festival of New American Plays at Actors Theatre of Louisville. It was originally directed by Michael Hankins with the following cast:

Joan	Peggy Cowles
Raymie	John Pielmeier
Dad	Daniel Ziskie

SETTING: The action takes place in July 1946, at Green Lake, a city park in Seattle, Washington.

CHARACTERS

DAD, 35: recently returned from military service in the Pacific

RAYMIE, 9: his son

JOAN, 11: his daughter

PRODUCTION SUGGESTIONS

The players, their personal props, and their costumes are all that is needed for this production. The crowd and the sound and light of the fireworks can all be imagined; if the actors "see" and "hear" these things, so will the audience.

If you are playing the role of Raymie or Joan, you will need to watch some children very carefully in order to portray them believably without either overacting or stereotypical behavior. The playwrights' advice on this problem is: "Direct the actors to look for the child within themselves: discover this quality and project it. I don't believe it is necessary to change voices, or to play 'at' being a child. It may be best to put the children's ages in the program to save audience confusion at the outset." Any gender may play any of the roles.

Address all inquiries concerning performances, readings, or reprinting of this work *or any portion thereof* to the playwright's agent: Tonda Marton, 1 Union Square West, Room 612, New York, NY 10003-3303.

For more information about Megan Terry, read *Women in American Theatre* by Helen Krich Chinoy and Linda Walsh Jenkins (T.C.G. Book, 1987), pages 285 to 292, and Phyllis Jane Rose's article in *The Dictionary of Literary Biography* (Gale Research, 1981), Volume 7, Part 2, pages 277 to 290, or contact the Omaha Magic Theatre at 2309 Hanscom Blvd., Omaha, NE 68105; phone/fax (402) 364-1227.

FIREWORKS

At rise: Dad, a muscular man of medium height, picks his way through the crowds at a beach. He is carrying a picnic basket; a beach blanket is thrown over one shoulder. He holds Raymie, a boy of nine, by the hand. The boy wears an officer's overseas cap with Captain's bars and he carries a lit sparkler in his free hand. The cap is too big for him and from time to time it falls over his eyes causing him to trip on other people's legs and blankets. [The crowd at the beach may be imagined by the actors.] Joan, a girl of eleven, follows— hopping over obstructions. She wears a white cowboy hat, red T-shirt and white shorts. Two six-guns in white holsters ride on her hips. Silver bullets line the back of the gun belt. She practices drawing and shooting as she moves. Her guns are loaded with caps. Firecrackers go off at random. There is the occasional whoosh of a small rocket and swirling light from Roman candles. Dad is dressed in a short-sleeved jungle fatigue shirt and officer's tropical slacks from World War II. He has great energy and genuine warmth in his voice. He radiates health and strength.

DAD: *(Putting down basket, he reaches in breast pocket for cigarettes and lighter.)* I'm having a nicotine fit.

RAYMIE: Quack, quack, I'm going to duck out of here.

JOAN: Stop it.

RAYMIE: Quack, quack, I'm going to duck out of here.

JOAN: You make me feel ferocious.

RAYMIE: You make me feel ducky!

DAD: Hey you guys, be nice. *(He spreads out beach blanket.)* I didn't fight the war just to come home to listen to you argue. Joanie, don't point guns at your brother.

JOAN: Sorry Dad. He gets on my nerves. *(Helping to smooth out beach blanket.)*

RAYMIE: I thought you didn't have nerves like "other girls."
   (They all sit on blanket and face the audience. They look out toward the lake. In the middle of the lake is a barge from which the fireworks will be set off.)

JOAN: I don't. Only when you...

DAD: Listen, Chicken Little!

JOAN: *(Lowering her guns.)* OK. OK.

DAD: Come here punkin. You hungry? What's this Grandma made for us?
   (Unpacking picnic basket.)

JOAN: Chicken, cooked in butter.

DAD: Real butter?

RAYMIE: Dripping with real butter.

DAD: I haven't had real butter in four years. *(Handing around plates, etc.)*

RAYMIE: Yippie!! I can eat two ducks.

JOAN: That's enough about ducks.

RAYMIE: That's enough out of you, dopey!

JOAN: Daddy!

DAD: *(To Raymie.)* You want a backhand?

RAYMIE: No, Dad.

DAD: Be nice.

JOAN: Pass the potato salad.

DAD: I've never seen so many people at Greenlake before.

JOAN: There's almost as many people here as were on the streets V-J Day.

DAD: Were you downtown then?

JOAN: Oh Dad, you should have seen it. Everybody was hugging and kissing.

RAYMIE: And they didn't even know each other.

JOAN: Three soldiers and ten sailors hugged me.

RAYMIE: You're telling stories.

JOAN: They did, too.

RAYMIE: It was Peter Ferris in his Scout uniform.

JOAN: Hey Dad, did you know I helped shoot the Japs in the two-man sub that was captured in Puget Sound?

RAYMIE: Those are just cap guns, you dumb Nazi!

JOAN: They didn't know that. These guns look real! Tojo Toejam!

DAD: Cut that out. I'm not going to tell you kids again.

RAYMIE: Did you see the big bomb drop, Dad?

JOAN: Did you see the mushroom cloud? We saw it on *March of Time* at the movies.

RAYMIE: Did you see the people melted into their own shadows on the sidewalk?

JOAN: Will the fireworks have mushroom shapes?

DAD: They usually look like flowers.

RAYMIE: Did you see it Dad, did you?

DAD: No, I was in Kobe City. It happened long before I landed in Japan.

JOAN: We didn't get to have fireworks for four whole years. We had to paint the headlights on our car black. I love the Fourth of July.

RAYMIE: I love the Fourth of July, too.

JOAN: Do I look different to you, Dad?

DAD: You're taller.

JOAN: Would you know I was your daughter?

DAD: I spotted you on the dock and waved, didn't I?

RAYMIE: Me too, you waved at me too.

DAD: Sure I did.

JOAN: Do I look the same as when you went away—or am I more grown up?

DAD: Well, you have these neat little curves at the corner of your mouth that make you look like you're happy, even when you're not smiling.

JOAN: I do. Where?

DAD: Here, right here, and right here.

RAYMIE: Do I have them too?

DAD: Your ears are smiling. You sure got a lot of hair. *(Massages his head.)* If we start the massage now maybe you'll keep yours longer than I will.

JOAN: Benjamin Franklin was bald. Bald men have lots of brains.

DAD: Yes they do, but I'm not bald. Not yet.

JOAN: I think you look real handsome. All the kids at school get jealous when I show them your picture in your captain's uniform.

RAYMIE: How many zeros did you get?

DAD: Ten, maybe twelve.

JOAN: They're going to start the fireworks now. *(She lies back to look at sky.)*

RAYMIE: Oh, Wow! There it goes.

(Sound of loud boom as fireworks are lit and shoot up into sky from barge in the lake.)

DAD: Hey, look at that one. It's like a giant chrysanthemum.

RAYMIE: Yeah.

JOAN: I wish they'd send up a marigold.

DAD: Watch up there. Right up there. Maybe the next one will look like a marigold.

JOAN: Can we have a garden again? We had the best garden before the war. We had an acre of marigolds and glads.

DAD: Two acres.

JOAN: Yeah. Can we do it again?

RAYMIE: I want a greenhouse full of tomatoes.

DAD: You ate all the tomatoes as high as you could reach.

RAYMIE: I did, didn't I? I haven't had any tomatoes since. Can we have a greenhouse again?

DAD: *(To Raymie.)* Hey, did you see that redhead?

RAYMIE: What?

DAD: Over there. Look at that redhead. She has a great figure. See there, how she's built.

RAYMIE: Which one?

DAD: She just sat down on that green blanket. I wonder if she's with anyone?

RAYMIE: That woman over there?

DAD: *Yes.* What a figure! She's built like a racehorse.

RAYMIE: She has a funny nose.

DAD: I'm not talking about her nose. I'm showing you how to spot a great figure.

JOAN: Momma has a nice shape.

DAD: She's turning around. I think she saw me.

JOAN: Dad, that woman isn't good-looking. Her face is scrambled.

DAD: I'm not looking at her face.

RAYMIE: Momma's beautiful.

JOAN: We can't wait to see Momma when she gets home from work. She's so beautiful.

RAYMIE: Which part of the lady are you looking at, Dad? This part? *(He makes round gestures at his breast.)*

JOAN: I love to watch her get ready in the morning. I love to watch her put on her make-up, and get into her stockings.

DAD: Look at the body on that woman.

JOAN: Why do you want to look at bodies so much?

DAD: If you had a body like that you'd know.

JOAN: I don't want a body like that. It's all lumpy.

DAD: Yeah...

JOAN: I'd hate to jiggle when I walk. All the nasty boys make remarks about girls who jiggle when they walk. They say that girls who jiggle will do anything.

DAD: Have you talked to your mother about that?

JOAN: About what?

DAD: You know, about *that.*

JOAN: What about what?

DAD: You're growing up. Wearing a T-shirt three sizes too big doesn't hide everything.

JOAN: Daddy!

DAD: Boys are going to want to sleep with you. Did your mother tell you what to do about it?

JOAN: I don't want to talk about it now. *(She gives a meaningful look at Raymie. She chokes and puts down her plate.)*

DAD: Boys are going to ask to sleep with you. Do you know how to protect yourself?

JOAN: I can beat up any boy my age.

DAD: The men down at the fishing dock whistled at you when we walked by.

JOAN: At me? I'm only eleven.

DAD: You're a pretty kid.

JOAN: *(Embarrassed.)* Oh Dad! Well, all I can say is, thank God I'm not a redhead.

RAYMIE: Don't swear.

JOAN: I'm not swearing. I'm giving thanks.

RAYMIE: Is that a good figure, Dad?

DAD: Where?

RAYMIE: That blond over there?

DAD: Not bad, but the redhead is still number one.

JOAN: Why don't you bozos look at the sky? That's where real beauty is. You two make me sick.

DAD: We're just healthy, red-blooded American boys.

JOAN: You'd get a bloody nose, if I was bigger.

DAD: Such talk. You're as tall as you're going to be.

JOAN: I'm doing stretching exercises every day. I'm going to join the Marines when I'm eighteen. I know judo. I used that judo you taught me. I dumped a big man on his can. This guy came up to me on the street from behind and put his arms around me. I did that thing you showed me. I reached down like this and grabbed his ankle and pulled. You could hear him bellow all the way to San Francisco when he hit the sidewalk.

RAYMIE: *(Pulling out German luger squirt gun.)* It's true, Dad, she really did it. I shot my squirt gun right in his mouth while he was yelling, then we ran like sixty.

DAD: Where was your mother?

JOAN: At work.

DAD: Things are going to change. You kids aren't going to be on your own anymore.

JOAN: I don't get scared at night. I'm not afraid of anything anymore. After they captured that Jap submarine in Puget Sound, nothing can scare me, 'cause I'm the fastest draw in Seattle. *(She whips out both guns and blazes away with her caps.)*

RAYMIE: When you coming back home, Dad?

DAD: I won't be coming back home, Raymie.

RAYMIE: But you *are* home. Why are you living at Gramma's?

DAD: Your mother and I...your Mother and I will be getting a divorce.

JOAN: Oh, no. We waited for you to come home from the South Pacific four whole years. You're back in Seattle. You should come home.

DAD: Your mother doesn't want me to.

JOAN: She does, she does. The whole war, all we lived for was you coming back home.

RAYMIE: It's awful to have you home, but not at our house.

JOAN: All the kids in the neighborhood think it's funny. They all love you and they're waiting to see your war souvenirs.

RAYMIE: The flags and swords and the Japanese rifle you captured. All the kids want to see them.

JOAN: We thought when the war was over we could have fun again.

DAD: I did, too. That's all I lived for, too.

RAYMIE: You don't have to be in the Army any more.

DAD: Have to sell the house.

JOAN: But it took us so long to build it…

RAYMIE: We all built it together…

JOAN: It took us a long time—my whole life, almost. We love our house—why would you want to sell it? I laid lots of the brick for the garage.

DAD: Yes, yes you did.

JOAN: I did. I laid it and I didn't even need plumb line.

DAD: That's right, Joanie—you have a good eye.

JOAN: That brick will stay up forever, won't it, Dad?

DAD: It sure will, punkin.

RAYMIE: Don't you love Mommie anymore?

DAD: She doesn't love me.

RAYMIE: Would you stay married if Mommie was a redhead?

JOAN: All the time you were gone we loved you. She loved you. We couldn't wait to get your letters.

DAD: *She* didn't wait for *me*. She entertained herself with Clint Berry.

RAYMIE: Uncle Clint?

JOAN: *(Kicks Raymie.)* When the Japs bombed Pearl Harbor, you remember that day? When it came on the radio, we were all scared, and Mommie was scared and you held Mommie in your arms on the couch right by the radio. And Mommie cried and you told her you'd protect us, and not to be scared.

DAD: I don't remember being on the couch.

JOAN: You held her like this. *(Demonstrating with Raymie.)* It made my heart break to see that.

(Dad wipes his eyes.)

RAYMIE: What's the matter, Dad?

DAD: Nothing. My eyes puddled up, that's all…

JOAN: Don't you remember? President Roosevelt came on and said…

DAD: Yes…I remember…I remember…

RAYMIE: *(Sotto voce.)* Dad, she's looking at us.

DAD: What?

RAYMIE: You know, Dad, the redhead with that great figure.

DAD: *(Smiles.)* I still got it. Sooner or later they give me the eye.

RAYMIE: What is it you do, Dad?

DAD: Watch me.

RAYMIE: But I don't know what to look for.

DAD: It's the way I hold my head and body. And my eyes, my bedroom eyes.

JOAN: Yeah, that's always what Momma said about you.

DAD: She did?

JOAN: She said she married you for your bedroom eyes.

RAYMIE: Do I have bedroom eyes?

DAD: You have refrigerator eyes. *(He pats his stomach.)* To develop bedroom eyes you have to stay out of the refrigerator.

JOAN: Hey, look at that one, Dad. That's the best yet. It's still shooting, two, three giant showers of colors. *(Boom.)* Oh great—it's making stars. Hey, it's a flag. In the sky, they made a flag!

RAYMIE: See the flag, Dad, see it?

DAD: I see it.

RAYMIE: How do they do it?

DAD: *(Holding them.)* It's good, it's good…

JOAN: Oh rats, it's starting to fade.

DAD: It's so good to be home.

JOAN: Dad, won't you come back to our house to live?

DAD: I can't.

RAYMIE: Please.

DAD: No, your mother and I can't make a home together anymore.

JOAN: What good was it then? What good was it your going away to fight?

DAD: I had to. I had to go and fight to protect you.

JOAN: But if you'd stayed home, we'd all still be together. It isn't fair.

DAD: I fought for you and I fought for the flag.

JOAN: But it isn't any fun without Mother.

DAD: I'll get you a new mother.

RAYMIE: We love Mommie.

DAD: I'm sorry. Don't get upset. We'll go phone this great woman I met. You guys can talk to her. She has a really great figure.

RAYMIE: Better than the redhead?

DAD: Better than the redhead. After you get to know her on the phone, I'm going to ask her to marry me. You'll love her.

JOAN: Does she know about us?

DAD: We're going to tell her. Come on. Let's find a phone.

JOAN: I hate to talk on the phone.

RAYMIE: Where did you meet her?

DAD: In the Philippines.

RAYMIE: Is she a Filipino?

DAD: No, a Bostonian.

RAYMIE: What's that?

DAD: Someone from Boston, Massachusetts. We live on the Pacific Ocean. Boston is on the Atlantic Ocean, clear across the United States.

RAYMIE: How did she get to the Philippines?

DAD: The Army sent her. She was in the WACs.

JOAN: Weren't you in Boston?

DAD: Cambridge. That's where the Army sent me to Navigation School. Your old man is a Harvard man. *(Uses Boston accent.)*

JOAN: You didn't meet till you were both in the South Pacific?

DAD: We met right after the invasion of Hollandia.

JOAN: Just like the movies?

DAD: I was born lucky.

JOAN: Did you date?

DAD: I took her out on my boat whenever General Kruger was away, which was most of the time.

JOAN: Does Mommie know she was on your boat?

DAD: Hey, look at that. Up to the right. That's a triple burst. Look at the colors change.

(They watch a moment. Dad stands.)

DAD: Come on, kids, let's pack up and go phone her. You'll love her. Come on, the fireworks are nearly over. We don't want to get stuck in this crowd.

JOAN: I don't want to talk on the phone on the Fourth of July.

DAD: Be a good sport and pack up the picnic things—*(To Raymie.)* Come on, pal—

(To Joan, he strokes her back and she pulls away.)

DAD: Hey scooter, we'll meet you at the phone booth over there.

(Joan picks up Raymie's squirt gun and empties it at them. She turns and begins to pick up the picnic things and throws them into the picnic basket as the lights fade. There is one last burst of fireworks.)

JOAN: *(Through clenched teeth.)* Well, at least the Japs didn't get him!

END OF PLAY

Eukiah

by Lanford Wilson

BIOGRAPHY

Lanford Wilson received the 1980 Pulitzer Prize for Drama and the New York Drama Critic's Circle Award for *Talley's Folly*. He is a founding member of Circle Repertory Company.

His work includes: *The Family Continues* (1972), *The Hot L Baltimore* (1973), *The Mound Builders* (1975), *Serenading Louie* (1976), *5th of July* (1978), *Talley's Folly* (1980), *A Tale Told* (1981), *Angels Fall* (1982), *Talley and Son* (1985), *Burn This* (1987), *Redwood Curtain* (1993), all directed by Marshall Mason, and the one-act plays *Brontosaurus* (1977) and *Thymus Vulgaris* (1982). *A Poster of the Cosmos* and *The Moonshot Tape* opened at Circle Repertory Theatre in May 1994.

His other plays include: *Balm in Gilead* (1965), *The Gingham Dog* (1966), *The Rimers of Eldritch* (1967), *Lemon Sky* (1969), and some twenty produced one-acts. He has also written the libretto for Lee Hoiby's opera of Tennessee Williams' *Summer and Smoke*, and two television plays, *Taxi!* and *The Migrants* (based on a story by Tennessee Williams).

Other awards include the New York Drama Critics' Circle Award, the Outer Critics' Circle Award and an Obie for *The Hot L Baltimore*, an Obie for *The Mound Builders*, a Drama-Logue Award for *5th of July* and *Talley's Folly*, the Vernon Rice Award for *The Rimers of Eldritch*, and Tony Award nominations for *Talley's Folly, 5th of July,* and *Angels Fall.* He is the recipient of the Brandeis University Creative Arts Award in Theatre Arts and the Institute of Arts and Letters Award.

Mr. Wilson has recently completed an entirely new translation of Chekhov's *The Three Sisters*, which was commissioned and produced by the Hartford Stage Company. He makes his home in Sag Harbor, New York.

ORIGINAL PRODUCTION

Eukiah premiered at Actors Theatre of Louisville in a 1991 Apprentice/Intern Showcase. It was directed by Marcia Dixcy with the following cast:

Butch ....Arthur Aulisi
Eukiah ....Jim Dubensky

Eukiah received its professional premiere at Actors Theatre of Louisville in the 1992 Humana Festival of New American Plays. That production was directed by Jon Jory with the following cast:

Butch ....Mark Shannon
Eukiah ....Shaun Powell

CHARACTERS
    BUTCH
    EUKIAH
TIME: The Present.
SETTING: An abandoned private airplane hangar.

EUKIAH

A dark empty stage represents a long abandoned private airplane hangar. The space is vast and almost entirely dark. A streak of light from a crack in the roof stripes the floor.
Butch walks into the light. He is a young powerful, charming man; everybody's best friend. He is also menacing. Nothing he says is introspective. Everything is for a purpose. During the indicated beats of silence he listens; for Eukiah to answer, for the sound of breathing, for the least indication of where Eukiah is. The play is a seduction.
Voices have a slight echo in here.

BUTCH: Eukiah? *(Beat.)* Eukiah? *(Beat.)* Barry saw you run in here, so I know you're here. You're doin' it again, Eukiah, you're jumping to these weird conclusions you jump to just like some half-wit. You don't wanna be called a half-wit, you gotta stop actin' like a half-wit, don't ya? You're gettin' to where nobody can joke around you, ya know that? What kind of fun is a person like that to be around, huh? One you can't joke around? We talked about that before, remember? *(Beat.)* Eukiah? What're you thinkin'? You thinkin' you heard Barry say something, you thought he meant it, didn't you? What did you think you heard? Huh? What'd you think he meant? Eukiah? *(Beat.)* You're gonna have to talk to me, I can't talk to myself here. *(Beat.)* Have you ever known me to lie to you? Eukiah? Have you ever known that? *(Pause. He might walk around some.)* Okay. Boy, this old hangar sure seen better days, hasn't it? Just like everything else on this place, huh? Been pretty much a losing proposition since I've known it, though. Probably you too, hasn't it? Hell, I don't think they have the wherewithal anymore, give even one of those ol' barns a swab a paint. You think? Might paint 'em pink, whattaya think? Or candy stripes. Red and white. Peppermint. You'd like that. *(Beat.)* This'll remind you of old Mac's heyday, though, won't it? Private airplane hangar. Talk about echoes, this is an echo of the past, huh? Ol' Mac had some winners, I guess, about twenty years ago. That must have been the life, huh? Private planes, keep 'em in your private hangar. You got your luncheons with the dukes and duchesses. Winner's Circle damn near every race. If they wasn't raised by Ol' Mac or their sire or dam one wasn't raised by Ol' Mac, I don't imagine anybody'd bother to bet on 'em, do you? Boy that's all gone, huh? Planes and limos and all, dukes and duchesses—good lookin' horses, though. Damn shame we can't enter 'em in a beauty contest somewhere. I know, you're attached to 'em, but I'll tell you they make damn expensive pets.

What was you? Out by the paddock when Barry was talkin' to me? You think you overheard something, is that it? What do you think you heard? You want to talk about it? I know you'd rather talk to me than talk to Barry, huh? Eukiah? *(Pause.)* Is this where you come? When you run off all temperamental and sulking? Pretty nasty old place to play in. Echoes good though. Gotta keep awful quiet if you're trying to be secret like you always do in a place like this.

Why do you do that? You got any idea? I'm serious, now. Run off like that. They're waitin' supper on you, I guess you know. You know how happy they're gonna be about it, too. *(Beat.)* Eukiah? What was it you think you heard, honey? What? Was it about horses? 'Cause I thought I told you never trust anything anybody says if it's about horses.

EUKIAH: *(Still unseen.)* I heard what Barry said. You said you *would,* too.

BUTCH: *(Relaxes some, smiles.)* Where the dickens have you got to? There's so much echo in here I can't tell where you are. You back in those oil drums? You haven't crawled up in the rafters have you? Watch yourself. We don't want you gettin' hurt. I don't think those horses would eat their oats at all, anybody gave 'em to 'em 'cept you. I think they'd flat out go on strike. Don't you figure?

EUKIAH: They wouldn't drink, you couldn't get 'em to.

BUTCH: Don't I know it. Pot-A-Gold, for sure. You're the only one to get him to do anything. I think he'd just dehydrate. He'd blow away, you wasn't leadin' him. We could lead him to water but we couldn't make him to drink, isn't that right? *(Beat.)* What are you hiding about? Nobody's gonna hurt you. Don't I always take up for you? You get the weirdest ideas. What do you think you heard Barry say?

EUKIAH: He's gonna burn the horses.

BUTCH: What? Oh, man. You are just crazy sometimes, these things you dream up. Who is? Barry? What would he wanna do something crazy like that for?

EUKIAH: I heard you talkin'.

BUTCH: Can you answer me that? Why would he even dream of doin' something like that?

EUKIAH: For the insurance.

BUTCH: No, Eukiah. Just come on to supper, now, I got a date tonight, I can't mess around with you anymore. You really are a half-wit. I'm sorry, but if you think Barry'd do something like that, I'm sorry, that's just flat out half-witted thinkin'. It's not even funny. The way you talk, you yak all day to anybody around, no idea what you're saying half the time; anybody heard something like that there wouldn't be no work for me or you or anybody else around here, 'cause they just lock us all up.

EUKIAH: You said you would.

BUTCH: *I* would? I would what?